ALMOST INVINCIBLE

DAN BETTS

Published by
Legends Publishing

E-mail david@legendspublishing.net
Website www.legendspublishing.net

Thanks to Panini for the use of the sticker images

CONTENTS

Foreword

I was pleased at the start of that 90/91 season. All of the lads were really. Most of us, after all, could remember what it was like following our previous title win. But hardly anyone had been signed. It was virtually the same group of players. It all felt a bit stale going into that campaign.

Nobody wants to lose their place to a new player. By the same token, though, you need some fresh blood to perk everyone up. You need to feel that the squad has taken a step forward.

And that's certainly how it felt when David Seaman walked through the door with a big grin. While it was sad to see John Lukic leave the club, it soon became apparent that Dave represented a significant step up.

Then there was Anders Limpar, the magical Swede of Hungarian extraction. Few of us had heard of the bloke up to that point. But I remember looking at Anders in training and marvelling at how quickly those size six boots moved.

Andy Linighan, fair to say, didn't cause such a stir. But the big man from Norwich would have an important part to play when Tony Adams went to prison that Christmas. So the mood was pretty good at the start of that campaign, even better after beating Wimbledon on their own patch to match the opening result from two years before, when the season ended in unspeakable glory at Anfield. Not a bad omen, we thought.

That whole title-winning experience, we felt, made us a better team. It provided the maturity and know-how to go with the talent. Even so, I don't think any of us expected to lose only one game. That just didn't happen. Not even Liverpool in their pomp managed to do that.

Yet a few months down the line, we sat in the away dressing room at Stamford Bridge feeling absolutely gutted. Our run had been halted by, let's face it, an average Chelsea team. But in all honesty, we knew we were pushing our luck when, in the skipper's absence, Steve Bould got injured and came off at half-time. We never looked happy after that. I certainly didn't after scoring right at the death. As consolation goals went, this one wasn't my favourite. 'Heads up lads', George Graham urged afterwards. 'It has been a brilliant effort. Congratulations. Now let's go again!'

And we did, to secure the championship trophy at something of a canter. At the end of it all, we looked back on a season none of us would forget, understandably proud of the tremendous consistency. The plaudits were fulsome. The newspapers wondered when this would happen again. It felt like an achievement to stand the test of time.

So who could have predicted that 13 years later it would be the very same club, not just equaling the record but having the cheek to go one better?

Alan Smith celebrating with Rocky Rocastle, a glittering trophy and some bubbly

Well, if someone was going to do it I was glad it was Arsenal. Not only that, I was glad that the finest team, for me, to ever grace England's top flight had got something special to show for their class. The Invincibles were born, arguably overdue. If it hadn't been for an off day in west London, they would have arrived a lot earlier.

Alan Smith

Introduction

Thirty years ago, Arsenal, George Graham and his multi- talented, but miniscule, squad began a campaign that should be ranked amongst Arsenal Football Club's finest achievements. The end result was the First Division Championship – but the sheer scale, and number, of obstacles put in the path of this Class of '91 adds a deeper lustre to this particular achievement.

True, football was vastly different to the sport as we know it today. From the contrasting levels of physicality within matches – to fitness regimens, diets and everything in between – football back in 1990 presented different challenges to nowadays. It doesn't lessen what the Class of '91 managed though. There were still 38 opportunities for failure – and for Arsenal to avoid that pitfall 37 times out of that 38 is on a level with The Invincibles team.

Does that sole loss really create a gulf between the two incarnations of Arsenal? Is the fact that the Class of '91 succumbed to a ridiculously unlucky loss a telltale sign that Wenger's team of 2004 was markedly better? Because, in all honesty, the rest of the numbers point to Graham's men being the superior team.

More goals scored, less conceded. A far smaller squad to navigate the season with. These are big indicators regarding the merits of that side that came so close to achieving the immortality that The Invincibles now enjoy.

Thirty years is a long time, but it isn't the length of time that has dimmed the spotlight that should always be focused on this side. It is that one little 'l' that stops the Class of 91 being talked about in the same vein as The Invincibles, the United Treble winners and others.

That loss was inflicted on a mire of a pitch, with our skipper incarcerated at Her Majesty's Pleasure. It was given to us with a shockingly brutal tackle on Steve Bould, which then forced George Graham to call upon a fresh-faced David Hillier (a midfielder) to act as a band-aid in the centre of defence in the absence of the injured Bould. This loss was thrust upon Arsenal by an offside goal and a flood of fixtures beforehand that left this threadbare squad exhausted. This side overcame a points deduction too, after the infamous Battle of Old Trafford.

It is tough to find another Championship-winning side that has had to endure, then overcome more, before achieving victory in such a comprehensive manner. You could even argue that the competition in 1990-91 was far more competitive than in 2003-04, when there was only two other contenders. Thirty years ago, Liverpool were the all-conquering Champions with 20 years' domination under their belts and a bulging trophy cabinet to prove it. The First Division also had an exciting Crystal Palace side with a forward-line to send fear into any defence. Manchester United were assembling something that resembled a challenge and even Tottenham, yes even Tottenham, had class in their side in the shape of Gazza and Lineker.

Chelsea's Graham Stuart celebrates with Dennis Wise after scoring the opener in 'that' game

As it's the 30th anniversary of this amazing side, my publisher and I thought it would be good to re-release the book – with some extra content and context to commemorate this brilliant Arsenal team. Beginning from the dying embers of the previous campaign, during which Arsenal had failed to regain the title – we look at how the squad was being put through their paces during pre-season – plus detailed coverage of the cup campaigns and the exhausting title race that followed.

This book also includes exclusive player insight from the heroes who we still, rightfully, adore. Alan Smith, Lee Dixon, Nigel Winterburn, David Seaman, Kevin Campbell and David Hillier share their memories, as well as (then) Arsenal coach, Bob Wilson, and renowned football journalist, Amy Lawrence. No stone is left unturned.

And, what better way to commemorate the 30th anniversary, than to include the unique insights of Kevin Campbell – a proud member of this illustrious Arsenal squad, and a man who contributed to a quite magic season? Enjoy our book and continue to raise your glasses to the Class of '91!

Thirty Year Anniversary

Does time diminish achievement? The chapters included in this book are written with one sole purpose – to raise awareness of a campaign that is arguably on a par with Arsenal's greatest ever achievement. Thirty years ago, as I write, Arsenal were preparing to embark on a very special season – although the word 'special' doesn't really do it justice, but I don't want to spoil the book for you. Let's just say that the journey that George Graham, his squad, and the club as a whole, had to endure only add to the glory that was achieved at the end of the campaign. 'Arduous' is another word that doesn't seem adequate either!

The season began with Arsenal having relinquished their grip on the First Division title to perennial winners, Liverpool. The Reds had regained the Championship they had so agonisingly lost themselves at home on May 26 1989, at Anfield and it appeared to be business as usual. But Liverpool had been rocked. They were not used to losing, especially titles and matches at their fortress of a stadium. Arsenal had not only rocked their boat – they planned on capsizing it.

Arsenal still had the 'Miracle of Anfield 89' fresh in their minds, however, former Arsenal striker, Kevin Campbell, told me that the environment was very different being Champions, then attempting to defend it. "Everyone knew that Liverpool would be hurt by the epic victory at Anfield in 1989, but you never fully understand until you go through it, that it is a totally different mind-set being the Champions being hunted, rather than the stalking contenders."
Campbell continued; "The hunger was 100% still there in the 90/91 season, and George trained us even harder, as he was all about winning and being successful, but it was a stronger league with more obstacles than just Kenny Dalglish's team to contend with."

Although fans still get misty-eyed over that era, I often wonder whether time has obscured some fans' ability to fully appreciate the scale of The Gunners' early-Nineties achievements – but surely three decades is not enough time to consign such historical highs to the irrelevance pile? As fans, we often seem to cherish certain things above others. It may depend if you were there in person, or it may be tied in with when you were younger and less cynical about things. Either way, you may hold our Double in 2002 closer to your heart, or it could the Five-Minute Final of 1979 that really gets your blood pumping. For some, it would be this season, the campaign when we were truly a cut above everyone else. For a player, though, has thirty years diminish the memories?

KEVIN CAMPBELL
ARSENAL

For Kevin Campbell the answer is an emphatic no, the title will always remain cherished. "We knew we could win the title again, as winning a title is never a fluke. Consistency is the key. We trained harder than ever and knew we could win it again. It was my first senior trophy for Arsenal and a League title, which I cherished immensely. Nobody was surprised we won the title though, as that team was special!"

The reference of hard training will be a theme which runs throughout this book. The boss, George Graham, was renowned for his ferocious preparation and his charges were put through their paces with little mercy – all of which ensured his team were well drilled and knew *exactly* what their role was in evolving situations throughout a match.

Campbell agrees, and his first-hand experiences offer an eye behind the scenes. Campbell confirms that the Scot didn't accept shirkers, but he valued performance above all else, and was fair in his approach. Campbell was promoted from the youth team after scoring a hat-full, but received no assurances over a place, although Campbell had fire in his belly thanks to his boss;

"I was promised nothing by George – everything had to be earned through good performances. That's what made us all so hungry to make the first team, because if you made it, then you knew you had earned it."

The squad that Campbell refers to was a tight-knit bunch and worked and played together, both on and off the pitch. When Arsenal suffered rare disappointment during this magical season, and whilst facing matches without their inspirational captain Tony Adams, Campbell describes how they coped.

"The determination was there and the focus had to be strong without our leader. The dressing room was full of character, and characters, who loved Arsenal... So there was no worry there! We were determined to do the business, although the FA Cup loss to Tottenham was very painful, because we had been so consistent throughout the season, yet the breaks in the game just never went our way. We were gutted, yet George was great afterwards, he said there would be no wallowing in self-pity. He told us to go out as a squad and have a few beers and he'd see us in the morning. We were totally refocused the morning after!"

I collected the opinions of many of the team about the Tottenham loss in the Cup and the sole League defeat, against Chelsea. This was a team of winners – losing didn't sit easy with them. Campbell was the same.

"The injuries had piled up and I think we played a large part of the game with young David Hillier at centre-back. We were gutted to lose a London derby and our first League game, yet things seemed to go against us all day." Both matches are sharply in focus during the course of the book, but judging from Kevin Campbell's answers, thirty years have done nothing to dampen his passionate memories.

Another flashpoint of the season was the infamous Battle of Old Trafford. Campbell spoke about the game and stated; "That was a proper North versus South clash – they thought they could win by getting physical and intimidating us, yet they got more than they bargained for! That was a defining moment because nobody could bully The Arsenal. Winning the game was great and then getting two points docked was great for the squad. We used it as fuel to win the League title despite our punishment!"

Listening to one of the squad talk of this incredible season, and the highs and lows, really brings it home. Yes, three decades is a long time, but I can vividly picture these moments as they are described, as you could feel the tension and focused determination from the stands too.

That season really did have everything. Arsenal won more than a title that year, they set the bar higher and allowed us, as Gooners, to have something to treasure – our side were the best by far that season.

Kevin Campbell agrees. "Good players can adapt and you need all the qualities to win a League title, losing only one game and conceding just 18! Coaching was so important, the preparation was key though. George had plotted getting the title back to Highbury!" You have to say, mission accomplished!

Thank you George, Kevin and the entire squad. Thirty years ago you lost just one game – but you were flawless to us and we remain so very proud of what you achieved for our great football club.

From The Ashes

Once the exquisitely dramatic events - particularly the ending - of Arsenal's 1988/89 title-snatching campaign had enjoyed time to settle - the next challenge that George Graham faced was to prove to the doubters that the Champions were not a flash in the pan.

Bringing the Gunners their first title in 18 years would have ensured the full support of the Arsenal Boardroom. It meant that George Graham could concentrate fully on keeping the Championship in the Arsenal trophy cabinet.

George Graham took the reins in 1986, but it wasn't a one-man contest. Arsenal Chairman, Peter Hill-Wood, had been sizing up the right man for the job, and in the frame at the time had been Terry Venables. The then Barcelona manager was under consideration, but George was the man the Board plumped for, and it had paid off.

Thanks to Harry Miller's book, 'Arsenal, the Champions Year,' Peter Hill-Wood can tell us himself about his thoughts on El Tel and the replacing of Don Howe.

"Don asked whether I was going to renew his contract at the end of the season. I said "no, we weren't." That was about a month before he went. He had asked me a direct question and I gave him a very straight answer. I don't regret what happened. What I did regret was when a reporter from The Sun telephoned me when I was on holiday in Jamaica. He asked some rather oblique questions about Terry Venables and I very rashly said I had spoken to Venables. It was absolutely true that I had. He was at Barcelona then. I had asked him in all innocence whether he was thinking of returning to England. If he was, would he be interested in Arsenal."

It was later revealed in the book that George Graham had actually been in with a shout for the job when Terry Neill left in 1983 - but he would have to wait three years before returning to the club that he had played for.

George Graham had proven to Hill-Wood and the rest of the club hierarchy that his appointment had been the best decision they had made. The Littlewoods Cup win in 1987 was the kindling on which this particular phoenix had risen from, and the title win had now seen the Gunners progress from also-rans to genuine heavyweights.

Now though, they would have their cards marked. When an opponent turned up to Highbury, they would play differently. Arsenal had become a scalp. Every team wants to beat the Champions, and so the difficult task in hand began. Could they reclaim the title?

George began his side's assault on the League well before any footballs had been kicked in anger. He expected his men to enjoy themselves in the football-

The famous yellow jersey worn on that special night at Anfield

ing hiatus, but not to take liberties. He set a limit on the weight they must be when they returned to pre-season training, with fines imposed if they were to go over.

The players were told in no uncertain terms that the forthcoming season would be harder than the last, but there were to be no influx of talent to boost the squad. Instead, the same squad which had lifted the title would again be the ones who would try and retain it.

The Charity Shield is the customary curtain-raiser, and Arsenal, after returning from their pre-season tour of Sweden, were to take on a foe which instantly raised the bar in terms of match importance. Manchester United had won the FA Cup, which granted them the right to see in the new season at Wembley. This showpiece had real gravitas which would do the new season justice.

Arsenal lost the match 4-1. It would be a theme for the whole year, as an underwhelming display saw Alex Ferguson's men draw first blood in this never-ending tussle between the two great clubs.

Arsenal would go on to finish fourth when the season ended. Injuries to key personnel, drama on the pitch and a heavier burden of expectation would all combine to overwhelm the Gunners. The usual firebrand football that had seen them onto success, had dropped by ten percent, and it served as an opportunity to pounce for their rivals.

Liverpool went on to reclaim the title they considered 'their own,' but worse news was in the form of Tottenham daring to finish above their North London neighbours. This would simply not do - in fact it would never do, according to the Arsenal faithful.

George Graham could point to a few things that would explain such a drop in performance. Midfield lynchpin, Paul Davis, missed a huge chunk of the season with a cyst problem on his thigh, which also affected his international prospects. Steve Bould, too, would miss almost half the season. This meant that the telepathy between Bould and captain Adams was not present and David O'Leary would play the role vacated. O'Leary had broken the all-time appearance record that season, and had shown that the faith Graham had placed in him was not unjust. The problem was that he wasn't Bould.

O'Leary would also play a big part in a precursor to Arsenal being handed the biggest punishment from the FA. Arsenal may have lacked fluency when they tried to defend their title, but their fighting spirit would never desert them. That very tenacious spirit bubbled to the surface in a match with Norwich, as a malicious opponent sparked wild scenes.

Malcolm Allen was the striker for the Canaries, and his elbows would make contact off the ball with Tony Adams, David O'Leary and Kevin Richardson. He was looking to antagonise the Gunners, and O'Leary reacted first. He grabbed Allen by the scruff of the neck after one particular incident and tried to drag him toward the referee to highlight what was going on. The match official was oblivious, and the roughhouse tactics from Allen were permitted to continue. O'Leary was even booked for his actions. This all happened in the first half in which Arsenal also found themselves two goals down.

The second half saw a marked difference from the Gunners - and a flurry of goals and penalties - as Adams and his men fought back to take the lead. It was when Alan Smith tried to grab the ball from the Norwich net after he had scored that the madness kicked off. The melee had begun. No punches were thrown, but the red mist had descended. Pushing and shoving from all players, with no backing down, It was anarchy.

There had not been any lasting damage in relation to the teams, but both clubs were given fines by the FA, and warned of their future conduct. This warning would dangle its ominous tendrils through to Arsenal's next season. Aside from the argy-bargy and injuries, there were dips in form too. Alan Smith, who had received the Golden Boot for his goalscoring exploits when they had so valiantly plucked the First Division title from Anfield, had complained about lacking a physical edge, and was sent for further tests. The results were unclear, but the lack of an answer meant that while he struggled on in the team, his usually reliable stream of goals dried up. He was subsequently dropped from the team, with Niall Quinn installed as his replacement. By the time Smudge returned to the team, fit and raring to go, valuable momentum had been lost.

Players would leave during the season, whilst others knew their days were numbered. For example, John Lukic was more than aware that George Graham had been chasing David Seaman to replace him. Niall Quinn moved to Manchester City in March of that year. Kevin Richardson and Brian Marwood, too, would have been under the spotlight. George Graham, as the season unfolded, saw that his side needed new blood.

The squad was so very nearly complete, but their undoing was ultimately a lack of reinforcements.

It wasn't enough to say they would fight tooth and nail for every point. They had done that and waved Liverpool off into the distance, no, what this team required was more firepower.

The summer of 1990 would see George rectify this, and give this band of men, clad in red and white, the last few pieces of the puzzle they were so close to completing. They stood on the precipice of something very special indeed, and the new signings would provide George Graham the final ingredients for First Division domination. The men that George Graham assembled would go on to achieve something very special.

George Graham's Gunners

The men detailed in this chapter were assembled by George Graham then drilled mercilessly, which transformed them from talented football players into an efficient machine. This machine was constructed with the sole purpose of destroying opponents with either a swift blow from the guile of Anders Limpar - assisting the prolific Alan Smith or Paul Merson - or the crushing grip of a defence which most teams had no answer to.

The machine however, was a sum of its parts. Without each and every cog working in complete cohesion, without the vital fluids which aided every moving part, this mosaic would be rendered useless. Opponents, who would be painfully aware of the fearsome potential of this team, instead of adapting to try to combat these weapons, would get ideas above their station. They would smell weakness. George Graham's methods and tactics were the oil which saw this engine purr through the entire season.

In short, this team was a match for anyone. The men who wore the jersey throughout this amazing season contributed so much. The following chapter is a rollcall - all the players who did so much. Every single hero who donned the jersey and took to the field are detailed and given just a few more words of appreciation. From Seaman to Smith - here is the squad who were mere minutes away from becoming the first Post-War Invincibles.

The Squad - 1990/1991

Signings

15/05/1990 - David Seaman from Leeds United - £1.3m
04/07/1990 - Andy Linighan from Norwich City - £1.2m
08/07/1990 - Anders Limpar from Cremonese - £1.2m

Departures

18/05/1990 - John Lukic to Leeds United - £1.17m
29/05/1990 - Martin Hayes to Celtic - £625k
01/07/1990 - Kevin Richardson to Real Sociedad - £723k

Defence

Thanks to the sheer bloody-mindedness and obsessional nature of George Graham, the defence upon which this team stood so proudly was the corner-stone of what was achieved in 90-91.

David Andrew Seaman
D.O.B - 19/09/63
Born - Rotherham. Signed for Arsenal - 1990
Position - Goalkeeper
Appearances in the 90/91 League Season - 38 - An ever present.

Seaman started his career at Leeds United, but never made an appearance for the senior side. He moved to Peterborough United, then Birmingham City, before impressing in his four years at QPR. A protracted move to Arsenal was his reward for his displays at Loftus Road and he came to Highbury replacing Gunners favourite John Lukic, who returned to Leeds

Nigel Winterburn
D.O.B - 11/12/63
Born - Arley. Signed for Arsenal - 1987
Position - Left-Back
Appearances in the 90/91 Season - 38 - An ever present.

Nigel Winterburn started his career at Birmingham City, but never broke through. A move to Oxford United resulted in the same struggle to get game time, so the left-back went to Wimbledon in 1983. Four years at Plough Lane was enough to catch the attention of George Graham and in 1987, Winterburn was made another piece in the puzzle of what was going to be the most effective backline in modern-day English football.

Lee Michael Dixon
D.O.B - 17/03/1964
Born - Manchester. Signed for Arsenal - 1988.
Position - Right-Back
Appearances in the 90/91 Season - 38 - An ever present. Goals - 5

Dixon made his professional bow at Burnley, but only four games in two years pushed him into the arms of Chester City. 57 games later, he had moved on to Bury. A season at Gigg Lane and then he was on the move again, this time to Stoke City. A flourishing partnership with centre-back Steve Bould was the impetus for George Graham to sign both and thus, another two players slotted into what was soon to emerge an almost impenetrable force.

Stephen Andrew Bould
D.O.B - 16/11/1962
Born - Stoke. Signed for Arsenal - 1988.
Position - Central Defender
Appearances in the 90/91 Season - 38 - An ever present.

Steve Bould spent eight years at Stoke City, with one year on loan at Torquay United. After establishing himself with the Potters, he moved to Highbury along with defensive partner Lee Dixon.

Tony Alexander Adams
D.O.B - 10/10/66
Born - Romford. Signed for Arsenal - 1983 as a Youth.
Position - Central Defender and Captain
Apps in the 90/91 Season - 30. Goals - 1

After three years as a schoolboy at Arsenal, Tony Adams finally made his debut in 1983, just after his 17th birthday. The rest of his story at Arsenal is encased in bronze.

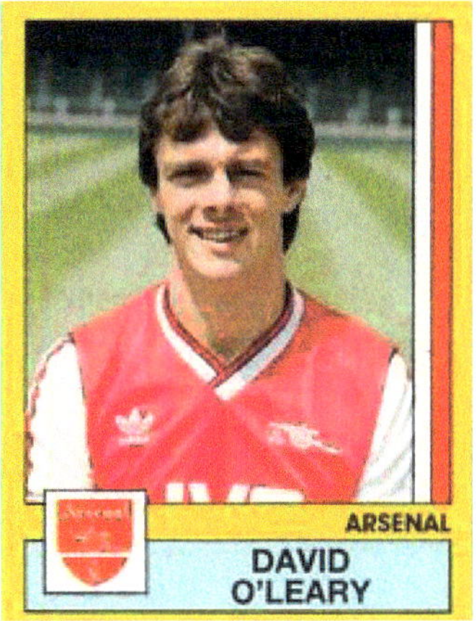

David Anthony O'Leary

D.O.B - 02/05/1958

Born - Stoke Newington. Signed for Arsenal - 1975

Position - Central Defender

Appearances in the 1990/91 Season - 11 (and 10 substitute Appearances) Goals - 1

O'Leary actually started his career at Irish club Shelbourne after moving to Ireland at the age of three, but signed his first professional contract at Arsenal. He made his debut in 1975, aged just 17.

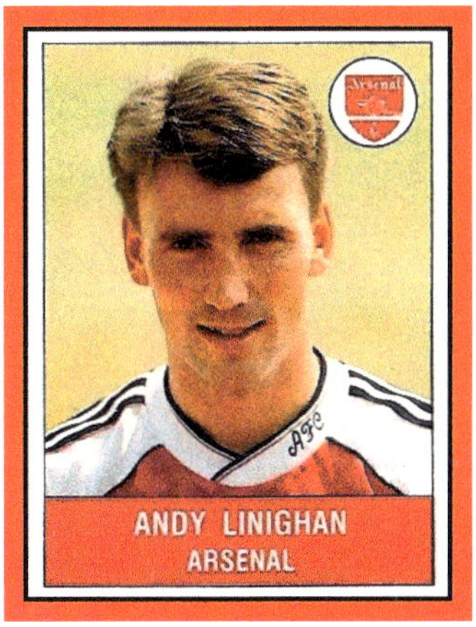

Andrew Linighan

D.O.B - 18/06/1962

Born - Hartlepool. Signed for Arsenal - 1990

Position - Central Defender

Appearances in the 1990/91 Season - 7 (with 3 substitute appearances)

Linighan started out at his local club, Hartlepool United, where he spent four years. In 1984, he moved to Elland Road, but two years later, was plying his trade at Oldham Athletic. It was his time at Carrow Road though - from 1988 to 1990 - that persuaded George Graham to add him to the Gunner's defensive ranks. Linighan had the same tenacity that Graham sought, and he would play a pivotal part in 1990/91.

Colin George Pates

D.O.B - 10/08/1961

Born - Carshalton. Signed for Arsenal - 1990

Position - Central Defender

Appearances in the 1990/91 Season - 1 substitute appearance.

Colin Pates had his most successful spell at his first club, Chelsea. 281 appearances were racked up over 9 years, before he moved South of the river to Charlton Athletic for two years. Then, in 1990, he moved to Highbury to add to Arsenal's defensive ranks. He also spent some time on loan at Brighton and Hove Albion during the 1990/91 season. Pate's arrival meant that Graham had a total of seven central defenders he could call upon in all. It still wouldn't be enough.

Midfield

With the perfect combination of raw power and enigmatic prowess, the centre of the Arsenal machine, was the peerless ally in attack and a warden protecting the already unrivalled backline. George Graham had it in spades - with Paul Davis and Michael Thomas, a seamless blend was found. They could both hound and harry opposing threats, but their link-up play is where they excelled.

Davis had an eye for a pass. That is not doing him justice to be fair. When under the cosh, a swish from his boot could ping the ball 60 yards and, with the aerial prowess of Smith waiting to receive, it meant Davis's long range passing was oft used. Converting our team from 'under pressure' to 'on top,' like footballing alchemy.

Thomas was younger and his effervescence was there for all to see. He was ridiculously hard to contain, but instead of launching missiles, Thomas ran. Then he ran some more. He carried the ball, and when he couldn't get the ball, his runs from deep would drag defenders from our attackers. It was his movement that caused the damage. Seeing as he was constantly in motion, it meant that he was always pivotal in matches.

Paul Vincent Davis

D.O.B - 09/12/1961
Born - Dulwich. Signed for Arsenal - Promoted from the Youth Team in 1980.
Position - Central Midfielder
Appearances in the 1990/91 Season - 36 (and 1 substitute appearance.) Goals - 3

Paul Davis was another player who dedicated his career to The Gunners. Signing as an Apprentice in 1977, through to making his first team debut in 1980, Davis became an integral part of the dramatic success of 1989 and also the near perfection of 1991. Quick, yet graceful, his passing was an underrated asset and had the ability to transform defence to attack in one flick of his boot. His testimonial year would be very special indeed.

Anders Erik Limpar

D.O.B - 24/09/1965
Born - Solna, Sweden. Signed for Arsenal - 1990
Position - Winger
Appearances in the 1990/91 Season - 32 (and 2 substitute appearances)
Goals - 11

Starting out at his boyhood club IF Brommapojkama, and staying for five years to complete his footballing education, Limpar honed his unique talents in Switzerland and Italy, before being recruited by George Graham in 1990 - totally against the grain of previous Graham purchases. The fleet-footed Swede instantly won over the ardent Gooner faithful with a vibrancy and trickery that wasn't evident anywhere else in the side. The outlet when games became mired in mediocrity, he blew teams away in his first season and cemented his place as a fans favourite. If minor injuries hadn't hampered him, it is a certainty that Limpar would have made an even bigger impact.

Michael Lauriston Thomas
D.O.B - 24/08/1967
Born - Lambeth. Signed for Arsenal - Promoted from the Youth Team in 1984.
Position - Central Midfielder
Appearances in the 1990/91 Season - 27 (and 4 substitute appearances) Goals - 2

Thomas signed as an Arsenal schoolboy in 1982, making his debut in 1984. He wrote his name in indelible ink upon the annals of Arsenal history with his last minute title winner in 1989 at Anfield and his dynamism in the centre of the park was the perfect companion to Paul Davis - strengthening Arsenal in the process. One of the best central midfield partnerships Arsenal have ever had.

Perry Groves
D.O.B - 19/04/1965
Born - Bow. Signed for Arsenal - 1986
Position - Winger
Appearances in the 1990/91 Season - 13 (and 19 substitute appearances) Goals - 3

Groves had family ties at Arsenal, but started his career at Colchester United, before moving to Highbury in 1986 and becoming George Graham's first signing for £50,000. Groves set up Charlie Nicholas to score the winner in the 1987 League Cup Final versus Liverpool to end a trophy drought spanning eight years, but he was used mainly as a game changer from the bench from the season after as Brian Marwood was preferred. Groves, though, was loved by the fans for good reason. Industrious and always bubbling with enthusiasm, he made things happen on the pitch. He would be used far more in this campaign, and his tireless performances could always be relied upon.

David Carlyle Rocastle

D.O.B - 02/05/1967
Born - Lewisham. Signed for Arsenal - Promoted from the Youth Team in 1984
Position - Winger
Appearances in the 1990/91 Season - 13 (and 3 substitute appearances) Goals - 2

Making his debut in 1984, it was only when his poor eyesight was corrected by contact lenses that 'Rocky' really started to blaze a trail at Highbury. An eye for goal and uncatchable with the ball at his feet, Rocastle earned England caps and adoration from fans for his work on the wing. He suffered with various injuries, but when fit and on the pitch, there was nothing Rocky couldn't do. His touch could unravel even the most composed of opponents, but this season would be bereft of the best that Rocky could do.

David Hillier

D.O.B - 19/12/1969
Born - Blackheath. Signed for Arsenal - Promoted from the Youth Team in 1988.
Position - Central Midfielder
Appearances in the 1990/91 Season - 9 (and 7 substitute appearances)

Hillier joined Arsenal as a youngster and progressed through the ranks until he made the first team squad in 1988. He had to wait for his debut, made against Chester City in 1990, but the grafter left his mark on George Graham's memory. His defensive bent allowed him to play a growing part in proceedings and he even filled in at the centre of defence, showing his versatility. He really earned his stripes during this season as injuries bit, and Hillier grabbed his chances with both hands.

Sigurdur 'Siggi' Jonsson

D.O.B - 27/09/1966
Born - Akranes, Iceland. Signed for Arsenal - 1989
Position - Central Midfielder.
Appearances in the 1990/91 Season - 2

'Siggi' made his reputation at Sheffield Wednesday, his sentry-like performances sitting in front of the back four, allied with his exocet of a shot, meant he impressed Graham enough to get the chequebook out in 1989. Injuries had a massive impact on his time at Highbury though, severely restricting his appearances in a Gunner's jersey. The Icelander never let anyone down whenever he donned the Arsenal shirt, and his two appearances in the campaign were the standard that the Gooners expected.

Forwards

Without Graham's attack, no matter how effective his midfield and defence were, then his plans for domination could not have come to fruition. An over-reliance on Alan Smith was perhaps the only weakness within the ranks that had been assembled by Arsenal's Scottish chief, but the other players who made up the Gunner's goal threat more than satisfied the requirement.

The man they call 'Smudge' had won the Adidas Golden Boot - the award for the league's top scorer for the season - when Arsenal had won the title two years previously. There were some very good reasons why Smith had become very acquainted with goals. Smudge was almost unrivalled in the air. He stands at 6'3" tall, so the genes his parents gave him obviously came in handy when going up for headers! There were many defenders who were taller than him, but allied with his leap, Smudge could pick the ball from the air with ease. That was only half the job though. You can win every ball that is launched to you, but if you then gift possession back, then it's a pretty useless skill to have. Smith had a built in sonar and he made nearly as many goals as he scored. His positioning, his finishing - you can see why George utilised him so regularly.

Anders Limpar and Paul Merson were genuine dangers cutting in from the flanks and they shared the goal burden with Smith, and the emergence of the powerful Kevin Campbell gave Graham the backup and variety in the striker department that a long season required. The attack was as well-armed as the famous defence.

Paul Charles Merson

D.O.B - 20/03/1968

Born - Harlesden. Signed for Arsenal - Promoted from Youth Team in 1985.

Position - Wide Forward (Often used as a winger when Rocky Rocastle was injured)

Appearances in the 1990/91 Season - 36 (and 1 substitute appearance).

Goals - 13

Signed as a schoolboy, then going out on loan to a Frank McLintock managed Brentford, stood Merson in good stead, and he made his debut in 1986. The dangerous forward had an eye for goal and an unpredictable nature that defenders struggled to read. He possessed the ability to produce defence-splitting passes, and his reading of situations were a huge asset, with Alan Smith nearly always profiting. The 'Magic Man' was one of the key players for the 1990/91 season and George Graham optimised him to full effect, making Smith and Merson a deadly double act which fired Arsenal to the title. He really left his mark on Gooners in his time at Highbury.

Alan Martin Smith
D.O.B - 21/11/1962
Born - Hollywood, Worcestershire.
Signed for Arsenal - 1987
Position - Striker
Appearances in the 1990/91 Season - 35 (and two sub appearances). Goals - 22

Starting out at Leicester City, the man fans call 'Smudge' always had a killer instinct in the box, but when he signed for Arsenal, he also perfected the art of the flick-on, which brought others into play in the attack. His aerial ability was unrivalled, his positioning in the danger zone was uncanny. As plainly and simply as I can put it, Smith was at the fulcrum of Arsenal's success. Top scorer in the league that year, Smudge was an explosive cylinder on George Graham's machine.

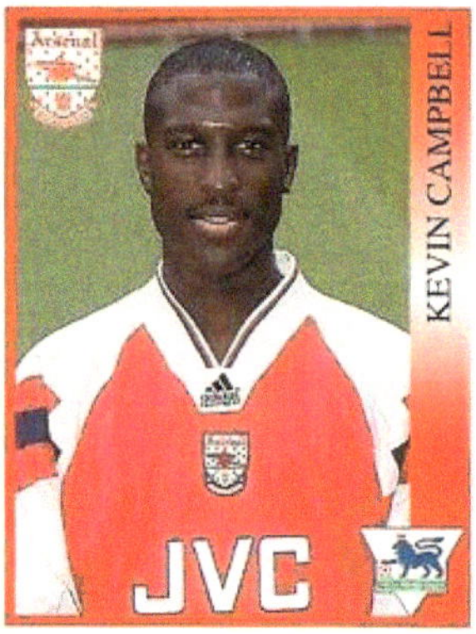

Kevin Joseph Campbell
D.O.B - 04/02/1970
Born - Lambeth. Signed for Arsenal - Promoted from Youth Team - 1988
Position - Striker
Appearances in the 1990/91 Season - 15 (and 7 substitute appearances). Goals - 9
Making his debut in 1988 was down to Campbell's prolific run in the Youth Team - scoring 59 goals in one season. The pacy youngster was to prove to be a valuable asset for the Gunners. Having two loans spells helped Campbell and he returned a far more accomplished striker than he was before. His pace and athleticism frightened defenders, and despite never managing to nail down a concrete place in the team - down to the fantastic form of Merson and Smith - Campbell would prove his worth in the near-Invincible season of 1990/91. Campbell's power and goals would be decisive in the latter months of that unforgettable year.

Andrew Alexander Cole
D.O.B - 15/10/1971
Born - Nottingham. Signed for Arsenal - Promoted from Youth Team in 1989
Position - Striker
Appearances in the 1990/91 Season - 1 substitute appearance.

Cole was an Arsenal schoolboy, before signing professional forms in 1989. Although fans are aware of his goalscoring pedigree now, back then, he made only one appearance - as a substitute against Sheffield Wednesday in 1990. There were no opportunities for the young Cole due to the presence of Smith, Merson and Campbell and he moved on. His story had only just begun however.

A total of 19 men were used in total. In comparison, the 'Invincibles' side used 34. Both had a league campaign of 38 games. In closer detail, this is how they measured up for the season.

	1990/91	
2003/04		
Players Used	19	34
Players Scored	11	15
Goals Scored	74	73
Goals Conceded	18	26
Goal Difference	+56	+47
Games Drawn	13	12

The comparative statistics highlight a glaring truth often overlooked regarding the Arsenal team of 1990/91 - they weren't simply about grinding down the opposition. They actually outscored the free-flowing Invincibles side of 2003/04. Throw into the mix a defence that conceded less than one in every two games and you have a recipe for domination.

The men who comprised this squad also performed the instructions that their Manager gave them down to the last letter, they had the winning mentality that all Champions require. They possessed the secret strand in their genetic makeup that doesn't allow for second best. From the seemingly insignificant wrong decisions on the pitch by a referee, or an over-zealous tackle by an opponent, they acted as a team to right wrongs and overturn bad karma.

A winning mentality, a squad that worked as a team full of cohesion, that took instruction and implemented it as requested - not to mention a desire so large, so bright, that it unified and drove these players to harness its strengths and hitch a ride to glory. This squad had it all.

The beginning of the season approached and George Graham had installed the final pieces of his machinery. Now that August was on the horizon, it was time to take it on the road for testing, and to see what it was capable of.

Summer In Sweden And Sweating Out Weakness

George Graham, who many of the players dubbed 'Gaddafi', had gathered the troops he deemed were fit enough to wrestle the Championship back from Liverpool. He had made his moves in the market, cutting the chaff from his squad and adding strength in the areas where he had seen weakness in the previous campaign.

Would these decisions prove to be the difference in what would be another compelling season? The 1988/89 season showed that any variable, no matter how miniscule, could be telling. Graham kept the same foundation which so enrapturingly captured the title on current Champions Liverpool's own turf, but could his latest recruits tip the scales back in Arsenal's favour?

The only proven method to testing fresh parts is to put them in action and gauge their effectiveness. To fit into an already successful contraption, the new pieces would have to be tested rigorously. It would not be an instant transition for them. They would have to work hard on and off the pitch.

David Seaman had long been a target of Graham's - his protracted signing was finally completed before the season began and Graham had his man. His previous efforts for QPR were precisely the reason why he was courted for so long, he had earned his first England cap whilst wearing the hoops of QPR. Seaman was also coached by a certain Bob Wilson at Loftus Road - the illustrious former Arsenal goalkeeper who won the Double in 1971 - and that relationship was to continue as Wilson rejoined the club he adored.

Speaking to Bob Wilson about Seaman joining the club, 'Gentleman' Bob said, "George and Don Howe both asked about David when we were at QPR. David obviously joined, and I did too just afterwards. David was always calm, and humble. You can never rile him. I can't recall ever seeing him lose the plot, even when I used to wind him up about being the only Arsenal goalie to win the Double!"

Bob and David's rapport was an integral as to why the Yorkshireman made a running start to affairs at the club, and it meant that Gooners soon got over John Lukic's departure.

Peace and Gunners love for new boy Anders Limpar

A notoriously strict taskmaster, George Graham would use pre-season to whip his boys into shape (figuratively speaking of course), and all of the squad would have been dreading the fitness drills!

Alan Smith stated that, "there were no poor trainers at the club, we weren't allowed to be! It was always a relief when he couldn't make training, although that was rare. George was a tracksuit manager and was always out there organising. There wasn't room for laziness!"

The challenge ahead of them was to overthrow the Scouse empire again. Arsenal had taken the First Division title from Liverpool two seasons previously, but the attempt to retain what was a surprise triumph went awry. George Graham would have to step up his work in order to repeat the feat, and devised a strategy to put his side one step ahead of the prestigious competition. Training was what he did best, intense training. The team would be put through their paces, to say the least..

The destination for this rigorous beasting was Sweden, and three fixtures had been lined up to help Graham determine where his team were in terms of readiness for the new campaign.

Sweden was a popular destination for English teams as a means for dipping their toe back into competitive football. Occasionally, there was an opportunity to visit a far-flung destination that could be lucrative for the club, but fanbases and sponsorship deals compared to the present day are immeasurable.

Besides, the Allsvenskan (the Swedish Football League) was in full flow, and the players would provide a stern test for English teams who needed to sweat out the excesses of a break where everything was let loose. With George Graham as manager, can you blame the players if they enjoyed themselves a little too much, with a backbreaking pre-season to look forward to?

So, the squad packed their bags and flew out to Scandinavia in July, with the start of the season mere weeks away. With new players to integrate and gauge, and fitness levels to raise, this would be no jolly-up.

I was lucky enough to be able to interview Arsenal's chief goal threat that season, Alan Smith, who said of his Scottish boss; "George was a hard taskmaster. He was out on the training pitch every single day. He was tough, and it was a relief to all of us on the rare occasions when he wasn't in!"

One of the new recruits to the Gunner's cause was enigmatic Swedish winger, Anders Limpar.

He had been brought in from Serie A, which was tactically superior at the time, but slower paced. Could the diminutive Scandinavian convert his talent to the English game? George Graham intended to find out.

Alan Smith said that George, "got into Anders in training. There were no shirkers on the training pitch, and he let him know in no uncertain terms." The Swede answered any doubters emphatically.

First up on this training exercise was a side called Varbergs Bois. The spectacle was over at half time, with Arsenal two goals to the good thanks to Paul Merson and Rocky Rocastle. Any fans holding out hope of seeing Limpar make an appearance were to be disappointed however, as he wasn't in the match-day squad. The little Scandinavian was still on honeymoon at the time, so his absence could be forgiven, I guess!

Graham seemed intent on utilising his whole squad while the chance was afforded to him, and this meant a return for Gus Caesar, who was to make his only start of the season in this game. He then disappeared back into the reserve squad before departing at the end of the season on a free transfer to QPR. Caesar was never recovered from his horror show in the Littlewoods Cup Final of 1988, and his departure had been on the cards for a while.

David Seaman started his first game, in what was to be a long and distinguished career with the club. He began as he would for the majority of his stay with Arsenal, with an assured display and a clean sheet.

Paul Davis and Siggi Jonsson formed the centre of midfield, with Merson, Groves and Smith the attacking threat. The result mattered little though. This game was a stepping stone to George's vision of a physically superior team and the Swedish tour, along with the fitness schedule, was in full swing and the next friendly match was on the horizon.

There was to be no respite for George's charges. Two days later, they played another top tier Swedish side, this time in the form of Vastra Frolunda IE.

The game ended with a handsome 4-0 scoreline in Arsenal's favour - the goals coming from Linighan and Smith, with Merson bagging his second and third of the tour. Graham had tinkered with the lineup, and gave two of his new signings a run out. Andy Linighan was partnered with Colin Pates in a newly forged central defensive duo, and the much-heralded Limpar was given his debut on the flank. Limpar made a startling impression on his first start for the club - assisting two of the goals. It heralded what fans could expect from the Swedish marvel, and to grab two assists on your debut was a mark of how quickly Limpar had adapted from the Italian game to Graham's methodology.

Siggi Jonsson made way for Paul Davis's more familiar midfield partner, Mickey Thomas, and Kevin Campbell actually slotted in ahead of Merson - but it was the 'Magic Man' who came off the bench to add gloss to the scoreline.

So far, so good. The three new recruits were showing promising signs, and all the men were dusting off the rust with each playing minute.

There was no time to admire the handiwork though, as a third game in six days, again against top flight Swedish opposition, was on the agenda. It was the final game of the tour, and to bring an end to proceedings, the opponents were IFK Varnamo.

A clean sweep of victories was to be denied Graham, as a tough 2-2 draw was to be the final result. Paul Merson, again, was on the scoresheet, and Limpar grabbed his first goal in a Gunner's jersey. The team had a more familiar feel to it, as captain Adams returned in place of Colin Pates, and Merson came in for Campbell.

Graham would have no doubt saw this excursion as 'Mission Accomplished.' He had utilised the vast majority of the men at his disposal, and had seen his new charges take to playing with a cannon on their chest successfully. He had also managed to regain fitness levels annually lost to the excesses of the summer break. Everything he had set out to do on the trip was checked off from his list, and with that, they returned to the UK.

Another added plus to the Swedish tour was the fact they had played three games in six days. It would be a more than familiar tale that Arsenal would be afflicted with during the coming season. Fixture congestion would play a huge part in proceedings.

A week after playing IFK Varnamo, another away friendly was planned against Wolverhampton Wanderers. The Black Country outfit were boasting Mike Stowell, a keeper with a burgeoning reputation and a respectable price tag of £250,000. It took just sixty seconds for Arsenal to deflate Wolves' new boy between the sticks however, as Paul Davis flicked on for 'Smudge' to finish with aplomb.

Arsenal had put Wolves to the sword, despite only winning by a single goal margin. David Seaman only had two saves of any note to make, and he was untroubled for the most part. Another clean sheet for the England goalkeeper, and another win for Arsenal as gameplans were being straightened out, players were sharpening their talents and roles were being decided. One of those roles was certainly decided at Molineux.

Brian Marwood had suffered an injury hit campaign in 1989/90, and it had resulted in the arrival of Anders Limpar. Marwood had earned the fan's respect after his assists were responsible for Alan Smith's goal haul in the epic season of 88/89. His injuries, though, were to deny him the chance to nail down the left hand flank for an extended amount of time. He played in the match against Wolves, but he was to be offloaded to Sheffield United just a month later, for £350,000.

Another match against a Midlands side was next up on the pre-season roster; a week later Aston Villa lined up against Graham's Gunners.

From this match onwards, Limpar's left-hand spot was undoubtedly his to lose. The game was part of the Makita Cup, a friendly tournament hosted at Wembley on an annual basis back then. It was organised by Arsenal, and its first incarnation took place in 1988. It ran until 1994, and the Gunners took the glory three times in that time.

Sampdoria had also won this seasonal warm-up event three times, and they would provide a tough examination of Arsenal's credentials. They were part of that year's tournament, as well as Villa and Real Sociedad, and whilst the trip to Scandinavia and the game against Wolves would help the Arsenal squad to raise their levels, the next two games would provide the sternest of tests.

The results would matter a lot more here. This is where all of George Graham's conditioning work would be stress tested. The calibre of team they would face would determine whether Graham had been successful in his summer's endeavours, or if there was room to be had for urgent improvement. So, the Villa game was first up, followed just twenty four hours later by a match against Sampdoria.

Some things never change, and one of them is speculation within football. The talk before the tournament began, was that Arsenal were expected to sign a striker. Arsenal had Smith, Campbell, Groves and Cole in their attacking ranks who could play in a striker's role, but the newspapers were of the opinion that Arsenal were light in the offensive spots. Would the doubters fire the Gunners to more goals?

The Villa game saw Limpar take centre stage, with a wonderful goal and his bag of tricks fully stocked. Kevin Campbell came off the bench in the second half to ensure victory, and set up a final against Sampdoria, who had beaten Sociedad on penalties to progress themselves.

The match was a good workout. Villa were under new stewardship, with Dr Josef Venglos at the helm. The Czech coach had led them to some fine results in pre-season, and the Villans were considered to be a force in the Championship. So a 2-0 win would have confidence coursing throughout the Arsenal side.

The press lavished praise on the Gunner's performance, and they singled out Limpar, Linighan, Davis and Rocky for special tributes for the way they had clicked together, and this was testimony to George Graham's thorough training schedule.

At this point in proceedings, Graham seemed to have settled on his chosen formula. Seaman had been showing why the comparatively large transfer fee had been spent on acquiring his services. Linighan was also justifying his price tag as he was chosen to partner Mr Arsenal himself - Tony Adams.

Looking back on this, the move to partner club captain Adams with new recruit Andy Linighan wasn't as surprising as it is now with the benefit of hindsight. Steve Bould had suffered a horrendous season the year before - missing five months through injury - and Linighan coming in from Norwich was seen, by many, as replacing Bould for the long term.

Hindsight is a wonderful thing, as it enables us to see that Bould was to emphatically prove all the doubters wrong. At the time, however, his fledgling Arsenal career - he had been at Arsenal for three years - was still in its infancy.

Lee Dixon and Nigel Winterburn had the full-back spots tied down, and Mickey Thomas stood alongside Paul Davis in the heart of midfield. Rocky was his effervescent self on the right, and super Swede Limpar was to wreak havoc on the left. Up front, despite being reportedly 'light' in attack, Paul Merson would ably assist ever-reliable Alan Smith. Merson's pliability in attack mean that he was just as effective out wide as he was when partnering Smudge. It also resulted in him giving defenders nightmares when tasked with marking him. Very scary ones in some cases!

This lineup was selected for the last three pre-season games. Aston Villa and Sampdoria in the Makita Cup, and the last warm-up fixture before the season kicked off - a testimonial for Steve Gatting, against Brighton.

The final of the Makita Cup was up first, and Sampdoria could boast of a fearsome attack, Gianluca Vialli and Roberto Mancini providing the threat for the Italian side, and with Gianluca Pagliuca in goal, Sampdoria went into the game as favourites.

The games, up to this point, were a growth chart of sorts, but this would be the litmus test for Graham and his work thus far. The result was disappointing (1-0 in favour of Sampdoria) but the Gunners came out of the match with their heads held high. Newspaper reports told of how Arsenal looked to have regained their speed of play after a poor attempt at regaining their title the previous season. The Guardian's match report mentioned how the Gunners struck the post three times during the game, despite being outplayed for large parts of the game.

Sampdoria were intricate and technically sound. George Graham, in his post-match comments, highlighted their interchanges up front and their triangular passing moves, which at times stretched the Gunners backline beyond breaking point.

So, Sampdoria were winners of the Makita Cup, but Graham's plans had firm foundations. They were a match for Sampdoria, they had defeated Aston Villa, and the side looked to have ironed out their creases ahead of the new campaign.

Liverpool and Manchester United - another two teams who looked likely to make up the Championship chasing pack - were to duke it out for the season's curtain raiser, the Charity Shield, which was to be the last opportunity the team's bosses would get to test the readiness for their sides. The Arsenal players, for their part, had one last chance to impress their manager and outline why they all deserved to play.

In this last chance saloon, against Brighton and Hove Albion, the Seagulls took a surprise two goal lead inside thirteen minutes, but Arsenal showed their fighting spirit was intact, by bringing parity to the scoreline before half-time. David Rocastle and Alan Smith were responsible for Arsenal hauling themselves back into the game.

The second half was a procession, but Graham would have been pleased that Smith was finding his touch before the big kick off.

With the Albion game wrapped up, all that was left was to look to their first game of the league campaign, which was a visit to Wimbledon in eight days.

Graham looked to have found a good formula, and the team which he had named for the last four warm-ups was identical. New signings were integrated, Smith and Merson were looking dangerous, and Limpar appeared to have taken to his new task with gusto.

The time for mistakes, for tests, was over. The league was to begin and the Gunners wanted their title back. Manchester United, Aston Villa and especially Liverpool, would have a big say on whether George Graham had done enough to wrestle power back from Merseyside again.

A visit to Selhurst Park, where Wimbledon were tenants at the time, was the first step to glory.

Ironing Out The Kinks

The gruelling fitness sessions, the new acquisitions, the experimental inclusions in pre-season, they were a means to an end. The end in question, ironically, being the start of the 1990/91 Division One campaign.

The defence of the title so heroically gained on that halcyon night on May 26th 1989 at Anfield had not gone according to George Graham's script. That is a huge understatement. The feelings of disappointment and anger as his Arsenal side limped to a fourth placed finish could quite possibly have manifested in more acrimonious ways, but the canny Scot knew what he had at his disposal.

The title that was relinquished with the briefest of struggles was not a flash in the pan, not in George's eyes. The squad that held the trophy aloft that season was largely still present, and stronger and wiser as a result. Upon interviewing one of the pillars that the Anfield success was built on - Lee Dixon - he shed some light on what was expected before the season began;

"After Anfield '89, every season we went into we expected to challenge for the League. George demanded a lot from his players, and it was hard to keep that intensity year after year."

George Graham was looking to build and tweak, improving the structure that he had already instilled. George had his finger on the pulse of every part of the club, and the youth system was another avenue that he looked to when strengthening his team.

The youth team was being managed by two Gunners who had the Cannon branded onto their hearts. Geordie Armstrong and Pat Rice had been vital parts of the Double winning team of 1971, and their roles of Reserve and Youth Team bosses would provide Graham with a bolstering of numbers that was a more organic method than the transfer window.

David Hillier, youth team captain the previous year, was given the chance that every starry-eyed kid dreamt of. He was promoted to the first team squad at the behest of Graham and with the stamp of approval from Rice and Armstrong. The same went for agile striker Kevin Campbell. Of course, transfer hype was almost as intense back then, but without the internet, there was no wildfire social media speculation or spurious click-bait news that exists today – and no 'Sky Sources'. The talk back then was mainly restricted to newspapers and pub chatter, but what it consisted of was that Arsenal were in the market for a striker, as previously mentioned.

Kevin Campbell's promotion from the reserves was merited, and it meant that the laborious task of integrating a new recruit would be avoided and full concentration could be spent on preparation for the new season. Campbell could instantly jump into the squad and was already au fait with the club's structure and the manner in which things were done. It was the perfect move. The structure for the season, and for training, would not have to be altered, George could set about his vision knowing each man in the team was under no illusions as to what to expect in training.

That instilling of structure was not to be underplayed however, and it had begun from the very moment he began his managerial role in 1986. The repetition on the training pitch, the defensive drills for different situations, it all stemmed from his first day at the helm of the club.

One of the most important factors of his early work is often missed though, namely his careful handpicking of playing staff - either from transfers, the youth setup, or simply who to offload. Guardian and Observer sports journalist Amy Lawrence touched on this when I quizzed her regarding this season;

"When George Graham arrived, something he did quickly was weed out the big egos and promote young, hungry players or purchase them. He wanted hunger. Like George was himself."

Graham had a reputation for not suffering fools, but his abhorrence of shirkers was even more ingrained into his methods. Since he took the reins at Arsenal in 1986, his raison d'etre was hard work gets results. It left his players in no doubt whatsoever as to what was expected of them.

I interviewed goalkeeping icon David Seaman for the book, and he said this of his first impressions of the training schedule;

"They were brilliant, but pure hard work. He knew what each player needed to do after another had moved. There was no room for slacking off, and it was a big difference from my other clubs, but I got used to it. I had no choice!"

His attention to detail meant that every scenario and threat that could be played out on the pitch, could be successfully negated with a shift in defensive movement. The bedrock of the 88-89 season was the Gunner's defence, so what had happened in the subsequent season?

Inspecting the final league table for that season shows us that Arsenal conceded a meagre 11 goals on the way to their fourth place finish. So the defensive stylings of George Graham had once again risen to the fore, but with only thirty eight goals from thirty eight games, was it a stuttering attack that had saw the Gunners title dreams bite the dust?

Perhaps, but as Lee Dixon mentioned, the intensity and battling qualities that were prized by the Arsenal manager and allowed his team to outgun their opponents through their sheer will to win - it was so very difficult to maintain that burning desire over a stretch of time.

Would the anguish of seeing their title return to the red half of Merseyside, after fighting so hard to win it, ignite that combustion engine which lay in every Arsenal players loins? After all, George had ensured the squad had put in the hard miles, so they were champing at the bit for the start of the season, and he had also seen fit to give his side's attack a boost with the acquisition of Anders Limpar. It seemed he had done all he could do.

Bob Wilson, who returned to Arsenal as goalkeeping coach on a permanent basis when David Seaman signed, thought as much;

"George Graham was incredible, and he had made sure that the budgets were all in place for the transfers he required. He was a tactically astute manager, but also a disciplinarian. The players knew who the boss was and the line was clear, but George gave everything to get the most out of each player."

So it appears as if the major work that Graham had identified as integral to their title hopes had been completed before the start line had been reached, but poring over the failure of the 1989-90 season allows a portal, of sorts, into what saw Arsenal stumble in their title defence.

After taking so much time to construct an impenetrable wall, Graham would have been distraught to see one of the cornerstones of his famous backline removed for half of the season. Steve Bould had played exactly half of the league games that season, as injuries bit the hard centre-back just as tough as one of Bould's tackles. This meant that the experienced David O'Leary slotted back into the defence. Not exactly a tragedy, especially with an understudy with the defensive merits that O'Leary had.

That was 1990 though, and David was 32. Those days, the very mention of a stretching session and a salad would see you booted from the training complex on the grounds of lunacy. Careers were not destined to be prolonged until another Arsenal manager came in six years later. The years of malicious kicks and pitches that wouldn't look amiss on a battlefield had worn away O'Leary.

He was still a part of the squad as he had been indoctrinated into George Graham's defensive mantras, and his experience allowed him to overlook the ravages of time his body would be suffering from. Steve Bould though, was the future, and his chemistry with Gunners Skipper Tony Adams bordered on telepathy at times. So whilst O'Leary was certainly capable of doing a great job filling in, capable did not cut it in Graham's perfect vision.

When he signed Andy Linighan from Norwich for a, then, massive £1.2 million, certain eyebrows were raised in the media. With England internationals Adams and Bould in the team, and with David O'Leary and Colin Pates as able deputies, what was Graham playing at spending that sort of cash on yet another centre-half?

Graham could see the potential for disaster if injuries hit his defence. Seeing as his entire team was built atop it, he moved quickly to avoid any possible repercussion from a lack of quality cover. With Bould missing such a large piece of the previous season, the chances of the same ailments recurring would also have to be taken into consideration. Being a man that made sure every detail was mapped out, he had done just that.

Linghan had been earning plaudits for his displays with the Canaries, and when he joined Arsenal, reporters and pundits alike were of the opinion that

Anders Limpar breaks through against Leeds United in January 1991

he would challenge the recently crocked Bould for the right to partner Arsenal's captain.

This is one of the main reasons Graham had set up so many pre-season runouts for his side. It wasn't just to obtain that magical level of match fitness in preparation for the season. It was to see how Linighan would fare when in the side, adapting to the Scottish Manager's finely tuned instructions for his back five.

The same reasoning can be applied to the decision to sign Swede Anders Limpar. There had been a few players who had missed large chunks of the previous season, with Paul Davis and Siggi Jonsson both suffering for differing reasons. Throw into the mix the departures of Kevin Richardson and Brian Marwood and there seemed to be a whiff of alarm in regards to midfield playing ranks.

Chief amongst any underlying motive to buy Limpar though, was the fitness of wing wizard David Rocastle. Fan favourite Rocky had struggled to play the full ninety minutes compared to his colleagues, and a severe knee cartilage injury Rocky had incurred early in his career had begun to swell and inflame after every game. Rocastle had got used to rough treatment from defenders as his touch beguiled and angered his opponents, but Graham had once again installed a failsafe to any potential pitfall that comes with being bereft of such an influential player.

Much like in his playing days, Bob Wilson told me, George was immaculate on the pitch as well as off it - Graham took into account the minutiae of variables.

He purchased Limpar, as without Rocastle, the sprinkling of stardust that every team needs would be largely missing. Merson could cut open any team, but Rocky was unpredictable and he could do it on his own at times. A replacement/backup would be difficult to locate, but Limpar had shown in the friendly matches he had took part in, that he was more than able to fill the void left if Rocastle needed time on the treatment table.

George had ensured that there was a level of immunity even when his teams polished outer shell was damaged. Cover for every conceivable circumstance had been put in place to allow Arsenal to wrestle back superiority.

The purchase of Limpar was two-fold as well. While his primary motive for signing the Swede was, no doubt, to lessen any impact that the absence of Rocky could land, Limpar could also weigh in with goals - something that was as equally important.

With any top side that could boast of an international class centre forward, the burden that they would carry for plundering goals would invariably weigh on their shoulders. This was no different with Arsenal and Alan 'Smudge' Smith.

Smith had banged in an impressive 23 goals in 36 league games when the Gunners were famously victorious at Anfield in 1989. The striker from Leicester was a real menace in the air and had an incredible knack for great positioning in the box for close-range finishing. He was a manager's dream; reliable, injury-free and always gave his side a threat.

However, the following season saw a drop in numbers for Smudge. He managed a total of thirteen goals in all competitions, from 42 starts. No less useful, but a slight blunting of what was a keen blade.

The next most effective arrow in George's quiver that campaign was Paul Merson, who had grabbed seven goals in 24 starts. It was an injury-hit campaign for the Magic Man, and this, in turn, saw the necessity for other players to pick up the slack in terms of making the net bulge.

The players who came closest to rivalling Smith and Merson for goals, were Mickey Thomas and Brian Marwood. Thomas could be relied upon to get between five to ten goals a season, but Marwood had left the club, so it meant that Graham had to act.

Limpar was seen as the shot in the arm that Arsenal needed to up the goal ante. His goal amounts for his previous club Cremonese were not enough to moisten the palate, but his electric movement and exquisite passing held the potential to bring his fellow attackers into the game, as well as finding them in the box.

His season in Italy was instrumental in honing the abilities that would hopefully invigorate Arsenal's attack. At the time, Serie A was at the height of its power, and its defensive teachings were amongst the best in the world. If you could score a goal or even find space in the final third, then you had performed above and beyond. Limpar would have benefitted from this cloistering football, and it meant he could very well flourish in the frenetic, but less taciturn First Division.

Graham had dotted the 'i's' and crossed the 't's'. He had found a way to refine a squad that was capable of much, but had misfired the season previously. The manner in which he did this though, is what was most impressive.

A plethora of gaffers would have reached for their trusty axe and cleaved what they perceived as under-achievers, before then going cap in hand to their chairmen with pleas of impoverishment and a malnourished squad number.

George Graham had not forgotten the miraculous season of 1988/89, and the herculean efforts his side - which he had manufactured - had performed in order to snatch a first title in eighteen years. The men who had taken his manifesto and allowed it to come to fruition were still at the club, and George knew he could once more depend on them. He still needed to bolster their shortcomings though. Did he grab his trolley and go wild in the aisles, purchasing talent as if it was going out of fashion? Did he grab the underachievers from the previous season and send them packing? No.

What he did do, was keep the chemistry and rapport that bound these men, and also reinforced it. The players he cut were the right players to let go. The players who were drafted in had been carefully selected, and if all went well, they would buy into the 'Arsenal Way.' So yes, George had done all he could.

Arsenal's great rivals, and North London neighbours, Tottenham, had been enjoying a revival under the stewardship of Terry Venables, and the season that saw Arsenal loosen their grip on the League trophy was also the year that 'El Tel' had masterminded a third place finish and decisively - finish above Arsenal.

Gary Lineker had joined the white half of North London, and his goals, with the guile of Paul Gascoigne behind him, meant that Spurs had added insult to the Gunner's injury, by reclaiming dominance over their shared constituency.

The fans were still the lifeblood in 1990, so this flagrant insult had to be rectified. George Graham would not have taken lightly the fact that, under his leadership, he had gifted their hated neighbours the bragging rights.

The time to iron out any kinks was over though. George Graham had tweaked, smoothed over, and rebuilt where applicable, and it appeared that Arsenal was ready.

Spurs, Liverpool, Crystal Palace, Aston Villa and Manchester United took to the start line with the Gunners to begin ceremonies, and one of the greatest season's in Arsenal's history was about to begin.

Title Rivals

It is the scale of adversary one faces that adds lustre to achievements. Snatching glory from a behemoth, a seemingly unbeatable foe, garners headlines and plaudits. No one harks back with misty-eyed adoration to a time when your team won the league with eight games to spare. When dusting down the tomes of memory, it is when the enemy's shadow looms large over you that the memory lends itself to greatness.

The 1990/91 season had plenty of worthy contestants that would provide stern competition and fit that exact bill, not least of all, Liverpool.

Six titles were garnered by the red machine of Liverpool in the 80's. Two European Cups, two FA Cups and four League Cups were obtained as the domination of the Seventies rolled on into the next decade. Kenny Dalglish's men were all-conquering, and the strike-force they had instilled a knife of fear into every team that lined up alongside them on the pitch.

Arsenal's defence though, was the perfect sheath for the keen blade of Messrs Rush, Dalglish and Barnes. As wily and merciless as the Liverpool attack was, they were matched by the stoic and intuitive Arsenal back four. They were blunted on that famous night at Anfield in '89, as Arsenal became the first side in over three years to win at the ground by two clear goals, and it was also the first time they had taken the points from Anfield in fifteen years.

The season after this miraculous achievement, Liverpool returned to winning ways, as they celebrated clinching the first League Championship of the 90's. They did so by finishing nine points clear of their nearest challengers, Aston Villa.

Arsenal? A massive 17 points was the gulf between the sides as the Gunners finished fourth. This was a reminder that the season before would be difficult to replicate, and Dalglish's Reds were not quite toppled from their perch.

Alex Ferguson is often attributed as being the man responsible for ending Liverpool's dominance over domestic proceedings, but Guardian and Observer journalist, Amy Lawrence, is keen to point out who should be acknowledged for drawing a line under the Merseysider's dominion;

"At the time, you couldn't tell this was Liverpool being knocked off their perch, which was of course the famous Sir Alex Ferguson quote. However, it was George Graham who knocked Liverpool off. It was Graham who, after Liverpool had won the title TEN times, won the League twice in three seasons. It was a four year tussle between the teams, which was very compelling."

A title apiece in the last two seasons, this year would see both sides square up together once again. Liverpool, eager to continue their supremacy over the rest of England, Arsenal, keen to show that 1989 was not simply an aberration, that they warranted their tag as contenders.

Fast forward to the start of the 1990/91 season, Liverpool were the presiding Champions. The team who were once again looking down from a lofty position, and sat comfortably back on a throne they had made their own.

Their rollcall of honours was long and illustrious, and their squad was the envy of their competitors. They had won everything, and had proved in the previous campaign that if anyone wanted to step up to the plate, their first port of call would be to pry the league trophy from Liverpool's vice-like grip.

In between the sticks, the miracle work of Bruce Grobbelaar had earned him a permanent place in Scouse hearts, and he still held the gloves and respect of teammates and opposing strikers, but the Zimbabwean was just the tip of this monolithic iceberg.

Every great team is built on a wall-like defence, and Liverpool were no different. Steve Staunton, Barry Venison and Steve Nicol were the cornerstones of this back four, and had been given the incredibly tough job of attempting to match the efforts of previous Liverpool defensive stalwarts Alan Hansen, Mark Lawrenson, Phil Neal, Tommy Smith and Phil Thompson. They had taken to it well though, and under the stewardship of Dalglish to impart his wisdom and experience, they had presented opponents with just as tough a task as in previous years.

The Reds also had a promising streak of youth in their ranks in Gary Ablett, who had done so well in their title win the year before. This powerful mix of abilities would see teams needing to be on their A-game if they wanted to pose a threat.

In the centre of the park, the Reds were blessed. A mix of mettle and guile, if on the rare occasion their lethal strikers were muted, the gargantuan menace of their midfielders and wingers would put the best defence to the sword. The strength of Jan Molby and Steve McMahon was the perfect foundation from which to launch strategic attacks, and with the speed and skill of John Barnes and Peter Beardsley, Liverpool were sufficiently armed.

It was their forward line that struck fear into any team that faced them though. Their reputation preceded them, and Ian Rush had a quite incredible record. For nearly six years up until the Littlewoods Cup Final in 1987, when the Welshman scored, Liverpool had never lost. The team that had ended that flabbergasting record? Arsenal.

It wasn't merely a one-man strikeforce that had earned Liverpool so much silverware however. The aforementioned Beardsley was adaptable and therefore difficult to pick up by defenders, and his switching from the wing to the foil for Rush was a nightmare for most teams.

Crucially though, it wasn't a patch on the former partnership of Dalglish and Rush, but the Scotsman's presence on the pitch had been on the decline since his appointment as Player-Manager back in 1985. His last official appearance was in 1990, but a club legend the size of Dalglish, now installed as full-time Manager, would surely inspire his troops? It had certainly done the trick from 1985, with three titles and two FA Cups to his name.

George Graham and Kenny Dalglish do battle again

There can be no doubt, the Reds of Merseyside offered the stiffest of examinations, but there were other teams lurking in the dark, waiting for their moment to strike.

Aston Villa had enjoyed a resurgence the season before, finishing as runners-up to Liverpool. The Villans had been managed by Graham Taylor, before becoming England boss he had revitalised this sleeping giant and in Paul McGrath, possessed one of the finest defenders in the League. The Villa legend would go on to win the PFA Player of the Year in 1992-93, but his presence within the side in 89-90 had propelled Villa to within a whisker of winning the title. Could the Irish defender again be the launchpad for a title tilt? It wasn't only in defence where the Midlands team excelled either.

Tony Cascarino and David Platt carried the goal threat for Villa, and England's Platt bagged 24 of them. Coming from midfield, that haul smacks of excellence. Not only was his domestic form blooming, the summer of that year had seen England go mightily close to glory in Italy in the World Cup, and David Platt had wowed the fans with his flair and presence at both ends of the pitch.

Cascarino had arrived in the summer from Millwall, and his burgeoning reputation was well deserved. An old fashioned centre forward who had a real thirst for goals, his partnership with Teddy Sheringham at the South London club had induced Villa to shell out a club record £1.1m to acquire his prolific services. His aerial ability would give the Claret and Blues side another arrow to their quiver in their pursuit to go one better than in 1989/90.

The question is though, could they learn from their previous efforts and go just one position higher? Could they bring the title back to Villa Park?

It wasn't just these three teams who would line up at the start line to chase the League trophy around a 38 match circuit. There were others who reckoned they could last the pace and outwit their fellow contenders.

North London neighbours Tottenham Hotspur had ended the previous season in the bronze medal position, and had real hopes of a first title since 1961. They had the league's top scorer in England striker Gary Lineker, and with Paul Gascoigne in midfield, they had the enigmatic presence which all great sides need. That unquestionable quality which defenders find a nightmare to contend with. His mercurial touch and unpredictable play would always give Arsenal's neighbours an outlet when under pressure, and Venables' tactical acumen would ensure the rest of the team stayed watertight. Gary Lineker and Paul Gascoigne gave Spurs a real edge in attack, as Lineker was amongst the finest finishers in the game at the time, and 'Gazza' was, at times, unplayable.

Tottenham had a reputation for blitzing teams with their verve and swagger, and Terry Venables had seemingly brought a slice of Catalonia with him when arriving from FC Barcelona.

Venables was a crafty Cockney who had revitalised the Lilywhites of North London. The cosmopolitan Londoner had returned from a successful spell as Barcelona boss, where he had won La Liga and reached the European Cup final and, allied with his earlier successes with Crystal Palace and QPR, 'El Tel' was a Gaffer in demand.

He had chosen Tottenham Hotspur as his next destination, and his decision to bring in two of the brightest England stars would reap dividends.

Venables' previous league finishes of 13th and sixth showed real improvement from the moment of his hiring, although it was far from where he wanted the club. The campaign of 1989/90, though, saw everything click, and a third place finish gave real hope to fans and proved they were a team to be taken seriously.

So, the runners and riders for the 1990/91 season would be Liverpool, Aston Villa, Tottenham and Arsenal. Quite an exciting list, and one hell of a gauntlet for the Gunners to run. It wasn't just the two-horse race of the previous few seasons, but the lineup wasn't complete yet.

There were other teams who were champing at the bit to grab glory for their fans.

Crystal Palace had assembled quite a team in reaching the FA Cup Final the season before and, in achieving safety after finishing fifteenth in their first season back in the top flight, they had found a striking duo who would torment the majority of teams they faced.

Mark Bright and Ian Wright bagged plenty of goals that season, despite their team struggling on the pitch, and with the danger they could create, Palace would always be in with a shout of silverware. The pair could be a nightmare for any team, and they would have walked into any team in the League. Goals win games, and Wrighty and Brighty had plenty of them.

The Eagles also had a quite brilliant skipper. Midfielder Geoff Thomas was tough in the tackle and industrious on the ball. Thomas was the safety net that allowed Wright and Bright to wreak havoc, but he also provided a goal threat himself. His form was on the rise, and his country were also beginning to take notice.

Palace really did have a strong lineup, but the fearsome duo up front could not do the job by themselves. The Eagles had John Salako and Eddie McGoldrick on the wings, and it was their endeavours which ensured the goal rush was plentiful. Salako in particular could deliver the ball on demand, and was the only player who took corners from both sides. His crossing was simply that good.

With Thomas, Wright and Bright, and McGoldrick and Salako rampaging out wide, Palace were on the up, and even though this was to be only their second season in the top flight since promotion, the Eagles would give any outfit the strictest of examinations. Then there was Manchester United.

Alex Ferguson had been going about his business steadily in crafting a team that would be capable of bringing trophies back to Old Trafford. His side's ascendance, season by season, should have acted as a warning to all comers.

The 1989-90 campaign however, was a season of contrasts for Fergie's men, as their 13th place finish was their lowest since their relegation fifteen years previously. The saving grace for the manager was to be found in the FA Cup, when they defeated Crystal Palace 1-0 after a 3-3 draw in the first game. If it were not for Lee Martin's winner, who knows what would've become of the now famous Scot? The FA Cup was the one thing that had saved Fergie's head from being placed on the chopping block.

They had a squad built to last the season, and they now had a taste for silverware. Manchester United had also built a feisty rivalry with the Gunners - which started in 1987 - and this feud would have a huge bearing on events for the season.

The bad blood seemed to originate in an ill-tempered match at Old Trafford, when United's hatchet man Norman Whiteside proceeded to kick lumps out of Arsenal winger David Rocastle, which prompted a reaction from Rocky. That reaction saw him red-carded. The Gunners' go-to reflex when one of their own was hurt was to protect, and the subsequent fixtures between the two sides were evidence of this. It was blood and thunder stuff from both teams.

From that game, the touchpaper had been lit. There was a sense that there was a potential payload of explosives that could ignite at any given moment. The detonation would happen this coming season, and the ramifications would ripple out over the rest of the campaign. It was one of the many incidents that would have been the ruination of weaker teams.

United though, were becoming a force again, and wily Scot Alex Ferguson was slowly constructing a side to be reckoned with.

Republic of Ireland full-back Denis Irwin was the club's only significant purchase, but his set-piece delivery and reliability was a real asset for the Red Devils. With the granite-like Steve Bruce - Gary Pallister central defensive partnership offering real security, it allowed the Old Trafford club to push up and really impose themselves in the centre of the park.

In midfield, Paul Ince and Bryan Robson provided guile and steel, and it was on the wings that Ferguson began showing his ability to blood a youngster, with Lee Sharpe and Ryan Giggs pressuring their more experienced counterparts for a place in the side.

Up front, Bryan McClair and Mark Hughes took the mantle to provide United with goals, and in the previous season, they had fired 23 between them. There was far more to come from United, and Alex Ferguson was only looking up towards the top of the table.

Looking back, it was abundantly clear Arsenal faced stiff competition to win the 1990/91 First Division Championship.

There was Aston Villa, with Platt and Cascarino providing a very real threat up top, as well as the reliable Paul McGrath at the back, to fire their title aspirations.

Crystal Palace possessed possibly the most fearsome strike duo in the League, with Wrighty and Brighty doing the business. John Salako and Eddie McGoldrick were loading the chambers from the flanks and Captain Geoff Thomas was the inspiration his side needed from their leader.

Tottenham had the enigmatic Paul Gascoigne and last season's top scorer in Gary Lineker in their pursuit for the title, and Terry Venables finally had the side he craved.

Manchester United were on the rise, and in their ranks they possessed Mark Hughes, Bryan Robson and some excellent youth prospects. After tasting silverware in the FA Cup the previous season, they would be hungry for more.

Finally, there were the giants of Liverpool. They possessed the squad, the experience, the desire of youth, the top class manager, and most importantly, they had the habit that is perhaps the most difficult to obtain - the habit of winning. The title resided at Anfield at the beginning of this tantalisingly poised season, and if any of these contenders were to have genuine aspirations, then they would have to duke it out with Liverpool before anyone else.

Arsenal had done it before, but never before with so much competition. The miracle of Anfield '89 was a two-horse race, and since the Gunners resurgence began with the Littlewoods Cup win in 1987, there had only been Arsenal, Liverpool, Nottingham Forest, Manchester United and Aston Villa finishing in the Top two. The crux of the matter was, there had not been a team that had provided Liverpool with a sustainable challenge. There had been a season here and there that saw a side rise above the tide of mediocrity to enjoy the lofty heights along with Dalglish's Reds, but it was never for long.

Arsenal though, from the phoenix-like rising from the ashes in 1987 with 'Champagne' Charlie Nicholas grabbing the glory, had given the Merseysiders food for thought. A cup to end the eight year drought in '87, a first title for eighteen years when the Gunners won so dramatically at Anfield, and a defence so watertight, it gave strikers recurring nightmares.

George Graham had been meticulous in the construction of his side, and his training methods were bearing fruit. Throughout his side, he had blended steel with ability, and if one cog in the machine was struggling, he could rest assured that the other parts would take the strain.

A title win in this season would cement he and his men into the annals of Arsenal history, and it would also underline Arsenal as one of the genuinely big teams of the era.

One title was fantastic, but two titles in such a short space of time? With far more competition trying to force their way into the picture, it would be a real test for George Graham's tactical expertise, and his team's mental strength.

The season's traditional curtain raiser had taken place - the Charity Shield match between Liverpool and Manchester United saw them both sharing the spoils in a 1-1 draw - and this meant that the season was ready to commence.

The starter pistol had been raised, with a finger on the trigger. The gruelling 38 game race had all the contestants primed on the start line, and Arsenal could have genuine belief they could keep pace with anyone.

Before they could take to their blocks in readiness for this sprint however, they would have to complete their preparations. It was all well and good knowing thine enemy, but if your own house wasn't in order then a capitulation was surely on the cards. Were Arsenal ready?

Start As We Mean To Go On

All the hard work and meticulous planning that George Graham had painstakingly performed was about to be put to the test. It was finally the 25 August 1990, and the Division One campaign was about to commence.

The expectations were always high where the manager was concerned, but Arsenal had not been habitual title contenders for quite some time. The aim, as the season began, was of course to win the title back from Liverpool and to oust the other contenders, but dreaming and lusting after something is entirely different from expectation or reality.

Could the Gunners actually turn their excellent team into title winners in a Division which had multiple outfits battling for supremacy? This season promised to be a battle royale and perhaps the toughest fought in some time between more than two combatants. Journalist Amy Lawrence describes the scenario succinctly...

"1989 was the exception, it wasn't the benchmark. It was a miracle. Prior to it, Arsenal hadn't won the league in 18 years. A fan could be 25 years old in 1989 and - depending on how good their memory was - have no memory of their team winning a title. It wasn't part of what the club did routinely. Liverpool had won it ten times from 1971 to 1989 and then again in 1990... 1989 felt like an aberration. Arsenal didn't go into the season thinking they were better than everybody else - but George Graham was positive and hopeful."

The men who made up Arsenal's squad may not have expected glory come May, but they were more than aware of what they were capable of. Battle hardened and well oiled, this team set out before each game with a mantra of sorts. David Hillier, promoted to the first team that season, told me that even with his lack of experience, he went into each match with one target;

"We approached each game the same and that was to avoid defeat - and nothing could have changed our focus that season. We all had the same mindset."

George Graham had implanted this tenacious seed, and it had flowered from season to season. The first buds of promise had begun with their Littlewoods Cup win in 1987, and in 1989 in Anfield, it had begun to bloom.

The first opponent for the 1990/91 season was Wimbledon at the decrepit Plough Lane. The previous season saw the Dons achieve an admirable eighth place finish, and the squad that Bobby Gould had guided to this overachieving placing was a real menace to any who lined up to face them.

There had been changes in the summer for the team which was affectionately known as 'The Crazy Gang.' Manager, and ex-Gunner, Bobby Gould, who had won the FA Cup in 1988 for the team and elevated them to the First Division in just four years, was replaced by former Luton Town gaffer Ray Harford.

Harford had taken a leaf out of Gould's book, by guiding an unfashionable outfit to silverware in 1988. Luton Town had lifted the Littlewoods Cup - as it was known in that year - and Harford was given the task of ensuring yet another year of progress for the South London team. The opponent in this Cup Final that the Hatters had surprisingly lifted? Arsenal. Just ask Gus Caesar.

It wasn't just down to the manager and staggering cup triumphs that the Dons had proved so many doubters wrong. The players had grown from inauspicious beginnings, and physically and mentally, they were more than a match for anyone. Harford would have to deal with the loss of inspirational midfielder Dennis Wise though, as he had been sold to Chelsea for a tidy sum in the summer.

In addition to the loss of Wise, Wimbledon had also sold defender Eric Young to neighbours Crystal Palace just ten days before the first match kicked off. They found a replacement in youth prospect Warren Barton from Maidstone. Young was a real loss to the Dons as he was one of the brighter gems in Wimbledon, but what was the Dons loss was their neighbour's gain. It is always a huge gamble to replace established talent with precocious potential, but the Dons placed extraordinary reliance on their scouts. A gamble it may have been, but one that would eventually pay off.

Dealing with the loss of an integral player is always difficult, but with a new gaffer in place, it also meant new tactics, methods and teamsheets. It would negate any possible shortcomings with the fresh scent of new beginnings. Wimbledon FC was full of positivity with what could be achieved.

That feeling encapsulates exactly what the first day of the season means to every fan. The memories of the previous season are cast aside to dusty memory, successful or otherwise, and new recruits and possible gullible hope precedes any negative notion that the coming season may hold doom for their team.

That is the beauty of football, it allows even the most fanciful of visions to at least temporarily become almost tangible, and the start of every new season wipes the slate clean for most supporters.

This match saw what would be Wimbledon's highest attendance of the season - 13,733 - and each fan that took to the stands of the soon to be defunct Plough Lane, would be envisioning the dream start for their respective sides.

If glory is to be brought that little bit closer, then a good start is mandatory. It isn't often that the captain of any sporting team is celebrating after suffering a demoralising result. All good stories must have a satisfactory beginning.

So it was perfectly apt that on the first match of the season, a marker was laid down by the Gunners, as they outfought and outmanoeuvred Wimbledon 3-0 at their now defunct home. John Fashanu, Lawrie Sanchez, Neil Ardley and co. were chasing shadows, as Paul Merson, Alan Smith and Perry Groves got Arsenal's epic journey off to a cracking start.

Paul Merson and Alan Smith, part of Arsenal's potent attack, celebrating at Wimbledon

As expected, George Graham went with what would be his strongest eleven. New signing, David Seaman, was the man between the sticks, and by his own admission, this match was the one that was by far the most memorable;

"The first game, away to Wimbledon. That was massive for me, I remember everything. It was probably one of my most memorable games. Making my debut for Arsenal was a special moment."

A first competitive game for his new side, and he was rewarded with a win and a clean sheet. Seaman had a 100% win percentage at Arsenal!

George Graham went for solidarity in the first game of the season, and the impregnable unit that was the back four was named again to continue the trend from the season before. Lee Dixon, Captain Tony Adams, Steve Bould and Nigel Winterburn.

In midfield, David Rocastle was named on one flank, with Anders Limpar on the other. Opponents must have seen these two names and knew that their own fullbacks would have to be at the very top of their game to get close enough to smell Rocky and Limpar, never mind stop them.

Graham knew that a solid foundation was the basis upon which he formed his plans, but without a sprinkle of unpredictability and a smidgin of flair, his team would be lacking. Rocky and Limpar would provide just that.

Michael Thomas and Paul Davis resumed their partnership in the centre of midfield and they both supplied the exact amount of aggression, cover and pressure conversion. They also possessed expert timing. Davis and Thomas. They were so tactically astute that no words need ever have left the others mouth when the team was on the attack or under the cosh.

Paul Merson was named as partner to Alan Smith in attack, and both prospered in this game, with each scoring. Whilst the overall notion that Merson was a wide man, his natural inclination to cut in and cause merry havoc saw him become the perfect ally to Smudge's dangerous presence in the box.

Perry Groves, the other scorer in this emphatic victory, was seen as able backup to Merse and Smudge, and with Kevin Campbell and youth prodigy Andy Cole in the squad, the Gunners did not lack the powder to light their cannons. Groves came on in the second half for the effervescent Anders Limpar, and his daring and desire to take on defenders was the perfect antidote to any tiring legs which had forgotten the rigours of top-flight football during the summer.

Groves, like Merson, was also thought of primarily as a winger, but his confrontational style and pace meant they were useful tools anywhere across the attack and Graham would utilise this across the season.

The Arsenal players had been put through the mill in pre-season by George Graham, and fitness was never an issue, but the last five percent, that is often labelled 'match sharpness,' is what every player loses in their downtime.

This match showed that they had re-found it rather quickly. Wimbledon were no cannon fodder, and could turn over any team looking for an easy ride. It wasn't just the abundance of flair that Arsenal had at their disposal, they also outfought a team which usually did the same to their own opponents.

George Graham would not allow any to bask in the rays of adulation however, and with their next match just four days after this win, he would need all of his men entirely focused.

That wasn't to say he would not acknowledge how well his side had manifested his instruction. Reading from the programme notes for the second match of the season versus Luton Town, Graham stated;

"What a way to start a season, at Wimbledon last Saturday. It's never easy to win at Plough Lane, so that 3-0 victory has given us just the focus we needed. We laid the foundations in the first half, when we kept things tight at the back. Seaman looked absolutely in charge on the crosses. After the interval, we took full control. Paul Davis's use of the ball was first class and we made great use of our spare full-back. Perry Groves's last minute goal was a gem, and I was equally pleased to see Anders Limpar looking so lively."

George had let the fans know that this was an excellent result, but it was exactly what was intended. A great start to the season's story, but up next was another potential banana-skin in Luton Town.

The Hatters had escaped relegation by the skin of their teeth the previous season, sacking Ray Harford halfway through the campaign and bringing in Jimmy Ryan. It was only goal difference that saw them avoid the hungry maw of relegation, and it had been clear to all at Kenilworth Road that changes would be required. They possessed the means to prosper however, and manager Ryan could call upon some truly talented individuals to change proceedings on the pitch. His strikers especially, could pose problems for even Arsenal's back five, and in Iain Dowie and Lars Elstrup, they were to give Adams, Bould and the rest of the Highbury defence a wake up call.

After the comfortable win over Wimbledon, the confidence would have been soaring, but the second match of the season - and first at Highbury - would be one of contrasting matters. Luton Town gave as good as they received from Thomas and Davis in the centre of the park and after twelve minutes, David Seaman had conceded his first goal for Arsenal.

A ball swung in from the left was aimed at Elstrup, but he was tightly marked by Steve Bould. It was near post territory, and as both men flung themselves forward to get a touch to deny or enable a goal, it found its way past Seaman.

This is where the resolve of Graham's men would be either found or forged. In losing situations, an ability to adapt to a troubling situation is one that may be beyond some - especially in the heat of battle. Luton were standing toe-to-toe with the Gunners, and were now a goal up. Could George's charges face up to and then quell the threat?

David Rocastle sparked the fightback, and it was his hounding of Luton Town's left-back which saw him take possession and put in a cross for the lurking Paul Merson. The Magic Man had found space in the centre of the penalty area, and his first time finish was lashed high above Hatters keeper Alec Chamberlain.

Crucially, it was also scored before half-time. That, arguably, would make the second half tactic far different than if Luton had held out for the remainder of the half.

That more positive approach paid dividends, and an Arsenal corner, which failed to find its target, bobbled to the edge of the box. Michael Thomas was waiting and his powerful shot evaded everyone in a packed box to find the bottom corner. It was the goal that proved to be the winner.

Tenacity to match the skill, but this game really was heavier in grit than silk.

The same starting XI for the 3-0 win over the Dons had seen off a spirited Luton. Even the second half introduction of Perry Groves for Anders Limpar, who was showing ominous signs of finding his tiny feet at this level, was mirrored. Yet, the result could have been so different.

It showed the two faces of Arsenal, however, they had ensured it was two out of two for the Gunners, a perfect start. Six points from six, and two tough games circumnavigated within a tough week.

Two games within the first four days of Division One beginning showed that any who avoided the lashes of losing had prepared well before festivities had commenced. George Graham had made sure of much, but two games in a season doesn't constitute even a slice of what is needed.

Only three days later, there was to be the visit of a familiar menace, and one which was looking to usurp the recent successes of Arsenal. Another match - this would be three in a week - would stretch every sinew of the squad which had achieved a flawless record thus far.

It wasn't only the hectic fixture list which would push Arsenal to the limit at the beginning of the season. The third match within seven days was against a formidable foe, and one that had aspirations of escaping the shadow which was created by Arsenal's recent glory. Tottenham were coming to Highbury, and they smelled blood!

Spurs Out From The Shadows

Whilst there were teams that carried a distinct risk to Arsenal's title hopes, there was one that carried more than just a hazard in regards to their aspirations. The duels with Liverpool in recent years had carried great weight, and each match promised much drama. They were prize fighters going glove to glove, and the purse invariably involved more than just bragging rights.

These matches garnered headlines, but there was something missing. It wasn't a derby, and although there was spice and fizz, the opponent still was not Tottenham.

The banter before and after North London derbies back in the pre-internet days was reserved to the workplace and school, however, the barbs that were slung at each other were familiar, and were centred around Arsenal's origins in South-East London, Tottenham winning the first double in '61, and Arsenal achieving the same in '71.

We all know that the rivalry started with Arsenal's decision to move from their home in South East London to Highbury in 1913, sharing the North London landscape with Tottenham. Obviously, Spurs were not too happy with having the share of fans potentially divided, but the move was simply necessary from an Arsenal point of view. The gates in the South East had been slowly but surely dying and the Arsenal hierarchy knew that a move away from their roots was essential if the club was to not only grow, but thrive. The move was a commercial success.

World War One put a halt to the Football League, but in the final season before football was changed in order to adapt to wartime conditions, Tottenham and Chelsea had finished in the bottom two. If World War One had not begun, then the next season would have seen both consigned to the Division below and Derby and Preston - the teams who finished in the top two of Division Two - would have taken their place. There was consternation amidst these final placings however.

A match between Manchester United and Liverpool in April 1915 - the last season before the league was broken up for the War - had been discovered to have been fixed by the players of Manchester United. It meant that United avoided going down and it saw Chelsea take their place.

The War ended in 1918, and the FA called for a meeting to organise how to recommence the top division and attempt to arrange clubs' concerns with the skullduggery of the fixed match which had rippled across the sport. Representatives from all teams, in both divisions, attended and several ideas were mooted before all agreed that the top two leagues should be grown to twenty two teams.

They also agreed that Chelsea would keep their place in the top bracket and that Derby and Preston would get the promotion that they had deserved. This left one remaining place up for grabs.

Arsenal had finished sixth in the Second Division when Tottenham had finished bottom of the First. Both clubs, along with five others, put forward their cases. It was hotly contested, as well it should be. A place at the top table, even back then, was a lucrative opportunity.

The Board voted to promote Arsenal to the First Division, and the animosity ripened instantly. It still rankles Spurs fans to this day and there have been several publications that have pointed the finger squarely at Sir Henry Norris for bribing the FA Board to gain approval for Arsenal. This has never been proven. In fact, there is not one shred of evidence that states Norris had anything to do with the vote. It did not help that Norris, in 1929, was banned from football - for incentivised payments to Charlie Buchan of Sunderland and for using club funds to pay for his chauffeur - but the events of that meeting in 1919 were not part of any charge.

Thanks to the learned fellows at www.thearsenalhistory.com - the real reason was found to be some shrewd lobbying of football journalists and the footballing elite. That meeting in 1919, which decided Arsenal and Tottenham's fate, took place in March of that year. Tottenham had begun pandering to people of influence in January. The only problem was they were dealing with the wrong people.

In fact, the reason Arsenal were victorious in 1919 was down to the actions of one very influential journalist and this was acknowledged by our greatest ever manager. Eleven years after the election in April 1930, a week prior to Arsenal winning their first piece of silverware, Jimmy Catton - the leading authority on sports in that era - gave a lecture in Hornsey entitled "Football, where from, where to?" Chairing the meeting was a certain Mr Herbert Chapman, who introduced Mr Catton to the expectant audience as "the man who got Arsenal into the First Division."'

It is a place that Arsenal have never relinquished. Arsenal enjoy the longest unbroken run in the top flight, and Spurs, as well as certain other clubs, have conjured up myths to argue their point about their rival's supposed skullduggery. The location move, the promotion and the shared fanbase from the relocation sowed the seed of acrimony, and the years that have followed have seen ample rainfall to enable rapid growth of this weed of contempt. Spurs simply cannot abide that Arsenal have taken what they see as rightfully theirs. Fast forward to the season of 1990/91, and the neighbours were still at loggerheads.

Once again, Guardian scribe, Amy Lawrence, expertly narrates the scene between the two clubs at the time; "The rivalry felt quite close, nip and tuck.

They had a glamorous team at the time as well. Gazza had signed for a record fee, and they had a few players with big reputations. Arguably, in terms of glamour, they had the edge. There was suggestions at the time that George Graham's side was merely 'functional,' which was a little unfair, especially when Anders was in the team. You also had Merson who was capable of brilliant things and Rocastle was beginning to struggle with injury but was still a wonderful player. Spurs also had that sparkle."

The history between the clubs was prevalent, but Gooners did not enjoy the ammunition to fire at Spurs fans that they enjoy today. Over two decades of finishing above 'the enemy,' would have seemed like a dream for fans during the time in question. It was only the previous season in 1989/90 that Spurs had finished above Arsenal, Tottenham finishing third to Arsenal's fourth.

There was a feeling of superiority, of sorts, that Gooners enjoyed though. From the season after Arsenal had won their first double in 1971 - matching the effort of Bill Nicholson's famous Tottenham side of 1961 - to the season of 1990/91, Arsenal had averaged a finishing position of seventh. Spurs average position was ninth in that time, and they were even relegated in 1976/77.

Neither Arsenal, nor Tottenham, could claim a title between 1972 until the miracle of Anfield in 1989, but the reputation of both clubs preceded them. They had stature, they had clout. There were trophies in that time, with Spurs winning the FA Cup in 1981 and 1982, and the League Cup in 1973. Arsenal had obviously won the FA Cup with, what is perceived by some to be, the most exciting Cup Final of all time, the 3-2 win over Manchester United in 1979, and had also won the League Cup in 1987 - which was the assumed catalyst for George Graham's late success.

Cup success is great for the fans, but the League is where the majority of battles between fans would be fought. It would always be the priority. All it needed was for one side to assert dominance over the other.

Tottenham could only claim to be better than Arsenal in six of those nineteen seasons between 1972 and 1989, but crucially, they had sat above the Gunners five times in the last decade. Where Arsenal had enjoyed supremacy virtually unchallenged in the Seventies, Tottenham had fought back from the ignominy of relegation and on the 1 September 1990, the balance of power was on the flip of a coin.

The cause for the revival in fortunes was primarily down to Terry Venables. The man known as 'El Tel', after his stint at the helm of Barcelona, had a firm grasp on tactics and his player recruitment had paid off in spades.

The improvement in the club's fortunes was there for all to see from Venables' first season. From tenth, he guided them to a top three placing, and aside from the following campaign where they finished 13th, he had overseen top six finishes in every season.

The calibre of player he could call upon had vastly improved too. El Tel had purchased England striker Gary Lineker during his time in Catalonia, and he had also done the same whilst at White Hart Lane. Aside from boasting arguably the Division's finest finisher in their side, they had many other strings to their now formidable bow.

Paul Gascoigne, another England starter, had been weaving his magic for Spurs in 1989/90, and was named as the club's player of the season for his exploits. Gazza was at the top of his game, and the summer's World Cup was the perfect showcase of his dazzling skills. He alone could prove decisive for Spurs.

They possessed the subtle blend, mentioned in the previous chapter, that all teams must have in their locker if they are to contend at the top. The tough, embattled outlook that Gary Mabbutt, Vinny Samways and Neil Ruddock all had by the crateload, combined so well with the enigma of Gazza and the effectiveness of Lineker.

Chris Waddle had been in a Spurs shirt up until the summer, but a desire to play European football was already a target for the wide man from Newcastle, and it only burned brighter within him after he played a huge role for England in their run to the Semi-Final in Italy. He took an offer from Marseille, and Tottenham were definitely poorer for the loss. What team wouldn't be, after all, Waddle played a huge role in the rise of the Lilywhites under Venables. El Tel had a plan though, and Spurs were not malnourished in midfield.

Spanish midfielder Nayim - a name Arsenal were to become painfully familiar with during the Cup Winners Cup Final of 1995 - had the capacity to weave similar paths of destruction from the flank, and young David Howells was continuing to impress when given a chance. They were genuine contenders, and their previous finish proved so. All the spice of a match between two genuine heavyweights, and with such a delicious prospect came some matchups that would provide the incendiary to spark a blaze that befitted such an auspicious and memorable occasion on the football calendar.

Gazza would keep Arsenal's back four more than busy, but could he be stopped at the source? Paul Davis and Michael Thomas were both upset to miss out on a call up for duty to England's glorious near-miss at World Cup 1990 in the summer, but both had risen above the disappointment, and had put early markers down with some imperious displays in the first two games. Both players had forged an exquisite balance in midfield, but could they shackle the man-child who so nearly inspired a second World Cup win for England? Teams during the season would hatch plans to mark Gazza out of the game, to adapt their own gameplan to stifle the playmaker.

Arsenal would find the same tactics would be unfurled against them as Anders Limpar unleashed himself on the First Division. The artisans that could undo any team if given an inch, could impose themselves on opponents before a ball was kicked. They instilled fear with just a mention of their name. It wouldn't be a one-man team though that took to the turf. Spurs were both well stocked in the talent department.

Both rivals had the luxury of true class in defence, it was Arsenal though, who had the edge. The famous back four had been cooking for a few seasons now, and they were now seasoned perfectly. Spurs did have men in their back-

Tottenham's Paul Gascoigne proved to be a thorn in the Arsenal side

line that would push Messrs Smith, Merson and Limpar to the limit, and Gary Mabbutt would marshal his troops well. When it came to the art of hindrance however, George Graham held all the cards and Arsenal were widely regarded as having the upper hand over every team when it came to defences.

So the scene was set, and in the programme notes for the match, the duel between Gazza and the Gunners core was touched upon;

"Today's midfield battle promises a fascinating contest, provided by a trio of England stars and England hopefuls. Paul Gascoigne, the nation's hero, Paul Davis – so close to an international place two years ago – plus Michael Thomas, who's won two caps and wants more." George Graham also paid special attention to Mickey Thomas in his programme column; "I was very pleased with Mickey Thomas on Wednesday. Not only did he score the winning goal, he was also one of our most influential players on the pitch. Yet, he only passed a fitness test on a groin injury a couple of hours before the game."

No such injury worries for Mickey for one of the biggest matches of this season, and certainly the biggest so far in this campaign's short life. George Graham obviously didn't quite embrace the notion of rotating the squad, and for the third time in a week, he named the same side. David Seaman in goal, a back four of Dixon, Bould, Adams and Winterburn, Davis and Thomas in the centre, with Limpar and Rocky on the wings. Lastly, Merson and Smith would occupy the attentions of Mabbutt and his Spurs cohorts in defence.

The match went pretty much to script. Both teams going hell for leather, but there wasn't much goalmouth action. It was frothing in the centre of the park, as each attack from both teams were crashing upon the rocks of the respective defences, leaving each side struggling to leave a mark on their opponent.

The first half saw the 40,000 plus crowd enjoy the sparks flying, but neither keepers were allowed to get too attached to the ball. The 45 minutes saw both teams trying to assert dominion over the other and the match teetered one way and then the other.

It wasn't really until the second half that the match spilled over into any goalmouth action, and it was David Howells who seemingly got away with committing a cardinal sin, by tripping Paul Davis in the Spurs box. Referee Joe Worrall ignored the Gunner's pleas for a penalty, much to the chagrin of George Graham, and the match continued to lurch toward an inconclusive conclusion.

The home side had time for another penalty appeal, this time it was Steve Bould who went down under what looked like a pull from Welshman Pat Van Den Hauwe. Again, no dice from the man in black, and Tottenham escaped once more. The game could have gone either way, but it was Arsenal who would be the more disappointed with sharing the points.

The next day the Daily Mirror covered the intricacies of the match, and Venables spoke of his happiness with his side's season so far, and of the point earned behind enemy lines; "We haven't had a good result here for quite a long time, so I'm quite satisfied, even though we can play better. It was a hyped-up game with not a lot of space."

El Tel had a good point. The game, which promised a midfield duel, saw all the action concentrated in that very area, or at least the lion's share. Paul Davis and Michael Thomas put a leash on the wildfire that was Gazza, but the aftermath was that the usual supply of long-range passes from Davis and the rampaging runs of Thomas, were conspicuous in their absence. It left Arsenal missing a vital cog in their attack, and Tottenham, in turn, were weakened by a Gazza who had two men standing sentry for his every move.

The match still had drama, but you do not go into a derby and expect a stalemate. Still, it extended both team's unbeaten runs in the Division, which underlined their prospects for success for the season ahead.

What was telling, in regards to the balance of the 90 minutes, was how Venables seemed quite pleased in his interview with the Daily Mirror to grab a point. With room only for winners at Arsenal, George Graham would not have rolled out the platitudes after drawing with the enemy. Terry Venables was a friend of Graham's, but there was no room for sentiment in derby fixtures.

No arguments were settled in this game, and no bragging rights were obtained. It was tense, and both sets of fans were left with questions that would not be answered for quite some time.

With the last few seasons seeing both teams swapping their league positions, who would once again win the key which grants North London freedom? Which gaggle of support would be going into work with a beaming smile on their face come May, struggling to contain the glee they would get from lording it over the other?

This match did not supply the ending to the tale, but it did add plenty of ingredients to the seething broth that was coming to the boil - as it did every season.

Arsenal did not get the points their Gooners craved, but they remained unscathed after playing three top-flight games in a week, and could enjoy a week's rest before their next fixture - an away match versus Everton.

George Graham had overseen a tough beginning on the climb to the summit. The path would get tougher, but it was 'job done' so far.

Keeping Pace, Staying Tight & Limpar's On Fire

In these modern times, where footballers who are finely tuned, athletic beasts, the managers who oversee these honed sports stars are increasingly frustrated. A congested fixture schedule is usually to blame, as games move to unorthodox days in order to fulfill the TV coverage, which fills the coffers of the same clubs who are complaining.

If we compare the scheduling of games though, it seems that clubs playing a shedload of fixtures in a short space of time is nothing new.

Arsenal's baptism to the 1990/91 season was three matches within a week. When you also consider that clubs nowadays have the luxury of a twenty five man squad, it means that managers can shuffle their pack in order to avoid burn-out and triggered injuries, which are the byproduct of such a heavy workload.

This highlights what a difficult task George Graham had in 1990/91 with his modest squad - and what heroic efforts his players had to put in to overthrow the effects of extreme fatigue. Twenty five men in a season is better than nineteen men.

George Graham had no such wiggle-room when he had to plot a course through the gauntlet of the Division One 1990/91 season. Instead he tried to ensure that his nineteen man squad (bearing in mind there was two players who made just one sub appearance throughout this campaign in question in Colin Pates and Andy Cole) were primed physically to cope with the demand, and the strenuous pre-season 'break' to Sweden was certainly paying dividends.

Arsenal's very own 'SuperSub,' Perry Groves, really came to the rescue in their next fixture, which afforded the Gunners a whole week's recovery before they had to travel to Goodison Park to take on Everton.

The Toffees were managed by Colin Harvey at that time, and he was under pressure. Everton had lost their first three games of the season, and the manager was copping the flak from the stands. Harvey had to get his team winning, and quickly. Everton were a successful team and possessed a wealth of stars studded in their side - their fans expected more.

Any team that included Pat Nevin, Neville Southall, Tony Cottee and Mike Newell in their team should be looking further up the table, so it was with a slight sense of trepidation that Arsenal fans would travel to see their team in the blue half of Merseyside. The team itself would have feared no-one though, a bullet-proof mental strength that was impenetrable from even the most explosive of siege's. That was again the work of George Graham, who was masterful at making his men feel bigger and more powerful than they actually were.

They had to withstand an Everton barrage in the early stages of the game. The Toffees must have been inspired by under-fire gaffer Harvey, as they came out and put the Gunners under instant pressure. The back five, which had played the last three, were again in place, and they stood firm, moulding and adapting to the movement of Newell, Nevin and Cottee. It was a fascinating duel, but it would be Arsenal who would break the deadlock.

From defence to attack with one swish of Lee Dixon's boot. He catapulted a ball to Anders Limpar. The speedy Swede had eluded the attentions of his marker as Everton had concentrated far too much on their own attack, and Limpar was intent on making them pay.

He was in the box before Southall had a chance to close down his angles, but the hairy-lipped Welsh keeper saved Limpar's venomous effort, which was high to his left, arrowing toward the top corner.

Southall could do no more, but the ball had not gone out of play. Perry Groves utilised his own burst of pace to latch onto the loose ball before any blue-shirted players, and his ginger bonce headed Arsenal into the lead.

George Graham would have been confident in his charges seeing out the rest of the game, but Everton conspired to spoil the Gunners plans. Andy Hinchcliffe could deliver a mean set-piece, and his corner saw Mike Newell leap higher than David Seaman and Paul Merson. In fact, Merson and Seaman showed a rare error in communication as both players went for the ball, leaving Newell to equalise.

Perhaps it was deserved, as Everton had created the better chances. However, the general consensus is that teams make their own luck through their endeavours. Arsenal had certainly worked hard enough to earn a favourable glance or two from Lady Luck during the game.

Either way, the match ended all square. George Graham could take heart that his side was still unbeaten, but so were Liverpool and Tottenham. Dropped points could be dealt with if the frequency was maintained, but defensive mistakes could not be allowed. The bedrock of all that was built, and still building, was the Gunner's backline and how watertight it was. If leaks started to sprout, would their title aspirations sink?

George Graham was nothing if not dogged. He would have had his men on the training pitch the next day, poring over the fallout from the game, and ensuring that they took all measures to rectify it.

The Scot had plenty of time to ruminate on the error that had cost his side two points. It may have been just one of those things, but the way he saw his men invite pressure upon themselves would have caused concern. With another week's respite, the training was as fierce as ever. From the early fixture congestion, to two games in two weeks for George and his boys. Plenty of time to iron out any creases, and preparation time for their next game - at home to Chelsea.

The Blues of South West London, much like Everton, had high hopes. Chelsea had just recruited their first ever one million pound players in midfielders Dennis Wise and Andy Townsend, and had finished just one place below the Gunners in the previous season's league standings. Chairman Ken Bates had a vision and he was moving ever closer to seeing that come to fruition.

There were a few Chelsea players Tony Adams, Steve Bould, and their brothers in arms, would have to pay special attention to. Graham Stuart, and new recruits Townsend and Wise, could pull strings and open gaps with alarming regularity, and Kerry Dixon had the ability to maximise any opportunities that would come his way.

George Graham opted to tend to this threat by shuffling his pack for the first time. Alan Smith was left out of the side, and Perry Groves was rewarded for his vibrant cameo in the previous fixture, and was given the nod. Groves had merited his selection after altering things from the bench in the games that had been played so far, but also because Smith had fired in a solitary goal in four games. The Smudge, that Gooners adored and relied on, was still trying to find his feet. The assistance he gave the team, at both ends of the pitch, was ever-present, but his clinical finishing and predatory positioning had been missing. There was no doubt from fans about those skills returning to the fore however.

To add to the changes, George had seen fit to issue a statement in his programme column for the game, to quell rumours surrounding Perry Groves and David O'Leary. The pair had to settle for cameo roles, which would not have left them feeling too happy, so the media had thoughtfully filled in the blanks. Graham set the record straight, stating; "And to quell any speculation; Perry Groves is far too valuable to be allowed to go. So is David O'Leary."

He also mentioned the fate of another player in the squad who had struggled to make an impact. Colin Pates was an experienced pro but wanted to play. He had failed to oust the raft of defenders at the club, so Pates had put in a transfer request, which Graham confirmed in his column in the match programme; "We have granted Colin Pates's transfer request. Colin wants to settle down at centre-back again, and with so many centre-halves at the club, we've agreed to let him leave."

Pates would be going nowhere though, although he would be consigned to the shadows of the squad. Oh, how this decision would come back to bite us.

That moment of regret was in the future though. Before that, Arsenal had the small matter of a home fixture against Chelsea. With Liverpool and Tottenham both matching Arsenal's unbeaten run, and Crystal Palace enjoying a good start, it was vital the Gunners kept winning.

And win they did. George oversaw his side's most comprehensive display to date, with the Highbury faithful cheering to the rafters after Arsenal hammered Chelsea 4-1. The 40,475 fans were treated to plenty of goals, and the Gunners put their London rivals to the sword.

Lee Dixon pinged in a great cross for the first goal, which Merson got his head onto. The Magic Man had the presence of mind to head the ball down

Perry Groves and Jason Cundy pre-radio punditry

instead of having an unlikely pop at goal. His decision paid off as Limpar had flown into the box and snaffled up the smart headed pass.

Then, a bone of contention. Merson was out wide on the left and squared it to Limpar - the diminutive winger ran. And he ran. His run continued into the box, where he was upended by David Lee and referee John Deakin had no hesitation in pointing to the spot, but this did not throw a fire blanket over the Chelsea player's arguments.

They were adamant that Limpar had dived, but there had been contact. It was in motion too, which always exaggerates any contact.

Regardless, Lee Dixon had no complaints as he stepped up to take the spot kick. He then calmly dispatched the penalty to Dave Beasant's left and Arsenal were two up.

Not quite finished with rubbing Chelsea's noses in it, Rocky Rocastle floated a delicious ball into the path of Mickey Thomas, who had made a trademark run toward Chelsea's box. He took a couple of touches to tame the bouncing ball, and unleashed a shot which Beasant did well to get down to. Limpar was the beneficiary of the loose ball and he squared to Merson who was standing on the six yard box. A simple finish and they were three goals to the good. Limpar was in an unforgiving mood and his returning of the favour to Merson had seen to it that Arsenal were now on easy street for the rest of the ninety.

Limpar still had a few tricks up his sleeve, and he danced across the periphery of Chelsea's box. He was choosing the most destructive moment to release the ball, and Rocky helped him to make the decision with a late run. Limpar played him in and Rocastle applied the succinct finish. Beautiful stuff.

Chelsea were not the vanquished enemy under the boot though, and a Kevin Wilson glancing header was a timely reminder that Chelsea could hurt our team. The loss of the clean sheet would have rankled these proud men, Nigel Winterburn would have especially been fuming, as it was he who was partly responsible for the taciturn Gunners defence giving away a goal with his soft clearance.

The late goal was a mere blot on a copybook that had become a stranger to errors. Arsenal had outplayed a strong Chelsea, and partnerships across the pitch were beginning to really gel. Thomas and Davis. Merson and Smith. Smith and Limpar, The entire Arsenal defence.

Referring to it as 'clicking into gear' would be doing George Graham a huge injustice, as he had gone to great lengths to ensure the plethora of games that marked the start of Division One in 1990/91 would be dealt with successfully. This wasn't his team finding their mojo, it was a glimpse of machinery hitting full steam, the oil at the right temperature, the pistons maintained perfectly. It was always going to happen as the hard work had left no margin for error. It was the manifestation of pure graft in the summer. After the game, sports journalist for the Daily Express, Barry Flatman, chose to concentrate on one particular element of this thrumming mechanism in the aftermath of such a complete show.

Anders Limpar was under Flatman's spotlight, and his particular brand of football was apparently at odds with Arsenal's more industrious reputation on the pitch. With the Swede in the side though, spectators were being treated to a different type of show; 'Flair, a commodity never really connected with Arsenal even when they won the Championship, is now flooding around Highbury. Drive and determination earned George Graham's Gunners the title two seasons ago. Now Anders Limpar's acquisition and David Rocastle's gradually rebuilt fitness are changing all that."

Even Rocky himself, partly attributed to the Gunner's new found form of entertaining on the pitch, couldn't help but wax lyrical about his wing partner; "Limpar is going to be the difference between us just winning matches and winning trophies. He can spirit a victory out of nothing in the last few minutes."

That is some praise from Rocky, who had been aware that England boss Graham Taylor had been in the stands for the game. Rocastle's improving fitness would have been chief among the reasons for Taylor to have visited Highbury, as well as the Gunner's defenders.

Limpar was questioned about his conversion from the more sedate Serie A to the frenetic pace of the English top-flight, and the winger had this to say: "The game is faster here than in Italy. There is not so much time on the ball and the tackling is far better."

He had a point. Even in games that the title contenders were expected to win, the amount of time to compose yourself when in possession was precisely nought, so when given the ball, your foot had to be ready to plunge down on the accelerator the instant you received possession. Limpar was beginning to grasp that he had to be more instinctive, to trust himself. He had the skills to wreak merry havoc, he just had to allow himself to let it flow. One week after this demolition of Chelsea, it was Rocky and Limpar who came to the fore once more.

Arsenal travelled to the City Ground to take on yet another team with aspirations of more than mid-table obscurity in the form of Nottingham Forest.

The iconic, and headstrong, Brian Clough was the manager who had brought so much to the home side, and even though their force was on the wane, he still had players who would walk into any side in the League. Defenders Des Walker and Stuart Pearce were the cream of England's crop, and Steve Stone, Steve Hodge and Ian Woan, on their day, could inflict pain on any foe. But could take Arsenal's cherry?

Not with Limpar and Rocky in imperious form. The talents of Walker and Pearce were chasing shadows on opposite flanks with the Swede and the England wide man intent on keeping up their recent record of mischievousness.

Rocky opened the scoring. A corner bobbled its way to him and his dashing footwork allowed half a yard to finish. Alan Smith was again missing from the lineup, and the Leicester-born striker would have loved to have taken the chance if he were on the pitch.

Away fans would have to wait until the second half for Limpar to leave his mark on proceedings. Alan Smith, a second half sub for goalscorer Rocastle, twisted and turned his marker wide on the left. The ball squirmed through to Limpar, who showed remarkable speed to get ahead of a host of defenders and shoot from an acute angle, through the legs of Forest goalie Mark Crossley. It was quite a goal, and only reinforced the new-found affections Gooners had for this tiny Scandinavian with the electric feet. One week later, and the growing Anders Limpar fan club would have a host of new members. After taking care of Nottingham Forest in a professional display, it was time for another away game. The destination? Elland Road. The opponent? You guessed it. Leeds United.

Keeping pace with Tottenham and Liverpool was proving to be difficult, as both teams were also unbeaten. It was taking a herculean effort for Arsenal to match their rivals, and Leeds United were also making a play for the top.

The Yorkshire side had only just returned to the top Division after an eight year absence, but Howard Wilkinson had not just assembled a promotion-worthy side. The boys in his team were genuine stars that would show everyone that they belonged. They would be a familiar obstacle as the season progressed.

The home side had the ever-reliable ex-Gunner John Lukic to call upon in goal, and Lee Chapman would supply a constant stream of goals if he was given the chances. Gordon Strachan and Gary Speed could provide the spark, and with Vinnie Jones and David Batty, they had plenty of dynamite in the middle of the park.

Leeds were well stocked, and Elland Road was always an intimidating place to go, but the sheer belief that George Graham had implanted, and helped to flourish within his squad, would not wilt under even the most oppressive of atmospheres.

When things are tight, the necessity for something a little unorthodox rises. The need to break the pattern of stifling play. Anders Limpar had quickly forged a reputation for being the maverick, and this match was exactly what Rocky Rocastle was referring to when he said that "Limpar is going to be the difference between us just winning matches and winning trophies. He can spirit a victory out of nothing in the last few minutes."

The match saw the home side take the lead, which was against the grain for Arsenal. Gary McCallister got free on the left and put in a ball that Steve Bould flung his telescopic legs out to block. He could only direct the ball further goalwards, where Lee Chapman tucked in from practically under the crossbar.

Arsenal were simply incapable of buckling, and Siggi Jonsson was the embodiment of that. The Icelandic international midfielder was making his first appearance of the season after continual injury woes. Mickey Thomas was the man who was left out, but the move paid off. Jonsson would show his battling qualities immediately.

Jonsson rode through two tackles. Part luck, part doggedness, with a dash of skill. His pass through to Limpar was exquisite though, and it completely cut out the Leeds defence. That is on first inspection though – it was in fact David Batty who had inadvertently put through Limpar as his close attentions on Jonsson saw him flick the ball into the Swede's path.

Limpar still had to adjust himself as he had bent his run to stay onside - which he marginally failed to do. Seeing as it had come off the Leeds midfielder though, it was completely legal. His tiny feet bewitched Leeds goalkeeper Lukic as he rounded him to score into an empty net. Lukic was still amongst the best goalkeepers in the country, but he had been mesmerised by the Gunners winger.

The second half was just as difficult for both teams as the first. Midfield generals not willing to down arms for a moment, and defenders on top of their game make fixtures a tactical masterclass, but a bit of a snoozefest. This is also when players like Limpar come in extremely handy. Like a Swiss Army knife in the wilderness, Limpar had a great habit of coming up with exactly what was needed at the right moment.

Lee Dixon lobbed the ball casually over a Leeds striker, before playing a pass over forty yards to Paul Merson. Merson steadied himself, before sidefooting a pass into the path of Limpar, who had made a characteristic late run into the box. He let the ball go past him before hooking a shot powerfully into the goal.

The Gunners had the lead, and with their rivals also maintaining a relentless pace, they would need to dig deep to keep this precious goal advantage.

Leeds kept at it and they were rewarded with a penalty. An aimless ball was not dealt with by the Gunners and when McCallister attempted to turn in the box, he fell to the floor. He claimed it was a combination of Jonsson and Tony Adams, who had blocked his run, and the match official believed the Scottish midfielder's claim.

Gordon Strachan, Leed's skipper, stepped up and hit the penalty to David Seaman's right. Seaman went the right way but it was just out of his massive gloved grasp. It was to prove conclusive, as the match finished all square again.

More dropped points, and despite the impressive fact that Arsenal still had not lost in the league, Liverpool were starting to build a lead and Tottenham were still breathing down their neighbour's neck.

If it wasn't for the genius of Anders Limpar, the still unbeaten Gunners would have been further behind reigning Champions Liverpool. Limpar was keeping Arsenal in the mix.

Arsenal's Swedish Magician

Although Arsenal had recently been crowned champions, and were again contending for the honour, the club were still synonymous with the more agricultural side of the sport. The media chose to concentrate on the battling and frugal sides of George Graham's defensive nature, and it was hard to look anywhere else in the side when attempting to locate the catalyst that had been firing Arsenal's cannons.

It was impossible to ignore that George Graham's ethos was to shut out the opposition. Indeed, all the players from that team agreed that the focus in training each day always had a defensive bent.

David Hillier, who made his first-team debut just weeks into the season, in that 2-2 draw against Leeds, said that George would remind the side before every game, "If they don't score you can't lose."

A fitting mantra from a tactically astute manager, and one who is aware of the strengths of his squad. He possessed genuine world-class defenders, who always performed their Gaffer's instructions effectively. They did exactly what he required, and it left him with room to ruminate on other matters. He did not need to worry about his backline, but with every training session came the same exercises, ensuring the level that they had reached was maintained through practice and sheer hard work. There was never any room for slackness.

The impressive defending may have been the fuel for Arsenal's upturn in fortunes over the last four years, but it meant that a stereotype followed the club around whenever they were mentioned in the media. Arsenal were simply not known for thrills and spills. Even with a team complete with Paul Merson and David Rocastle, the Gunners carried the tag 'Boring, Boring Arsenal' with them. Alan Smith admitted that he and his teammates were "not known for being entertaining!" That was, until Anders Limpar joined the club - and ripped up the script.

When Arsenal performed their miraculous season in 1988/89, the instigator for this memorable title win was desire and organisation. The midfield, the attack and especially the defence - each part took to the pitch with their own role firmly in their mind. It would be unfair to say they were not capable of

Euphoric Anders Limpar scores against Norwich in September 1990

footballing magic though. Every team that garners glory has a smidgin of footballing magic in their midst and the Gunners in that season looked to Merson and Rocastle to mesmerise their opponents. These two bewitched many an opposing fullback, and it wasn't just their pace and trickery which was concealed in their twinkling feet.

What good is defeating your marker and earning that precious yard of space, when you then proceed to put the ball out of play or gift possession back? All great widemen can fuse their artistry and slight of foot with a reliable end product. Rocastle and Merson had that and then some, much to opposing teams anguish. They were equally adept at pinging crosses in for Smith, and cutting into the box and going for goal themselves. When your enemy doesn't know what you are going to do, then the battle is already half won. Unpredictability is a defender's weak spot.

Rocky and the aptly monikered Magic Man could perform tricks that allowed their team to avoid the tightest of corners. Every team, no matter how industrial their approach, needs one or two within the squad who have the ability to pull a coin from behind a startled person's ear, or a bunch of flowers from their billowing sleeve.

When Anders Limpar joined, it became quickly apparent that the Swede could conjure up anything, and he dispelled the belief that the Gunners lacked flair. Of course, Graham still held firm that his defence would win them the lion's share of points, but with Limpar leading the way, closely followed by Merson and Rocky, they now had that unpredictability that opponents dread.

Arsenal were no longer just defence merchants, turning up to matches, challenging the opposing team to break them down. They could still counter at speed, but when Limpar received the ball, he had that lucrative quality that saw fans slowly rise from their seats in expectation - their eyes never leaving the tiny man.

When a player can do this to fans, it means he has won them over, but also, it means he truly does have magic in his boots. What other way to explain that mysterious skill that draws grown adults under his spell - that sees them rise from their haunches with nary an instruction given? It is hypnotism, but no pocket watch is seen swinging nor enticing words are uttered. All there is to be seen is the blur of legs and the swoosh of leather hitting the net. Football at its most mesmeric.

His bountiful array of skills ranged from sublime stepovers, to a subtle shift in his body weight which opened up avenues of escape or simply diversionary tactics, which shielded his true intentions. Master deceiver he may be, but in amongst his tricks he also possessed excellent vision which would often pick up the sly runs of Alan Smith and Merson.

Alan Smith, one of the main beneficiaries of Limpar's vision and his roommate that season, said "His feet moved so quickly, but when he joined he wasn't known. He was so clever, and his feet were tiny! He wore size six boots! He was kind of like Mesut Ozil today, as he liked to disguise his passes and create chances."

Nigel Winterburn commented on the cumulative effect the Swede had on Arsenal, saying "Anders had a huge influence on the team, and he scored some crucial goals. He had the quickest feet and scared the life out of defenders."

Young David Hillier would have benefitted from watching his daily exploits on the training pitch, and spoke in glowing terms about the talented winger, "Anders brought the trickery to our side and was the cream on our cake."

Limpar had spoke of his trouble to adapt quickly to the pace of English football when he joined, coming from the intense, but sedately paced, Italian league would have required a settling in period. George realised this and acted swiftly.

Anders was taken off early in his first two games as the flow of the game threatened to submerge him. He did not play badly, quite the contrary in fact. He did tire though, and his efforts would have to be timed in order to last the match. By the time Arsenal reached their fifth game of the season, though, Limpar was in tune with the team and had scored his first goal. The next four matches saw Limpar grab four goals, and his rapport with Smith and Merson began to strengthen. George Graham preferred structure, but with Limpar flitting in between the lines, he could see that his unpredictability gave his side so much. He was the grey area that you cannot account for, he was a fly in the ointment for anyone who faced Arsenal.

George Graham signed him, so he obviously saw Limpar as the last piece of the puzzle, but his exhausting training methods, and focus on organisation, will always be at odds with a maverick of the team. Alan Smith confirmed that Graham, "got into Anders in training. George was a hard taskmaster." Was Anders a poor trainer?

Limpar had not stayed at a club for more than two seasons, other than his boyhood club IF Brommapojkarna. It was his move to Orgryte that alerted scouts across Europe however, and it allowed him passage to Bern in Switzerland to play for Young Boys. Twenty seven appearances and seven goals later, in his only season for the Swiss side, he was again packing his bags, this time for Italy.

Cremonese had just been promoted to Serie A and were looking to maintain their presence in the top flight, so signing a young, hungry talent such as Limpar was a transfer that made sense – Limpar made 24 appearances that campaign – but Cremonese went straight back down.

Limpar did not go down with the ship though as George Graham threw him a lifeline with an offer to join Arsenal, and he settled in quickly. Transfers involving foreign talents often require a 'bedding in' period. Two of the best players ever to grace the Cannon crest - Thierry Henry and Dennis Bergkamp - both took months before beginning to show everyone what they were capable of. Anders Limpar had almost hit the ground running in comparison.

His manager's training methods may have been a shock to the system, but Limpar had also sampled training methods from across Europe, so would have his own strong ideas. His lack of longevity at each club may, or may not, point to problems under the surface, but it was abundantly clear that Anders was doing exactly what Graham had bought him for.

If a player is producing on the pitch, as Limpar was, then a certain amount of leeway would be expected, but Graham did not allow any player to shirk his training.

The Swede was interviewed by the Guardian via a Swedish News channel in 2012, and his comments regarding George Graham leave no illusions as to his feelings on his Scottish manager at the time; "George Graham's regime was like living in Iraq under Saddam Hussein", Limpar told Aftonbladet TV.

"He was disgusting. You would turn up for training one day and he would call a player into 'his room,' although it wasn't a room because everyone could hear what he was saying. Then he would say 'I have sold you to Leeds.' So the player replies 'I don't want to join Leeds.' Graham then says 'Well, you just have to pack your bag and leave.'" "What a swine. I have never seen a guy (player) like that. Tears running down his cheeks. He had been at the club since he was 16. I think it was Leeds he was sold to."

There may be a touch of vitriol left over after Limpar did not agree with the manner of his departure from the club in 1994, but his efforts on the pitch in 1990/91 must have papered over the cracks of a relationship that saw both men come from different ends of the spectrum. Regardless of whether they had a good relationship, Graham was intelligent enough to realise that his team benefitted from Limpar's unique input.

Anders Limpar's goals and assists had been pivotal in Arsenal's unbeaten start, and allowed them to hang onto the coattails of Champions Liverpool. He was undroppable on the form he was showing. As Guardian journalist Amy Lawrence so succinctly explains, Limpar was "that X-factor player."

That certain strand of genius had an obvious effect on the fans who were treated to his footballing delights, but the effect he had on teams was perhaps more telling.

When a team changes their tactics to deal specifically with a certain player, then that speaks volumes. Paul Gascoigne was one who always received extra attention. Anders Limpar was another. Before big games, the managers of the teams due to face the Gunners were asked about plans they may have hatched in order to curb the destruction that Limpar would seek to reap. Extra holding midfielders were named so they could squeeze the life out of Limpar's natural game.

Limpar had them running scared. The Swede was again the man that would prove the difference in perhaps the most titanic, and memorable, game of Arsenal's season.

Fisticuffs at Old Trafford And Slapped Wrists

Bundle... The infamous incident against Manchester United that led to the deduction of points

Liverpool and Tottenham had continued their merciless pace and both were unbeaten in the league, so it was pretty handy that George Graham was also able to navigate his side to a flawless start. It was mandatory as dropped points at this stage would have seen a chasm forming at the top of the First Division table.

The competition was proving to be just as difficult as was first envisioned. Crystal Palace were proving that this horse race would include more than three runners, and Alex Ferguson's Manchester United were keeping pace with the frontrunners too. The front end of the table was looking rather congested, and the Red Devil's well balanced team were showing to all and sundry that they belonged in the mix.

United had won their first piece of silverware in five years when they lifted the FA Cup in May. It smoothed over a disappointing Division One campaign, which led to a 13th place finish. The squad Ferguson had assembled were better than this mediocre placing. The FA Cup had given them a taste for the finer things, and had cast aside doubts that Ferguson was the right man to bring about a revolution. It was the validation his work needed.

Denis Irwin had been the sole noteworthy purchase in the summer, as Ferguson had cultivated some promising youngsters, who looked primed to make a splash that season. Lee Sharpe had already made his debut and was in the first team picture, and 17 year old Ryan Giggs was champing at the bit to sign his first pro contract. They would both go on to make their mark, and this approach from Ferguson was a brave one. The FA Cup win may have brought about a stay of execution, but surely he would need more reinforcements than he had purchased? However talented these fresh-faced youths may be, would they be able to last the distance or provide the contribution that would make all the difference in a gruelling campaign?

Remember, you don't win anything with kids!

United had the luxury of being able to combine true flair with the hunger of youth. In defence, the partnership of Gary Pallister and Steve Bruce was reaping dividends. Midfield saw Paul Ince provide the bite and Lee Sharpe the skills. Up top, they had Bryan McClair and Mark Hughes to provide the goals. It was a strong team, and one that would again be looking to crash the party at the top of the league.

Arsenal travelled to Old Trafford on October 20, knowing that a win was much-needed, pressure was mounting, for what had become something of a grudge match. The animosity between the two sides had been bubbling over during the previous few seasons. Largely because of a routine cup clash between the clubs.

When I asked if there was an undercurrent before the game kicked off, Alan Smith explained, "There was an edge. It came from a cup match in 1988. Nigel (Winterburn) and (Bryan) McClair were both really feisty, physical and no holds were barred between them. It started because a ball was played to me and Gary Pallister went over the top of me. Nigel started and it went from there."

Guardian journalist Amy Lawrence has dug a little deeper though, and has found earlier traces of bad blood between the sides, which she revealed;

"The history came from an FA Cup game and McClair missing a penalty kick. You can go back a little further to 1987, when Norman Whiteside got David Rocastle sent off in a provocative match at Old Trafford. A lot of bad feeling stemmed from that. Nigel Winterburn had words with McClair. Players tend to wait to make a point to someone when they feel wronged." Those words of Amy's perfectly sum up what happened next.

Michael Thomas resumed his midfield partnership with Paul Davis, with Siggi Jonsson making way. Aside from that it was the same lineup which had dealt with Norwich so professionally two weeks before, with a Paul Davis brace proving to be the difference between the Canaries and the Gunners.

Graham certainly believed in the old adage 'if it ain't broke don't fix it,' and they would need every ounce of the winning mentality that they had cultivated.

The first half of the match was pretty much one way traffic, with the home side probing and stretching Arsenal's rearguard at every opportunity. It was a huge testament to Seaman and the back four that they repeatedly repelled United's advances. The 'rope' technique, regularly used in George Graham's defensive drills, was being put under the severest scrutiny.

It usually takes something special to turn the tide in football, and that season there was nothing that fitted that bill more than Anders Limpar. It was the mercurial Swede who silenced the home crowd, and the goal he scored could still be argued over to this day.

Paul Davis lined up to take a corner, one of the rare forays into United territory that Arsenal had enjoyed up to that point. The first eyebrow-raiser was the manner of the set-piece. Paul Davis had swung in many a pinpoint cross, but this time, he opted for the short corner to Limpar, who waited just outside of the penalty area, wide on the right.

It caught out a napping United, who were clearly poised for another Davis specialty. They had numbers in the box, but when Limpar shifted the ball and shaped himself to clip it into the near post, it wasn't only the Red Devil's backline which failed to foresee the coming events.

United keeper Les Sealey was also waiting for an airborne delivery, remaining in his position to claim the ball in the box and no doubt start another attack. However, United were wrongfooted by the sheer unpredictable nature of what Limpar did next.

He had moved the ball onto his favoured left boot, and the ball left his left peg with intent. It wasn't an exocet of a shot, but the dip and curl of his effort was enough to outwit Sealey, who got to the ball with a desperate lunge, but only after it had crossed the line.

Or did he? Without the benefit of goal line technology back then, a juddering replay was the best that could be offered to any fan afterwards, but it was not conclusive. Either way, referee Keith Hackett adjudged that the ball had indeed crossed the line, which only served to incense the aggrieved United players further. They had bossed the game, and were now behind to, what they perceived to be, a dodgy goal?

There was no time for reciprocation, as the half-time whistle blew soon after the goal. It was the perfect time for an Arsenal goal, and it would vastly change what would be said in each changing room. If the goal had not occurred, Ferguson would have asked his men for more of the same fare they had served up - a patient and querying tactic which had probed and passed in front of the stoic Arsenal defence, looking for a chink in the impressive armour that had kept them at bay thus far.

George Graham would have been all set for a motivational diatribe in an attempt to induce more of an attacking presence into his team. There could be no doubt he would have been satisfied with their close monitoring of the home side's attack, but could George Graham himself be satisfied with a point away from home against a valid rival?

The question was redundant, as a sprinkling of Limpar had ensured any provoking speeches formulated by either manager would have to be hastily edited. The goal had put Arsenal in the ascendancy.

The second half was a more even affair, and the Gunners had a fantastic chance to wrap up the points. Limpar was again involved, and his peach of a through ball set Rocastle in on goal. He only had Sealey to beat, but United's keeper, this time, read the situation well to defy Rocky's shot.

Ferguson could see he needed to change things. His side had lost their previous match and looked to be losing even more ground to the frontrunners in this game. He introduced Mark Robins to the game, and although it would give United more presence up front, it would also allow more chances for Arsenal to hit them on the counter as his men piled forward in search of the equaliser.

The game exploded soon after the substitution, with about 25 minutes left on the clock. As Anders Limpar was collecting the ball, Denis Irwin attempted to tackle the Swede from behind. Nigel Winterburn steamed in to aid his teammate, and his sliding challenge went in hard on the United man.

The fuse had been lit, and within seconds, every home player, and ten of Arsenal's eleven, were embroiled. McClair had taken umbrage with Winterburn (the history between the pair, and McClair's missed penalty, perhaps prominent in his mind?) and he thrust himself into proceedings, kicking Winterburn whilst he was still prone on the floor. Limpar had offered his hand for Irwin to shake, but he refused it and knocked the Swede away.

The only way to get to the bottom of the issue was to speak to one of the men who was in the heat of the fire. In my interview with Nigel Winterburn, I asked him if the McClair penalty incident in 1988 was in the back of everyone's mind?

Nigel said, "You are right! McClair missed a penalty and I thanked him for it! He did not take too well to that. The tackle at Old Trafford had nothing to do with previous games - although I suppose Man United players saw it as a way to get some revenge on me. The game felt like it was waiting for something."

The plot thickens! Amy Lawrence was right it seems - players do like to wait for the perfect moment to serve up that acerbic dish of revenge.

Back to that moment in question, and Irwin had just refused Limpar's offer of a handshake. The mass of seething players grew, with only one man left out of the bundle. David Seaman. So what did Safe Hands see from his position?

"Not much!" he tells me in his deep Yorkshire tones. He went on "I was 60-70 yards away at the time, and I wasn't aware of the previous incidents. We were all aware that United were getting stronger though."

Back to the brawl, and the growing gaggle of anger gravitated toward the touchline where both managers resided, along with their backroom staff. George Graham became involved, as well as his Assistant Stewart Houston, Alex Ferguson could be seen out of his touchline area, in heated discussion with Arsenal skipper Tony Adams. Paul Davis and David Rocastle were in the thick of it as well, but the majority were there to calm things down before it really kicked off.

David Rocastle was one who had the red mist descend, and he was another who had suffered previous dealings with United. He was being held back by none other than United goalie Les Sealey, who could see that Rocky was keen to live up to his boxing namesake!

David Hillier was on the bench that day, and he said "It was a naughty tackle by Denis Irwin on Anders and there was already beef with them. I remember jumping off the bench and joining in! What team spirit! The gaffer always said we should have each other's backs and we certainly did."

The Arsenal squad had taken offence to McClair and his kicking of what was a stricken player, as well as the tackle from Irwin, which was made with no real attempt to gain possession.

The United squad had umbrage with Winterburn's zealous tackling of Denis Irwin. Guardian journalist Amy Lawrence says of the incident, "the kick on Nigel Winterburn was a pure consequence of the match in 1987. Things escalated so quickly, but to kick someone when they are down seemed to cross some sort of code."To that end, the eventual punishment meted out to both teams was unrivalled. After such an explosive incident, how would the rest of the match unfold?

The remaining minutes were played out calmly and without much incident. It was a strange, almost eerie setting. There were only two yellow cards shown during the entire match, and referee Keith Hackett had done a commendable job in placing a lid on the boiling pot. It is a rare occurrence indeed that a match official receives praise, but the subsequent minutes after the incident were played on frayed nerves and still ignitable embers - Hackett should be applauded for his tight leash on the game.

The match ground to a halt and Arsenal had grabbed the points, but there were far larger ramifications to consider than the winning of the game. The Football Association were under real scrutiny to stamp this behaviour out of football, and here were two sides who should be carrying the flag for English football. Instead, they had muddied its reputation with their aggressive actions. The book would be thrown at both teams, and it was talked up in the papers over the coming days.

The Daily Mirror, three days after the match, ran with a two page special with a garish headline, intimating that Arsenal were 'sweating on video verdict', as the FA pored over replays of the brawl. Mirror writer, Harry Harris, also wrote of how Europe's then disciplinary soccer chief, Rene Eberie, had implored the FA to sanction a points deduction for both teams. The fact that the major governing bodies of football were commenting on what had happened shows how critical the potential punishment could be for both sides.

Manager's Graham and Ferguson were both singing from the same hymn sheet, by issuing statements to the media underlining how they read the riot act to their respective men, and they wholly supported any action that the FA may or may not take. The Daily Express featured an article by writer Kevin Mosely, which was a focus on Graham and his answer to the backlash he and his men faced.

The Arsenal Gaffer said "One of the British strengths is competitiveness. We don't want to take that away, but you've got to act with responsible control whether it's as a team or as an individual. It's down to pressure. It's a matter of handling it."

Graham had offered the media the soliloquy of peace they had required, but simultaneously, he had also thrown down a challenge to his squad. Could they keep their head in the heat of battle? Were they made of the right stuff? Graham seemed to be always finding opportunities to push his men further.

He also touched upon a previous indiscretion, one that would ensure that his Gunners copped it heavier than United would when it came to doling out discipline from the FA. "Our disciplinary record is outstanding" Graham stated, before going on to say "apart from that Norwich incident last year which was again a group thing. Team spirit is always a good thing, but it is also a collective thing. We have to stamp this out."

The incident George referred to was a similar brawl at Highbury, during a match between his side and the Canaries. The bust-up cost Arsenal £20k and Norwich £50k, with a warning to both that if similar events were to transpire in the future, then the punishment would be much heavier. Which brings us onto the FA's eventual decision.

They docked Arsenal two points and Manchester United one point. It was a first, and it still has yet to be repeated. Arsenal, as a club, fined Paul Davis, David Rocastle, Michael Thomas, Anders Limpar and Nigel Winterburn. They also fined their own Manager, with George Graham asked to pay £9,000.

When asked about his decision to fine George, Arsenal Chairman Peter Hill-Wood defiantly said "Twice in two years is too often. The name of Arsenal has been sullied and that is why I have taken this action." Both clubs also had to pay £50k, but this was not newsworthy. The fact that United and the Gunner's had been slapped with a points deduction was huge, and hit them both where it hurt most.

Arsenal were particularly impacted by the deduction. They were in second place at the time of the points being taken away, and one point ahead of fellow unbeaten team, North London rivals Tottenham. The points Arsenal were immediately bereft of saw the gap to Liverpool greaten. That was hard to swallow as it felt, at the time, that the FA had handed the title to Liverpool on a plate. Tottenham then took advantage of the Gunner's punishment by slipping above them.

That was unacceptable. Good can come from adversity, and Graham grabbed whatever he could whilst slipping underfoot. He used the negativity that was being directed at Arsenal, at his charges.

He had wanted each and every member of his squad to stick up for one another, to generate a feeling of camaraderie. This was the foundation for the ferocious reaction that was seen at Old Trafford. Guardian scribe Amy Lawrence again describes it best; "There was a sense of brotherhood, to stick up for your teammates. Even little Anders was involved! It was the reason they were so successful."

What was not really featured in many reports was the TV cameras visit to London Colney to cover George Graham lambasting his men for their part in the disgraceful scenes on the Old Trafford pitch. It was a press event designed to show that Arsenal were doing the honourable thing and ensuring this ghastly behaviour would cease. George Graham would castigate his troops in front of the camera, and the media would have the tasty titbits they would need to fill a few back pages. Headlines involving 'Naughty Arsenal told off by teacher' or words to that effect, were the order of the day, and would be a plaster to cover what was becoming an ugly scab thanks to the non-stop coverage in the papers.

Anders Limpar disclosed afterwards what happened when the cameras had completed their recording. George changed his expression from grave and serious to utter elation, his teeth bared with delight at the snarling Arsenal that had refused to let United bully them.

He was congratulating his men, fists balled in delight. He wanted to see his boys stick up for each other and that was exactly what they had done. It was the fighting spirit he had cultivated, in tangible form.

Lee Dixon was also on TV after it had occurred. The England defender responded comically when asked about what had happened; "We won the game didn't we?"

I asked him if the history between the teams had played a part. Dixon said "No. The game was big but so were all the others. We could play, but we could also fight if we were prodded. United prodded us!"

After all the messy aftermath, there was still the small matter of football to be played. Liverpool may have had a healthy lead, but all was not lost. It was time to forget the previous week and crack on again. They wanted to switch the focus from fighting, to passing and goals.

A week after the Old Trafford fiasco, their wish came true as Arsenal welcomed Sunderland to Highbury. Game on!

The Wall Stands Tall

The reaction that followed the Old Trafford fracas did overshadow what was shaping up to be an incredible title run-in, and Arsenal - slapped with a points penalty and the ire of the footballing world - were readying themselves for a fight of a different sort than was seen at the home of Manchester United.

So fierce and all-encompassing was the news trail that followed the events of that United match, it dwarfed any actual football that was played in the days after. Liverpool, as expected, were leading the way and had an unblemished record to boot. Tottenham also had a record which was yet to taste league defeat and with the Gunner's points deduction, it meant they were breathing the same air as Arsenal, and looking to take advantage of Arsenal's self-inflicted wound.

Crystal Palace and Arsenal also boasted unblemished records. The Eagles were in second place, four points behind the current champions, and that meant that the job was not finished, not by a long shot. With four teams going strongly and the chasing teams by no means cut adrift, it showed that this season in the First Division was to be the most hotly contested for some time. It also succinctly demonstrates what standards would be necessary to be victorious come May.

George Graham was - at least behind the scenes - delighted with his men and how they stood up for each other at Old Trafford. No amount of threats or challenges would splinter this group - and that was what the canny Scot had been building since he started at Arsenal, and had been reinforcing ever since.

The Reds of Merseyside claimed the honours of top scorers at that stage. Peter Beardsley and John Barnes had been eviscerating sides with their dynamism, and with six and five goals respectively, they sat atop the scoring charts.

Anders Limpar, fast becoming a Gooner fan favourite, had also bagged five goals, but the team had not shared the goals as evenly as Liverpool had. Alan Smith, Paul Merson and Kevin Campbell had not hit their flow yet, but with the fixtures occurring with alarming regularity, these attackers were about to aid Limpar and alleviate the goal burden from the Swede's delicate shoulders.

It hadn't been an avalanche of goals that had seen the Gunners ride on Liverpool's coat-tails thus far. It had been George Graham's brainchild, the Arsenal Back 5. They had conceded just five goals up to this point, with only Spurs bettering that amount, conceding only three. The men who comprised Graham's work in tangible form had been carefully selected, hewn from the hardest granite and shaped in the fires of George's sustained scrutiny, when the seeds of which were sown way back when Graham first took the job in 1986.

From his first day at Highbury, he could count on club Captain Tony Adams, but his signing of Steve Bould, Lee Dixon and Nigel Winterburn was the purest proof that he knew exactly what parts he needed to construct a line of defence that would cause the finest attacks in football to stumble.

The final brick in this imposing wall had been David Seaman. By George Graham's own admission, when he was asked about the purchase of Seaman and the sale of fan favourite John Lukic, he stated that "John is one of the best goalkeepers in England. It is just that I believe David is the best."

It made life at the beginning tough for Arsenal's new Number One. A record fee for a goalkeeper hanging over his head, attempting to replace a player who the fans adored - a weaker character may have crumbled. David admitted that at the beginning, he struggled saying, "The problem was winning the fans over. I had to show them what I could do. I was also friends with John Lukic from my time at Leeds. It was difficult."

Gooners needn't have worried. George Graham picked his transfer targets with accuracy, and one criteria his purchases always ticked was mental strength. David Seaman began strongly, and he never let his foot from the accelerator.

One factor that would have helped was goalkeeping coach and Arsenal legend Bob Wilson making the leap from QPR to join his protege at Arsenal. The relationship between the two was strong, and with Wilson constantly producing more and more from the big Yorkshireman, the results showed on the pitch.

When I interviewed Bob Wilson, he could not have spoken higher of the man who dominated his penalty area that season, telling me "David was calm, and always is. You cannot get him riled. I cannot recall ever seeing him lose the plot. I used to wind him up incessantly about being the first and only keeper to have won the Double at Arsenal, so I know he is unflappable! He is also incredibly humble."

Guardian and Observer writer Amy Lawrence had this to say on the man we now know as Safe Hands; "A sensational goalie, he had that unflappable temperament. You wouldn't call him a leader in any sense of the word, but having that presence behind you of total cool reliability, it gives you leadership in itself. He was vital."

David Seaman shared the same level of respect for his goalkeeping coach and mentor, "We had two years at QPR, then thirteen years at Arsenal. He has been my Best Man twice, and he has an incredible knack of giving you confidence in training."

The training ground was where Seaman's hard work and Wilson's knack of eking out the best from his protege meant that, on the pitch, the goalie could prove to the fans he was up to the task.

Now that Seaman was integrated into the side and George had established his first choice centre-back partner for Tony Adams, the relentless repetition of training was bearing fruit on the pitch. Even when one of the components in this impenetrable wall was missing through injury, the countless exercises they did at London Colney meant that it was a seamless transition for the backup when they were called upon. Everyone was aware of their job.

Rocky Rocastle in full flight against Norwich City in October 1990

George Graham had a fixation on defence. It must have been tiresome for the players on the training ground, but the results showed that it was worthwhile. The 'Tuesday Club' that the players took part in was a necessary letting off of steam, and whilst drinking and banter would occur on other days through the week on occasion, the Tuesday Club allowed players to further strengthen the bonds of friendship. It meant that at work and out of work, these men were spending time together, subconsciously learning all there is to know about each other. If that didn't help on the pitch, then the training regimen would fill the gap.

Bob Wilson told me about the regular exercises that would fill a day at London Colney, saying, "They were an amazingly strong and well-knit team, and George's defence was the perfect base. The defence was solely down to George Graham and his work. Every player knew their role. They did countless routines where they worked without the ball, focusing on movement and reactions."

Amy Lawrence had this keen observation about the melding of this five part combination; "George had drilled them within an inch of their lives. Everyone knew what they were doing, they could help Linighan integrate, or anyone else who came in."

Speaking to another member of this impregnable unit, Nigel Winterburn touched on the work that was involved to get to this stage; "We did a lot of team play and back four work, which when you look back, you wonder how could we do that for so long as some of it was boring! But I will say it made us into a very strong unit . George used Tony, his captain, to pass messages on to the players throughout the week as he liked to keep his distance between manager and players."

The conduit then, was Tony Adams. The man who had been at Arsenal since youth, had made his debut in 1981 and had been ever present ever since. George relied on his Skipper to ensure the instructions he put in place were made real on the pitch - and to a tee. Speaking to the players and experts on this team, you get the distinct impression that perfection was what George demanded - and it was a very real target.

David Hillier had finally made the leap from Youth Team Captain to the first team thanks to George Graham. The gap in quality would normally see the kids in question struggle initially. Did the gruelling training help him to bridge the gap?

Hillier told me, "It was tough, he was like a headmaster although he was the first to praise or reward, but he was fair and honest. The best manager I've worked under no doubt." Upon quizzing these players, one thing was mentioned repeatedly, and it was a training exercise that was used so often, it has obviously never left them, even after twenty five years.

It involved a rope, and the back four. It was tied around each of them, and various scenarios were played in and around them. The key trait that was highlighted with this exercise was the movement between each man, and how a shift to the left or right by your fellow defender can create a gap that can be punished by your opponent. This exercise would place a tangible link to each of them, but after countless times of being tied to your teammate, eventually, the rope would tie their minds together too.

Performing this routine repeatedly would inevitably see these men being able to predict the next move his comrade would make. This would create a domino effect, which would see the whole back four mirror the initial movement.

Like a school of fish, or a mass flock of starlings in the sky, the defence would move as a whole, reacting in strength to any threat with one large movement. It was the amalgamation of four defensive minds into one, coalescing the intelligence into one hive.

This hive, with the addition of the solid presence of David Seaman, would be the undoing of the sharpest of strikers. Instead of a fractured reaction, which would see one of the defenders going to the man in possession and therefore opening a space which could be used against them, they all moved relatively to their teammate. It required much work to implement, but the fruits of labour were there for all to see.

This was on display at Old Trafford, though you would be forgiven for missing it with the fireworks that took place. Adams, Bould, Seaman, Dixon and Winterburn withstood an onslaught of United pressure, especially in the first half. Mark Hughes was one of the deadliest sharpshooters in the Division, but he was supremely shackled by Arsenal's defensive efforts. United had tried in vain to stretch and contort the Arsenal line, but whatever direction they tried, Adams and company were impervious to this possessional pressure.

They had also accrued another clean sheet in the previous fixture, a 2-0 home win over Norwich. Two tough games and two normally productive attacks had been blunted by the Gunners wall, and the next fixture for George Graham's well-oiled machine was the visit of Sunderland at Highbury.

Graham saw no need to change his eleven, and the unchanged team took the game to struggling Sunderland, who were well organised at the back but, aside from Marco Gabbiadini, posed little threat. The Mackem's defence stood firm but with all the home side's pressure, it was perhaps surprising that the game contained only one goal.

Paul Merson had possession on the right flank and chipped in a ball that the Black Cats looked to have dealt with. A cushioned defensive header saw the ball come alive again, and Sunderland defender John Kay and Anders Limpar scampered after the unclaimed ball.

In a foot race there was only ever going to be one winner, and so it proved as Kay dived in, in his mind knowing that probably Limpar would get to it first. He did not connect with the ball, but his legs did trip the Swede, who was sent tumbling.

A penalty was awarded by referee Vic Callow, and regular penalty taker Lee Dixon stepped up to smash the ball just off the centre of the net, with goalkeeper Tony Norman falling to his right.

The rest of the game was relatively risk free for the Gunners, and it was another three points - and yet another blank slate for the Gunners defence to add to their growing collection.

Another week of rigorous training followed which preceded an away game at Coventry. A change was made in the lineup, with perennial substitute Perry Groves installed into the side in place of winger David Rocastle, who was beginning to struggle for fitness. Fans looking back on this fixture, who I have spoken to, remember this match not for yet another clean sheet, but for the sheer genius of Anders Limpar.

The tricky winger had truly found his feet at this level, and his continued influence in games was telling. He was an alchemist who was able to transform the dullest of fixtures with a swish of his tiny boot or a drop of his shoulder. His electrifying brand of magic would be the difference against the Sky Blues.

Limpar picked up a short pass from Paul Davis and attempted to wriggle free down the right, but Sky Blues man Dean Emerson used his physical prowess - and quite a bit of an armlock - to hold the Swede at bay. This illegal resistance would last about six seconds more.

He decided to cut in after freeing himself from Emerson's grasp, and his speed whilst on the ball was far better than his opponents without. He dummied a shot, which gave him the yard of space he needed, and he swung his left boot at the ball. Twenty five yards out, it had a faint curl which took it out of the despairing reach of Coventry keeper Steve Ogrizovic, and it buried into the net.

Arms outstretched high in the air, Limpar realised he had scored a fantastic goal, and an important one.

The same half saw Limpar strike again. Nigel Winterburn broke up a promising Coventry attack and carried the ball deep into enemy territory. More than capable of launching a goal-bound effort, he decided against going for goal as Anders Limpar showed up on his shoulder. Nigel offloaded to the Swede, who was visibly full of confidence after his earlier effort.

He cut in from the left past one startled defender, and decided to pull the trigger. Would Limpar have chosen to shoot from this distance again if his earlier effort had not gone in? It certainly would have had some bearing. These little facets may be buried underneath stats and other facts, but they have as much heft in deciding glory's path as other factors.

Fate may have played a part, as another little facet decided to chime in. Limpar's shot was deflected, and Ogrizovic could only watch as he fell agonisingly out of the spinning ball's trajectory and the turning leather sphere nestled into an empty net.

It wasn't just good luck that got involved during this match. Striking lynchpin Alan Smith injured his ankle during the match, with Kevin Campbell replacing him. Losing Smudge would dent any side, would this factor override the hard work that had gone in to continue the side's impressive start? Despite Arsenal starting the season impressively, would an injury to one of their key men prove more decisive? Fans the world over have seen the object of their affections ultimately crumble at one point or another after being deprived of a certain player, and losing Smith could debilitate George Graham's setup.

The match had thrown up a huge problem for the Gunners. Arsenal had to keep fighting even in the face of losing such an important player, and the decision to not sign a striker and keep faith with what he had at his disposal would be put to the test. Smith was out for the next few games, and Campbell would get his shot to justify Graham's conviction in him.

The Coventry game could have seen the Gunners drop points and further strengthen Liverpool's position at the top of the table. The events of the game though, secreted factors that emboldened Graham's confidence in his men, and why they would continue to apply pressure to the leaders.

Nigel's long run. Limpar's inclination to shoot from a long distance. The exquisite deflection that could have carried the ball anywhere. All things that may not have necessarily happened on a regular match day, but both conspired to give Arsenal another win, continue their unbeaten run to eleven games - and it also meant another clean sheet.

These coincidences, these slices in time that could have splintered in any other direction than the way they did - it emanates an overwhelming whiff of destiny. The defence that was beginning to constrict the life out of any who stood in its way did not require coincidence however, and another potential victory was on the horizon. Not just any win either.

Crystal Palace were tipped at the start of the season for great things and while they had a taciturn defence and competitive midfield, it was their strike-force that was the main reason for such optimism toward the Eagles.

Mark Bright and Ian Wright had fired Palace to Division One two seasons ago. Ian Wright suffered serious injury the season after, a double break to his shin which had hampered his international prospects and also the South London club's aspirations, although Mark Bright continued to plunder goals - 17 for the season.

Wrighty and Brighty were reunited this campaign, and with Geoff Thomas behind them posing another threat, they were thought of as contenders for silverware. They were going well in the League at the time they faced the Gunners, in fourth spot and keeping up with the breakneck speed of the unbeaten teams, with Tottenham in third who had lost their first game of the season.

George Graham was forced to shuffle his winning hand, as Alan Smith and Perry Groves both were carrying knocks. The Scot also changed formation for the first time in the campaign, opting for a 5-4-1, with Kevin Campbell filling the gap left by Smudge, and David O'Leary starting his first league game. This formed a three man central hub of defence, and the plan was to give Winterburn and Dixon free rein to bomb down the wings and cause merry havoc.

Arsenal's left-back and right-back were integral to the team's excellent defensive record, but they provided an important outlet when the Gunners were attacking. They both could convert pressure into promise with a delivery from deep, and they overlapped with timed precision in order to supplement forays on the flanks. Their metronome-like runs were in sync with the rest of the team, so they were rarely caught out of position and they were always ready to lend a hand to their respective wingers when the need arose. They would need all of these in their armoury to contend with the Eagles' frontmen.

The game finished at an impasse, with neither side managing to add to their own 'goals scored' column in the league table. George Graham, in his programme column for the next game against Southampton, paid compliments to his newly constructed defence, but also lamented his side's lack of presence in the box when crosses from Limpar and Merson came whizzing in.

Campbell would need time to adapt his own positions and runs in order to benefit from the supply of Limpar and Merson, but Graham's call to use a five man defence stifled Wright and Bright. It was the first time he had utilised this change in tack to his tried and tested formula – and the rest of the season would see Arsenal's manager use this formation in some vital matches.

George said of his side's display against Crystal Palace; "We looked more secure than at any point this season - no mean feat against Wright and Bright." The new-look Gunners defence, instead of being weakened through unfamiliarity, had instead silenced what was possibly the most potent attack in England.

It was testament to the hive mentality and qualities that the Arsenal defence - first choice defenders and their backups – all shared. O'Leary had come in, the whole match instruction changed as well as the positioning, but the result was still the same. An emphatic shutout.

The next target lined up on Arsenal's cross-hairs was a Southampton side who were underachieving, given the ability which resided in their squad.

Up front, Saints manager Chris Nicholl had an embarrassment of riches. Young striker Alan Shearer was grabbing the headlines with his eye for goals, and the amazingly talented Matt Le Tissier would always provide. With Rodney Wallace, hatchet-man Jimmy Case and Neil Ruddock in their side, the South Coast team had class, clout and the capacity to win any game.

George Graham would have been well aware of this, and the fact he had the returning Smudge in his first eleven earlier than expected would have boosted his hopes for another victory. Perry Groves also came back into the team, with Kevin Campbell and David O'Leary back on the bench as Graham reverted to 4-4-2.

The rotation and shift back to the more conventional formation of 4-4-2 obviously suited Arsenal, even though they had played well in the 0-0 draw with Palace using a 5-4-1.

The Gunners demolished Southampton 4-0 in a clinical display of finishing. Smudge in particular was effective, grabbing a brace. It was a huge boost to the returning striker, who had not enjoyed the most fruitful of starts to 1990-91. Smith's goals would go on to be a recurring theme for the rest of the campaign, but this double was the start.

Anders Limpar and Paul Merson were Smudge's fellow goalscorers and it was a real showing of strength from Arsenal. It had been a reminder to their rivals that they can be just as powerful in attack as they could be in defence.

It was the sixth consecutive clean sheet for Arsenal, and it enabled them to cultivate hope of catching Liverpool. The seasoned veterans of title run-ins were ten points in front of the Gunners, and Beardsley, Barnes and Rush had peppered their opponents to the tune of twenty two goals. In plain terms, the Scousers were smashing it.

If it weren't for Arsenal's defiant rearguard laying their own brand of smack-down on strikers across the country, the pride of North London would be collectively choking on the dust created by Liverpool's vast speed toward the title.

Instead, both of these teams, proudly carrying an unbeaten record, were heading straight into choppy waters and the vessel which survived would stand the greater chance of lasting the voyage.

The two teams were due to face each other, with only one fixture to play before this potentially season-defining ninety minutes. When a decisive fixture looms into view, players and managerial staff can often place the majority of their attention on preparing for this huge game. They then lose sight of the nearest hazard and instead of impeccable preparation, they are handed a loss in confidence and greater pressure going into the match.

George Graham would not allow this to happen. Never remiss when it came to the finer points, the team would be more than ready for the tussle with Liverpool, but not before ensuring their next test would be passed.

This examination of their credentials was a real brain-teaser though, and one that came within a whisker of ruining Arsenal's flawless record.

A week after humbling Southampton - and with the media focusing on the next game versus top of the table Liverpool - George Graham took his team to Loftus Road to take on Queens Park Rangers.

QPR were no fools, and if Arsenal decided to let their foot off the gas, even a little, to conserve energy for the Liverpool game, the Hoops would make them pay.

Just before half time, it seemed as if this was actually going to happen. American striker Roy Wegerle picked up the ball and took on Tony Adams. It was initially right of the penalty box, but Adams retreated so the pair were now in the box.

Wegerle then made his move. He put the ball past the Arsenal captain, and intended to follow. Adams may let the ball pass him, or the man - but he would not let both pass. They went shoulder to shoulder and Wegerle went down rather easily. Referee Ray Lewis pointed to the spot and the man who earned the spot kick took it. The American striker scored, and QPR were the first team in over six games to score a goal against Arsenal. They were also perilously close to being the first team to inflict defeat on George Graham's team.

The second half was frustration personified for half an hour, until parity was restored with twelve minutes left. A Davis free kick bounced around the box, before a Tony Adams shot found its way to Paul Merson, who lashed high into the net. The ball could have gone anywhere, but again, fate decreed its path was meant for Merson, who did not need a second invitation.

Twelve minutes to go before the Gunners would have registered their first loss, but the team continued to grind, to probe and press. The appetite of these men was on display, and they seemed ravenous.

Arsenal then seized the initiative. Nigel Winterburn rampaged down the left and cut back to substitute Kevin Campbell. Campbell attempted to turn and get it onto his favoured foot, but fell under pressure. The ball travelled two yards parallel, to where Smudge was waiting. He made no mistake, with a first time shot which found its home in the bottom left of the keeper's goal.

The dam had burst, and Arsenal were not finished. Like a lion with fresh prey, they were merciless. A long punt forward by Lee Dixon was chased down by Campbell, who was showing heart but QPR defender David Bardsley had it under control, surely?

No, he didn't. His nightmare encapsulated about three seconds in total. He failed to simply pass the ball, well, anywhere. He failed to dump it into Row Z. He instead hesitated, and let the ball roll under him. Campbell was not going to pass this opportunity up, and he advanced toward the goal, where he calmly slotted it past Jan Stejskal. This response, this roar of defiance from Arsenal, happened in a neatly wrapped twelve minutes.

George would have been hurting after seeing his side concede their first goal in over five hundred and eighty minutes, but those twelve minutes would have reinforced his belief that his side were more than capable of reeling in the giants of Merseyside.

It took a penalty to break Arsenal's run of clean sheets. Six in all, and even though the six zeroes had failed to add a seventh, the fact remained that it was now seven games where teams had failed to break this team down from open play. George Graham had constructed a beast of epic proportions. Now QPR had been dealt with, the match of the season was upon them. Liverpool had earned a points buffer that they were more than accustomed to enjoying, and were showing their usual ominous signs.

If Arsenal wanted to keep their title dream alive, they would have to not just take points from the Reds. They would have to first silence their forwards, and then blast them away with their own firepower. The top two in the league, with two unbeaten records – something had to give.

Shifting The Tide And Taking A Beating

The two pacesetters and last remaining unbeaten sides were ready for battle. Fists had been taped and gloves were on, the ringwalks had been impressive and the baying crowds were hungry to see these heavyweights go toe-to-toe.

Before this mammoth match took place, George Graham had not just been preparing his side for a title tilt. He had been plotting a course aimed at winning every match his prize-fighting squad showed up to. It wasn't just a horde of Division One matches that had caused selection headaches amidst fixture congestion. The Rumbelows Cup had begun back in September, and the ties only added to the strain placed on Graham's men.

The first obstacle the Gunners had to hurdle in the League Cup was an away match to Chester City. The 'home' side didn't quite get to claim to be the home side, as they had sold their Sealand Park stadium that year to cope with debt problems. They shared Macclesfield Town's Moss Rose ground that season, and this was where this Rumbelows Cup tie was played.

This wasn't the rollover that Gunners fans were expecting. It was the quintessential cup tie against lower league opposition, and Chester put up a real fight. What made their display even more impressive was that the side Graham picked was a strong one. Arsenal, just three days before this tricky game, had put in a great performance to defeat Nottingham Forest 2-0, but a tough away tie at Elland Road just four days after, shaded this fixture in terms of importance. Despite this, the Arsenal gaffer did not go easy on what could be perceived as a straightforward game, nor did he rest the majority of his first choice team and prioritise the tough match to come against Leeds.

Instead, George trusted in the work they had done and continued to do so. He knew the limitations of each and every one of his men and he was obviously confident that they could play these three matches in short succession.

Nevertheless, the Gunners toiled for the majority of the game, and even used up a fair bit of luck as Chester hit the post from a direct free kick. It was the wake up call Arsenal needed. Paul Davis soon after clipped a ball through the Chester defence and Paul Merson raced onto the pass, his touch putting him a couple of yards ahead so he had time to pick his spot and score.

It was the bare minimum Arsenal needed to gain an advantage for the second leg at Highbury, which took place on 9 October.

This game was the polar opposite of the first leg as Arsenal walked through what seemed like a broken Chester. All the fight from the first tie was missing, or perhaps the Third Division side were overawed by the setting. Either way, it didn't take long for Lee Dixon to wing in a cross and Perry Groves to head home at the back post.

The lead was doubled when Groves was again the beneficiary of a great cross, this time from Rocky Rocastle. Speedy Perry volleyed in the cross and his confidence was high, it was a fantastic finish.

The Gunners were three goals up when the same right hand side combination produced another pinpoint cross. Dixon picked up a backheel and pinged in a pass which Merson did well to head back into the danger zone. Alan Smith was alive, as always, to snaffle the chance up and it was three goals in the half.

Arsenal were not finished punishing Chester. The second half saw more goals as the full Highbury crowd enjoyed the show. A lofted central ball found Smith with his back to goal. He flicked the ball on and an adventurous Tony Adams chested the ball down before bundling the ball home. Time for a fifth course maybe?

The Gunners really spoiled the home crowd with the final strike. Merson drove toward the Chester goal, but with about thirty yards to go, he chose to shoot. The ball flew from his right foot and arrowed into the top corner over a despairing dive from the Chester keeper.

Game over. Progression obtained. Arsenal had not only overcome a stubborn Chester side, they had also avoided defeat against Leeds. Graham's gamble had paid off.

The fourth round of the Rumbelows Cup was a top-flight affair, with Manchester City welcoming Graham's team to Maine Road. Liverpool had exited the tournament at this stage, and when the Reds went out, teams across the land pricked their ears. It meant that everyone's chances improved ten-fold. This opportunity for silverware had just become very real. Thus, another strong side was selected for this game.

There were no second leg affairs in round four. Just a straight knockout match. Liverpool had lost 3-1 to Manchester United at Old Trafford, which may have actually benefited Liverpool as it meant one less game to play at the very least.

In that era, the bigger clubs normally rotate the much larger squads they have to play with when it comes to the League Cup and lower league ties in domestic competition. Graham did not have that luxury, nor did he want to rotate. He and his men wanted it all.

A hectic calendar was not even on Graham's agenda. The cup tie was, again, precariously sandwiched - this time between a match against Sunderland (which Arsenal had won 1-0) and then, three days after this cup tie, Graham took his team to Coventry.

Even in the face of these headaches, the fitness work that George had installed in the summer was paying off. He picked a similar side to the team that had won just three days earlier in the league. It was a similar hero too, as Merson put in a tantalising cross that Groves popped up to slot away to give Arsenal the lead.

Manchester City could, and should, have drawn level. Former Gunner Niall Quinn put a header just wide of the post, and then Adrian Heath cracked the crossbar with a volley with David Seaman beaten. Arsenal didn't need telling again.

They doubled their lead, with a corner coming into the box with both Smith and Tony Adams going for it. Smith got the touch, but the ball fell flat in the path of Adams, who punted the ball into the net.

Two goals up, but City would not let go of their chance that easily. A free kick was put into Arsenal's box, and Quinn, again, got his head to it. It fell to Clive Allen with his back to goal, but he swivelled and his volley fizzed past Seaman.

A goal back, but with six minutes left, it was too little too late. Arsenal had rode their luck but the next round of the League Cup had been assured.

If you bear in mind that was all achieved as the Gunners maintained their unbeaten start in Division One, then it only underlines what Arsenal were capable of. Liverpool had popped their losing cherry by that stage, but George Graham's men carried on and bettered their run. It was a feat that didn't garner enough respect at the time.

This takes us seamlessly to the eve of the tussle with Liverpool. The top of the table clash tha... Hold on a minute. There was the small matter of another Rumbelows Cup tie to navigate before Arsenal and Liverpool would put up their dukes. It wasn't just any tie either.

After Arsenal's last League result - the 3-1 victory over QPR on 24 November - it left eight days to prepare for the biggest test of the season with a Cup fixture against none other than Manchester United in between.

If this had taken place twenty years later, Sky Sports would have billed it as the week that would determine Arsenal's season, 'Judgement week.' It would have been on every advert break and the buildup would've included an opinion from everyone willing to offer it.

As it was though, there was still plenty of attention on both fixtures. If Arsenal were to lose to current champions and title favourites Liverpool, then they would have been nine points behind and the confidence, which was oozing from every pore, would have been sapped. It would potentially break the spine of their title challenge.

Then there was the burgeoning rivalry with Manchester United to contend with. Going out of the Cup to Ferguson's men would not sit well with anyone at Arsenal, and with the Old Trafford debacle still fresh in their minds, Arsenal would go all out to ensure that United would be denied again.

The previous fixture between the two teams brought this game to the boil. There could be no chance whatsoever that Graham would let anyone take their foot from the throttle with the opponent being United. They would have as much of a point to prove as United, even though Arsenal had actually won that game 1-0!

Eyes were on Arsenal. Three days and two crunch matches. Could they do the unthinkable and remain unscathed as they had done thus far?

At least with having played one another so recently, it meant that the teams knew what to expect from proceedings. It didn't mean that a surprise couldn't be sprung on each other though. Alex Ferguson thought so anyway.

Fergie made a bold decision to leave his skipper Neil Webb on the bench. He switched up his formation and made room for 19 year old Lee Sharpe in the team. He also tried to harness the pace in his side by opting for Danny Wallace to play alongside Mark 'Sparky' Hughes up front.

Arsenal were on the cusp of breaking a club record of eighteen matches unbeaten in all competitions. With the notorious fixture at Old Trafford still fresh in the memory - and how they had won - Davis touched on how big this matchup was in an interview that was included in the match programme.

"Our win at Manchester last month gives us extra confidence, but it's a new game tonight and United seem to have a flair for cup competitions. I've played in plenty of big games before, so I don't feel any special pressure because I've been out for a while. I've been pleased with my form so far. A big game like this provides a big stage to play on and I'm looking forward to it." Paul could not have foreseen what was to come next.

Football perpetually lures us all into thinking that sense can be applied to its parameters, that convention has a place within its confines.

Then its mask falls momentarily and its true anarchic visage can be seen. This match was one of those moments. Within 80 seconds of this madcap match beginning, Fergie's men had taken the lead.

Clayton Blackmore received a short layoff from an indirect free-kick, roughly 30 yards from Arsenal's goal. He produced a daisy cutter of a shot, but it had enough fizz to squeeze past the Arsenal wall and past David Seaman's massive hands to nestle into the bottom corner.

The shellshocked Gunners battled to regain a foothold, but United were just as pumped for this grudge match. There was to be no repeat of the fisticuffs at Old Trafford a month beforehand, but there was no holding back from either set of players.

A goal at the start of the half had the Gunners on their heels, and it was a goal at the end of the half that had Arsenal gasping for air. Lee Sharpe had the ball wide on the left and he found Wallace in space in the box, Wallace did not hesitate to square it to Hughes, whose first time shot rifled past Seaman to double United's lead.

If Arsenal were on the deck begging for a reprieve after the second, then what happened next saw them facing a count from the man with the whistle.

Welcome to the big leagues, Sharpe. It was a huge call to include the precocious teenager, but after Wallace had carried the ball into Arsenal's third of the pitch with seconds to go in the first half, the ball bobbled to the youngster. He chose to shoot from 25 yards, and what was produced from his boot was something to behold. It arced, it curled and it found its home in Seaman's goal in the top corner. It was unstoppable, it was untouchable. And it was the purest form of revenge.

The half time whistle blew from the lips of referee John Martin with the events of the half going against what most fans had envisaged, and seconds too late to avoid the last blow which had put Arsenal on the deck. If supporters could not have predicted this outcome, then spare a thought for George Graham, who had seen his defence concede just six goals all season, only for this particular 45 minutes to buck that trend quite spectacularly.

What was said in the dressing room is not known, but one thing that can be taken for granted is that George would not have let his men give up. Even with the gargantuan task ahead of them, he would not let the Arsenal name be sullied by a thrashing at Highbury at the hands of a team fast becoming the Gunner's biggest rivals in terms of fan hatred, well, other than that lot down the road obviously...

The match would be another log that fanned in the flames of hostility that licked lasciviously at the feet of every fixture these teams would play. The second half then saw a mighty load of wood placed within the flames. It was compelling viewing.

Arsenal came out of the blocks with a point to prove. Never better than when they had their backs to the wall, a free kick came in to the United box, and it eventually found its way to Alan Smith who fired home after Michael Thomas's shot was parried by Les Sealey. Game on?

The Gunners were feeding off the fans and the rising atmosphere that had been extinguished in the first half by the Red Devils goal blitz. They soon had a second and the wind in their sails.

A Davis corner was met by Adams and he headed it low toward goal. Merson got a touch before the United keeper could grasp it properly, meaning that Smith - a yard out from the goalline - could get a toe on the ball and grab a scrappy second for the home team.

From an apparent humiliation to a real chance of recovery. Arsenal were flying, and in a post-match interview with the Daily Express, this is where it went wrong for Graham's men. The Scottish gaffer revealed "They got off to a fine start, it gave them confidence. They outplayed us in the first half but for twenty minutes we got back to 3-2. I thought we should have calmed it down then, but we were flying, trying to get the equaliser. There was too much gung-ho."

The Gunners WERE flying, but Sharpe had a shotgun cocked and ready to fire to bring the home side down to earth.

With fifteen minutes left on the clock, the progression of either team to the next round was on a knife edge. Denis Irwin found space as the tackles were flying in, and his perfect cross found an airborne Lee Sharpe at the front post. His glancing header flew past Seaman and the wind that was in the Gunners sails was hushed instantly. The Arsenal fans were silenced by the goal.

From nobody to superstar in just eight minutes, Lee Sharpe scores the opener for Manchester United

Arsenal had gotten the habit of winning. They had not tasted the bitter fruit of defeat all season. They were about to be force-fed this acrid berry before the fat lady started her funeral dirge.

Arsenal were in a frenzy and on the attack once more, not knowing the meaning of 'give up,' but good work by Hughes set the pacy Wallace free in midfield. He bore down on the Arsenal area, before setting Sharpe free, who had kept up with Wallace all the way.

Sharpe picked the ball up with a deft touch, before drilling a low shot across goal. Seaman managed a touch, but he could only direct the ball into the far corner. 5-2, at home. This was a hell of a way to lose your unbeaten record.

It really was a madcap way to follow what was a groundbreaking, violent match the month before. The matches between these two sides had noteworthy incidents harking back to 1987, but even in 1979 they produced what some still regard as the greatest FA Cup Final last five minutes ever played.

Two matches in this season had seen these sides produce nearly everything that could possibly happen on a football pitch. That figurative fire that encompassed fixtures between United and Arsenal was now burning with white hot abandon. United could see Arsenal were swaying, and could not resist a final insult.

The Gunners were seeking some solace as they were again on the front foot, but a backheel from hat-trick hero Sharpe sent McClair clear. As he rampaged through midfield, he could be seen urging his teammates forward, even with a three goal lead and minutes left on the clock. This was a chance to leave a lasting mark.

McClair passed to Hughes, who crossed low, through Seaman, for Wallace to finish from inside the six yard box.

Six goals. At Highbury. A hat trick from a player who hadn't scored in the League as yet. Unbelievable!

The United fans were chanting "we want seven." You could not blame them. If the boot was on the Gooner's foot, they would have relished the chance to rub our faces in it. I asked Smith about this incongruent result. His response pretty much fit the bill.

"I haven't a clue what happened! I remember the Cup wasn't a priority, but it was such a strange game! You could play that game ten times in a row and you wouldn't get the same result again!"

Ferguson commented in the Daily Express just as Graham had, and his delight could barely be contained, "It must be one of the best United results for many, many years. It was one of my most satisfying!" If the Old Trafford battle was 1-0 to The Arsenal, this reverse was certainly an equaliser for Manchester United.

Of course, the League Cup wasn't placed as high as a league match against Liverpool in Arsenal's vision, but it was still a match against United. With all that had passed under the bridge, it could not be treated as just another game. This can be seen by the feverish attempts to grab an equaliser by the Gunner's players. The margin of defeat meant they desperately tried to claw back a goal so that they could save a little dignity. Any ideas about conserving energy for the match against Liverpool in just four days was vanquished.

George took the opportunity to talk up his side's chances in his programme column for this huge match. This game represented a chance to bounce straight back from the realms of misery, and it was an opportunity he fully intended to grasp. "We've always bounced back from setbacks in the past. It's time to do so again. Wednesday's defeat by United was a crazy result. No one could have dreamed that a side with our great defensive record would concede six at home. It was my biggest defeat as a manager. I can only look at it as an aberration, taken against our magnificent start to the season."

He mentioned that the Double season of 1971 shared certain parallels too, and that magnificent side had gone on to achieve Arsenal's greatest accolades that season. They had lost 5-0 at Stoke City and had then lost at home to Crystal Palace. But what a recovery. That is the response he was yearning for, what he expected. He knew what his men were capable of, but the opponents would provide the toughest examination so far.

Liverpool also shared an unbeaten league record, and with John Barnes, Peter Beardsley and Ian Rush in their ranks, it was almost a certainty that they would score goals. No other team had managed to deny them.

George highlighted the task ahead of them with a sentence in the programme that resonates even now, "We won't face tougher opponents, because Liverpool have come to represent the standards by which we all measure ourselves."

To be the best you have to beat the best. The league's most prolific attack, facing off against the league's tightest defence. Yin and Yang. Both managers opted to change things up a little.

Kenny Dalglish chose not to attack beleaguered Arsenal from the off, leaving Beardsley on the bench and having Rush on his own up front. He, instead, went

Alan Smith scores Arsenal's third goal against Liverpool in December 1990

for midfield solidarity, inserting Barry Venison into a stoic-looking centre. It had worked recently for him too, in a win against fellow high-flyers Spurs. It was an attempt to wrestle control of the game in the middle and use that as a base.

George had obviously seen something he liked in his team's recent stalemate against Crystal Palace, as he again selected David O'Leary in a sweeper role. It did not impact on Arsenal's attacking intent either, and Dalglish would be paying special attention to Smudge, who had a great goalscoring record against the Reds.

Smith had tripped up the Merseysider's in his Leicester days, and had plundered four in his previous four games in Arsenal colours. Smith seemed to have the beating of the Liverpool backline.

Arsenal had not beaten Liverpool at Highbury in George's three and a half years at the club, but this was to end in spectacular fashion.

The first twenty minutes were cagey, like boxers feeling each other out before wading in with haymakers. Liverpool had the first chance, with Rush setting David Burrows clear, but under pressure he fired wide of goal and it was the home team who struck the crucial first goal.

Thomas, who had grabbed the game by the scruff of the neck, darted into Liverpool's third, and it took a Ronnie Whelan clearance to stop the midfielder, at the expense of a corner. Thomas's corner was partially cleared by Glenn Hysen, only for Thomas, again, to get involved. He hooked the ball back into the area and wily veteran O'Leary headed on to Paul Merson. The Magic Man headed at goal and it was saved well by Bruce Grobbelaar, but Merson had followed on. He got there first after Grobbelaar's parry, and he headed the ball past the Red's keeper from his own touch. Barry Venison was on the goal line to clear, but the linesman judged the ball had already crossed the line.

A huge decision, but rightly or wrongly, Arsenal had the lead. Liverpool could have grabbed an instant response, with Molby's corner headed just over by Ronnie Whelan, but Liverpool were not dismayed and continued to press forward.

Venison saw his shot well held by Seaman, and Rush dragged another shot inches wide of the far post as Arsenal's five man defence struggled to keep Liverpool at bay. They had done enough to hold them at arms length for the first half at least, as referee Alan Gunn signalled for the half time interval. The Gunners had battered their way to a small lead, and then had all hands to the pump to stop Liverpool doing what they had done to every other team they had faced. It was at times last-gasp defending, but Arsenal did not buckle.

The same pattern continued for the second 45 minutes. Liverpool tried their patient build up, and Arsenal threw everything in the way, before looking to set free either Thomas, Limpar or Merson on the counter-attack.

And it was on the counter that Arsenal broke Liverpool's hearts. A ball forward saw Merson and Limpar vying to claim it on the edge of the Liverpool box. Merson was deceived by the spin of the ball, but Limpar carried it forward a touch, before Gary Gillespie lunged at the ball. Limpar's speed of thought had moved the ball on, and instead of Gillespie valiantly snatching the ball, he clipped a running Limpar. The Swede had thought quicker and moved quicker than Gillespie, which meant the Liverpool man had to thrust out a leg.

Gunn blew for a penalty without hesitation and Whelan was spitting fire. He went straight for Limpar, and words were indeed exchanged. Limpar remained calm and didn't respond, but the calmest man in the stadium was Dixon, who slammed the penalty high up the middle of the goal to give Grobbelaar no chance.

That was the turning point for the game. Liverpool felt aggrieved, Arsenal were elated. Just like United had been four days earlier, Arsenal could smell blood and wanted to leave a scar. Dalglish then made some changes, with Houghton and Rosenthal coming on, but to no avail. With ten minutes to go, the killer blow was struck.

In what was fast becoming Arsenal's signature move, Seaman punted forward and Smith flicked on expertly. His aerial prowess was not wasted, as Merson picked up the ball and back-heeled to Smith, who had not rested on his laurels and continued his run. He knew he would get the ball and his first time shot found the far corner expertly.

Three goals to nil. It was Liverpool's heaviest defeat for a year. It was also a reminder that Arsenal, even with the points deduction, were not going away.

In the battle between the top two, Arsenal were the emphatic victors. What a message to send, to both the doubters who envisioned a hangover after their Rumbelows Cup mauling - and to the Reds who they had most resoundingly beaten.

Liverpool were still adamant that Limpar had dived to win the all-important penalty, and the next day's tabloids were full of their outcry regarding 'justice' failing them. Limpar was dubbed 'an actor' in the Daily Mirror by Venison. He also stated that the Swede 'deserves an Oscar.' Quite a statement.

It wasn't just Liverpool bemoaning Limpar's apparent antics either. The Gunner's very own O'Leary said of the incident, "Honestly, I don't know. I see Anders in training and I watch him take a tumble off his own back. He has got to be very careful in the way he reacts. By rolling over more than he should, it could work against him."

The Daily Mirror hardly helped by doing a diving feature in the paper, looking at various other attempts to coerce the match official into awarding a penalty. Did Limpar dive, though? Through the delights of video replays, it does seem as if there is contact, but it is unclear.

What is undeniable, is that Arsenal struck a huge claim for the title in this game. It would be, perhaps, the instant that Liverpool were reminded of their mortality, as they did not have the same air of infallibility as they had enjoyed before.

Three points now separated the teams in the table, but it wasn't the points tally that held more weight. It was to be seen in the losses column. Liverpool had one little L, compared to Arsenal's O!

After fifteen games, they had still not lost in Division One, and they had faced every conceivable obstacle that could be thrown at them. A severe case of fixture congestion so bad, it made lunchtime on the M25 look like a picnic. Injuries to key men. Matches against giants, even points taken away.

Nothing had managed to stop them thus far, but what could fate conjure up to test them further? How about sending their Club Captain to prison halfway through the season?

Coping Without The Captain

The 3-0 win over Liverpool had turned heads as well as the destiny of the Division One title. Liverpool had built a lead, gone unbeaten and were showing the familiar signs of all of their previous title triumphs. George Graham's tinkering of his side was the proverbial spanner in Liverpool's works.

They had been looking ominous and it was a heroic performance from their nearest challengers that had loosened the unyielding grip that the Reds had enjoyed over domestic competition for quite some time.

Guardian and Observer writer, Amy Lawrence, once again captures how pivotal the triumph was; "The 3-0 win felt important at the time. The teams had had some titanic battles over that period and that match was yet another. It was one of the few games where Arsenal absolutely battered Liverpool though."

Arsenal's win refreshed hope that the Liverpool juggernaut could be halted. Graham could feel he deserved a break after masterminding what could well have breathed new vigour into the title race. Anyone who had ever experienced the work of the aforementioned Gaffer would not believe that a rest day was in his repertoire though. The season was in full swing and Kenny Dalglish could not ignore that the main obstacle to regaining what most people regarded as Liverpool's title, was once again Arsenal.

Graham, although he may not take a day to enjoy his most recent spoils of war, could take a certain amount of pride. His decision to play David O'Leary as sweeper meant that Arsenal could control the midfield. His hunch gave Arsenal the edge in the centre of the park and this swing in control meant that chances dried up for Rush - and Alan Smith, Anders Limpar and Paul Merson could truly test the Champions at the back. It worked a treat and the door for the title was unlocked.

Seeing as the League waits for no man, the next match was brewing, and Graham used the same formula against Luton Town. The corresponding fixture had seen the Gunners tough it out in a 2-1 win, and the Hatters once again gave Arsenal a game.

Arsenal took the lead through Smith, who had well and truly returned after his spell out through injury. He stooped low to head in a Davis free kick and Arsenal were on track.

The rest of the game completely changed when Skipper Tony Adams was sent off, as he grappled with Ian Dowie who had a yard headstart on him. It was a definite penalty, but when the referee called Adams over, the surprise amongst everyone was genuine when he held the red card aloft.

Perry Groves was warming up on the touchline as Adams departed from the pitch, and a pat on the back was the last we would see of the Arsenal captain during this game. Arsenal would soon have to get used to his absence, and the loss of the Gunners captain could have had catastrophic repercussions.

John Dreyer swept the spot kick into the top corner but Arsenal held on valiantly for a point as Luton made the most of the unfamiliar surface on which both teams played. Kenilworth Road had an artificial pitch, and it added to the difficulty away teams faced when visiting Luton.

Graham mentioned the plastic pitch in his programme notes for the next game versus Wimbledon at Highbury. a week later; "The outcome at Kenilworth Road was a huge disappointment. All I can comment about Tony Adams's dismissal is what I said after the game. Does the referee's decision now mean that every player who brings down an opponent for a penalty will be sent off? I'm not complaining. I'm just asking for more consistency. There hasn't been much of it where Arsenal are concerned. We showed our resilience to hang onto a point with ten men. We'd probably have settled for that before the game. Luton are a useful side - and they're particularly useful on that plastic. Fortunately, that was the last league game we'll have to play on it."

It seems that apart from the foreign body that was the playing surface, some things never change. Graham crying out for consistency in refereeing decisions is a plea that can still be heard every week in today's Premier League matches.

Under the same scrutiny that was used to judge the harshness of the match official, it could be decreed that this game was the closest Arsenal had come, so far, to dropping the ball in terms of their unbeaten record. Going down to ten men, losing the organisation and defensive merits of the captain, and gamely hanging on for a point. This match could have quite easily been the first defeat of the League campaign. The 'never say die' spirit that burned within each Arsenal man was the last wall of resistance that had carried on the flawless streak to 16 matches.

Liverpool still had a lead over the Gunners of two points and had a game in hand. The run would have to continue in the face of such relentless pace from the team at the top. While Liverpool were asking their nearest challengers to show them that they were up to the chase, it was also vital to continue to put every ounce of pressure onto the Reds. If the gap were stretched, then it would have been Liverpool's title.

Could any more be done to upset Liverpool? An unbeaten run and a vicious hammering were apparently not enough to sway Dalglish's team from their tunnel vision. Graham would ensure that his charges would keep battling away, and Wimbledon provided their next opportunity to extend their run.

The Dons had been Arsenal's first competitive opponents of the campaign, and were dispatched in comprehensive fashion to the tune of a 3-0 win. Would home advantage and the memory of this thumping give the Gunners enough to repeat the feat? Arsenal would have been confident, but their previous match had eroded the Gunner's belief a little.

Luton Town had taken more out of this Arsenal side than just their physical edge. George's constant work had ensured they were amongst the fittest in the land, but the draw at Kenilworth Road had sapped the batteries, and Wimbledon never needed a second asking to take advantage of a team not at 100%.

Arsenal got off to a solid start and they broke through the rugged Dons rearguard quickly - Smith turned provider to see Merson through on his own with just the keeper, Hans Segers, to beat. He chose to shoot early with his right and it was enough to find the net. They doubled their lead when a Davis corner went deep into the box, and Adams slammed a header past Segers. Wimbledon had a reputation for being strong in the air, but Adams could not be stopped for his goal. The same could be said for the Arsenal backline, but they had a momentary lapse aerially, as a John Scales cross from the left found Detzi Kruszynski, who headed powerfully and David Seaman could only parry the ball into his goal.

Two games played and two goals conceded. It was most unlike Arsenal's regular pattern, especially that season. After earning a two goal lead, the constant movement and mental focus had switched off, and that small window was enough for the opportunistic Dons to fight their way back into the game.

It was to get worse, as a free kick from their own half was flung into the Arsenal box and an uncharacteristic error from Seaman allowed an equaliser. He came off his line to punch, but was beaten to it by John Fashanu and the ball looped into the empty net vacated by the straying Gunners' keeper.

There was no time left for Arsenal to regain the lead they had given up so softly, and another two points had been dropped. Would one of their finest hours be all in vain after those two results? Would the 3-0 victory over Liverpool be all in vain?

It appeared as if this may have been the Gunners most challenging part of the season so far, and it was underlined a few days after this result, as their Captain and leader, Adams, was sentenced to four months in prison for drunk and reckless driving. Adams has since released an autobiography chronicling his time in jail and his struggles with alcoholism, entitled 'Addicted.' This part of the book is not a focus on what is already well known. What isn't so commonly understood is how his forlorn team mates dealt with the very large void on the pitch - and off it.

Adams *was* Arsenal. He had already been at the club since 1980, and had made his debut in 1983. The armband had its rightful home on his arm. He embodied everything that a George Graham team contains, and he was the middleman through which all of Graham's instructions would be passed. Could any team cope without such a player?

With his team giving away initiative and breathing space to their rivals at the top of the table, could his sojourn at Her Majesty's Pleasure have come at a worse time? Technically, yes.

With his sending off at Luton, Adams was due to sit out three games through suspension. If he had been sentenced any later, he would have missed three games, and with his prison term, very likely have missed the rest of the season.

I'll back Adams

Boss Graham stands by fallen Arsenal idol

REPORT By STEVE CURRY

ARSENAL manager George Graham last night insisted he would stand by his jailed captain Tony Adams.

But 24-year-old Adams, once tipped as a future England captain, won't receive the same strong backing from his international bosses. Adams, convicted on reckless and drink-driving offences yesterday, was due to start a three-match suspension this weekend for being sent off at Luton on December 8.

Now he is likely to be out of First Division football until April ... and international football for good. Graham, who groomed Adams to stardom, was devastated by the sentence which will hit Arsenal's Championship bid severely.

"I could not wish for anyone better to be my captain," he said. "He has been the complete professional on the field and in training and, as a sportsman, he has my complete backing.

Down in the dumps: Arsenal boss George Graham with Tony Adams earlier this year

That could well have sounded the death knell for Arsenal's title dreams. So could Graham's band of tight-knit brothers deal with the loss of one of their own? Could they still steer the ship when rudderless?

Bob Wilson, goalkeeping coach and man behind the scenes, delivered his verdict. He told me; "Tony had set the tone, so they all knew what was expected. When they were up against it, it became a collective thing. In terms of who stepped up, well, Nigel Winterburn was always noisy! Lee Dixon was a real leader though, and he could have been Captain himself."

So, obviously upon hearing this, when I spoke to Lee Dixon, I asked him how the team coped without the man dubbed 'Mr Arsenal.' Lee said "It was difficult at first. but the essence of the team was when we were backed up against the wall, we came out fighting, George Graham style!"

It seems the siege mentality George had bred at Arsenal was fiercer than previously imagined. Fellow members of the famous Arsenal 'Back 5,' Nigel Winterburn and David Seaman, also gave their thoughts on how the team dealt with this demanding period of the campaign.

Nigel stated that "the players did not worry about it too much. Although Tony was the Captain, we had a duty to keep our run in the league going. You put your trust into any player that comes into the team to replace a teammate. There is more pressure on the individual to perform particularly when you are replacing the Captain."

It appears as though the team used the circumstances as a positive and would carry on as their Captain would have wanted. David Seaman had this to say about who stepped up to fill the 'unfillable' void left by Adams; "We all did. We felt for Tony. The only way was to keep winning. After our game against Spurs, he managed to get a message to me, saying 'well done goalie.' That meant a lot." The Captain was inspiring even when he wasn't in the dressing room!

Alan Smith told me that Tony Adams's dad came into the dressing room whilst his son was serving his time, and his words had really resonated with the team. Smudge went on, saying "No one could do what Tony did, nobody was the same. He had a big voice! We all shared the responsibility, and we took it on the chin. The day he was sentenced was the day of the Christmas party, we all debated whether it should go ahead!"

Smudge never told me whether it took place, but if they were acting on what Tony would have wanted, then I'm sure a few drinks were put away in his honour.

There wasn't just a gap in the dressing room with the Captain gone - Arsenal's unrivalled defence was now broken. His presence was missed throughout the club. George Graham would have relied on his men to keep up their motivation and unbreakable team spirit, but in terms of matters on the pitch, he had a decision to make. Would David O'Leary - the man who held the record for most appearances for the club, and had recently appeared as sweeper in the team to great effect - be the man to shore up the gap? Or would Graham opt for Andy Linighan, his summer purchase?

In came Linighan. It had been thrown around in pre-season that Linighan had been purchased as a replacement for Steve Bould, who had missed a fair few games through injury. It was with a fair sense of irony then, that when he did manage a run of games, it was to replace the captain and that he partnered Bould.

Linighan was a reputable defender and certainly no lightweight, Amy Lawrence says of the former Oldham Athletic, Leeds United and Norwich City defender; "He wasn't a 16-year-old plucked from the youth team. He was a good pro. Everyone raised their game in Adams's absence and they all knew exactly what they were doing on the pitch. That was down to George Graham."

The relentless drills, the rope, the exercises without the ball. It was all to create an impregnable defence that could operate minus a link in the chain. Adams was a mighty big link, but Linighan had been indoctrinated for six months in The Arsenal Way. He knew exactly what his role was.

Tony's sentence was judged to be a little harsh at that time, and no one had expected such a long duration. Perhaps it was because it was an England and Arsenal player that had been in the dock? It had taken six months for the case to go to court and the papers had enjoyed every lurid detail. The Arsenal had never been a media darling, and the relationship worsened with every sentence printed on the subject.

Graham's programme column for the match with Derby County was telling of the mood at Highbury; "The fate of Tony Adams overshadows everything at Highbury this week. We don't condone what Tony did and the club has fined him for it, but some of the reaction in the tabloid press has gone way over the top. Tony has accepted his responsibilities as captain with great dignity and professionalism. Everyone at the club respects him as a player and person. We're going to stick by him. Everyone will welcome him back when his sentence is over, and so will the fans. When he returns to Highbury he'll go straight back to being our Captain."

Lawrence describes what it had been like back then with sports stars and drinking; "Players DID drink driving at that time and if he had done that today, it would've been difficult to come back from. They went out on the lash in their sports cars. It was a heck of a punishment for him though. Some people felt he was being made an example of. There was a strong core of Arsenal fans who defended him, but that is part and parcel of football's tribalism." What he had done was undeniably wrong, and he was serving his punishment. How would Arsenal be punished though, with missing what was possibly their most important player?

Three matches came quickly for the Gunners as the fixture list decided this was the best time to test Arsenal's mettle. First up was an away match at Villa Park to take on a dangerous Aston Villa side. Three days later, Derby County would be at Highbury and finally, after another three days, another home game against Sheffield United. If Arsenal were going to get through the gauntlet, this would be the litmus test.

On the back of two underwhelming draws, the first match against Villa - and the toughest match of the three - was a stern test for the makeshift Arsenal defence.

There was a moment of consternation during the game as Groves was taken down in the box and, to all and sundry, it looked a penalty. The referee disagreed and it was the nearest Graham's men would come to scoring, as both defences outwitted each other's attack and the game finished 0-0. The only other moment of interest in the game came by way of a save from Seaman, who acrobatically denied David Platt to keep his side's unbeaten record intact.

Linighan had been dropped in at the deep end after making sporadic appearances since he had joined. He had no match sharpness and no rhythm, but he was singled out for praise by his manager for his presence and tactical nous. Graham said that Adams' replacement had done a top class job, and Graham's decision to bring in yet another centre-back in the off-season had been vindicated.

Linighan's assured performance was the chief reason why Arsenal had still yet to be beaten in the League. They had sailed close to defeat before, but the Midlands side had tested the Gunners severely. With Adams missing, and the sticky form they had been going through, a point was not so negative after all. The league table would prove a contrasting point of view entirely. However, it was still a case of more dropped points, and Liverpool must have been enjoying the rut their rivals were stuck in. There was not time for moping though. Derby County were ready and waiting at Highbury.

There was one piece of good news to lighten the mood, David Rocastle finally returned to the first team after yet more injury woe and some cameos in the previous games. He replaced Groves in the side and Rocky's return must have boosted his comrades, as Arsenal got back to winning ways.

Limpar and his trusty crosses supplied the first goal, and an even trustier Alan Smith glanced in past Peter Shilton, 1-0 to The Arsenal! The usually reliable Mark Wright had been caught out by Limpar's pinpoint cross, and 'Smudge' took the gift without a second's hesitation.

The second goal was a scrappy affair, but the Gunners would not have minded. It was sheer bloody-mindedness from Paul Davis, who challenged for the ball in the box, and the loose ball fell to Paul Merson who swung the ball in first time out wide. The prone Peter Shilton, who had gone up with Davis to contest the first ball, could only watch as Merson's effort went into the goal.

The third goal belongs in the comedy annals - maybe a football blooper DVD hosted by Nick Hancock - and anyone who had seen the goal will not forget it. David Seaman kicked the ball out, and the ball flew a fair distance. It looked like the Ram's defence had it covered, but they conspired to miss the hurtling ball. The ball kept travelling and Shilton, who was off his line, could only get his fingertips on the goalbound ball. His touch put it onto the crossbar, and who was there before anyone else? Goal-getter supreme Alan Smith.

It looked like an easy finish, but what goes under the radar is his positioning. He was primed for any sort of chance or deflection that would come his way. Smudge was like a bloodhound in the penalty box.

It finished 3-0 to the Arsenal, and after three consecutive draws, the win was more than welcome. It also represented a valuable and confidence-boosting clean sheet, a second in two games for Linighan and co.

The win against Derby was nothing but good news. Rocky was back, it was another shutout for the defence, and it was number nineteen undefeated in the league, at the halfway marker. It was a hell of a record already, to go that length of time in such a competitive league was worthy of high praise, but it would mean nothing if they did not finish at the zenith come May.

Match number 20, and the third in six days, was another home game versus Sheffield United. Before the game, 'Rocky' received more bad news, as his long awaited return in the previous game was tempered with more ill-luck. He had suffered a broken toe in the first minute of his comeback, and would again be sidelined. Groves once again filled in for 'Rocky' on the flank, but that change aside, it was the same side who had defeated Derby.

Sheffield United were bubbling with confidence after two wins on the spin, and took the lead with a low header which found the far corner. Not exactly according to Graham's plan, but his side did him proud by hitting straight back. Another testimonial to the team's incredible willpower.

Smith dinked a ball over the Blades defence, and Groves looked to run onto it. His shirt was pulled by Vinnie Jones, and R.L Hamer, the referee, pointed to the spot. Dixon stepped up and sent Simon Tracey the wrong way and the Gunners were level. It didn't take long for the natural order to ring true and the home side were soon in the ascendancy.

A nice passage of play ended with Winterburn scampering down the left and putting in a low cross which Smith dispatched with a first time effort. It looked effortless and Smudge was enjoying a purple patch - his fourth in five games. It had been Davis that had made the difference though, his pass had sliced open the underbelly of United, and Winterburn duly laid it on a plate for Smith.

Then it was three. Merson could not be caught down the left of the area, but his cutback evaded everyone. It eventually stopped at the feet of a back-

Andrew Cole pictured against Sheffield United – his only appearance in an Arsenal jersey

tracking Michael Thomas. Mickey swung a hopeful boot at it whilst off-balance, and the ball curled and dribbled into the net. The fans wanted four, and they got their wish.

Davis was once again the conductor, and his chipped ball to the back stick was read by one man. Smith had stole in, with the Sheffield backline unaware of his run. The penalty box ninja from Leicester planted an unopposed header past Tracey for his fifth goal in five games, and it gift-wrapped three more points for the Gunners.

That was seven points from nine in the space of six days. George could not have asked for much more, but he would still have the match against Villa buzzing in his mind like an errant fly. He would be pleased with overcoming so many problems, but he was also a perfectionist. He wanted nine from nine.

The points his men had worked hard to gather had been enough to close the gap to Liverpool however. One solitary point was what separated Arsenal from the top. The Reds had a game in hand still, but it was another firm reminder to Dalglish that the Gunners would not go away. Arsenal were like a jack russell at this point. They were relentless and did not let go. It was like the Championship was the Vicars tweed-clad leg, and they clapped eyes on his limb and their jaw was set on it before they even realised they had chomped down.

A game away to Manchester City on New Years Day was a fourth game in nine days for Arsenal. Could they welcome in 1991 with a win? Would they carry on this unceasing gnawing of the vicar's trousers?

City at Maine Road was a significant mark up in difficulty when compared to Sheffield United and Derby County at home. It wasn't a lack of respect to be aware of your enemy's strengths and weaknesses. It was evident that, whilst Derby and Sheffield carried as many arrows as City did, they had more gaps in their armour than the Mancunians. It was the difference between good sides and contenders.

The blue half of Manchester were firmly established in the top half of the table, and they were within touching distance of the top six. This called for a change in tack from Graham, and the Scot again opted to include O'Leary as a sweeper to provide that extra cover at the back.

The opponent would be difficult for Arsenal, but what would be just as big a hindrance to another positive result was four games in nine days. What an exhausting schedule to complete, even the finest teams would surely stumble when faced with this proposition. George's team never saw problems though, they saw challenges waiting to be conquered, and they set about hurdling this particular hazard with as much vigour as the last twenty matches.

It was all hands to the pump at both ends of the pitch for the Gunners. The game could have gone either way, but the subtle blend of experience and hunger edged a tight game. After sending on Groves for O'Leary in the second half as Arsenal hunted the winner, a corner from Davis found a lurking Smith to smash high into the net, which proved to be the winning goal.

In four games, and within such a short time frame, Arsenal had won three and drawn just one. They had conceded just one goal in that time, and scored eight goals. All of this was obtained without one of their finest exponents of creative football, 'Rocky', and the lynchpin for the entire side, Adams. Quite remarkable, and it was a testament to the rod of steel which was Arsenal's backbone.

The last match they needed next, even with confidences riding high, was a clash against North London neighbours.

Spurs had enjoyed a good start to their season, but had fallen away a little, sitting in sixth place. This was not an indicator of their quality though, and the last derby was on a knife edge. Graham would be expecting the same level of competition in this game. It was at White Hart Lane too, so Tottenham would be looking to get one over their rivals, just as Arsenal would be aiming for the same bragging rights.

Terry Venables's men were always slick in possession, and so Graham (again) went for O'Leary as sweeper as he had done against Manchester City. This would hopefully clog midfield and not allow Paul Gascoigne the space he thrived on. Gazza had been a marked man by all teams since the start of the season, and it was a necessary precaution.

Graham again got his tactics spot on, and his team were unlucky not to take the lead when Limpar showed a flash of what he was capable of, destroying three Spurs players with skill before trying an audacious shot which narrowly missed the goal.

But it was the home side who came closest to nicking the points - and how their fans would have lapped up ending Arsenal's unbeaten run! Clive Allen

Mickey Thomas hurdles a desperate lunge from Justin Edinburgh at White Hart Lane in Januray 1991

found himself unmarked late in the game, and his header forced Seaman into what could be perceived as his finest - and certainly his most vital - save. Every sinew in his arm stretched to deny Allen. Such was the manner of the save, that the normally ice-cool England stopper clenched his fists with delight and roared to his fans. That was why Adams sent a message of congratulations whilst still behind bars! Seaman had saved the game for Arsenal, and thanks to his heroics, he not only denied Tottenham some serious bragging rights - but Arsenal, after twenty two games, were still undefeated.

The squad had been stretched thin during this festive period. There had been many games and not many days to play them. The fringe players had all featured at some point, with David Hillier, Kevin Campbell, O'Leary and Groves playing big parts in maintaining the Gunners title focus. Every member of the squad was pulling in the same direction. It must have been consolation for their imprisoned Skipper, who would have been watching every moment with intent - and pride.

After such a rigorous schedule, George could look forward to resting his men a little, but a poorly executed Italian League versus English League friendly match three days prior to their next game - a home match versus Everton - meant that the hectic nature of the fixture roster had continued. Graham's men desperately needed a rest, but thanks to this moronic planning, it meant there was no respite in sight for some Gunners.

Davis, Limpar, Seaman, Dixon and Thomas were selected for the dubious honour of playing in this needless fixture, and Graham voiced his displeasure in the matchday programme. "I've already made my feelings clear about this Italian verus English League fixture, and it has done nothing to help our preparations for today (the Everton match). We did try to have today's game postponed to allow more time for any injured players to recover, but the best we could get was a delay until Sunday, so we decided to go ahead with the match as planned."

The Everton match went ahead, and so did Arsenal, as their imperious form continued. The first half saw a little fatigue factor into Arsenal's normally breakneck pace and pressing, O'Leary was playing his third game as sweeper in a row, and the firm grip in midfield was the foundation Arsenal needed to push on in the second half.

It was a showing of squad strength which edged this game for the Gunners. Second half substitute Groves chased a flick on he himself had performed. Groves hounded the Toffee's backline who regained possession, but the ball was suddenly nicked back thanks to Groves's refusal to give up. Merson was onto it in a flash. If there was tiredness in his bones, he did not show it as he finished easily to give his side the winner.

Another tight match, but yet again Arsenal produced the goods. So many matches and so many detracting factors were seemingly intent on derailing the Gunners train, but there was only one stop on this line - glory.

It was an amazing feat to escape from this series of matches with no losses. The calibre of opponent, the loss of their leader, and injuries aplenty would have robbed the best of teams of any impetus they had fought to gain.

Not Arsenal though. Not Graham's side. He wouldn't let them buckle, and the fire he had instilled inside each and every one of them would not go out. It didn't flicker, even in the fiercest of winds.

As it stood after this severest of scrutinies, Arsenal had gone twenty three matches without the ignominy of a loss. It was unheard of. In such circumstances, in the face of competition of the highest nature, Arsenal had managed an incredible feat.

The table was the reward for such a wonderful run. They had finally acquired top spot, sitting one point ahead of Liverpool, though they had that valuable game in hand. The Gunners had also conceded just TEN goals in those twenty three games.

At some point, you run out of fitting adjectives. You just have to try and soak in what an achievement it is. It should rank among the best of what Arsenal has ever done, but it could have been even better. Sadly, that run of twenty three games unbeaten would stay where it was.

All thanks to an FA Cup tie straight from hell, a hazardous tackle from a Chelsea defender, and a clearly offside goal.

The Leeds Cup Saga, Losing Bouldy And Losing, Full Stop.

In the midst of Arsenal's League offensive, the flurry of matches they had faced and overcame was also intertwined with the beginning of the FA Cup. Sandwiched uncomfortably between a trip to Maine Road - which Arsenal had won with their signature scoreline of 1-0 - and the fans most eagerly awaited fixture of a game against the old enemy of Spurs, the Gunners began their quest for Cup glory with a third round welcoming of Sunderland to Highbury.

The Cup draw had not been kind to George Graham. There was plenty of lower league opposition that could have had the misfortune to come up against Graham's soldiers, but it was fellow top-flight team Sunderland who were given the task of defeating the undefeated. If the Cup was to be lifted then First Division opposition would be inevitable, and Arsenal were certainly gunning for the trophy. They had last won it in that famous final in 1979, eleven years ago. It was high time that Arsenal once more had their name engraved upon the most famous domestic cup in world football, but the path to Wembley was not exactly a cakewalk.

This cup tie meant that the Gunners squad would have to manoeuvre around six games in nineteen days, which worked out roughly to a game every three days for nearly three weeks. It was a schedule cut from the devil's loincloth. With the benefit of hindsight, we can see that this was preposterous organisation from the FA, but what is in even bolder print is that Graham deserves massive credit for not only avoiding defeat during this torrid timetable, but for maintaining the Gunner's iron grip on Liverpool's coattails as they once again sat atop the table after winning their game in hand.

Arsenal and George wanted everything and would not lower their standards, so a strong side was sent out against the Black Cats, who had given a good account of themselves in the league match between the two sides in October, which was in stark contrast to their plight in the First Division. Arsenal showed their hunger for the Cup and the task ahead with the first goal, which came from an incredible counter attack.

Sunderland had taken a corner, but Paul Merson was switched on and he intercepted an intended pass, which was the signal for his comrades to maraude up the pitch. Alan Smith offloaded to Paul Davis, who let rip with a twenty yard pass to the gallivanting Perry Groves on the left.

His raw pace saw him to the byline, and his cutback evaded the majority of the Sunderland defence. Smith had run the whole length of the pitch, and he was rewarded as he was first to Groves's ball and he bobbled the ball home to give the home side the lead. Fatigue was the enemy which was being held at arm's length by Arsenal. At least for the moment.

Anders Limpar had hit a dry spell in comparison to his blazing hot form at the start of the season, but he returned to goal duty to give Arsenal a two goal cushion when he was set free from the grips of the Mackem's defence. He couldn't be caught, and he confidently finished high into the net. Sunderland may have been two goals down and low on confidence, but they had not given up hope of staying in the competition.

The second half saw some long ball tactics from Sunderland, and a hopeful ball lumped forward saw David O'Leary being hassled. Just before the penalty area, he attempted to clear, but - dependant on your outlook - his connection was either sumptuous or horrific. He lobbed David Seaman and the ball fell perfectly over the line. A striker would have been proud of the finish, but O'Leary could only dump his hands on his hips in disbelief. In terms of comical own goals, it must rank highly.

The plucky Gunners would hold on though, and the fourth round of the FA Cup was guaranteed. Sunderland had showed grit, but just like their earlier league encounter, they had just fallen short. Arsenal wanted it more and it was their hunger rather than their superior levels of talent that had seen them over the line ahead of a gallant Sunderland.

The Cup draw obviously had reservations about Arsenal, as again it conjured up a hellish tie for Graham and his boys. Arsenal would have the solace of playing at Highbury, but their opponents would be Leeds United.

The BBC cameras were covering the game, and they had picked the tie of the round. It was first place versus fourth in the league, and Graham whet the appetite of Gooners at the match with his match programme column; "This is the tie of the round. I hope we provide the cameras with a spectacle to set before the nation. Most of all, I hope we're in that draw for the fifth round later that afternoon. We could hardly have asked for harder opponents, so I'm glad we have home advantage. Howard Wilkinson has done a terrific job, re-awakening a sleeping giant. He's bought some fine players. Leeds and Tottenham have given us our toughest games this season. I was pleased with that 2-2 draw at Elland Road in September. Very few teams have subjected us to the pressure Leeds did that afternoon."

Graham also mentioned how his squad seemed to be taking strength through the bouts of adversity that had plagued them for the last two months or so. Minus their influential skipper and fellow first team members, and with a calendar packed with matches leaving little room to recover, his side had steeled themselves with the 'us against them' mentality. The last few games they hadn't been at their most fluent, but they had won through gritted teeth and buckets of elbow grease. The players who normally eked out enough flair to squeeze Arsenal through the tight games, had been stifled but they had not downed tools. They had instead rolled their sleeves up and thrown themselves into the Gunner's cause.

Every top team had to go through a spell where they would inevitably struggle - no club can claim to have serenely sailed through the gauntlet of a season in top flight football. Arsenal had buffeted against the high winds and broiling seas and still remained on course. Even better, they had remained without loss. They were also still in the hat for cup glory.

Now, if they wanted their names on the FA Cup for the first time since Alan Sunderland scored that golden-tinged winner in 1979, they must overcome a team that Graham gauged as their toughest test so far.

Steve Bould, as well as Seaman, Lee Dixon and Nigel Winterburn, had been ever present in the league so far. The centre back had come off the field in the last few minutes in their win over Everton, but he was named in the team. He would be vital in this tie, as both teams fiercely competed for the right to stay in the FA Cup. This was a battle royale, and there was no room for shirkers. Blood and thunder were the dominant ingredients in this match, and it made for a no holds barred contest, where both teams showed their hunger for the right to progress.

Two former Gunners returned home, with John Lukic and Lee Chapman both playing, but they both failed to make any measurable impact on proceedings. What denied both teams a goal and passage to the fifth round, was an offside flag and Seaman.

The first half was a turgid affair, and both teams seemed reluctant to stretch themselves and potentially leave gaps in defence. Instead, it was a rigid display and defences were on top. The second half was where both sides decided to wake up and avoid a banana skin of a replay, and it was the home team who drew their sword first.

Stand-in skipper, Davis, in his testimonial year to boot, broke through enemy lines to loop a header over the stranded Lukic. Replays were inconclusive, but it was borderline whether he was offside. The linesman denied Davis the goal, and it was Leeds who nearly added salt to the wound.

Gary McCallister was teed up on the edge of the box and his rocket of a shot was saved expertly by Seaman. Arsenal's keeper had been in imperious form in the last few games, and his rise to prominence had coincided with this difficult period. He had been one of the biggest reasons why his side were undefeated and now, still in the FA Cup.

The match ended goalless, and Graham was correct in his prediction that Leeds would provide a stern examination. The impasse on the field ensured Arsenal were included in the next draw, just as Graham had hoped.

It also ensured that this current bout of matches in quick succession was prolonged. The replay would only add to the already hazardously-packed fixture list which was in danger of destroying all the good work George Graham and his charges had valiantly produced thus far.

Another three days were generously awarded to the Gunners before the Arsenal versus Leeds rematch. With the hard yards comes wear and tear, and Groves had succumbed to injury in the first tie, so 21 year old David Hillier came into the side. What a huge ask for the former youth team captain, but it showed that Graham held no fears in throwing him into what was a lion's den.

Hillier had been battle-hardened in his debut season, and he gave a fantastic account of himself in the Elland Road cauldron. Midfield was where the action had been in the first attempt at separating these two clubs, and Hillier seemed at home in the centre of the park and dealt with the home side's impressive engine room.

Howard Wilkinson had overseen an eleven match unbeaten run in home games coming into this match, so Arsenal were up against it from the start.

Leeds started brighter, buoyed by the vibrant home support, and it was another ex-Gunner - Chris Whyte - who nearly made the difference. A Gordon Strachan corner eventually made its way to Whyte, whose volley went through the legs of Chapman and into the net.

Whyte could be forgiven for celebrating, as his five years at Highbury had been blighted by injury and a struggle to find a place in the team. He did indeed celebrate, but the linesman, just as he did in the first tie, was not content with letting any player have the limelight. He flagged for offside, the contrast between the first decision and this was that this one was clearly correct. Chapman was a yard beyond the last Arsenal man when he hurdled over Whyte's effort and he had interfered with play. It was back to square one in terms of finding the tool to untie these tightly knotted teams.

The former Arsenal players in Wilkinson's team seemed adamant that they wanted the honour of dumping their old side out of the Cup, and it was Chapman who broke this deadlock, rising highest to head home from close range.

Leeds deserved their lead. They had abandoned their stoic approach and gone at a fatigued Gunners side. No amount of fitness regimes and conditioning could have kept weariness at bay. It had only been a matter of time before the slew of matches and miniscule recuperation periods would chip away. That extra ten percent which had seen Arsenal through in the last month or so had been whittled away by a relentless assault which was indefensible.

The Arsenal were far from finished however. What they may have lacked in energy levels, they would always make up for with their attitude and competitive hunger. This was never in doubt with George at the helm, as he would not allow anything less than full-blooded commitment.

The home side had scored an offside goal, had a goalbound effort cleared by Winterburn, and scored a legitimate goal, all in the space of five minutes. They had Arsenal on the ropes, but the indomitable spirit which resided in every single

Arsenal player roared into action, within a minute of going behind. Bloodied, but not beaten.

Winterburn, again, was involved, and it was the all-action left-back who stole possession from Leeds. A couple of passes later and Limpar had been sent scampering free. His pace took care of one defender, and his beautiful cut in gave him the best angle to put the ball past Lukic.

The Elland Road faithful had been in fine voice, but just for that moment, the noise was gone, smashed to smithereens by the Super Swede and his twinkling feet. The scoreline would finish 1-1, and Arsenal had done all they could to remain in the FA Cup.

The fightback required everything Arsenal could summon, but they had again managed to avoid defeat. This saga had another episode, a third match and fourth in total between these inseparable teams so far. Arsenal must have been incredibly wicked behind the scenes, as there was to be no rest for them. There was a chance to take a breather in between, and how the Arsenal boys must have relished it.

The second replay would be played on Valentine's Day. That was two weeks away, so players could finally unclench and take a well deserved short sabbatical. This saga had not reached its conclusion.

There was only the small matter of a League match against Chelsea at Stamford Bridge to get through, and they could put up those aching limbs for a few days and regroup. Chelsea were a distant seventh in the table, and had been sent packing from Highbury in September, after conceding four goals. Would these exhausted Gunners get caught napping with one eye on that heavenly hiatus? After a schedule that had taken all that they could offer, Arsenal could be absolved for having their mind on some creature comforts rather than yet another match.

We all know that this would never be the case. What is illustrated is that with every game that was played when there wasn't adequate rest beforehand, it meant that every game that came in quick succession sapped at the power which had seen Graham's side to the top.

Arsenal had gone twenty three games unbeaten. They sat at the top of the league. They had the superior squad. If this was played on paper, Arsenal would have gone to The Bridge and continued their impeccable run.

Matches are not played on paper though. Graham took his men into this fixture with many mitigating circumstances that would amalgamate into a formidable foe indeed. The obstacles were plentiful and it seemed that events out of the team's control had conspired to ensure Arsenal would not go unscathed through the season.

Firstly, there was just two days between this tie and the gruelling second FA Cup tie against Leeds. Then, when you consider the team were without their talismanic Captain, then the odds grow ever steeper. Add the growing injury list into the mix and with the final game of this arduous run being played at a venue they had not won at for seventeen seasons - it paints a pretty gloomy picture for the Gunners' chances.

Yes, that last startling stat is correct. For seventeen consecutive seasons, Arsenal had not won a match at Chelsea's home. A fair portion of the game was played mentally. Did this apparent hoodoo affect the players before the game? Were they even aware of it for them to be destabilised?

I asked the players I had interviewed whether they had this in their mind before they took to the field. It was an amusing mixture of answers! Nigel Winterburn was completely unaware of Arsenal's poor record at The Bridge.

Hillier defiantly proclaimed, "we were too strong a group to be bothered by hoodoos, jinxes or superstitions!"

Smith told me that some of them were probably aware of the record, but it didn't affect them greatly.

Whether it was burrowing in their subconscious or not, Arsenal were not optimised for this game - that much was apparent. Their fighting spirit had been enough to see them through thus far, but would it topple the Blues?

Chelsea midfielder and captain, Andy Townsend, spoke to the Daily Express's Barry Flatman on the eve of the game. He commented first on the reported demise of Liverpool, and he believed those claims were greatly exaggerated, "Liverpool are still the team to beat. A lot of people are talking about their demise, but I think they are as good as ever... The main reason for all the doubts is actually credit to Arsenal. They have established themselves as a strong side and proved they are no flash in the pan. Winning the league gave them a taste of it, they know what it's like to be up there."

Considering the paper ran the headline, "Chelsea Captain Andy Townsend put down Arsenal's title chances", and you can see the media were trying to ignite interest in the game. It looked like a regular match between two London sides, but the supporting cast for this black comedy was the mitigating circumstances which had Arsenal at a distinct disadvantage before a ball was kicked.

Townsend went further in his appetiser for the game. The Chelsea man was complimentary regarding our season, and had reserved glowing terms for Anders Limpar too after his FA Cup goal at Elland Road; "That goal proved he is one of the cleverest players in the First Division. Defenders are even worried about tackling him in the box now because he has such great balance. They know once he is in the box they are in trouble. If they touched him, it could be a penalty. If they let him shoot, it could be a goal. He does not cheat, what he does is a skill."

Townsend's words were a double-edged sword. He laid praise at the Arsenal flanker's door, but he also shrewdly implanted the larvae of doubt with the game looming large on the calendar. He placed emphasis on Limpar's dealings in the box, and his comments could well have altered any decisions made during the game.

The Chelsea boss, and former Arsenal coach, Bobby Campbell, also spoke to Flatman at The Daily Express, saying "We crumbled a little bit at Highbury. Limpar is in great form, but we kept Paul Gascoigne quiet when we played Spurs in the Rumbelows Cup last week. There is no reason why we cannot do the same job."

Tony Dorigo, persued by Perry Groves, gets a cross in at Stamford Bridge

A special focus would again be placed on Anders. His displays had placed him on the 'Most Wanted' list for managers across the First Division, a list reserved for only the most dangerous of players. Complimentary it may be, but it would also make it a damn sight harder to make an impact upon proceedings.

Campbell was also asked about his striking options, with Gordon Durie suspended for the game. It appeared as if Campbell was forced to play an untested Graeme Stuart as a forward, but when commenting on this unorthodox choice, the Blues boss had an air of confidence that his gamble would reap dividends; "I think everyone is in for a treat. He can play in many different positions, and I reckon he will do well."

Did Campbell have a crystal ball concealed in his jacket? Was it an inconspicuous portent of what was to come?

Back to Arsenal matters, and Groves had rapidly returned to fitness, so youngster Hillier dropped to the bench at Groves' expense. Hillier had let no-one down in his last game, but Groves and his pace would be crucial against a cynical Chelsea defence. Hillier would also get his chance as the game wore on...

O'Leary had enjoyed a run in the side as sweeper, but that option was taken from George before the game kicked off. Instead, the conventional Arsenal back four was put into place, with Linighan partnering Bould in the centre.

Steve Bould had been in great form in the face of intense competition, and his presence would be fundamental to Arsenal's cause.

The late injury to O'Leary was yet more evidence of bad luck being the major suspect in Arsenal's plight. The 5-4-1 which had been implemented by Graham in six League games so far - and in the last three games alone - was George's concealed weapon. It was used in matches where he perceived a threat in terms of possession, and he combatted that with numbers in the final third and an optimal setup to counter attack. It had proved to be effective, but with O'Leary missing, this option was robbed of him.

Adams behind bars. O'Leary injured, and his hand forced in terms of tactics. Graham and his boys were accustomed to having their backs to the wall at times, but with their hands tied as well?

The game began, and the Stamford Bridge playing surface was not conducive to playing the ball to feet. This hampered the effectiveness of Limpar, who was heavily marked throughout. Merson was on the flank as opposed to being a partner for 'Smudge' up front.

The press had criticised this decision, as his best play had come from playing further up the pitch, but Merson was not one to hug the touchline. Difficult to mark, and with a tendency to float between midfield and attack, the 'Magic Man' would not stay on the right hand side all game. With the mire of a pitch making control an issue, Merson had his work cut out, but he stuck gamely to the task ahead.

He was intent on causing havoc. Chelsea were at home though, and the sandbox masquerading as a football pitch was their playground. Merson was more adept on Highbury's kempt turf, but he would have to make do with the stage he had.

Arsenal's wide men were being shackled well by Gareth Hall and Tony Dorigo. When the Gunners' wingers were having no joy in previous games, it saw the emergence of Davis and Thomas as an attacking threat. This game was not seeing them as a forward force though, and it had these two midfielders tied up trying to contain Townsend and Wise, or just trying to string a pass together. This match was probably Davis and Thomas' weakest that season. They had their hands full keeping an eye on the Blue's middle men, and when they did get the ball, they were not their decisive selves.

There was no shortage of endeavour. They worked as hard as they always had done, it was after all, the least that their Gaffer expected. They could not exert themselves on proceedings though. Chelsea were still more than busy, and Perry Groves had a shot which was well gathered by Dave Beasant in the Chelsea goal.

Limpar did manage to escape from the clutches of his captors once in the first half, but his effort was narrowly wide. In the face of adversity, Arsenal were still giving their all and were looking to end that obscene run at The Bridge. The game was on a knife-edge, although the Gunners were looking the more likely to end the war of attrition that was taking place on the turf.

Andy Linighan and David Hillier give it their all without Tony Adams, David O'Leary and Steve Bould against Chelsea at The Bridge

The first half drew to a close and the away team were again surviving through sheer will. Chelsea were matching the physical side of the Gunners, but their new-look attack of Graeme Stuart and Kerry Dixon had not troubled the assured presence of Bould and Andy Linighan. It may not be according to the plan George Graham had set out, but his men were still on a level with Chelsea, and they would have their eye on another favourable result as they had done all season. It was the second half of Arsenal's twenty fourth League game in which a hairline fracture appeared - precisely one minute after referee Vic Gallow had resumed the match.

Gareth Hall had done well to contain Limpar, but his next act was as heinous as any can commit on a pitch and expect leniency. He went into a challenge with Bould - actually, to call it a challenge would be complimentary - he flew into Bould with reckless abandon.

Steve Curry of the Daily Express called it correctly, describing it as "late, high and unpunished, which changed the complexion of the game completely." It saw Bould take no further part in the game, and his replacement was fresh-faced David Hillier. Hillier said of the task that was in front of him, “It was tough. Kerry Dixon was a handfull and Graeme Stuart mobile, so they dragged me and Andy around a bit, but credit to Chelsea they saw we were weakened when Bouldy went off and stepped up the pressure.”

Adams missing, O’Leary injured before the game and now Bould carried off in the second half. With the willing but green Hillier slotting into the backline and the score still at 0-0, the mission for the Gunners was clear - to see out this game. Bad luck had been the major instigator in this match above any on the pitch, and the Gunners would have to perform heroics to avoid any blemish on their copybook.

It may have been criminal that Hall got away scot-free, but Chelsea saw that yet another of the famous back five were absent from duty - and they began to circle what was now a weakened prey. Arsenal were limping. Smudge said of the game, post-Bould, “we were struggling after Bouldy went off. The balance tilted after that.”

Chelsea began to turn the screw. Linighan was a polished professional who had settled well at Arsenal, but this was the first time Arsenal had to cope without Adams, Bould or O’Leary in the team for many a year. It saw the former Norwich man alongside a talented but raw Hillier, and no amount of training in the world could prepare them for this exceptional set of factors.

They held out heroically as the home side and their roaring fans tightened their hunting circle and began to concentrate their attacks. Twenty minutes after Bould had departed for treatment, Chelsea took the lead. It had been coming despite Hillier and Linighan’s best efforts.

A deep free kick was flicked on - 'Smudge' style - by Dixon. Winterburn went up to head clear, but instead, his header stayed in the danger zone. It was hoovered up by surprise striking inclusion Graeme Stuart, heading in above Linighan. Winterburn’s header could have gone anywhere. That may have been in the lap of the gods. Linighan being outmuscled and outjumped by Stuart however, was the mistake that Chelsea had been waiting for, and how they cashed in. There was still over twenty minutes to go to rescue this dire mess of a game. Graham had overseen his team go behind on many occasions, there was no need for alarm... yet.

For Arsenal to drag themselves into the game, they would have to commit men forward, but Chelsea produced wave after wave of attack. Arsenal could not escape this dangerous loop. Over-exerting themselves on an attempted break would be the perfect opening for the home side to finally kill off their hampered opponent. Would Arsenal get a chance to rectify the scoreline and save their unbeaten status?

Dennis Wise, Dixon and Stuart were pulling Linighan and Hillier out of position. The rope technique in training had been severed. This was backs to the wall, instinctive defending. It also meant space for Townsend to spring more and more passes into the apertures in the Gunner’s backline.

With all the misfortune that Arsenal had to deal with, they could well do without another mistake from a normally ever-reliable player. Dixon was next to make an error that went against the grain. An attempted pass out wide from the Gunner's man did not find its intended target. Instead he found Wise, he passed to Stuart, who had floated out on the left. He squared to an open Damian Matthew, who then cut inside a half-hearted - or perhaps exhausted - tackle from Linighan - with Dixon completely unmarked on the six yard box.

Arsenal appealed for offside. Hillier had been dragged deep and so was playing Dixon onside, or it appeared so. Replays showed that Dixon was lying in wait but in an offside position. The Chelsea frontman had the simple task of putting it into the net and he wheeled away after shooting, knowing that his eighty-eighth minute goal was the one which had cemented the win for Chelsea.

Mistake or no mistake, the goal which looked to have earned Chelsea the accolade of the first to beat Arsenal in the League was an illegal one. Injuries, fixture congestion and the luck of a team who had smashed many mirrors whilst walking under a ladder had conspired to seemingly end Arsenal's famous run.

Martin Tyler, the commentator for the game, uttered the sentence, "Chelsea know they have won, and Arsenal know they are beaten." Heads hung in dismay, this was not a feeling they were accustomed to.

One of the few positives about the game from a Gooners point of view was the reaction from the Arsenal team when they scored what was purely a consolation.

Smith was put through by substitute Kevin Campbell, and he made no mistake by shooting low past Beasant. It was his first clear sight on goal and he did what he did best. With mere seconds to go, Groves made a dash for the ball which had been put into the Chelsea net and the rest of the team hurriedly ran back to their positions so they could begin their hunt for an unlikely equaliser posthaste.

It was remarkable to see, and it was evidence that this team never knew when they were beaten. Even when they were actually beaten! They had forgotten the ugly face of losing after going twenty three games without meeting defeat. There couldn't have been more than seconds to go, but Groves, Smith and the rest intended to use every precious one to change this scoreline.

The whistle from Vic Gallow blew its shrilling but sombre sound.

Arsenal had lost.

From the start of the season way back in August, to this fateful game in February, George had taken the North London club from respected contenders, to all-conquering giants. They had taken on all comers, faced every team in the Division, and had won fifteen, and drawn eight.

The old adage goes, "winning is a habit." As fans in this day and age, we have seen seemingly unbeatable teams enjoy a run of games, only to see the first slip-up transform into a full blown crisis. When the acrid taste of being thwarted is first introduced onto the palate after a long absence, it can ruin whatever plans were in place. It can darken the outlook, it can sour the future.

Arsenal's Invincibles of 2003/04 were foiled in their fiftieth game without loss in similar acrimonious settings, and they struggled for some time after. Could George Graham steady the ship? This loss would have devastated each and every one of them, and to summon the strength they would need to continue would have seen lesser men wilt.

To add insult to injury, Liverpool regained the First Division One top spot after that result, but they still had to go to Stamford Bridge, and one of Arsenal's vanquishers - Kerry Dixon - offered this morsel to mourning Gooners in the Daily Express; "We will beat Liverpool the same when they come here."

Quite a bold statement. Dixon carried on though, and his next sentence was surprising. In today's age of vitriolic rivalries, this sentiment from a player hailing from a London rival club was so very refreshing; "They will find it just as difficult and, hopefully, we can do Arsenal a favour."

Anders Limpar, who could not weave his magic on proceedings, gave his verdict in the same article, stating "I think there was a psychological barrier for us. The other players had been telling me how hard we find it to win here. But just because our run has been broken, it doesn't mean the world has ended. You know, Liverpool lose matches occasionally too."

If Limpar had winked at the end of this interview, it would have been a perfect fit for the tone his words came across in that paragraph. The cheeky devil.

It was fitting that Graham would have the last say in this interesting piece in the Daily Express, written by Curry. The Arsenal gaffer had this to say on finally losing, "If someone had said at the start of the season that we wouldn't lose a game until February, I would have said thank you very much. Today we were capable of extending our run until we lost Bould, but we will react positively to this defeat, and we must make sure that we get into the right pattern for our game next week."

With the way this incredible sequence had ended, it was abundantly clear that Arsenal would have to be similarly strung up to fall foul again. In a strange way, it may have sent out a message to the teams in and around them in the table, especially Liverpool. They would have to hope that misfortune would again take arms against the Gunners, and that injuries would befall them like a plague. They would also have to be missing their captain and hope dearly that the match official and linesman were as ignorant as the ones who were present at Stamford Bridge. Then maybe, just maybe, they might be able to overcome the Highbury boys.

Even after this huge setback, losing the game, Bould, and the top spot in the league, Graham wanted to rectify what had happened. The best medicine for such a setback is to return to winning ways, but it seemed fate had other ideas once again.

With Crystal Palace and Liverpool the next foes for Arsenal, it couldn't get any more difficult to jump back on the winning horse.

Double Dreams, Replacing Kings and Championship Form

A rest after a vigorous workout is almost as important as the exercise itself. After playing eleven games in 41 days, George Graham could allow his troops a little R and R for the first time since mid December. They had played admirably through the pain and relentless fixtures, the loss of their captain and muse, injuries to key personnel and some punishing opponents. Not to mention fighting through the adversity of some questionable officiating, which had cost them dearly.

However, it would have been easy to be disheartened if you were an Arsenal player at this moment of the season. After that monumental effort, and after losing just one game in 24, not to mention coping with some farcical rostering of matches by the FA, they were still behind Liverpool in the table.

After conceding a paltry 12 goals in 24 games - an average of a goal every two matches - they could still see Kenny Dalglish's team above them when they arched their neck to the heavens of the league table.

What more could be done? If superhuman exertion and a nigh-on flawless record of results was not enough to overthrow Liverpool from their accustomed position, what else could the Gunners muster? It must have been a challenge to stave off the negativity at times.

These Arsenal lads were made of stern stuff, and instead of feeling resentment and pity for themselves, they used the gloom and potential pessimism as a launch pad for a wondrous run of results that would send the Liver Bird among the pigeons.

After Graham had ensured his men were fit and ready to resume their assault on the First Division - after all, a huge eleven days off was something of a luxury that season for the Gunners - they once again did battle with a familiar foe. Leeds United in the FA Cup.

Their Fourth Round tie had still to be settled, after a 0-0 and a 1-1 at both Highbury and Elland Road. These teams could not be split apart, and the third

David O'Leary and Lee Chapman during Arsenal's FA Cup 4th round 2nd replay against Leeds United in February 1991

attempt to declare a winner was played, again, at the home of Arsenal. All in all, it was already the fourth match already between these teams so far in this campaign, and in each of these games, no winner could be found.

Would anyone have been surprised to know that this game once again finished with the scores all square? Arsenal did let the away side off the hook though, as the normally reliable Lee Dixon fluffed his lines with a penalty which would have made all the difference. It was a missed opportunity to write a conclusion to this cup tie which really needed to end, it also meant that Arsenal would again travel to Elland Road.

Another game which had ended with both teams inseparable. It is said that familiarity breeds contempt, but the only feeling that resided in the Gooner camp was boredom, as it meant yet another match against the same opponent.

Three days later, it was Round Four in this Yorkshire versus London saga, and Arsenal had some injury worries that would force Graham to use his powers of ingenuity to cope. Anders Limpar and Perry Groves were both sidelined, so Kevin Campbell came into the team and Paul Merson occupied the left hand side. The talent that Merson had at just 22 years old was staggering, but it also allowed him to fit in seamlessly wherever he was selected. All he needed was the ball.

Steve Bould's injury, that was thuggishly inflicted upon him at Stamford Bridge, had not been as severe as first feared and he had played in the previous fixture against Leeds. He was named in the side again alongside Andy Linighan and David O'Leary, as Graham opted for his 5-4-1 again. In amongst all of the tactical talk, the biggest piece of news surrounding the club was just the pick-me-up that Arsenal needed.

Tony Adams had been released from prison after serving half of his sentence, and he was being put through his paces by the club, a reserve team clash against Reading was his first game back, in order to get the club captain back where he belonged - leading his men into battle. Match sharpness would be lacking, so Adams would be returning back to the Gunners fold under no illusions as to what his demanding coach would be expecting. The hard yards would be put in prior to the skipper getting game time.

Before that could happen, though, another fight with Leeds was about to commence, and it was Arsenal who - for the first time in this never ending cup tie - were going to draw first blood. It would be Merson who underlined his adaptability and importance to the side by scoring the opener, on a pitch worse than at Stamford Bridge!

A stymied Leeds attack was the source, and Paul Merson was set free on the halfway line. He ran down the left hand side and cut in, just outside the penalty area. His jinking feet bewitched the Leeds defence, before he bobbled in a 20 yard shot which gave the Gunners the lead.

The matches beforehand provided a pattern which was quite easy to read, and although they had the lead, Arsenal would be well aware that their opponent had matched every action they had produced previously. It was paramount that they held the home side at bay. Luckily enough, that was the thing that Arsenal's defence did best. They did so, and it allowed the Gunners to push on and finish off Leeds.

Dixon doubled the lead - the first time in four games that either team had scored two goals - but not through his conventional manner of a penalty. This effort was far more artistic. The right-back picked up the ball just outside the box, and instigated a one-two with none other than Linighan. Quite how the defender was permitted to leave his station and rampage up the pitch is an unanswered question, but the former Norwich man's chipped return ball was perfectly in line with the running Dixon, who held off his marker to finish confidently into the far corner. It was a goal befitting Limpar, but Dixon had scored it, with more than a little assistance from Linighan. It was also a redemption of sorts for Dixon after missing a penalty in the game before. Arsenal could see an end to this epic, but they still had another 45 minutes to see off a team which had been the epitome of stubbornness.

Leeds didn't come back into the game until the second half, as Gordon Strachan put in a tantalising ball which Chapman did well to convert, especially under the amount of duress he was under from Linighan. This was now verging on the ridiculous. The odds for an equaliser must've been preposterously short.

Thankfully there would be no more equalisers. The game finished 2-1, and it was the end of Leeds' FA Cup journey, as Arsenal finally ensured progression in the Cup.

The Gunners could continue to dream of a Double, although both parts of the equation were still some distance away to being achieved. If it was possible though, George and the boys would gun for it. They had shown more than enough substance so far to give supporters reasons to dream. At the very least, the consolation prize was that Arsenal wouldn't have to face Leeds again for a month.

Arsenal could now focus on something other than Howard Wilkinson's side, as league matters returned to the fore. Crystal Palace were at Highbury a week after Arsenal's FA Cup win - and the Eagles were flying high.

The target of the title was very much the plan for Graham and his men, but quietly and without warning, Palace had swung into the Gunners rearview. Before kickoff, the Eagles were just two points behind and, with a win, would fly above Arsenal in the table. Liverpool were three points ahead of Arsenal in top spot, so with both teams posing the utmost threat, it was fundamental that maximum points were gained. The matches were coming thick and fast again, and there were to be no gimmes in the fixture list at this point in the season. Crystal Palace were surprising everyone and the league table was unable to lie - they were worthy of the tag of contenders.

The day before the match, there had been a surprising development, one which would have ramifications on the course of the title, and it did not play out on a pitch. Two days after a quite incredible 4-4 derby draw with their Merseyside neighbours Everton in a Fifth Round FA Cup tie, the man that Reds fans knew only as 'King Kenny' resigned from his position as manager of Liverpool Football Club.

With his side sitting in their customary top spot in the League, and with a very real possibility of a Double on the cards, to say Kenny Dalglish's announcement was a shock was a huge understatement.

In a fascinating article in the Guardian newspaper, published 20 years after Dalglish's resignation, journalist Louise Taylor covered the story of how the man responsible for creating Liverpool's empire came to fall on his own sword.

Ray Houghton, who was on the bench during the 4-4 draw, had a great view of the last acts and emotions of Dalglish whilst still at the helm; "I had no idea what was to come and neither did anyone else, not even those who knew Kenny best. Ask Alan Hansen, he was his closest friend and he didn't have a clue. Kenny's resignation came out of the blue, you could have knocked each and everyone of the Liverpool players down with a feather."

If it had such a huge effect on the Liverpool players, would they be able to carry on in the same manner which had garnered so much success in years gone by, in the same vein that had them still top of the league? Was their dominance simply a matter of continuing their day-to-day routine, which had seen their rise to prominence, or did a change of leadership mean a change in fortunes?

In the same piece, Kenny Dalglish commented on just what had pushed him to the precipice in a job that he could have claimed for life if the fans saw fit; "After we had taken the lead for the final time I knew I had to make a change to shore things up at the back. I could see what needed to be done and what would happen if I didn't. I didn't act on it. That was the moment I knew I was shattered. I needed to get away from the pressure."

If his job could have that effect on a man who had seen and done it all in his career, in a position which his job had never been under scrutiny, just imagine what it must have been like for a mere mortal? Dalglish had, perhaps, the safest position in the top flight, and the rigours of managing such a huge club had wore him down.

Looking at developments through Arsenal-tinted specs gave it a positive hue. For the sport to lose Dalglish was lamentable, but for Arsenal, it must have given them a real boost. The King of Merseyside, who had lain waste to all and sundry repeatedly over the years, was gone. Who would take his crown? The crown of Liverpool, but even more pertinently - the crown of England?

The match against Crystal Palace was almost akin to a boxing title eliminator. The winner would earn the right to duke it out for the belt. The loser would have to build their reputation up once again and come back to fight another day.

The day after Dalglish's bombshell, the Gunners set their sights on the Eagles at Highbury.

Steve Coppell had built an impressive side, one which had proved their worth with their lofty position in the First Division. They were feared for their attack of Mark Bright and Ian Wright - 16 league goals between them at that point in the campaign - but they also had Geoff Thomas in midfield, Andy Gray and John Salako on the wings, with Richard Shaw in defence, a player who gave anyone a torrid time who faced him. Even their goalkeeper, Nigel Martyn, had found inspiration, whether it was down to his attempt at a Seaman-esque moustache at the time is debateable! They were more than just two strikers, they had men throughout the side who could hurt you, and their position in the league served as a reminder of their powers.

The Palace keeper may have had similar lip furniture, but he could not recreate his opposite number's exploits on the pitch. Evening Standard Player of the Month, David Seaman, was enjoying a fantastic debut season at Arsenal, and he would win the battle of the keepers in this game too.

George again fell back on his sweeper system, as O'Leary came back in, with Bould and Linighan just ahead of the Irishman. Limpar, again, missed out, with Campbell partnering Alan Smith so Merson could occupy Limpar's spot.

Arsenal got the decisive first goal early doors, and it came from an overhit Merson corner. It was rescued by Linighan's head at the far post, and it was O'Leary whose bundled finish provided a fillip for the Gunners. Thirty seven minutes later in the first half, Merson had made it two and Palace were in disarray. Thomas toepoked it through midfield and when Eric Young attempted to clear, he missed completely. Merson didn't say thank you for the gift as he was too busy bearing down on Martyn, before finishing calmly. Young had been playing well all season, but that mistake had cost his side dearly.

Two goals to the good, and Arsenal were clearly enjoying the space that Palace mistakenly provided them. Coppell relied on his side's capacity to attack, and this allowed Arsenal - if they could turnover possession quickly - to bypass Palace's midfield with a single swoop. It seemed as if Coppell did not have a plan B.

The second half saw no change in approach from either team, and Arsenal continued to compose a fine demonstration. O'Leary battled in midfield and sneaked a pass to Campbell. He fought and wrestled with his marker, before deciding to come a few yards infield. Smith was his backup, so Campbell laid it off to his strike partner. The defence was thoroughly occupied with Campbell, and it gave 'Smudge' a yard to shift it to his left, before letting fly with a superlative curler from 20 yards, which sailed around and over Martyn on its way to the executive suite of goal areas - the top corner.

The adventurous streak had been teased out of the home side with this comfortable beating of a team tipped to really test Arsenal. This luring out of Arsenal's more aesthetically pleasing talents was manifesting itself in tangible form when Nigel Winterburn was sent clear and his ambitious shot, from an acute angle, was parried by Martyn, only into the path of a prowling Campbell, who poked the ball away from close range and got the goal his efforts had well earned. The cake had been iced and it was proving to be delicious fare for the home fans, but a cherry on top was about to be applied.

David 'Rocky' Rocastle was a late substitute for Merson, and it was his first league appearance since December after a toe injury. Gooners adored Rocky, and his high-jinks on the wing were hard to replace. With Rocky back, and the form the team had shown in this imperious ninety minutes, it seemed Arsenal had gotten through the squall.

George had seen off a real challenge in Crystal Palace. Coppell's side now sat on their haunches, five points behind the team who had tonked them so convincingly. His opposite number could now devote his energy to Liverpool, especially as they were the next team the Gunners would face in the First Division.

The endless Cup replays with Leeds had created a backlog of matches however, and Shrewsbury Town were waiting to try their hand at a cup upset.

The Shrews were in the Third Division, but Graham did not take these lower league opponents lightly. He went with a system of solidity and picked O'Leary as sweeper once again. He would also have been delighted to recall club captain Adams back for his first competitive game since being released from prison.

Holding midfielder, Hillier, also started the game as stand-in captain Paul Davis was rested, and Campbell, Smith and Merson took the same slots they had so effervescently occupied in their demolishing of Crystal Palace four days earlier.

They had played on the terrible turf at Stamford Bridge, and the lego pitch at Kenilworth Road presented its own difficulties, but what was passed off as a pitch at Gay Meadow looked like a field, post-Glastonbury. Massive chunks of pitch rising from the bed of soil. Trenches that could cause serious injury. If Arsenal were not prepared for a battle, they would come unstuck. The game was tight, with The Shrews defending well, but there was a marked difference between the sides as well as in scoreline.

Merson tracked back on the left to cut out a pass, and Winterburn hotfooted it through midfield. His pass found Mickey Thomas on one of his foraging runs, and he half-volleyed the bouncing leather sphere into the net with aplomb.

The goal made the game a more comfortable affair, as it really was a smart and accomplished move and finish. It also kept alive Arsenal's Double dream. It was that little bit nearer now. The Gunners were in the sixth round of the Cup and would face another Third Division side in Cambridge United in ten days time. It would be for the right to take part in a Semi-Final at Wembley - something George Graham had never achieved in his time as manager of Arsenal or Millwall.

It was now the business end of the season. The cut and thrust of every game meaning so much more than before. There was no room for error anymore unlike earlier in the season. All the hard work and sacrifice meant nothing if they could not press home the issue from here on in.

Every game was the proverbial cup final. Every ninety minutes carried the capacity for utmost tragedy or halcyon days that would live on forever through the history of the club. The mentality, physicality and every fibre of every man would be put to the fiercest of tests from this point forward.

It was a watershed moment that took place every season. A cutoff point that every team fought to make, but only a select few managed to grab an escape pod from mediocrity. The 'business end' of the season is its customary term.

Arsenal had now done it twice in the last three seasons. It meant a chance to aim for history, but there was a distinct reason why only the best made it. It was because the last steps were always the hardest. To illustrate this point precisely, the next game was against Liverpool.

There was time to prepare, but after a great performance in a decisive fixture, tiredness does not fit into the equation. The majority would just want the next game to come along as quickly as possible.

Arsenal would be bouncing after their complete domination of Crystal Palace. Every player would want to be on the field to prove themselves again against Liverpool. The keepers of the title for so long, Arsenal were intent on proving that the Miracle of Anfield 1989, wasn't such a miracle after all.

In their minds, it had been their title to take all along. George Graham instilled belief in his men, which was the fuel for their incredible spirit and ability to endure levels of fatigue and stress that most would buckle under.

They would have one source of inspiration in the side, as Tony Adams made his first League start since December after incarceration, but another would be missing. Limpar, the tormentor of Liverpool in the corresponding fixture - when the Gunners gave the Reds a reminder of their strength via a 3-0 thumping - was missing through injury. It meant that Hillier would play the biggest game of his fledgling career, as he partnered Thomas in the centre, with Merson and Campbell supporting Smith from out wide.

This strategy paid off in spades in the previous game, and again George went for O'Leary as sweeper - just as he did when they had last played Liverpool.

The onus was on Liverpool to find a way past Arsenal's fortification. They had failed the first time, and as both teams sat precariously placed on 54 points, the Liverpool of old would have got the job done.

The personnel at Liverpool was the same, but King Kenny was not there to guide the way. Could they prove that the club did not rely on one man - as the Gunners had done when their own leader had been sent to prison?

Ronnie Moran was taking temporary charge of team affairs whilst the Liverpool Board decided on the appropriate replacement for the unreplaceable. The man was steeped in the club and if anyone could keep this current title bid on course, it was him. So, on the afternoon of March 3, 1991, Arsenal played Liverpool. Even on points. Level on the playing field.

If this had been played in the era of Pay-per-view TV, it would have been plastered across every form of media for weeks beforehand. It was that big, clearly.

Liverpool, with their expectant fans singing their name loudly, got off to a good start. With John Barnes and Peter Beardsley supplementing the prolific Ian Rush, even the reputable Arsenal defence would get a good stretching. Liverpool knocked it about with the swagger that came with being comfortable in their own skins and being Champions.

Seaman had shown the whole country recently why George had branded him the best keeper in England when he signed him in the summer - and he reinforced his burgeoning reputation by keeping the Gunners in it in the first half.

Ray Houghton was causing Thomas a headache and Hillier, put on sentry duty to nullify Jan Molby, had his hands full. Adams wasn't quite at the races, and Bould and O'Leary were being rushed into losing their usual cool heads.

The solution, though, was keeping Barnes and Beardsley under lock and key. If George could set his side up to manage this herculean feat, then all the wonderful passes in the world would fall dead before they got through to David Seaman.

When Barnes did evade his captors, as he did in the ninth minute, he found that there was another layer of captivity. Liverpool's England winger flicked toward goal at the near post, Seaman saved it despite looking second favourite.

Jan Molby was next to test Seaman's credentials and Graham's theory, this time with a long range fizzer which 'Safe Hands' dealt with. Then he showed the intelligent side to his game rather than agility and technique, as he reacted before anyone when Beardsley chested down to a hovering Barnes. Seaman was showing everyone that he was the best goalkeeper in England.

It was pretty much backs to the wall for the first 45, but Arsenal held firm. They were content in the knowledge that they would get a chance as the game wore on, but it was Merson who was profligate, shooting over the bar when well placed and wasting a header. He would make amends.

The home side had chucked their best at Arsenal all half, but they still hadn't scored. It was not an invitation to admire their handiwork though, as they had escaped by the skin of their teeth. Graham would have been pleased, but his nerves would have been frayed. You would never know though, his facade remained icy-cold.

Arsenal lost Campbell to a dead leg ten minutes before the half time whistle, but the returning Rocastle was a dab hand in these titanic tussles, and he slotted in as if he had never been away. Rocky always had the deftest of touches, but his defensive covering was one of his finest attributes.

The second half came from a different mould to the first. The away side started to come out of their iron-clad shell, and the first shot across the Liverpool bows was well saved by Grobbelaar from a Thomas shot.

On 66 minutes, Arsenal once again found they had the ability to silence the Anfield faithful, nearly two years after sending home fans into an involuntary vow of silence.

Smith had been ploughing a lonely furrow up top, but he had not been idly waiting. Any sniff of the ball and he was alert and hounding Moran's men. When Beardsley's pass to Gary Gillespie was cut out by the lively Merson, Smudge got a yard ahead of his man. He knew what was coming.

Merson passed to Smith, who used that valuable distance to excellent effect, completing the one-two with Merson, whose continued rampage could not be stopped. He fizzed on until he got to the box.

Time seemed to stand still as he got closer to Grobbelaar. It transformed from a few seconds of a football match, into a Western movie. Merson vs Grobbelaar in a deadeye shootout. Both men waited for the other to make a move. Merson continually touching the ball ever nearer, the Zimbabwean keeper taking flitting little steps backwards on the balls of his feet. Merson's body language looked like he was going to go to the keepers right. He had been bluffing. He flicked the ball nonchalantly with his right foot past a now stranded Grobbelaar and into the net.

Bruce Grobbelaar had been wearing a 'Candy' branded cap to shield his eyes from the blinding low rays of the sunshine. He was safe from the light, but he had not been safe from Merson's unbelievable levels of composure. He had outwitted the Red's keeper. There was still over 20 minutes to go, but this game had seen strong manoeuvring from both sides and Arsenal had proved their armoury was more potent. Arsenal's defence had yet again caged Liverpool's all-conquering attack.

On that unforgettable night on May 26 in 1989, Arsenal had shaken the Merseyside club to their roots. And it was happening all over again. England had been a one club dominion for too long, and Liverpool didn't like to share.

The last three seasons - this one included - was Arsenal forcing their way into the club with the special handshakes and commemorative keychains. It was a one-member club, prior to Arsenal busting their way in.

The game was seen out professionally as the Gunners had dealt with Rush, Beardsley and the rest of their cohorts. Graham had once again concocted a mixture that had been too heady for even Liverpool to sample.

Liverpool were left licking their significant wounds. It was the first time in five years that they had lost more than two games in succession. To outline what an achievement that result was for Arsenal and George Graham, this stat pretty much shouts it out.

Since Arsenal had won the league at Anfield in 1989, Liverpool had played 42 games at Anfield and had lost just once, to Coventry City. This meant that in four years, or 44 matches, Liverpool had lost thrice, and Arsenal had had the gumption and fortitude to do it twice.

Arsenal were now three points clear at the top of the league. There was still twelve games to play, but it was definitely in their hands now. Even if they did not go on to win the Championship back from Liverpool, they had shown that Gods do bleed.

Moran was cynical and forthright in his post-match interview with the Daily Express. His role as Caretaker was not going according to plan.

He said "I don't go along with this claptrap about the ball not bouncing for you. You have to make it bounce for you. There are only three points in it and there are twelve games to go. It's different from this being the last game and giving you no chance to get back (it seems he couldn't help but subconsciously reference Anfield 89!). We came up against Neville Southall last week for Everton and today Arsenal had David Seaman producing saves. But that's what goalkeepers are for. I don't think Arsenal deserved to win, but good luck to them. We conceded a bad goal and we've had a talk about it. The lads are downhearted but we've just got to get on with it."

The Gunners boss was tight-lipped on his team's title chances, stating "Both defences looked a little slack. We've just got to win every game now."

Given a few days to savour the victory, Graham's comments were a little more open in his programme column for the next match - the FA Cup Quarter-Final against Cambridge United; "There's not much I can say about our win

Steve Bould, David Seaman and Paul Merson
celebrating another famous Anfield victory

at Anfield - except that it was fantastic. We're getting used to these pressure games now, long may they continue. That will prove we are one of the top sides in Europe. Our players have shown their character in so many tense matches. They could do very well in Europe next season......if we get there. Maybe I'm being cautious, but we must win a domestic trophy before we can look forward to that new challenge."

I happened upon a VHS of this extraordinary season recently, and Merson and Hillier both commented on this wonderful, tidal-shifting victory. Merson said this with a wry smile, "They're the Champs, but we've beat them twice and they haven't scored against us, so it was nice to take points from them."

David Hillier was more pragmatic in his offerings, concentrating more on his long term prospects after his great performance, "I've a contract until the end of the season. My first target was to get my contract extended and get a couple of games!"

It was clear he had achieved more than that, but it shows how far the lad had come in a short space of time.

It was time to switch focus again, as Arsenal were gunning for the Double. Six days had passed and it was the day of the FA Cup Sixth Round and Cambridge United were the visitors to Highbury. This game appeared a surefire win with home advantage and lower league opposition. It wouldn't be criminal for the Gunners to be expecting to win, but the dangling carrot for the winner was a trip to Wembley.

It was perhaps one of the biggest matches in the United's history, but they were not fazed by the occasion, nor the calibre of opponent. The match turned out to be far more fraught than anyone could have imagined. It wouldn't be Arsenal if they did it the easy way, every Gooner is painfully aware of that.

Paul Davis returned to the bench after being rested, with David Hillier keeping his place, and Kevin Campbell was back in the starting lineup after going off with a dead leg against Liverpool. But it would be Campbell who would give Arsenal the lead the crowd expected. A Winterburn cross was met by Campbell, leaping like a salmon with a jetpack. His header was well directed and it found the far corner. Job done? Not quite.

Cambridge United had a player in their ranks that would go on to great things. His goal could be construed as a signal of intent of sorts.

Dion Dublin found space in the box and his volley, via an Adams headed deflection, looped over Seaman and into the back of the net. It was not going to script. Cambridge had done the one thing Liverpool had failed to muster in 180 minutes - score against Arsenal.

Paul Davis was introduced in the second half, and he had a hand in the goal which sent shivers of relief coursing through Highbury - and potential for one of the biggest upsets of all time was lessened.

Davis's corner found its way to Adams, who tried to make room for a shot. Cambridge were back in numbers, so the Captain's only option was a short pass to Bould, who looked up and chipped a ball to the back post. Bould's pass was

Paul Merson finds the aerial battle a little tough against Cambridge United in the Highbury FA Cup clash

perfect and Smith headed down powerfully, only to see United keeper John Vaughan produce a magnificent save with his fingertips low down. Adams had used his initiative to follow up though, and he headed in from just underneath the crossbar. Scrappy, ugly, but worth its weight in gold. Arsenal were on their way to Wembley.

It was heartbreak for Cambridge who had done magnificently to get that far in the competition, but their ultimate aim was promotion - and they won the Third Division that season. They had done themselves proud and come closer than anyone could have predicted to booking a spot at Wembley in the Cup, and Arsenal had struggled to overcome their challenge.

For Arsenal, they were now favourites for the FA Cup and the League. They were infinitely nearer to the Cup win they so craved as they still had twelve games to play in the league, but neither was a gimme. Bookies odds have never been a precursor to success.

Nonetheless, this was turning out to be one of Arsenal's most thorough and convincing seasons in an already illustrious history. One defeat so far in the league and now in the FA Cup semi-final. And the home straight was beckoning.

Fighting For The Line And Cup Anguish

Two massive wins over fellow title contenders had buoyed Arsenal for the run-in to the title, and they now had a Semi-Final date at Wembley with rivals Spurs to pen into an exciting looking April and May.

George Graham had made some bold decisions in these games on which their whole season had hinged, and the comprehensive results which had followed were the purest form of vindication that he had made the correct choice. However, there had been no luck involved where the Arsenal Manager's calls were concerned. Each time he had made a change which seemed routine at the time, would have been fastidiously thought through. There was nothing left to chance, or at least as close as the always prepared Graham could achieve. The sport itself meant that no matter how well you crunch the numbers, there is always something that can go awry.

Every choice made represented chips on a roulette number. Not every variable could be accounted for, so managers became as close to experts on estimation as they could possibly get.

Graham's switching to a central back three in the big games had bamboozled the Champions on both occasions they had played, and the emergence of David Hillier had allowed overworked midfield artisan Paul Davis to rest. If George had not decided to show belief in yet another prospect that had rolled out of the Arsenal youth setup, it would have surely meant curtains to the Gunner's impeccable record in this campaign. Putting so much faith in youth could have had repercussions, as even when the lucky starlet is supremely blessed with talent, there are so many pitfalls that can befall the inexperienced. It was just another indication of what odds Graham faced every time he made a bold call. This season though, had seen the Scot manage to beat the house almost every time. Arsenal's midfield carried on the way they had done from August, and Hillier did a fantastic job of covering in the centre of the park.

Davis and Michael Thomas had been imperious in their domination of matches. Each game they had played together, the bond had become stronger. Such was their all-encompassing grasp on midfield, they attacked and defended like lions. The amount of matches would have taken their toll on any player, and with Hillier showing he was ready to stand in, it gave Graham the breathing space he needed to invigorate his team when the games were coming every three days.

They had just defeated Liverpool at Anfield, and had then squeaked past plucky Cambridge United to book their Wembley Cup match.

The task that Graham set his men was simple in words, but oh so demanding to actually achieve. Twelve league games and two Cup games. If Arsenal won all of them, they would etch their names alongside the greats of the game.

Mission Implausible Part One had gone swimmingly. It was always the sequel that contrived to be more convoluted than anyone could deal with... Eight days after pipping Cambridge United, saw the return of this season's Groundhog Day foe - Leeds United.

The teams had played each other five times already, with the score aggregate, thus far, 5-4 to Arsenal - thanks to the third replay of their fourth round FA Cup tie.

Howard Wilkinson was onto something at Elland Road. He had taken the Yorkshire side up and his first season back in the 'big league' had been sink or swim. United were not only swimming, they were lapping some of their more illustrious competitors.

They were in fourth spot in the First Division, and they could go into this game safe in the knowledge that they could keep up with whatever Arsenal managed to throw at them. As they'd proved numerous times already!

George seemed to be favouring the David O'Leary sweeper model in these crunch fixtures, and he named the same side which had defeated Liverpool and Crystal Palace. Why change what worked so beautifully?

The game was predictably tight and Arsenal fans had to wait until the 77th minute to enjoy a goal. Lee Dixon was the spark as he passed to Alan Smith on the right - Smudge had moved out wide to try and gain some space in the heat of some tight Leeds defending. Smith then displayed some neat footwork before putting in a delightful sliderule pass for Kevin Campbell, who collected and arrowed in a low shot that whizzed through John Lukic's legs and into the far corner.

Previously, the team that made the breakthrough normally were pegged back, but Arsenal had evolved, they were wise to Leeds this time.

A return of an Arsenal favourite gave the home side the points. A Seaman kick was flicked on by the aerially unequalled Smudge. The Leeds defence should have dealt with the ball, but a mixture of hesitancy and Campbell's persistence, saw the ball break free enough for Campbell to toe poke the ball in the air over an onrushing Lukic.

Campbell was coming into his own, and his brace had seen off another team that had aspirations of taking points from Highbury. His power was proving too much for the majority of defences, and his intuitive positioning meant that he was perfectly placed to feed from the ample chances Smith and Merson were creating.

Arsenal had been polished and professional and had done exactly what was needed to successfully see off a potential usurper of their hopes. The team had been set up perfectly yet again by George Graham, and it meant that another game had been chalked off the list. Another rung was climbed on the ladder to success.

The Leeds win was the aperitif in a course of three matches within six days. Horrendous scheduling execution had also befallen the Gunners earlier in the season on multiple occasions and they had expertly avoided catastrophe. In fact, on closer inspection, they had excelled in these testing conditions. Graham was right, once again, when he said that this Arsenal team were getting used to these tense times.

Nottingham Forest provided the next match for Arsenal. George mentioned in his programme column for the game about collecting his 'Manager of the Month' award for February and how Campbell collected his Man of the Match award for his two goals against Leeds United. Both of these accolades came with a bottle of champagne, but neither men would have time to enjoy the spoils!

Arsenal's injured were returning, with Anders Limpar, Andy Linighan and Perry Groves taking part in reserve fixtures. Siggi Jonsson had also returned to training, and Hillier was singled out for praise for holding down the position he had won from Davis. He had fitted in superbly, and his future was bright, but it was inevitable that the England hopeful and Arsenal's midfield dictator, Davis would win his place back. It would also be the game that had Groves and most excitingly for Gooners, Anders Limpar, on the bench.

Liverpool had drawn level on points with Arsenal, even though the Gunners had not dropped any points. The Merseysiders, and current champions, had played one game more than Arsenal, and had used it to close the gap. Dependant on whether you are a glass half-full or empty type of person, a game in hand represents very different things.

When Arsenal had four games in hand over Manchester United in 1997/98, but were ten points behind, Alex Ferguson famously declared he would much rather have the points in the bank than games in hand, which involved risk and luck. The work still had to be done. Arsene Wenger agreed with this statement - and then set about overhauling United to win the title.

George was an optimist, but he was grounded in reality. Even the most pessimistic of fans in 1991 would have seen what their beloved team had done all season and been left with no doubt that they would give everything to the cause. That extra game Liverpool had played heaped pressure on Arsenal's shoulders, but pressure had brought the best out of the players. After all, Arsenal had still only lost ONE game all season in the First Division. The very real threat of a loss, and handing valuable initiative to Liverpool, hung in the air of every game, and Forest were next up at Highbury.

The home side took the lead through Campbell, but the move started from Seaman's long goal kick, which was flicked on by - you guessed it - Smith. The touch that made the goal though, came from Thomas, who was aptly placed to receive Smith's header. He had taken up residence between enemy lines, quite literally between their midfield and defence, and his first touch was all he needed to loop a ball over Des Walker and Steve Chettle with the outside of his boot.

The pass was so righteous that Campbell could let the ball bounce so it was a perfect fit for his shot, which was low and hard and enough to convincingly beat Forest keeper Mark Crossley. That goal was his fourth in three games, yet another youth product coming good for Graham. His policy on blooding these promising starlets was looking like shrewd business.

The second half saw the much heralded return of Limpar to the side, replacing Paul Davis as a substitute. Groves also came off the bench in place of Merson, but their presence on the pitch did not stave off Brian Clough's Forest side, or stem their attacking inclinations.

A free kick wide of the penalty area was snapped up by Nigel Jemson, whose smart turn and shot caught everyone by surprise, including Seaman and the matchday cameraman! It was a good goal that no one could have stopped, but it meant that two points had slipped through Arsenal's fingers. It was pivotal with so few games left to make a difference, and with Liverpool so close in the table. Just like in that unforgettable season of 1988/89, Arsenal were dropping points and letting Liverpool steal a march on their position. Had the lesson from that year been learned?

The last game of the three within six days was at Carrow Road. Mid-table Norwich had been polished off at Highbury in October thanks to a Davis brace, but this game was the polar opposite of that cakewalk.

George included Limpar from the start and kept Campbell in the team because of his impressive recent form. It meant there was no place for Merson in the eleven, but there was ample gunpowder in the Arsenal cannon.

The match was an awkward affair, with the home side stifling Arsenal's wide men. The nearest the Gunners came to a goal was a O'Leary header, which Bryan Gunn saved. It was a display that was devoid of the usual urgency Graham instilled in their play. Norwich could even have inflicted only a second loss of Arsenal's league season after some late pressure, but it was to no avail.

After the match, the 29th of the First Division, Liverpool had clambered over Arsenal and sat astride the top spot, a point in front. This position was a comfortable one for Liverpool. They were more than familiar with this lofty spot after a decade of dominance. Crystal Palace, in third, had also refused to go away, only four points away from Graham's side. It was out of Arsenal's hands.

In the face of Arsenal's record at that point, it was damning to see Liverpool still above the Gunners and serves to highlight what a challenge Liverpool posed. Even though there was just one blot on Arsenal's copybook, Liverpool always seemed one step ahead. It sapped belief from the team - after all that hard work and yet the Reds were still lording it over them.

Arsenal could continue with their near-flawless league record, but if the Merseysiders were to win all their remaining fixtures, as they would no doubt expect to, then the title would stay at Anfield. The next three games would contain many clues regarding the destination of the title.

Arsenal would face bottom club Derby County at the Baseball Ground, followed by a home game against Aston Villa three days later, and finally, after another three days, Graham would take his troops to Bramall Lane to take on Sheffield United.

Liverpool had a slightly easier calendar to manage. Their next matchup was with Queens Park Rangers at Anfield. They also had another game three days later, where they would face Southampton at The Dell. The advantage they had over their title peers was that their third match allowed for eight days of recovery, instead of Arsenal's three. Liverpool faced Coventry City after a precious spell of recuperation.

Arsenal travelled to Derby on the back foot after two previous games without a win. Derby County were cut adrift at the bottom of the First Division, so the scheduling gave the away team a fair chance to rediscover some form and confidence. The week before, County had been taken apart mercilessly by Liverpool in a 7-1 mauling. It was the perfect scenario for Arsenal to get their groove back. Derby were not without their danger, and striker Dean Saunders was amongst the top scorers in the league, so there was still cause for concern for any who didn't give their all.

Smith was also amongst the hottest of goal-getters, and his haul had seen him with a real chance of grabbing the accolade of top goalscorer. It wouldn't have been on his mind, such was the nature of the modest striker, but his goals had made the difference time and again.

It was to be the case again. Smudge's brace came straight from the training ground, as both were manufactured from corner routines. A flick on at the near post from a teammate and a late and impeccably timed run from Smith to head home. Carbon copy goals, which had been perfectly executed by the team. The game finished in a 2-0 victory for Graham's men. Arsenal had done their part. What did Liverpool have up their sleeve?

QPR had never won at Anfield, and were perilously close to the drop zone when they met at Anfield. The game was as close to a home banker as any match in history. One omission from the Liverpool lineup gave the Hoops a boost before the match proceeded - John Barnes was out of the team through injury.

The away side produced quite comfortably their best display of the season. Two goals up with twenty five minutes left to play, Jan Molby pulled one back from the penalty spot and everyone expected the fightback, but Clive Wilson re-established the two goal lead for QPR, and Liverpool had, unbelievably, fallen at home again.

Arsenal had their noses in front once more, and three days later, the previously infallible Reds crumbled to another loss. Southampton held on for a famous 1-0 victory in front of their own fans, which meant that if Graham could inspire his men like he had done all year long, then the pride of North London would have a five point lead with seven games to play.

This gift that no one could have foreseen was not about to be returned. Arsenal turned on the style against Aston Villa, sending them back to the Midlands with red faces after scoring five unopposed.

Hillier came back into the side, but the rejig did nothing to hamper Arsenal's fluency. The goals were bagged by Smith and Campbell - who both got a brace - and Davis scored what was a beautiful turn and volley that crashed in off the post. Limpar also showed a welcome return to form, having a hand in two of the goals. Aston Villa were not helped by their goalkeeper Nigel Spink going off injured. With no subs left to use, it was left to David Platt to put the gloves on - he was the one who let in the fourth and fifth goals!

Something worthy of note that may crop up in a pub quiz also happened when Platt took the gloves in that game - it was the first time he would put on an Arsenal jersey, four years before he eventually signed for the Gunners. His stint in goal saw him don a spare Arsenal goalkeeping jersey, and whilst he may have been dressed like Seaman, he thankfully could not recreate the Gunners stopper's heroics!

It was the complete package on the pitch, and what truly giftwrapped the win was the gap that had grown between Arsenal and second place: five points. It was hardly curtains for Liverpool, but Arsenal had the novelty of breathing room and their own destiny back in their hands.

Those extra few days of rest that was mentioned earlier for Liverpool? They would have needed them after successive losses, but it is doubtful they could have made it count, as their recent bout of uncharacteristic nerves continued, only drawing with Coventry at Anfield thanks to an 82nd minute equaliser from Ian Rush.

All of a sudden, this gasping Reds team was unrecognisable. Had opponents finally realised that there was weakness that could be utilised within the side? Had Arsenal shaken things up to such a degree that the previously untouchable Red machine was now relying on late equalisers to salvage a point? Liverpool had been masters of the home straight. They had ran this race so often. This time though, Arsenal had refused to let them get away. In the face of countless hardships, the Gunners had bravely faced the best that Liverpool could muster, and then proceeded to launch it straight back.

Could Arsenal compound the misery in Merseyside by winning their third game in six days? It was certainly a factor for Liverpool's dropping of points against Coventry, as the pressure was heaped high by Arsenal with yet another win. It seemed that whilst Liverpool were adept at dishing out the strain, their chin was looking decidedly glassy.

Bramall Lane would be the venue that decided if the Gunner's could dish out a telling blow to Liverpool, or rather, it was again Campbell and Smith who provided the succinct riposte.

Both strikers continued their rich vein of form in a 2-0 victory. Campbell picked up a Smith flick-on to score the first, then Campbell kindly returned the favour, squaring to Smith to curl a wonderful effort into the top corner. Campbell had seven goals in eight games and was unplayable, and Smudge had now grabbed his 18th goal of the league season.

Arsenal had the wind beneath their wings, and in the process had taken it from Liverpool. They had pressured and squeezed them, and demanded they

A surefire quiz question – the night David Platt played in a Gunners' jersey five years before signing for Arsenal

perform in each and every game. They had not been up to the task that Graham had set.

It had been an excellent three games, and maximum points had swung the pendulum firmly in Arsenal's favour. Nothing had been won yet though, and Liverpool's pedigree was reminder enough that any slip could well be fatal in the title race.

Yet another customary three day gap in between matches saw Southampton - who were bouncing after beating Liverpool - welcome Arsenal to The Dell. The Saints were just as pumped to grab another title contending scalp, but Alan Smith grabbed a point for the Gunners and he had ensured his team did not befall the same fate that Liverpool had. It was a difficult match with a confident and dangerous Saints side, but Arsenal's indomitable spirit was enough to snatch a point.

Another probable reason for Arsenal not making it four consecutive wins was them having one eye on the FA Cup semi-final. The occasion could not be much bigger, and the same could be said for the opponent. It was just five days after the draw at The Dell, and Limpar and Thomas had been recently rested with a view to this North London slug fest at Wembley. The tale of the tape before both teams walked out on the hallowed turf made for interesting reading.

Arsenal were top of the league, and had the Division's joint top scorer in their ranks in Smith. Tottenham were a distant 27 points behind in the table after initially matching their neighbours in the early stage of the campaign. Gary Lineker had also grabbed a fair amount of goals, ably abetted by the enigma that was Paul Gascoigne.

Whenever Spurs had played a fixture that 'Gazza' was in the lineup for, the opponent was always asked how they would deal with his unique threat. That is one of the marks of a gifted player. Teams really did make plans to stifle the midfield man, even the mighty Liverpool planted David Burrows on him on both occasions they had met.

George rarely had to get the whiteboard out to devise a plan to stop Gazza. Only 35 days had passed since the England whizz had gone under the knife for a double hernia operation, but Terry Venables made a huge gamble by selecting him for this semi-final.

It was Tottenham's, and Venables's, last chance to salvage what had promised so much that season. If they wanted to view the year as anything other than wasteful, they simply must win the Cup.

Arsenal were huge favourites for the Double. Holding the bragging rights over their rivals in the league, they still had eyes on both prizes. However, some things are simply not meant to be. As much as it pains us to admit, Spurs deserved to win the game. They drew their strength from the irrepressible Gazza and his free-kick, which stunned the Gunners, was impeccable - and unsaveable. Seaman had stopped some shots in his first campaign that he had no right to do, but he could not get a finger on that exocet.

Gazza only lasted 60 minutes, as the reality of recent surgery buckled him, but his hour-long show was enough to give his side - and their fans - a rare moment of happiness. They were a goal up, at Wembley in an FA Cup semi-final. The team that had been put to the sword was the team who had always been in their sights, ever since 1913 when Arsenal had taken residence in North London.

Arsenal were on the ascendancy in recent years, but that match gave Tottenham fans something to cherish as they would fade into Arsenal's shadow in the years to come. We can let them have that game, even if the manner in which they broke the deadlock was not exactly pretty.

It had been Tottenham's malicious intent that had gotten them the opener. Vinny Samways had taken Limpar out of the equation within a minute of the game starting. It was a message to let the Swede know he was in for a pasting. Whilst prone on the floor, Samway's teammate Van Den Hauwe kicked the diminutive winger, but it was not spotted by anyone other than Limpar, who had revenge on his mind.

He had been fully briefed on the Arsenal Way, so he felt retribution was needed. In the fifth minute, Limpar made a late tackle on Paul Stewart - and the resulting set-piece was art, even Gooners would have to recognise it.

Gazza stepped up to the free kick and shaped up to shoot. It was 35 yards out, and with David Seaman in goal, Arsenal were not exactly over-worried. But the shot fizzed, curled and arced – it had deceived Seaman – and it found the net.

He was at it again when he led Arsenal's defence on a merry dance so Lineker could score the second. George had done what every other manager had done and stuck a man-marker on Gascoigne, but the man dubbed 'England's Clown Prince' was unstoppable. His assist for Lineker to double their lead was mesmerising

He showed his mastery was not resigned to set-pieces only, and his flicks and tricks, not to mention his vision, meant that Lineker had the easiest job to push Tottenham to the brink of the Cup final. The ball eventually came within Lineker range in the box and the England hotshot reacted nanoseconds before Adams to score.

This was not in Graham's plan. Or even in his Plan B. Arsenal had not played badly, but Tottenham had a riddle in their team that had every Arsenal player scratching their heads trying to solve.

Arsenal began to grind into gear, the ominous sounds of their fearsome engine roaring into life were in the form of Smith firing over and Davis and Thomas getting their grips on midfield. It was very much game on just before half time, as Smith picked up a defensive clearance from Spurs and squirted it out wide to Dixon. The right-back put in a tantalising bait, which drew Spurs keeper Thorstvedt out just enough. Smith had gunned it back into the box and he bested Gary Mabbutt in the air to nod in a lifeline. The first half was over, and amidst George Graham's shaking head and grimace, the ending to the half would have been cause for optimism. Arsenal were awake, and snarling again.

The second half began with Arsenal leaping out and starting their assault on the Tottenham goal early, but Mabbutt had organised his men well at the back.

Paul Gascoigne shakes Tony Adams' hand at the final whistle after the 1991 FA Cup semi Final at Wembley Stadium

The turning point of the entire match fell to the tiny feet of Anders Limpar. Anders had the best chance to draw the Gunners level, but his weak finish did not trouble Thorstvedt much.

Limpar was soon replaced by Groves as Graham tried to force the issue. Gazza had gone off, and Tottenham were fighting for their lives. So it was with shock that the lilywhites scored the next goal, and in doing so, broke Arsenal's resolve.

Mabbutt had the ball and Samways took an Arsenal defender with him on a dummy run, which opened a pocket of space for lethal Lineker to fire home.

That was the end of the Double dream for Graham. 'Gazza' and his team-mates danced and sang on the pitch, driven on by the mania in the Spurs end of the stadium. Arsenal were out, and the hand on the hilt of the dagger had been their hated rivals.

It was the lowest point of the season by a country mile. I asked Alan Smith what had perturbed him more when looking back on this season with the benefit of hindsight; losing the unbeaten run or the Cup Semi-Final to Spurs? Smudge responded "We were just pleased to win the title, but there was more annoyance at the time at not lifting the cup. We all expected to win the game as we were in great form, so it hurt. We soon got over it though!"

George's next column in the match programme, for the home game against Manchester City, was dominated by the FA Cup exit; "We've got to bounce back again after last Sunday's disappointment. We've recovered from far worse setbacks than losing to Tottenham - the points deduction for a start. Football is about highs and lows. We'd been on a high til Sunday, winning regularly, scoring plenty of goals and building a lead over Liverpool. Now we've got to recover from a low. Our success has been about overcoming the odds. We lost the game in the first twenty minutes. It's asking a lot of any team to come back from two down - though after that spell I was quite pleased with our display. If we'd begun the game the way we started the second half, there wouldn't have been any problems."

The Gaffer went on to wish his neighbours and his old pal Venables well in the Final, and implored his side and the raucous fans to turn up for this game.

When I asked Dixon about the Cup exit at the hands of Spurs, the fullback admitted "It was my worst moment at Arsenal. Gazza won it for them, and we did think after the game that we would have to win the League now, because they will win the Cup."

Once again, Arsenal were required to come back from something that had been alien to them for the majority of August through to April. A loss would have taken the breath and momentum from any side on a run, and the iron will that was instilled by Graham would have to come to the rescue in order for the Gunners to see the season out victorious. It had been a bodyblow to lose, but for the punch to be administered by their nemesis? George Graham would be ensuring his side did not lose sight of the target.

There was still the biggest prize to claim, and Arsenal wanted their name on it again. They deserved it, and the proof in the pudding was in looking at the league table. Five games left. As Dixon said, they HAD to win the league now.

David Seaman is helped off the pitch in tears by David Rocastle after his mistakes handed Tottenham victory at Wembley

Champions

After a fall from a horse, or a crash in a vehicle, the toughest task is always to attempt to jump back on your steed, or drive that car again. A break in pattern, a sudden jolt that tears you away from the path your brain had set, is enough to give you a soft reset of sorts. It jars the senses.

Think about when you turn your phone quickly on and off when it freezes, and that pause as the white screen blazes into your retina. This is what happens when a team or sports star who is accustomed to winning, loses. It is a reboot of sorts, as the brain frantically grabs at anything to regain the position it once had. Liverpool had been turned off by Arsenal, and now Tottenham had done the same to Arsenal.

How quickly could George Graham boot his team back up? They had no time to waste, as Manchester City were the visitors to Highbury just three days after the shattering defeat at Wembley.

Their record of losing just one game would mean nothing without the title. To go through the thirty-eight games that comprises a season, and to lose just one, would be one hell of an accomplishment, and if it went hand-in-hand with the Championship, then George Graham would be responsible for the most dominating and complete league campaign that Arsenal had ever accomplished. The Championship made everything else worthwhile.

The title was the aim, and if they wanted to grab that trophy with both hands, then winning the next five games - or at least avoiding defeat - would be mandatory to stave off perennial winners Liverpool.

Talking of the Reds, they had now hired the man who had incredibly large shoes to fill. Graeme Souness was the man who left Glasgow Rangers and had five games to heap as much pressure on the Gunning frontrunners as possible. Souness carried similar stature to King Kenny; he was part of the all-conquering Liverpool side who had taken England and Europe in their grasp. He commanded respect and he seemed the obvious choice. It could not have gone to an outsider at this crucial stage, they needed a legend to lead this iconic team.

The new Red's boss had games at Norwich, a tough tie at home to Crystal Palace, followed by three tricky games at Stamford Bridge, the City Ground and ending their season at Anfield against Spurs.

In the other lane, George had games against Manchester City first, then a home game against Liverpool-humblers QPR. The last three games were away to Sunderland, a pivotal home game against Manchester United and lastly another home match against Coventry City. It would have been far more difficult if the United match had not been postponed and had been in its original slot, but this formidable Arsenal team had grown accustomed to the various slings and arrows that fate and luck could throw at them. They had overcome so much already, but it is always the last yards that are the hardest, isn't it?

The Gunners had the slightly easier run in with four of the five games at home, and they had a five point cushion to boot. If they could win the first three, then there was a conceivable chance to win the title when Alex Ferguson and United were at Highbury, if Souness contrived to drop points. The prospect of the United players forming a guard of honour was a tantalising one for Gooners. Just imagine how the players felt after the matches that they had played? Scores would never be settled between the sides, but what a chance to slip a body blow square in the ribs.

Bouncing back, as Graham had instructed after the loss to their nemesis, was perhaps the biggest stumbling block on the path to the title. The first attempt to swing their feet back into the stirrups was versus Manchester City.

Graham reverted back to a trusty 4-4-2, with the typical Arsenal back four in place. Michael Thomas and Paul Davis were in the engine room. Paul Merson and Perry Groves on the flanks, ably supporting the flying Kevin Campbell and Alan Smith. A gameplan that was more than recognisable, but opponents could not find an answer to. Arsenal used this to great effect to grab the lead.

David Seaman punted long. Alan Smith got the better of his marker to flick on and a hungry, racing Kevin Campbell outmuscled and outpaced his man to get in a shot and score. It was his eighth goal in his last eleven First Division appearances. Smith had performed this assist repeatedly, and markers would be painfully aware of his aerial ability. They would go out of their way to stifle this particular weapon in Arsenal's armoury, but time and again, 'Smudge' would get the better of whichever defender was tasked with silencing him. The next goal showed that he wasn't just good in the air either.

Arsenal grabbed a second when Groves crossed and it was again Smudge who found himself in the perfect position. He juggled the ball as he waited for Merson to get into space and then laid it off for Merson, who still had plenty to do, but he let his shot work for him, sidefooting a sumptuous volley into the far corner.

One of the team's best goals of the entire campaign. It should have been curtains for the visitors, but Arsenal took their foot from City's jugular, and in this most competitive of arenas, any combatant you face will make you pay.

Whoever writes the scripts for fate usually has a taste for comedy, as former players are usually front and centre when it comes to haunting their former places of employment. This game was no different, as Niall Quinn earned a penalty for his new team which was converted, much to the chagrin of Seaman who was agonisingly close to keeping it out.

City weren't finished and had dazed Arsenal. They really shouldn't have been able to lay a glove on Arsenal, as the Gunners weren't known for giving up a lead, especially a two goal advantage. This game was the exception, as Groves took a throw in but missed his intended target. The ever alert David White snapped up the ball and was through, and he put it past Arsenal's number one to grab a point.

Liverpool had won their match against Norwich, and had converted their own two goal lead, even bettering it to three. They had piled more pressure onto Graham and his boys. They were doing what was expected. The gap between the teams was now down to three points, with four to play. This was building up to a cinematic finish. Next up for Arsenal was Queens Park Rangers.

Hardly what Graham needed before kickoff was an injury to Thomas. Hillier had performed well when called upon so far, and the youngster was given another start. Anders Limpar also came back into the side, at the expense of Groves. These were the only two changes from the City game, but the result would be far more contrasting than the team selection.

QPR had improved in recent games and were on a run which had given them some breathing space above the relegation zone, but Davis' fancy footwork had them spellbound in their own box, and he was unceremoniously dumped to the turf. The referee, John Moules, pointed to the spot and resident penalty taker Lee Dixon slammed the ball home.

Arsenal pressed for the comfort of a second goal, and they were rewarded when Campbell used his lightning reactions to snatch a spare yard. He took the shot at the first opportunity. Jan Stejskal, who had repelled his fair share of attempts that afternoon, did the same again as he parried from Campbell, but Merson had the presence of mind to follow up any possible spillage from the Hoops keeper. The 'Magic Man' had a second to mop up and he duly obliged.

You couldn't say that this Arsenal side failed to learn from their errors. The two goal lead they had surrendered against Manchester City had stuck in their mind, and there was no risk of the same thing happening, although pressure does strange things when applied, and Liverpool had been breathing heavily at the window, looking in on Arsenal at the top. The condensation on the window may have distorted their vision, but Arsenal could still operate their defence, which had become second nature. They saw out the rest of the game and it meant that the finish line drew ever closer. Another win. Another clean sheet. Another three points and another rung climbed on the ladder.

If the theme was repetition, then Liverpool couldn't resist in joining in. They earned their second 3-0 home win in succession, and the gap remained at three points. A solitary win from the Reds and an Arsenal loss would leave these tusslers level on points. The ending to this film was indeed building the tension, and what thriller would be complete without a twist? The season had thrown up several so far. The unpredictability of England's top league was the one thing you could count on.

Next up was Sunderland for the Gunners, and Liverpool went to Chelsea, the place which had registered the sole 'L' in the league table for George Graham's side.

Could Graham expect any favours from Chelsea? George wasn't the type to rely on anyone else to do the hard work for him and his side. He would concentrate on the one thing he could affect and that was to see his side continue to win. It was in his side's hands with only three games left to go. If he had been offered that in August, he would not have refused.

Perry Groves goes round the Sunderland goalkeeper, Tim Carter, at Roker Park in May 1991

Chelsea striker, Kerry Dixon, in the aftermath of his team's multi-faceted victory over Arsenal which broke the unbeaten record, had said to the papers that Liverpool, too, would be beaten at the Bridge, and that his Blues comrades would try and do Arsenal a favour. There was the twist in the storyline. Dixon stayed true to his word.

Arsenal went to Roker Park to play second from bottom Sunderland, and although their defence was as true as ever, they failed to break down a rugged Mackems team. It could have been much worse, but yet again, David Seaman came to the rescue with an acrobatic, fingertip save to keep the scores level, and his team's incredible record in the league intact. Meanwhile, Chelsea had put Liverpool to the sword. Stamford Bridge was not just a nightmare for Arsenal to take points from, as Souness's Reds failed to deal with Graham Stuart, Dixon and Denis Wise.

Dixon's promise had come true. Just as it had looked like the gap was going to come down to one point with two to play after Arsenal had failed to put down Sunderland, Chelsea showed that their word was their bond as they sent Liverpool packing after winning 4-2. Who saw that coming other than the Chelsea players? The Gunners and their fans would have expected Liverpool to creep ever nearer in the table after the Sunderland result, but The Bridge was something of a fortress and Souness couldn't conjure a plan to take the points away.

It's party time for David Seaman, Kevin Campbell and David Hillier

Expectations were reaching a crescendo. This film's ending was coming into view, and could any scriptwriter have come up with a more perfect ending than playing Manchester United?

That season had seen Crystal Palace, Leeds, even Luton Town, give Arsenal a real headache and a genuine reason to circle their team's name in next season's fixture list. Tottenham and Liverpool were self-explanatory in their position as games that Gooners most looked forward to, but Manchester United had a special spot reserved in Arsenal's 'affections.'

From 1987 to the present day, each and every match between them included bones of contention, tackles of the purest dark intentions, bouts between evenly matched players, and games that are still talked of years after. The grudge between the two was growing exponentially, each match was a potential for revenge after the last game, thus the cycle never ended, it only grew. Gooners packed the matchday pubs hours before they were due to pack the rafters at Highbury. They, of course, wanted to see the next installment of this explosive series.

After Chelsea had defeated Liverpool, it meant that their next game - the early kickoff against Nottingham Forest - was a veritable must win. The gap was four points, so if they wanted to force an Arsenal response and hope that United would help them the way Chelsea did the Gunners - they had to first beat Brian Clough's FA Cup finalists.

Forest drew first blood, as Steve Staunton gave away a penalty, which Nigel Clough put past Grobbelaar. Liverpool were now seeing Arsenal drive off into the distance, cursing themselves as their mistakes were costing them valuable impetus. They were beginning to choke on Arsenal's dust.

Nottingham Forest defender Steve Chettle slid into Ronnie Rosenthal in the 55th minute to gift Liverpool a chance to grab an equaliser they hadn't looked like taking, and Jan Molby stepped up to score his eighth penalty of the season.

A team of the stature that Liverpool enjoyed did not simply accept a trophy in their possession switching hands. They had earned that reputation through years of success. They were fighting to make things as uncomfortable as possible for Arsenal. On this occasion though, their fighting spirit was not enough.

Ian Woan, the Forest midfielder, who hailed from Liverpool, would be the man destined to unwrap Liverpool's rigid fingers from the title. The Scouser waited at the back post for a wide free kick, and an errant headed clearance fell to him. He chested it down and thumped a half volley into the top corner, and kill off, the Scouser's title hopes.

Arsenal were Champions for the second time in three years. Some people branded the achievement as 'Liverpool chucking it away', however, if a team who had lost just once in the season didn't deserve to win the League, then no one would. Liverpool in the first half of the season had chucked everything at the Gunners, but what had earned Arsenal the glory was that they had answered every single question that the all-conquering Merseysiders had posed.

Bob Wilson, goalkeeping coach at the time and bona fide Arsenal legend, said of the welcoming committee as they pulled up to Highbury in the team coach, "The streets were packed, it was an amazing reception." The Gooners had watched it all unfold from the various pubs around Highbury. They were poised to kick off an unforgettable day and make sure they were waiting for the Arsenal coach as it arrived at the home ground.

Did this welcome skew the match before it had even been played? What was it like to play a heated adversary, knowing that your ultimate target had already been achieved?

'Smudge' was interviewed on the official club VHS for the season, and said "We had listened to the Liverpool game on the coach on the way to the ground. There was a big crowd already at Highbury who had all done the same as us, so it made for a party atmosphere after the final whistle."

Campbell commented on the closeness of the behind the scenes staff, coaches and players, who all watched and listened to the game together, "We were all just praying Forest would hold out!"

Hillier had been the Youth Team Captain when they had won the Youth Cup the season prior, and this was his first as a fully fledged first teamer. What was whirling through his mind? "I didn't know how to feel! I just looked at the other lads and asked them what to do and how to act!"

Not every player was so pleased that the pressure had finally been lifted before the United game. Thomas was also interviewed on the VHS tape, and he said " It was an anti-climax! We had the celebration before! It was hard to get geed up, but we did!"

George, though, was just pleased to have another title, to prove they were not flashes in the pan. "Would I have preferred Liverpool to have won before the United game? You must be joking! We went into the United game knowing we were Champions!"

There was a small matter of a game to play against a team who had caused Arsenal problems in more places than the pitch. The guard of honour that the United players would have to form as Arsenal stepped foot onto the Highbury pitch would have been something that every Arsenal player and fan would have taken great pleasure from. The purest form of humble pie.

Thomas needn't have worried about motivation either. Arsenal put on a show for their fans worthy of the moniker of Champions.

Smith scored a hat-trick as Arsenal defeated Ferguson's men 3-1. He had scored his first two with a trademark header and a clever shot, but when Arsenal were awarded a penalty, Dixon made a huge gesture. The team's official penalty taker gave the ball to Smith so he could complete his hat-trick and give him the edge in his chase for the Adidas Golden Boot Award. He would go on to win this accolade for the second time in just three seasons.

Smith later said, "It was my first penalty, as I've never liked taking them! I was on my hat-trick though, so there was no pressure. I wouldn't have liked to have taken it otherwise!"

Smith may have had second thoughts on taking penalties after this, as his effort hit the top left corner and gave the keeper no chance of saving it.

It was officially party time once the whistle blew. United unsurprisingly left sharply and it left a stadium full of Gooners. The staff were just as elated as the fans who now rejoiced in unison. Some worked for the club, some played for the club, some made tea for the club. All of them supported the Club. The Club that were now title winners yet again.

An Arsenal fan for over fifty years, blogger and Gooner Gary Lawrence described to me the day that Liverpool fell to Forest; "I remember the day we won the title in 1990/91 that all the pubs around Highbury were banged out and The Woodbine - the pub I was in - was no exception. People were standing on seats in order to see the TV. We were all hoping to see Cloughie's Nottingham Forest turn Liverpool over to clinch the title for us before even playing Manchester United and they duly obliged. I recall the roars going up and the pub erupting when Forest scored their goals."

"It was a party atmosphere as we made our way to Highbury for the game and it was the same inside the ground. The United players formed a guard of honour for the new Champions. The players could relax and they wiped the floor with United as Smudger scored a hat-trick in the 3-1 win. I couldn't drink too much as I had work the next day, but I made up for that on the Saturday after. We hammered Coventry City 6-1 with Anders scoring a hat-trick this time. I got absolutely slaughtered that night!" Just imagine what he would have been able to recall if he hadn't drunk his own body weight that night.

Paul Merson with a beautiful trophy but questionable choice of headwear

The streets were a carnival, and a sea of red and white in Avenell Road, that was where the epicentre was. Fans were given more time to fully appreciate this title than when the ultimate heist took place at Anfield in May 1989, and by the way they raucously heralded the team coach, it seemed as if they were embracing the occasion.

A second title in three seasons meant that the Arsenal could now claim to be a force to be reckoned with in Europe, and Graham's men would be competing on the continent the season after the Euro ban was lifted.

It wasn't just matters on the pitch in which the Gunners were pulling up trees. Arsenal had opened up a swanky new club shop, they were redeveloping the North Bank and were champions of England with some of the best players in the land on their books.

Make no mistake, this was the Gunners moving into the upper echelons, preparing for the future.

What of the past however? Arsenal had a rich historical tapestry which was littered with cups and trophies. Did this league win rank alongside, or even dwarf their previous accolades?

With every season, and with more interest and money pouring into the league, the First Division was becoming increasingly competitive and difficult to win. It gave this title more lustre.

What really added the polish though, was the style and panache in which they won their final league match, against Coventry City.

Highbury before kickoff was serenaded by a wonderful brass band, and the fans enjoyed part two of the Arsenal title-winning show, as the players treated them to a buffet of goals.

Another treble, this time from Limpar, who was back to his impish best, Smith, an own goal and a Groves goal, gave Arsenal six of the best on their coronation as Champions. They may have won the league before they kicked a ball, but this game was where they would have THAT moment. The sepia-toned image that every single person connected to the club would be unable to, or want to, forget. It would be placed in images on walls, and more importantly, engrained in memory.

The players applauded the rapturous fans before going into the tunnel. They had a natter - and an egg fight - with some of the staff as they waited for the pitch to be arranged so they could be awarded the First Division trophy. They were visibly unwinding after a season fraught with tension and peril. They deserved to enjoy themselves.

About ten minutes passed, before Tony Adams led his men out. Medals were put around necks, and beaming faces were in every corner of the ground, including on the turf from the players. The work they had put in to get to this particular slice of time was forgotten. Every person who had contributed was intent on making the most of the celebrations.

Adams took the trophy that he was made to hold. He faced out to the fans and his arms locked into place as he lifted it over his head to signal that this

The sweet feeling of redemption for Arsenal captain Tony Adams

Michael Thomas and Nigel Winterburn celebrate after the Manchester United title clincher

was for them, just as much as it was for the players. Could the Skipper have imagined this as he sat in his bunk earlier in the year? It was impossible to have made it any sweeter for him. Redemption.

To say it was well received in the stands was an understatement. That moment would never leave the men who had moved mountains, and bureaucracy, to make that a reality.

It would never leave Gooners either. The complete team had the complete League season, and it was the perfect platform to grow into the giant power they knew they had the potential to become.

The title was theirs, and it was glorious. Looking back on the entire season, that sole loss, which looks like an incongruous typing error, may have robbed a history-writing team the extra bit of attention that they warranted.

There are many superlatives you can aim at the team who won the title, but Invincible should have been one of them.

Just one loss in the League. So many different things had come together to rob Arsenal of the cleanest of slates. The title was just reward for their gargantuan efforts, but after the Invincibles achieved what this team should have, this sole defeat rankles more than it should.

Even though it is a question that is nigh-on impossible to answer, does the title winning team of 1990-91 rank alongside what many see as Arsenal's greatest team of all time?

Which begs the question, how would the footballing landscape have changed if the 1990-91 team had done the unthinkable and become Invincible?

As Good As The Invincibles?

The dust has had ample time to settle on the remarkable achievements of George Graham and the Arsenal team of 1990/91, although hindsight is a double-edged sword. It can skew and warp events out of recognition, making them far more grandiose or insignificant depending on the original standpoint. It can also figuratively laminate those memories that you would like to cherish, saving them for flitting through ad infinitum.

Looking back on the entirety of the season, as this book has hopefully done so thoroughly, the passages of time have faded what was achieved. You can tell this has happened as you leaf through each result, each occasion of adversity which these men clad in red and white faced without fear or hesitation. It has been overlooked what a stupendously formidable task they performed.
Do Arsenal's more recent accolades merit the larger share of attention that they get? Or does this season back at the start of the Nineties earn a place on the same shelf as the Invincibles?

Having written a rather excellent book on Arsene Wenger's team of perfectionists (entitled 'Invincible'), Guardian and Observer writer Amy Lawrence is best qualified to speak first on this chapter. She has had the distinct pleasure of interviewing George Graham in the past and her experiences shed a light on what made this notoriously concealed man tick.

She told me, "One thing I remember vividly when I spoke to George. He had a shrine of sorts dedicated to Arsenal in his house. There was lots from his playing days and as a manager. Rare books, memorabilia steeped in history. He was a collector. He also had on his wall a copy of the League table from 1990-91. He stopped to look at it, whilst saying quietly "just one loss." It was interesting as it was the closest any team had come to it, but if you don't do it, you don't get the same credit. That team had to overcome two massive hits of adversity. To lose your captain and to be deducted two points. I didn't remember any other teams ever having points taken. It's remarkable what they achieved. It cemented that siege mentality and George Graham fostered it."

Amy has a knack of making a point. She pretty much explained what I had wanted to highlight in this book, but in one paragraph. Damn, she's good.

I wanted to show that this team deserves just as much of the limelight as Wenger's Invincibles.

Alan Smith celebrates scoring one of his three goals against Manchester United in May 1991

It is foolish to compare teams from different era's. The parameters were so vastly different, but hopefully the chapters that have brought you to this point have allowed you to realise that George's near-immortals could hold more than a flame to Wengers Invincible's.

The opposition was different. The team was different. The coach was different. Hell, even the boots and footballs were different. It is a fool's task to even put these triumphs up against each other, but they were so good, so far ahead of their respective competition, it also seems that they were the only team that could be a match for each other.

Both teams played the same amount of games, and the points tally was similar, with George's team obtaining 83 points - if no deductions had occurred it would have been 85 - and Wenger's heroes gathering 90.

In terms of goals, George's team really discarded their tag for boring football, as they actually scored one more goal in the league than their swashbuckling brothers from the future, grabbing seventy four to the Invincible's seventy three. As was mooted in 1981 cult hit 'Gregory's Girl;' "numbers make the world go round."

Stats may be able to be taken out of context, but they also help us to visualise and understand. Every facet of football is now under the spotlight and we can find out so much at the click of a button. Let us harness the power of statistics to go deeper in this analysis.

They may have scored nearly exactly the same amount of goals, but was there an over reliance on certain players? Both teams had lethal strikers, how did the whole team fare in bolstering the goals scored column?

The Unbeatable team of 2003/04 had a total of thirteen goalscorers in their flawless league campaign, compared to 90-91's total of twelve. This may have come as a direct symptom of the larger squad Wenger had at his disposal, although it is a small difference. It shows Graham's men really shared the goal-scoring out amongst their brethren.

A telling factor in footballing fluency and how a team conducts themselves in terms of tactics is who scored the goals. Steve Bruce in 1990/91 scored thirteen league goals, showing that Manchester United were a real threat from corners - as well as gaining a lot of penalties that season - colour us all surprised.

Where did the goals come from in both Arsenal teams? It is no surprise to say that Thierry Henry and Alan Smith were top goalscorers in their respective teams, with thirty and twenty two respectively. They also shared the honour of picking up that season's award for top scorer in the competition.

For The Invincibles, the other forty three goals were a pretty even share, once you take out Robert Pirès who pilfered an impressive fourteen goals. The percentage of goals from the other team mates amounts to just over thirty nine percent.

Graham's Wonders obviously relied on Smudge, but his twenty two goals accounted for just over twenty nine percent. The rest was shared pretty evenly amongst the attack, with Anders Limpar and Paul Merson both reaching double figures and Kevin Campbell hitting nine.

It means that whilst the intricate play and aesthetically pleasing build up from Wenger's men was far easier on the eye in comparison to Graham's team, they did not even the load in terms of goals. This is not a criticism, far from it. If you have a Thierry Henry and Pires in your team, then you must milk that cow for all it's worth. They were celestial beings born to change football.

This is just to highlight how close in all areas they were to a team that actually achieved what Graham's title winners came so close to doing.

In terms of being Invincible, the team of 1990/91 were a Steve Bould injury away, or an offside goal, from being the first. The stereotype of 'Boring Boring Arsenal' that stuck to George's team in 1991 was wholly undeserved. It was borne from defensive excellence and a string of clean sheets.

Speaking of defence, Graham's rigid and relentless training, and the formative years from 1987 onwards, saw his side concede a measly 18 goals all season, compared to Wenger's 26 conceded.

The Invincibles flew close to the wind on many occasions, none more so than when Ruud Van Nistelrooy smacked a late penalty against a still wobbling crossbar late in the game.

The same goes for the match against Portsmouth, when a dubious penalty was awarded which saved the Gunners skin. A hairs width lower from Van Nistelrooy's spot kick, or a referee who waved away Pires's pleas, and they would have had the same record as Graham's nearly men

Or would they? The Invincibles were no shirkers, and their mental strength was put under examination on many occasions, but who is to say that losing at Old Trafford or Fratton Park would not have derailed their impeccable record? The same goes for the side of 1990-91 of course, but then, this is all hypothetical.

It is written just to open up a thought process. To entertain the idea that it wasn't just The Invincibles that Gooners have to hold up as poster boys. The side that Graham assembled were just as complete across the pitch.

The fixture congestion that Graham had to wriggle around to give his boys a chance to recover. The refereeing decisions. The fact that his squad of nineteen players was far smaller than what Wenger had at his disposal (even if one of them was Pascal Cygan).

It just adds credence to what this book hopefully does for every one of you that bravely reads my meandering words.

The title winning side of 1990-91 was one of the greatest Arsenal - and England - has ever seen. The lack of a zero in the losses column - cruelly robbed from them by a shocking pitch, terrible match scheduling and some refereeing decisions that bordered on unlawful - has dimmed the light of adulation that they should be permanently placed under.

Even the media seemed to dismiss George's boys. Only David Seaman and Lee Dixon made it into the PFA Team of the Year. Mystifyingly, where was Golden Boot winner Smith? He was left out and in his stead, Mark Hughes and Ian Rush were the strikers for this select band of the finest the First Division supposedly had to offer. Even though both were outscored by the technically brilliant 'Smudge'.

When I spoke to Smith, he of course held no grudges as that is the mark of the man he is, but it is hard to swallow given they were clinically outperformed. He simply said to me calmly about the outrageous ignorance from the media; "There was no anti-Arsenal agenda, I can't recall any. Maybe it was a grudging respect."

What about the rest of the Arsenal back four? Nigel Winterburn and Steve Bould both played every single game of the league campaign. Who had been deemed to be the cream of the defensive crop in the First Division? Stuart Pearce and Mark Wright. That is correct, Mark Wright of relegated, bottom of the league Derby County.

The injustice does not stop there. Tony Adams was reviled by the media and after his brush with prison, he had been sullied as far as they were concerned. Arsenal's player of the year and inspirational captain was of course left out of the 'best of the best'.

Paul Davis and Michael Thomas, the engineers in the engine room, the architects of so many goals, and the gatekeepers that opposing attacks had to pass. They encompassed everything Arsenal did in that year. Where were they in not only the Team of the Year, but also in the England setup? Gordon Strachan and Gazza were given the slots instead.

That moment! Tony Adams lifts the Championship trophy with David Seaman after the 6-1 win against Coventry City

Limpar, twenty two year old Merson. They both terrorised defences and were a nightmare to pick up as they continually switched positions. Both also grabbed double figures in goals in the League. How could they be overlooked?

Seaman conceded just eighteen goals in thirty eight games. He was named in the PFA team of the year, but he had enjoyed such a wonderful campaign that if he were to be left out, it would have been a travesty. He had claimed twenty four clean sheets from thirty eight games! He was head and shoulders above his goalkeeping peers and would go on to chisel his name into the Marble Halls forever.

His future in the annals of the club were assured, but what of his team mates? What happened to each of his comrades that had given so much to the cause? The wages were ample at the time but far from enough to allow an easy life after they hung up their boots. What did they do once they left Highbury?

Seaman of course went on to become probably Arsenal's greatest ever keeper. Winning silverware regularly and making the transition into the Wenger era, Seaman left in 2003, for a final season at Manchester City.

He never managed to finish that season for City as injury culled his playing time, but on a return to Highbury with City, he earned a rapturous ovation from his Gooner fans. He earned seventy five England caps and he also cut his famous ponytail off for charity! The nickname of 'Safe Hands' was fully deserved.

Dixon also continued his career with Arsenal for quite some time, alongside Tony, Seaman, Steve Bould and Nigel Winterburn. The famous Back Five would not be split until Steve Bould left in 1999 to join Sunderland.

Winterburn was next to depart, in 2000 to West Ham United. Tony Adams would go on and retired at the club after winning the title yet again in 2002. Adams was a one-club man, but the whole group and their paths extolled the belief that once you find Arsenal, it doesn't let you go.

Davis had been at the club since 1980, and it was only due to declining fitness at thirty four years of age that Davis left Arsenal. He played for a short stint in Norway, before returning to England for a season - his last as a player - for Brentford. Arsenal lured him back in 1996 as a coach, and Davis stayed to lend his experience until 2003, when he was invited to become part of the PFA Coaching setup. Davis in 2005 then became Assistant Manager to Paul Gascoigne at Kettering Town. The tenure did not last, as two months later Gazza had left his post.

Davis was asked to stay on as he had impressed the clubs hierarchy, but he chose to return to the PFA coaching team. Davis had earned the highest set of coaching badges, and with his extensive knowledge of the game, he eventually joined the FA, where he continues to ply his coaching skills and his excellent work with anti-racism organisations, such as 'Kick It Out' and 'Show Racism the Red Card.'

Davis's midfield partner Thomas was lured to the very team who he had helped to dethrone. Thomas transferred to Liverpool in the summer of 91, staying at Anfield for seven years. He had a short loan spell at Middlesbrough in 1998, before being allowed to move to Benfica. His sojourn in Portugal lasted a

David O'Leary and Tony Adams celebrate in front of the Clock End

season, and the midfielder ended his playing career at Wimbledon in 2001. He received two caps for England, and in retirement he has set up a security firm in Liverpool.

Limpar left the club in acrimonious circumstances in 1994, to join Everton. His relationship with Graham had broken down and the result was a transfer to Goodison Park. He helped his new team win the FA Cup in 1995, but his stay was not long, eventually he joined Birmingham City in 1997, but the move was not prosperous. Just three months later he had left the Blues to return to his native Sweden. AIK was the club who had acquired his services and he helped them win the Allsvenskan in 1998. MLS side Colorado Rapids then signed Limpar for over a year before the pull of home became too strong. His last club was Djurgardens, although he did not manage an appearance. He had earned 58 caps for Sweden, and he has coached at Swedish second Division side Sollentuna United.

Merson enjoyed a longer stay than the title-winning Swede, leaving in 1997 for a longer contract at Middlesbrough. He had been offered a two year deal by Wenger, but the security of a better contract appealed to Merson. The extra years in the end were not needed, as he left Boro to join Aston Villa in 1998. where he spent four seasons before signing for Portsmouth in 2002. It was a short stint on the South Coast, as he moved down the leagues to aid Walsall as both a player and Manager in 2003. 2006 saw Merson see out his last season in the National Conference with Tamworth. He has since forged a career as a pundit on Sky Sports.

Smith scored a total of 115 goals and picked up just one solitary booking in his career, before retiring at Arsenal in 1995. He won thirteen caps for England and is now known to an entire generation as the voice of uber-popular video game franchise FIFA, and in his co-commentating capacity at Sky Sports.

Campbell enjoyed a fruitful career, with Arsenal at first, but with a host of others too. In 1995, he left Highbury for Nottingham Forest and stayed at the City Ground for three years. He departed for foreign shores, joining Trabzonspor in Turkey, but the club's chairman forced Campbell to leave after his racism reared its ugly head, directed at Campbell himself. Kevin's escape route was Everton in 1999, and his impact allowed the Toffees to escape relegation. His stay was long and he enjoyed a great relationship with the grateful fans for his endeavours and goals. In 2005, he left for West Bromwich Albion and immediately into another relegation dogfight. He again led the fight and they stayed up, but a move to Cardiff City in 2006 in the second tier occurred and this was his last club before retiring. He is also the player who has scored the most goals in the top flight without receiving a full England cap. He has run various companies – from a security firm to a record label – in his time since playing, and has also made appearances in front of the camera in a punditry capacity.

David 'Rocky' Rocastle left his adoring fans in 1992 after injuries had taken their toll. He went to Leeds United but injuries had left the talented player a shadow of what he was capable of. Manchester City signed Rocky a year later, and his amount of appearances improved, but Chelsea signed his services in 1994. The limbs were not as fresh as his heyday at Arsenal, but he managed 29 league games for the Blues, before he ended his career with short spells at Norwich and Hull. A move to Malaysian side Sabah was technically his last club, but he never turned out in their colours. David was capped fourteen times by England, but he was to suffer tragic news as he was diagnosed with non-Hodgkins Lymphoma and passed away on the 31st of March 2001. His mark was so profound at Arsenal that the fans and club now celebrate his life every year on the first of April - David Rocastle Day. Never forgotten Rocky, thank you on behalf of every Gooner.

Groves had been the willing winger who could run and run at defences. He left Arsenal soon after winning the League in 1991, joining Southampton and staying down South for two seasons. Groves had only made fifteen starts with the Saints in his two years at The Dell, scoring twice, before he retired from professional football after a serious problem with his achilles tendon. He did turn out four times for Conference side Dagenham and Redbridge, but his career effectively ended at the tender age of twenty eight. Post-football, his work in radio and TV punditry has been prolific, and in 2014 he showed his entrepreneurial skills by starting 'Play With a Legend,' which offers people the chance to play football with the idols of their childhood.

Hillier flourished at first in his career infancy at Arsenal, but left Highbury in 1996 to gain more first team opportunities at Portsmouth. He spent three years at Fratton Park, and after a loan spell at Bristol Rovers, signed for the Pirates

Almost Invincible Arsenal – the class of 1991

in 1999. Another three years passed before he picked his last club, Barnet. He retired in 2003 and tried his hand at management in the amateur ranks. He is now a fireman in Bristol, and is an occasional pundit for various channels.

Andy Linighan stayed at Arsenal until 1997, signing for Crystal Palace. A three year spell at Selhurst Park ended with a loan spell to QPR before signing permanently for Oxford United for one season. He ended his playing career at St Albans City, and he now runs his own plumbing firm.

Siggi Jonsson, the Icelandic midfielder, had his Arsenal career cruelly disrupted by injury, and left the club in 1992. He rejoined his former club Ia Akranes in Iceland for three years, until in 1995 he signed for Orebro SK in Sweden. His season in Sweden impressed and he was snapped up by Dundee United in 1997, enjoying three years in Scotland. His last season in 2000 was spent back at IA Akranes, and he achieved sixty five caps for his national side in his career. He has had an extensive managerial career in Scandinavia and Iceland, and is currently manager of Kari Akranes in his home country.

David O'Leary is still Arsenal's record appearance maker after playing for the Gunners for two decades. His last seasons as a player was at Leeds United in 1993-95. When his former gaffer George Graham became Leeds United boss in 1996, O'Leary was named as his Assistant. He remained at this post until 1998, when he was handed the reins himself. He took Leeds to a fourth placed finish in his time as Leeds manager, as well as the Champions League semi-finals, but financial difficulties at the club caused chaos, with club chairman Peter Ridsdale ending his tenure in 2002. He took the Aston Villa hotseat in 2002 and lasted until 2006. His last managerial job was with Saudi side Al-Ahli in 2010.

Colin Pates made one substitute appearance in the season this book refers to, and mid-season he went on loan to Brighton. The summer of 91 saw the move become permanent and he stayed at the seaside club for two years,

David Rocastle, with his wife Janet, and their daughter during the Arsenal Parade through Islington

before ending his career with non-league sides Crawley Town and Romford in 1997. He also took the manager's job at Crawley in 1995, but currently coaches football at a school in South London.

Andy Cole also made one solitary substitute appearance, before going on loan to Fulham. He moved to Bristol City in 1993, where his twenty goals attracted Newcastle United. He then hit his stride, scoring fifty five goals for the Toon in just seventy appearances. He was controversially sold to Manchester United in 1995, and in his six years at Old Trafford, Cole won everything possible, scoring ninety three goals in the process. Cole left in 2001, and subsequently played for Fulham, Manchester City, Portsmouth and Birmingham City. His last appearance was for Sunderland in 2008, before retirement beckoned. It is safe to say we maybe should have shown a little more patience with Cole! He has since dabbled with coaching and has done much charity work in Africa.

Graham wasn't finished at Arsenal, but this title was perhaps his finest hour. He won a cup double in 1993 and then achieved an unlikely UEFA Cup-Winners Cup win in 1994 – only the club's second European trophy. His Gunners ties ended acrimoniously, but he carried on in the managerial world, with two years at Elland Road. A move which may have sullied his reputation at the club amongst the Gooner faithful was his decision to take the manager's job at North London rivals Tottenham. He stayed for three seasons at White Hart Lane, winning the League Cup in 1999. He was dismissed in 2001 and has had sporadic work in front of the TV cameras since. His golf handicap has no doubt improved as well!

Assistant to George, Stewart Houston actually had the manager's job at Highbury in a caretaker capacity. He decided to manage QPR in 1996, but he didn't last long. He was sacked in 1997, and was offered a position as first team coach at Ipswich Town where he stayed until 1999, when he reunited with George at Tottenham. He has also worked as a scout for Arsenal since leaving Spurs.

The men mentioned above all played their part in the title win. They all added something to the melting pot which produced a season in which the side lost just one game.

Do these men compare to The Invincibles? Can we hold these 'Almost-Invincibles' up as examples on the highest pedestal as a team which were intertwined with winning? It is perhaps fitting that the last words of this book should go to Amy Lawrence; "I will always remember the expression on George Graham's face when he gazed at a framed copy of the league table from 1990-91 that adorned the wall of his study. The 'lost one' seemed to rankle a little bit. This was a few years after that championship, and a good few more before Arsenal managed that feat of going a whole league campaign unbeaten."

"Like Wenger, the perfectionist streak in Graham held the idea of going a season without defeat in the highest esteem, as an extra attainment. To most - players, fans, pundits, managers, whoever - just winning a title is enough. The be all and end all. But Graham came close enough to appreciate just what it was to add extra historic resonance to the joy of being crowned as the season's best. Lost one... And he knew that bad luck played a part in that one as well. Would Arsenal have lost at Chelsea in 1990-91 had the famous back four not been so badly disrupted? He would have good reason to doubt that. Without wishing to draw comparisons between different eras, different players, different styles, the aspect that binds the 1990-91 team to the 2003-04 Invincibles is a tangible sense that the squad would give everything to avoid being beaten. They were teams who played fearlessly, based on a resilience and a team spirit that meant anyone who could absorb a defeat casually would not be tolerated in their dressing room. That is not a bad foundation - one that any title-winning team should be proud of."

Would Football Be The Same?

It is all well and good hearing just one opinion on a matter, but on a subject as contentious as football - and hypothetical football at that - the rule of the pub applies strongly. When a conversation manifests itself amongst friends, one view alone is blinkered. A multi-faceted beauty such as football requires a variety of different standing points, otherwise all will be at risk of missing out or even worse, getting it completely wrong.

By now, you should all know my view on whether the Arsenal side constructed by George Graham in 1991 had the capability of going unbeaten throughout the season. The many variables which affected this incredible team during the season did more than attempt to sidetrack them, and the sole loss should never have occurred. But what would Arsenal be like today had it happened?

The Invincibles, crafted by Arsene Wenger almost thirteen years later, is still talked about in revered tones by experts - and rightfully so. They didn't just win games, they left an indelible mark of panache on each opponent.

So, if it had happened thirteen years beforehand, would the achievement, and the team, be put up on a pedestal like the 2003/04 Champions?

Would Graham be given a job for life? Would it have sent fear through the chasing pack and left Graham's Gunners to cut a swathe through the First Division and later, the Premier League?

It is impossible to say. Just look at what happened to Wenger's incarnation once they achieved footballing immortality. The team broke up over the next two years, leaving only a few players to fight on in the face of tightening belts and stark realism.

It is a momentous accolade to have earned. To battle through an entire campaign without incurring defeat does send shockwaves through the sport. Arsenal are now famous for that side, but the fanbase is much larger than it was in 1990/91. Would this achievement have received as many plaudits with a smaller audience?

The Premier League has changed inexorably in recent years, but the Premier League itself changed football from the moment of its inception, the 1992/93 season.

Ultimately, it is down to every single fan and how they perceive it. In my mind, what George and his boys achieved is as near as you can get to matching the Invincibles. They swatted teams aside with a potent blend of power and incisive skill, just like Wenger's men. Enough of my own views though.

I have assembled some level-minded and well-informed Gooners to share what impact they think Graham's 'Almost Invincibles' would have had on the sport, or even if they think they could have managed it.

Think of it like an Arsenal Think-Tank of sorts. Much like the pub analogy I used earlier, this varied spread of stances will give you the perfect opportunity to come to a conclusion yourself.

How would Arsenal - and football in general - have changed if George Graham's side had gone unbeaten in 1990-91?

Well, Geoff Hollefreund is of the opinion that Graham's side deserves a little more respect, even if they didn't quite manage the unthinkable. Geoff has been supporting Arsenal since the mid 80's. He has blogged for Arsenal sites 'A Bergkamp Wonderland and Smrteta.com and can be found on Twitter at @ Hollefreund. Here is what he had to say on the matter.

In today's frenetic and sanitized Premier League, it is a daunting task to look back at the period before all of this came to be. The current Arsenal is vastly unrecognizable from the team that nearly were Invincible in the 1990/91 season; from players to pitch, just about everything about the club is different.

The wheels of change had already been set in motion for a major change to the League by the time Arsenal lifted the title in May of 1991. The Taylor Report on all-seater stadiums had been delivered and the vast untapped marketability of the English League was already being explored by the top flight clubs at the time.

Perhaps the biggest advantage to an unbeaten Arsenal would have been more keenly felt off the pitch. A case for right place, right time could be made for an Invincible team as the Premier League marketing executives looked for a compelling story to expand the reaches of the newly begotten league to the farthest corners of the globe.

As it happened, it was Manchester United, leveraging their 1991 European Cup Winners Cup win, which became the golden boys for the new and flash Premier League. United successfully transitioned that success into both on field success as well as off field marketing opportunities; a position that has elevated the club to one of the richest in the world today.

Could Arsenal have been that team? Certainly the Invincible moniker would have opened the door to greater revenue, but additional funds are only one part of the picture for any successful club. True success can only be characterised by trophies when it comes to football.

In that sense, Arsenal may have been able to springboard the additional confidence of an unbeaten season into the 1991/92 campaign to greater effect; but even that may have been negligible. After all, we are discussing the League Champions, not a team that finished a distant fourth. If, however, it had been enough to overcome a third round loss to Wrexham in the F.A. Cup that season, I'd take it.

Gooners singing their hearts out for the lads during the parade

For the players, the feather in the cap of an unbeaten season would have stuck with them for life. I often find that the exploits of our 1990/91 team are criminally under-appreciated. To be deducted points and lose the greatest ever Arsenal captain in Tony Adams for four months, and still win the League while losing only one game, is one of the most remarkable achievements in the modern game.

As for George Graham, the water is muddied in terms of his place in the club's history. His eventual acrimonious dismissal in 1995 and subsequent management of bitter rivals Tottenham, only serve as distractions from the fact he won six trophies in eight years at Arsenal.

On the field, Graham was one of Arsenal's greatest ever managers, and perhaps going one better in 1990/91 would have been enough to overcome the controversy of his departure. The feat of that team, and the success he brought to the playing side of Arsenal, would have certainly been undisputed.

There is a romance connected to the term Invincible; strong, resilient and emphatic - much like the qualities of the 1990/91 side. It would be a term that would characterize so much about that squad and its manager and would have served as a beacon for future generations of Gooners to look back on with greater understanding of just how good that team truly was. As it stands, there is a tiny asterisk next to the 1990/91 title; a blemish on the face of a remarkable season that deserves a much higher status in the memory of Arsenal Football Club and those that support it.

Amongst the opinions I've collected, the next is the most personal. Linus Morris is the man behind Arsenal site www.arsenalvision.co.uk. He can be found on Twitter at @ArsenalVision and he remembers the season fondly indeed.

I was a little late to that famous campaign unfortunately. My earliest memories of football began at Tufnell Park Primary School, I didn't know much about the game but wanted to join in the Panini sticker swapping craze at school, so I adopted Liverpool as my team of choice as they were the dominant force in England at the time. It would be a few years later that I would see sense when I looked at football beyond football stickers.

I had made my first trip to Highbury as a 14 year old kid on a sunny day in 1992, a 4-1 thumping of Crystal Palace had me well and truly hooked. We were not lucky enough to have the internet in the nineties so I had to digest as many video tapes as possible. Luckily my friends had been collecting the season reviews years earlier.

We had all watched them so many times that we knew almost the entire commentary throughout all the videos from 1988-89 to 1991-92. We would then repeat those phrases back on the pitch when one of us would recreate a moment from a match.

The 1990/91 title winning season was a firm favourite of ours and one that would have had the most plays I'm sure. I can remember vividly being frustrated about that one defeat at Stamford Bridge in the league. Almost every time I watched it, I would kick myself and ask why didn't we just snatch a point? We would have gone the entire league season unbeaten and surely that chance wouldn't present itself again, or so I thought.

We had beaten Chelsea convincingly 4-1 at Highbury earlier on in the season, Anders Limpar, my all time favourite Arsenal player, tore the West Londoners to shreds that afternoon.

On the 2nd February 1991 the tables had been turned. The Gunners had played a difficult Cup replay against Leeds United at Elland Road only three days earlier while Chelsea had a full week to prepare for this game, so perhaps fatigue played its part.

Graham Stuart, who was deputising for Gordon Durie, scored the opener. Every time I watched the highlights, I kept hoping that Nigel Winterburn would head the ball out instead of in the direction of the Chelsea forward, even though I knew what was coming. The second Chelsea goal came after yet another full back error, this time it was Lee Dixon's misplaced pass that Chelsea capitalised on.

Our defending, for once, was a shambles and Kerry Dixon was on hand to tap past David Seaman from close range. Alan Smith's goal in stoppage time only added to my frustration, as another late goal would have resulted in the unthinkable.

If Graham had gone the entire league season without defeat, I'm not sure we would have witnessed the same hype as Arsène's team years later, partly down to the arrival of Sky Sports. In many ways I think the Chelsea defeat back in 1991 may have impacted the Arsène Wenger of the future more than it would have done Graham, in the sense that going unbeaten wouldn't have been quite the unique achievement in 2003/04.

It would have been a huge personal achievement for Graham, no doubt about it, but I'm not sure his path would have been any different either way.

Even with the blue stain on our title 90/91 triumph, that season and those around it will always be fondly remembered by myself and many Gooners of that generation."

Those halcyon days Linus described as he first became enthralled with football, intertwined with this special season, so his recollections on what could've been are tinged with sepia tones and memories of childhood. It means he'll never forget that year. The next person on the rollcall is a certain Daniel Cowan. Daniel runs both www.Goonersphere.com and www.NorthLondonIsRed.com, and is on Twitter @theDanielCowan. When I asked him to offer his views on the subject, Daniel preferred to go down the scientific route.

Arsenal's undefeated campaign of 2003/04 undeniably changed the face of English football as much as the introduction of continental management, coaching and preparation that came with Arsène Wenger in 1996. How different then would English football look had, a mere 13 years earlier, George Graham's charges achieved the same feat as their immortalised successors?

Would Arsenal have gone to win nine major trophies under Arsène Wenger? Would Arsène ever have joined the club his name seemed to have destined him to manage for over 20 years?

Would George Graham's legacy at Arsenal remain unsullied for all time? The premise poses interesting questions.

The ignominious departure of Graham from Arsenal, fuelled in part by inexplicable avarice and stupidity, seemed on the cards for a couple of seasons before his exit. A certain David Dein had grand plans for his beloved club and it was believed that George's philosophy jarred with those plans. His fate was sealed by the vision of Dein who wanted to create a dynasty for the Gunners. Would an undefeated title win have saved him from that fate? I believe not. Perhaps the executioner's blade may have been stayed, but only for a while. As long as Dein remained at the club, George's departure was inevitable.

Graham always insisted the affair was a misunderstanding yet reimbursing the Club with interest instead of returning the payments to Rune Hauge did not logically follow the protestations of innocent naivety. In an alternate version of history though, could an undefeated season have saved Stroller's Arsenal career and legacy? Perhaps the prestige of such an achievement would have seen him command such a contract that illicit payments – solicited or not –would never have had the chance to even be a consideration. For what interest could Pal Lydersen or John Jensen hold to an unbeatable team?

In that reality, perhaps Graham would have survived the designs of Dein and his schemes to bring the professorial talents of Wenger to Arsenal. Or perhaps he would simply have left of his own accord or moved upstairs. Certainly his legacy would have seemed far less dispensable. Arsène Wenger enjoys patience and trust unequalled to any manager in the league and much of this is owed to that immortal season.

Then there is the question of Arsenal's dominance under Graham. Would the pressure of defending an unbeaten title have spurred them on to win further league titles? Would the attraction of playing for invincible champions have seen Arsenal bolster their ranks with the cream from the continent? Would that have killed the chase for Crystal Palace's Ian Wright? How different would history look without the goals of the man so good we named him thrice?

In chaos theory, the butterfly effect suggests that small changes to the initial condition of a deterministic nonlinear system can result in large changes in later conditions. For Arsenal, not losing to Chelsea in February 1991 could have resulted in George Graham staying as manager and Arsenal's history books not featuring Wenger's nine trophies, the talents of Messrs Bergkamp, Henry, Pires, Vieira et al, or the creation of the Emirates Stadium.

There is much Arsenal supporters would love to change about Arsenal's history, but the results of those changes could be worse than our current reality. Perhaps, then, it is best that Arsenal's 1990/91 squad remain 'Almost Invincible.'

An excellent and informed view from Daniel. Perhaps it was for the best that it didn't happen in 1990/91 after all? Well, hold your horses before you decide, I've lined up some more Gooner minds that may sway your decision.

David Faber blogs as @TheGoonerholic and his site can be located here - www.goonerholic.com. David has taken a different stance to others, and laments the break up of this incredible team. Would it have been different had they just won that one match against Chelsea?

I remember being asked how Arsenal, and the English top flight, would be different had Arsenal achieved the 'invincibles' tag in 1990/91. It would be tempting, but lazy, to point out the deterioration in Arsenal's fortunes after they finally did complete an undefeated Premier League season thirteen years later. However, the circumstances the club faced in the wake of that triumph included the not inconsiderable upheaval created by the move from Highbury to their vast new home at Ashburton Grove.

George Graham's impressive champions were not an ageing side and there was a feeling among the supporters then, that having dethroned Liverpool twice in three seasons, we had established a platform to dominate English football and impress in Europe for the foreseeable future.

Arsenal were the first English club to compete in the European Cup following the five-year ban imposed after the Heysel disaster. Graham was looking forward to pitting his wits against the top coaches in Europe and, with the benefit of hindsight, we might have been distracted by our involvement in the competition.

A team that had fallen at just one hurdle months earlier managed to lose three of the first eight league fixtures prior to trouncing Austria Wien 6-1 at Highbury in the first round of the European Cup.

The second round provided a jolt for Graham and his team. Benfica were held to a 1-1 draw in the Estádio da Luz and expected to take full advantage of that away goal in the second leg. Sven-Goran Eriksson, by Graham's own admission in his 1995 book 'The Glory and the Grief', out-manoeuvred the Scot. At Highbury his team produced a wonderful performance to end the Gunners European dream, coming from behind to win 3-1 after extra-time.

Graham had already altered the Gunners attacking focus with the September acquisition of Ian Wright. Jimmy Carter arrived from Liverpool the following month as Graham's relationship with Anders Limpar started to deteriorate.

Following the Benfica debacle, Graham then signed Norwegian full-back Pål Lydersen. Most surprising of all was the sale of Michael Thomas to Liverpool in December, followed by that of David Rocastle to Leeds United at the end of the season.

It is hard to argue that any of this would have been different had we avoided defeat at Chelsea in February 1991. The significance of the defeat to Benfica was to have an impact on Graham. It kick-started a change in his

George Graham, Tony Adams and a sea of Gooners
by the Hare and Hounds pub on Upper Street

approach to the game and he reconstructed Arsenal as a more pragmatic side in style.

David Hillier, not the stylish Paul Davis, replaced Thomas. John Jensen arrived to replace Rocky Rocastle. Arsenal turned from exciting champions into a dour, but successful, cup side, landing the domestic cup double in 1993 and the European Cup-Winners Cup against holders Parma a year later.

The top flight itself was shaped by the arrival of the Premier League, put together with the full support of Arsenal, and David Dein in particular. From the initial breakaway meetings in the summer of 1991 it took just a year to sign the lucrative new television deals and establish a new 20 club format away from the umbrella of the Football League.

Arsenal's sun was to set for a few years, until the arrival of a bespectacled football professeur.

David's offering has highlighted another shared factor between the 90/91 team and the Invincibles. Both teams disintegrated rather rapidly, and this would have happened whether the unbeaten campaign had been achieved, or not.

Jeanne Francis is firmly in the opinion that George Graham's team would not have been able to go on and complete this feat. Jeanne is the COO for the Atlanta Gooners branch of fans in the US, and can be found on Twitter @KittyGlitter. Jeanne is of the opinion that George's managerial methods were the reason why it simply wasn't possible.

When Dan asked me, "Could the Invincibles have happened under George?" without the slightest pause my brain responded, "Absolutely not, are you mad?" My DNA-level response is there is no way George could have gotten that performance from those players, but not because he was a poor manager.

Consider some history: 1995 was the cusp of individual-management, not just in football, but also in human performance development overall. Every sport and industry was seeing a shift from Management by Fear to Management by Personal Investment. If you're my age, you may remember a sudden burst of "Team Culture" in your workplace.

New generations of players brought the need for the game to evolve. To borrow a phrase we've heard often in the 16/17 season, it was time for change. George was the classic style of manager that was common of the day: technical structure, one-size fits all, carrot or stick.

Fear had become such a limited way to manage. After a time, one builds a callus at the back of the knee from that stick every week. When they no longer feel it, what's left to use for motivation? In motivating the individual through validation, they feel trusted and prepared. Feeling protected and understanding their role as part of the team, they'll take risks and responsibility. Players have a sense of ownership in both the play and the win. They self-motivate. It's impossible to accomplish if you fear losing influence by deferring to the individual, which is how George and others of earlier eras were forged.

We saw the evolution from other managers and it proved successful. Sir Alex built a culture at United where the players were invested in what they were fighting for every week. Terry Venables focused on getting the best out of the individual in order to get the best of out his England squad. The stage was set for the innovations of Wenger. He created an environment where the players were learning from each other, creating cohesion and partnership, which has continually been The Arsenal's secret weapon.

That is what made the Invincibles possible. They were a literal interpretation, the physical embodiment of Victoria Concordia Crescit. I do not believe George would, or could, have ever evolved that far. He was not built for this era.

There are so many facets that make a great manager. In 2017, we're at a time where again the game is changing. Men like Klopp, Pochettino, and Conte are the innovators displaying the next phase: Man Management + Enforcement = Responsive Tactics driven by Personal Investment. Men in new positions. Using fear when it's effective. Building a culture of loyalty and work ethic. A mélange of the past's Structure with the Individualism of today. (#WhyNotBoth)

When we consider greatness, context is crucial as greatness is not a static measure. Something I dearly love about our history is the many shades and hues of greatness, from brilliant champions to tenacious underdogs and back again through the years. Onward, Arsenal."

An intriguing offering from Jeanne, and the managerial approaches from both Graham and Wenger truly couldn't be more different.

The last opinion is in contrast to the previous one. Kris Carpenter thinks that the 90/91 'Almost Invincible' team may well be responsible for what happened thirteen seasons later. Kris is a Ligue Un aficionado. He is part of the 'A Bergkamp Wonderland' podcast group and is host and founder of the Football-Hipster podcast. Find him on Twitter @AFCFreddie8.

The Arsenal vintage of 90/91, Champions, played 38, won 24, drew 13, lost 1... But ask yourself this question, what if? What if that one blemish, a 2-1 defeat to Chelsea at Stamford Bridge had not have happened, just how different would the future have been?

The truth is we will never know, but it does pose the question would we have seen Arsene Wenger's reign? Would George Graham have been given the freedom of Highbury and a longer run as Manager, not withstanding his later indiscretions? Would the class of 2004 have happened sooner or even at all? Could English Football have taken a completely different path even? So many variables and different opinions could be offered, my take is this.

The squad Graham was able to utilise during this incredible season was largely built on the triumph of Anfield 89.' Adams, Bould, Merson, Davis, Smith, Seaman etc were winners, they were instilled as such by a driven, focused and relentless Scotsman, this planted the seed for what would follow some five years later under Arsene Wenger, a talented yet largely under rated group of players with one common goal, success! Something The Frenchman would take on to an even greater level in 2004. Graham's winning mentality was etched in the Marble Halls from that day forth and would shape the club for the next 20 plus years, but it is with a heavy heart that I say this, the GG era was simply not at the level on the eye of Wenger's future Invincibles.

So what would have transpired if the 90/91 side had gone a season unbeaten? Hard to say, the cup double in 92/93, as well as a Cup Winners Cup triumph in 1994, would be Graham's last trophies as Manager, suffering eight losses and a fourth place finish the following season would lend itself to suggest the 90/91 success was a shot in a million, but equally not something you would expect to see again, nor did it change the face of English Football - but did it shape what was to come in terms of Arsenal adapting a new style, a continental style, a Wenger style...

I fully appreciate those who say the Graham Arsenal was the glory days to follow the club, especially those from that generation looking back, but myself, as a child of the early 80's, my feeling is the side built in 90/91, that went so close to doing the seemingly impossible, only galvanised the club in cementing immortality in English Football with what was to come in 2004. The club knew that, to build on the success of The Scotsman, they had to make the next step both on and off the pitch, European competition was giving a rebirth to attacking, open and entertaining football - sponsorship

> was pumping big money into the game, stadiums were getting bigger... Arsenal had to move forwards, retain the drive for success the class of 91 created and be THE team, the world was talking about - enter The Invincibles....
>
> Here's to you George, Arsene. The Club and us fans will always remember where the dream of being unbeatable began..."

A wide range of opinions that should illuminate you enough to decide for yourself. Would Arsenal be any different had they managed to become Invincible under Graham?

Once you have mulled this poser over for a while, I've got another question. Which team do YOU think had to overcome more? Are both on an even keel after all? After reading this book, I hope you can find an answer a little easier. Send your answers to @JokmanAFC #AlmostInvincible.

Acknowledgements

I'd like to make one thing abundantly clear, the pages you have in your hand would not have been written without the help of the people I am now going to mention. The most important person I reserve for first mention is my wife Jo. You see, she would dearly love for me to be the typical man and utilise my DIY skills so the house we have purchased doesn't resemble a 'before' picture on a DIY show on early morning television.

The problem is that I have zero skills pertaining to home improvements. I have only recently learned how to rewire a plug (wait a minute, the brown wire is earth right?) and seeing as our 'house' needs new walls, floors, wallpaper, and someone from the original Jurassic Park film to see to our overrun garden, she would do well to find a replacement for me.

Instead, she has gritted her teeth and allowed me to waste valuable time and write a book about the one subject that she couldn't be more sick of hearing about. She has shown incredible patience with me. She has also ensured that my notorious lack of a spine has not conspired to see me quit this often laborious project. It has taken six months to write, and anything that takes longer than three seconds I usually abandon. She has not let me do that. She knows me inside and out and thus, is aware that my dream has been to write a book (I've always wanted to eat an eighteen egg cheese omelette as well, but she won't let me do that). So thank you Jo, you really are my everything.

Next up is my mum. I've always been a dreamer. Instead of grafting in the many jobs I've had and hated, I have opted to keep my head in the clouds and escape by daydreaming and thinking the unreachable are within my grasp. Most told me off for not being realistic, but my mum Irene has always made sure I don't lose sight of what I've always wanted to do. She made me aware that real life grinds the best of us down, so it is important to dream a little. The confidence she has given me has seen me through to the finish line. So if you hate the book, you have my mum to thank for your wasted hours! Thanks mum!

A really vital part of the research hails from the players themselves. I can only firstly apologise to them for pestering / stalking them for prolonged amounts of time so I could wear them down by asking them repeatedly for their precious time. The ex-Gunners who are contained in these pages obviously took pity on this particular fanboy, and they so graciously let me peer behind the veil that fans don't often get the chance to do.

Alan Smith, you were a delight. The foreword was quite excellent, and every time you responded to me, it was a real pleasure. I will always remain a huge fan of yours so the fact that I've met you and spoken to you has been a personal highlight.

Lee Dixon, Nigel Winterburn, David Seaman and David Hillier, the time you gave up to help me has helped inexorably. I know that my name must be subconsciously tied to negative thoughts by now as message after message has plagued your phone, but just know that this Gooner is overjoyed that you have spoken to me and helped this book hopefully become that little bit better. Also, thanks for not taking out that restraining order.

Bob Wilson, the reputation you have as a gentleman within Arsenal ranks is well deserved. What great insights you gave, I could have listened to you all day. You have my utmost gratitude.

Amy Lawrence, I have been reading your work for a few years now, as I want to improve my own writing and why look anywhere other than the best examples? The morning you consented to an interview in a North London cafe blew my mind with your extensive knowledge. Keep up the excellent work and I hope to one day meet you again so I can wrack your grey matter again.

Geoff Hollefreund, you were the brave soul who agreed to look over my words and let me know in no uncertain terms if I have made a real mess. Your attention for detail and your ability to tell me the truth without crushing my confidence is very much appreciated! Thank you Sir!

My Dad Charlie and my brother Paul deserve a special mention. Despite my father having zero amount of enthusiasm for anything at all in the world, he has shown remarkable interest toward my project. He has even shown belief I can actually see this through to the end, even though he is of the opinion I can't complete a colouring book (to be fair to him, I am utterly useless).

My brother Paul came to my rescue when I was continuing my research for the book and there were moments in the season I could not dig up from the internet, the library or my network of great people on social networks. Paul had the answer in the back of the garage. He still had his VHS copy of the 1990-91 Arsenal season. Lifesaver. Cheers Bro!

James Durose Rayner. You have shared, supported and enjoyed my articles prolifically. You have also given me a cause and confidence I didn't have before. I've loved the books you have written and they inspired me to do the same. You have even employed me to write too! You are a treasured friend and a great motivator, thank you.

Les Crang, you've been a fountain of knowledge I have supped at regularly and more pertinently - you've supplied a library of books. You've helped this book hopefully avoid being a meandering mess and at least be well-informed. You're a true pal.

I have been writing an Arsenal-based blog for about four years now - www.upthearsenal.com if you are so inclined - and the support I have received from the people on Twitter has kept me tapping away at the keyboard. I've met some amazing people thanks to Twitter, and they deserve a mention on here. I wouldn't have believed I could write a book without the lovely stuff you have said about my articles, so a huge Gracias to; @jasondavies71 @apnelson1 @raygfox @anarsenalchap @Steve1886 @kaltume_b @TheGunnersPub @morethanagame66 @Arselona @Gooner_In_BCN @Yoii @Kittyglitter @Dfresh10 @tjaffry @AFCfreddie8 @ColonialCannon @TheGoonerTalkTV @boyd_d1 @AnuNande @Gooner-

Girl1969 @GunnerFaithful @catyeboah @Garythegooner56 @TheGoonerholic @DarrenArsenal1 @TheN5Library @LePhantomMenace @TheRealGunner @ The_Tsar_Cannon @Dinklage_Afc @fazjac_debra @SuburbanGooner @The-GunnersPub @PieburyCorner @CojaboBerlin @RoyalArsenalMRA @KYJB87 @ kmwood02 @TheGoonerette @SweetAFCJane @Boblex @ScottyBoyGooner @ ExpatGoonah @Highbury_74 @timjbharg @The_GFP @EvaMcL3 - If you are on Twitter, you could do a lot worse than follow these peeps. Thank you to you all. There are many more to mention, but a huge list of Twitter names does not make for interesting reading.

Speaking of social networks, there are five people who have annoyed me so much that I have often envisioned grievous harm upon them. On the other hand, I consider them very dear friends and together we form @GoonerspherePod - by far the best Arsenal-based podcast in the land. Daniel Cowan and James Raul Stokes are the men behind this assault on your ears, and the day they invited me to become a part of the podcast was perhaps the worst mistake they've made. Daniel - @thedanielcowan and James - @JamesRaulStokes are both bloggers as well and their advice, their constant jibing about my oversized head and penchant for gravy have kept me going when I have struggled. Mike - @GreeneBantern Sim - @SimplyEnigmatic and Devon - @Devon4Real you guys suck, but have been invaluable. Keep up the humourous and annoying work.

Thank you also to the many people who bridged the gap and allowed me contact with my Arsenal heroes. You know who you are.

Luke James, you not only have fixed my awful house, but you allowed me to meet Gentleman Bob Wilson. You are quite clearly, if I am using youth vernacular correctly, 'da man.'

I was not a fan of the club, or even football in general, when we won the title in 1990-91. I was an eight-year-old kid who was far more interested in climbing trees and eating copious amounts of sugar. Since becoming a Gooner in 1996, every bit I have learned about the club I love dearly has shown me that Arsenal has a history that no other club can boast of. I knew already we had won the title, but the more I learned of this amazing season when researching it, the more I became infatuated with it.

As fans, we are always seeking new ways to best our rivals fans. Chelsea have won the Champions League, United won the treble etc. We use these accolades to lord it over the other. I believe the season of 1990-91 is another arrow to Gooners quivers. It was an incredible year and a record that stands up to scrutiny.

There will be nuggets of info that may open your eyes to how difficult it was to achieve.

All I can wish for is that you really enjoy the words I have written, and that you end up sharing the same affection for this remarkable team and feat that I do.

Word to your respective guardians.

Dan Betts
@JokmanAFC

Arsenal Fans Roll Of Honour

Stefan Leverton
Dave Seager
Joshua Stanley
David Bloomfield
Emma Hayes
Warren Benson
Andy Selby
Philip Decatris
Tony Daisley
Stephen Cooper
Arif Azim – Pakistan Supports' Club
Darren Palfrey
David Watkins
Martin Weekley
Sachin Sapat
Jon Gibbs
Scott Joseph Bellamy Nimmons
Shane O'Driscoll
Robin Sargent
Matt Griggs
Peter McGarry
Steve Kell
Geoffrey Barratt
Anthony Kendall
Jill Brown
Shonelle D'Nailz
Theo Valaydon-Pyke
Karen Pond
Michael Williams
Phil Malcolm
Thomas Walker
Bradford Miller
David Sells
Jimmy Stevens
Keith D Henderson
Andy Barnes
Aasheesh Bailoor
Paul Heaton
David Corke
Michael Salmon
Clive Livermore
Daniel Bissett
Douglas Kerrigan
Lee Robertson
Tom Wragg
Liam Bush
Joe Kelly
Gerard Kelly
Robert Cope
James Light
Stephen Beynon
David Esteves
Stig Michelsen
John Abbott
Web Expression
Linus Morris
Stelios Stilianou
Joanna Denham
Marvin Berglas
Chris Grove
Kunal Patel
Sydney Roberts
Bryan Anderson
Sunil Patel
Bryan Anderson
Tony Sharpstone
Davy Boyd
Jake Casey
Jeanne Francis
Michael Flood
Andy Barnes
Michael Peters
Jeff Sutherland
Jens Bellmann
Drew Dawson
Edward Bawtree
Danny Rose
Martin Levy
Alan Knight
Stephen Randall
Liam Kennedy
Aasheesh Bailoor
Jeremy Coker
Glyn Taylor
Becky Toomey
Simon Barham
Ian Gordon
Peter Styles
Stephen Shaw
Karen Chatterley
Aisling Gervin
Kevin Heatherington
Mark Rayner
Pål Louis Yarra
Andy Mitchell
Gary Lawrence
Graham Goodhew
Nick Goodhew
John Best
Robert Wheeler
Philip Cook
Nigel Shaw
Paul Bezant
Brian Phillips
Geoffrey Hollefreund
Frances Johnson
Frode Hagen
Joshua Sng
Michael Rusling
Lee Armitt
Mark Crawley
Antony Smith
Mark Brindle
Stephen Conroy
Mark Horner
Lucas Pinks
Paul Bunce
M Rose
Clive Needham
John Ratcliffe
Patricia Cleary
David Wallis
John Moody
John Culleton
Jonathan Cousens
Sydney Roberts
Tony Link
John Justice
Vip Mair
Liza Marchant
Ilhan Mazlum
Derek Reader
Todd Grange
Robert Taylor
Austin Winch-Furness
Leonard Goodyear
Julia Morrow
Pervinder Johal
Chris Davies
Paul Antino
Shaun Murray
Gavin Moore
Andreas Jalstrand
Frank Stubbs
Stephen Steer-Smith
Simon Roome
Martin Redford
John Tester
Patrik Strandberg
Joanne Tester
Rob Martin
Doug Farfaglia
Matthew Wallace
Roberto Puzzi
Arron Moon
Paul Bezant
Terry Moy
Danny Sweetman
Christopher Smith
Nick Whitehead
David Clark
Steve Martin
Paul Heaton
Elliott Hurst
Neil Benwell
Simon Hill
Brendan Delaney
Peter Gregory
Michael Deasy
Ian Fassl
Darren Bennett
Raj Thaker
James Stokes
Peter Copsey
Paul Beaman
Annie Nelson
Michael Deasy
Craig Paxton
John Collins
Jonathan Brooks
Marcus Evans
William Estes
Ivan Medak
Leslie Crang
Catherine Yeboah
Mark Wilcox
Demetrios Savva
Daniel Burrows
Ken Helie
Adam Whyte
Danny Ruch
Mark Ingram
Daniel Burrows
Daniel Cowan
Stephen Pavelin
Richard Mulvaney
Alan Thompsett
Victoria Scott
Lucy Grattan
Una Hoyle

FLIRTING WITH FIRE

PIPER RAYNE

Cover Photo: Wander Aguiar Photography

Cover Design: RBA Designs

Line Editor: Gray Ink Editing

Proofreader: Shawna Gavas, Behind The Writer

Everyone knows that if you play with fire you'll end up getting burned...

What happens when you attend a first responder's bachelor auction with your best friends? Well, if your name is Madison Kelly like me, your friends end up bidding on a date for you with your high school crush.

That's right. Even back when I was 'Fatty Maddie' to all my classmates, I had eyes for the quarterback of our football team. Not like I was the only one.

Mauro Bianco may fight fires for a living, but he still sets my heart ablaze. One look at the rugged, muscular man he's turned into and I want to slide down his pole.

One date. That's all I'm committed to. A few hours and I can tuck him back into that tattered old shoebox in my closet.

As always, the universe has other plans. I never would've predicted that in a matter of days he'd turn from my dream guy into my business partner-***and that's when things got interesting.***

Flirting WITH FIRE

xo,

Piper

&

Rayne

PROLOGUE

Nine years ago...Highschool—AKA Hell

Madison

"I don't want to go," I whine for the hundredth time tonight.

"Get out of the car." Lauren stands on the driver's side of my dad's beat up Wrangler that he gave me last week for my sixteenth birthday.

I push up my glasses. "It's a *senior* party. I'll let you pick the movie if we can please go back to my house. I'll even let you sneak into my dad's liquor cabinet."

Since this is my dad's weekend, I get a tad more freedom with the newfound single life he's embracing. It's meant either late night or early morning arrivals back home depending on how easy the women are.

Lauren grabs my hand, yanking me out of the truck. "I'm not sitting around watching some dumbass romantic comedy again."

I stumble out, my feet landing right in a puddle. My white

trainers are now caked with brown mud. "Great. My mom's going to kill me."

"It's fine." Lauren looks cool as usual. Lucky for her, the style of baggy pants and t-shirts are in, although she's sported the same look since we were in kindergarten. Tonight, when her mom dropped her off, I knew there was trouble on the agenda when I noticed she had on a sheer layer of lip gloss.

"Says you, who won't be spending the next couple hours with her soaked socks squishing in her shoes."

She rolls her eyes. "If you would have let me dress you," she singsongs.

"Yeah, well my stomach doesn't look like that in a tight t-shirt." I point to her lean waist. "My back fat would be squeezing out the sides."

Lauren and I have been friends forever, but we're completely different. After school, Lauren's day is filled with soccer, softball or volleyball depending on the season. Mine is spent at home with the exception of the theater club where I'm a set designer. Did you think I have the leading role? Think again. Girls like me don't get center stage.

"Shut up. You're perfect." She swats at my shoulder like she usually does.

I let the topic go because I don't want to be the friend who brings other people down.

The bonfire is roaring and a bunch of kids from our high school are sitting around on logs. Fall came early to Illinois this year.

Some couples are making out and I glance away quickly. Other kids are enthralled in Keeten Berkshire's telling of some urban myth about a girl who ventured into the woods years ago and was found cut up in pieces the next morning. We've all heard it a million times, but he adds his own spin to the story about how no one missed her because she was such an ugly loser.

My stomach rumbles with nerves. I don't belong here. Hell, Lauren only half belongs herself. The seniors from her soccer team invited her after she made the winning goal last week in a clincher. At least she actually talks to some of these people. Me, on the other hand, I'm way out of my comfort zone.

"Let's grab a beer first." Lauren drags me the opposite way of the bonfire and part of me suspects she heard Keeten telling the story and she's worried I'm going to run off scared and be the one found cut up into little pieces tomorrow morning.

All the liquor is stashed in the woods so that if the cops come to break up the party, they won't find any evidence of underage drinking.

Sometimes I wonder about the intelligence of the police force. Don't get me wrong, my classmates go to great lengths to cover it up. There's a garbage can spray painted in camouflage that covers the keg. Different liquor bottles are set on opposite sides of the log with a green and brown tarp that someone took the time to sew together. But if I know this, how do the cops not?

"I'm driving," I say.

She stops at the back of the line for the keg. Intrigued eyes scan over the two of us, probably wondering why the hell I'm here.

"Oh yeah, well, hold a cup to look like you're drinking." She tosses me a red Solo cup.

I hold it in my hands.

"Not upside down." She snatches it away and turns it over, shoving it back into my hand.

"Jeez, calm down," I grumble.

I push my lips out over my braces because they've been more irritating than usual lately. I kind of wish I had that wax stuff so I won't cut my lip again. Another six months and I'll be free of these train tracks.

My cheap-ass dad refused to get them for me when I was in middle school. His lame excuse was that I wasn't responsible enough. Maybe he should be the one to visit the bonfire tonight and feel like an outcast compared to the others my age.

The line takes forever to move, mostly because of a few girls at the front complaining about how their beer has too much head and the guys joking about wanting head themselves.

I roll my eyes while Lauren interjects into their conversation with some crude comment of her own making them all laugh. The girl can fit in anywhere. It's a constant reminder that I'm holding her back from being a 'cool kid.'

The other kids disperse, heading back to the bonfire with their filled Solo cups. A few giggling cheerleaders stumble over some branches, but their strong football player boyfriends come to their rescue.

My heart aches to be one of those girls, but when babies in utero were handed the traits of a homecoming queen, I must've been missed.

Sure, my mom is always rambling on about how people peak at different times in their lives. I keep telling myself that I'm smart and I'm going to get into a good college. I just need to believe once my braces are off and I convince my dad that he's not wasting money on contacts, things will improve.

Okay, and maybe get my act together by running with Lauren when she asks. Maybe then I won't have to wait until my hormones finally wake up and let me peak.

"Maddie!" Lauren hollers and I'm dragged from my thoughts.

I stare down at my cup overflowing with beer under the tap. "Sorry." I take my cup from her but stay in place.

Why is she filling my cup?

"The tap is fucked up and it won't stop. No one wants to miss out, so move along." Lauren motions with her hand and my brain finally processes the sighs behind me.

"Sorry," I say, stepping out of the way, my beer sloshing over the side of the cup. I push my glasses up on my nose.

"Let's head back to the fire." Lauren slides her arm through mine, leading the way. Her athletic and coordinated stride means she doesn't trip over a single branch in the dark but saves me from falling on my face twice.

The fire grows larger. I know this because I've been studying it for the past half hour since Lauren said she was going to head back to refill her cup and never returned. Not in the mood to risk my ankle again, I chose to stay in place.

The night is going fine. Lauren introduced me to her senior soccer teammates who smiled politely and carried on talking about the team they're playing next week. I'm not standing alone and the other people around aren't mean so I can't complain.

Then Lauren asked if I wanted a refill. I'd dumped half my beer in the grass and pretended to sip on the rest.

"Nah, I'm good."

"Well, I'll be right back." Lauren tightened her hand over my forearm to assure me she wouldn't be long.

I took a spot across from the make-out couples. Somewhere between the mesmerizing orange and yellow flames I forgot where I was, letting my mind drift to a time in my life when I wouldn't be the awkward loser. It was hard sometimes to believe that there ever would be such a time. Why wasn't I born gorgeous? Why were my hips so wide and why didn't the skinny gene run in my family? Having a cheap-ass father only added to my problems.

Something caught my eye and I glanced up over the flames. My heart leaped in my chest right before it lodged in my throat.

Mauro Bianco.

He's staring back at me.

I look away but sneak a glance back a second later. That's when I realize that he isn't staring at me, he's mesmerized by the fire as well.

I study his face. The way the fire reflects in his blue eyes transfixes me so that I don't notice right away when liquid is pouring down my back.

"Ugh!" I stand up, grabbing the fabric from the back of my dress.

"Oh shit, sorry," Kami whoever from my physics class says. "Good thing the dress is ugly as fuck."

The other girls in her group all laugh, remarking how funny her comment is and confirming how ugly my dress is.

My shoulders slump and though I wish I could stand up to them, I only turn around. Mauro is gone.

I search the area for Lauren, but she's nowhere in sight. At this point, I'm cutting my losses and leaving this bonfire with the hopes that she never drags me anywhere like this again. I've been meaning to read the hot new dystopian series everyone is raving about anyway.

Wandering around, I try to ignore the feeling that everyone is staring at me, whispering to their friends with wonderment as to why I'm here. Once I reach the treeline, I contemplate if I want to chance heading back by the drinks. Lauren's been gone for forty-five minutes now and I've reached the conclusion that she's lip-locked with a jock somewhere.

Squinting—as if that ever helped anyone see better in the

dark—I peer through the trees, not seeing anyone. Not the keg, not the alcohol and not the line of kids. Could they have moved it?

Pulling out my phone, I shine it through the trees to see if my usual sense of direction is playing tricks on me.

"Mind not blinding me?" a deep voice asks, and I can only make out a large guy shielding his eyes as he walks out of the foliage.

"Sorry," I mumble, feeling like an idiot.

The closer he gets the clearer the person becomes. His letterman jacket. The worn jeans that cover big brown boots. His backward baseball cap and the scruff along his face that a high school senior shouldn't have.

"Hey." He snaps his fingers and points to me, as if he's trying to remember my name.

Of course, I've daydreamed about our wedding and he doesn't even know my name.

"Maddie," I say.

His hand lands on the tree behind my head and my stomach tingles with anticipation until the rancid smell of alcohol surrounds me when he breathes.

He's drunk.

"Right. Maddie. Never seen you at one of these things."

I push up my glasses for the millionth time. "Yeah, uh. Hopefully you didn't rub against any toxicodendron radicans." I point to the forest behind him as my face heats.

I finally get the chance to talk to him and *this* is what I come up with?

"What?" He shakes his head like he didn't understand me. "I'm having a bad night. I don't usually drink but..." His words trail off and I'm not sure if he lost his train of thought or is just choosing not to continue.

"It happens." I nod at the woods. "Did you see anyone else in there?"

He looks back toward the woods like he doesn't remember coming out of there.

"I try not to check out other people while they're taking a piss." He chuckles and his eyes light up in that aqua color that makes me tongue-tied.

"Oh, I thought the alcohol was back there."

He chuckles a deep rumble and an energy charges between my thighs. The sensation is one I'm not familiar with.

"This is the piss stop, that's the refill station." He points to the other side of the woods past the bonfire.

Shit.

"Okay, thanks." I head in the other direction to look for Lauren, praying to God he doesn't remember this encounter tomorrow.

His hand grabs mine before I get far enough away, igniting a rush of goose bumps along my skin. "You seem sober."

"And you could tell that how?"

One side of his lips tick up into a smirk. "Funny and smart, huh?"

"How do you know I'm smart?"

"Those two fancy words you said earlier. Why not just say poison ivy?"

I can't help the smile that spreads across my face and I'm sure that if someone snapped a picture right now, I'd be looking up at him in adoration. "How do you know they mean poison ivy?"

His smirk grows and turns wildly attractive and has me involuntarily clenching my thighs. "What else could I rub against that would cause me harm in a forest? Not all jocks are dumb."

My head snaps back in surprise. "I never said that."

"You stereotype I'm sure." His tone has done a one-eighty from moments before.

I stare down at his hand on my arm and he follows my vision, retracting it.

"Sorry."

"I am sober, so what do you want?" I ask, happy to change the subject.

"A ride home? I need to sleep this shit off."

In a car alone with my crush? I glance around for a camera crew to charge out of the woods and tell me I'm on Punk'd. Jocks only fall for the geeks in the movies. That's not real life, but that doesn't mean I'm going to say no. I didn't get my 4.0 grade point average for nothing.

"Let me grab my friend and I can drive you."

"Cool." He walks alongside me toward the bonfire and I can't help but wonder what everyone else here is going to think when they see us together.

I should've known things would not go as smoothly as I hoped.

After tracking Lauren down with Jay Hewitt, the captain of the varsity soccer team, it confirmed my earlier thought that I truly am holding her back. Even worse was that Jay said he'd drive her back to my house after the bonfire died down and Lauren agreed.

This leaves me alone with Mauro. I can't be trusted not to make a complete ass of myself. I don't know what it is about him. When he's around, it's like I'm incapable of forming a complete thought.

He decided he didn't want to walk around the party with me on a wild goose chase, so I gave him directions to meet me at my Wrangler. I told myself it wasn't because he didn't want to be seen walking around with *me*, and that it's probably just because he's so drunk.

I'm still wondering if he'll be there when I make it back to where I parked.

Hightailing it back the other way through the muddy grass area, I find Mauro leaning against the truck.

"It's locked." He wears the most bored expression on his face.

"Sorry."

Since my Wrangler is old as hell, I have to actually insert the key into the passenger door before heading to my side.

"Don't go thinking you're getting lucky," he jokes, sliding his large form into my car.

He sure takes up a lot more space than Lauren.

"Don't worry, I won't take advantage of you," I say in response.

Wow! Did I just flirt with Mauro Bianco?

I start the car with shaking hands. Other than a shoulder brush near his locker that sent my heartbeat in a tailspin my freshman year, I've never been this close to him. I'm trying my best to concentrate on the road and not the fact that my entire body feels like I just ran a triathlon.

"Tell me about yourself." He reaches down, grabbing the lever of the seat and adjusting it so he's leaning farther back.

"There's not much to say. I'm a sophomore."

"You must know my brother then. Luca Bianco?"

Um...he can't be that naive to think that the Bianco brothers aren't known by every female between the ages of fourteen and eighteen within a fifty-mile radius. I mean they're three attractive Italian brothers, each a year apart from each other. All of them accomplished athletes and gorgeous as hell.

"I think I have PE with him." I think I pulled off a casual vibe with my response which is hard when almost every girl in school tries to get her schedule changed to have PE with any one of the brothers.

"He's cocky and arrogant, right? We're not all alike." His voice is fading like he's growing tired. "Take me, I'm going to graduate this year and have no clue what the fuck I want to do with my life. No football scholarship doesn't leave me with a ton of options. I'm thinking about joining the army."

I'm hoping he ignores the fact I'm driving to his house without any directions from him, but everyone knows where the Bianco brothers live.

"That's very...heroic." I'm sure my voice betrays my worry.

"You don't make it sound that way. My mama is pissed. Like beat me with a frying pan pissed for even thinking about joining. Not that she's against me serving my country, she worries about me not coming back. You know moms." He runs his hand through his hair.

The thought of something happening to him overseas and not coming back sends a chill through me.

"What makes you want to join?"

A low stream of air flows out of his mouth and I'm reminded once again that he probably wouldn't be speaking this freely with me if he weren't drunk.

"All I know is I don't want to run a sandwich shop when I'm older." He shrugs.

The Sandwich Place is the Bianco family business and is located downtown across from the courthouse. I'm sure as the oldest son in an Italian family the pressure to take over the shop is immense, but he doesn't seem like someone who would shave meat for a living.

"Nothing else has ever piqued your interest? No classes?" I put my blinker on to make a right-hand turn, looking in all directions before I finally push down on the gas pedal.

"I've lived through high school one party at a time. My future seemed like something so far off in the distance...like it would never actually come." The melancholy in his voice suggests that thought haunts him. "What do you want to do?"

"Well, I have a little longer than you, but no way my dad won't make me go to college. I'm not sure what I want to do with my life either. Does that make you feel any better?"

One corner of his lip tips up. "A little. I figured you'd spit out doctor or some shit where you'll be in school for the next ten years."

"So are you relieved that I'm as indecisive as you?"

He chuckles again, turning the radio up a notch. "Chasing Cars" by Snow Patrol plays and Mauro sings softly along to the lyrics. "I know it's selfish, but it does relieve me."

I turn down Irving Park Road to head to his house.

"You're easy to talk to." His forearm flexes as he rolls down my window. The cool fall air flows into the car. "Sorry, I feel like I'm gonna puke."

My fingers wrap around the steering wheel even tighter. "Tell me and I'll pull over."

My dad would kill me if someone puked in my car.

He leans back again and as the song continues to play, his voice fades. I chance a look to find his eyes closed.

A few minutes later, I pull up to the curb of his bungalow. Three football helmet signs dot the yard with Bianco at the bottom and each of the siblings' numbers.

The residential street is dark and vacant when I climb out of the Wrangler. I open the passenger side door and nudge Mauro.

His eyes snap open, wide and blue. "Shit. I'm sorry." He bolts up.

"Hold on, be careful." I step back.

"I'm good." He gets out—a little wobbly, but able to walk. "Want to go to the park?"

He poses it as a question, but he's already heading into the darkness, halfway across the street.

"I think you should probably go lay down."

"Nah." He waves me off. "Come on. Let your hair down a little."

I follow him because when you're a girl like me and a guy like Mauro invites you along, you go.

The park is barely lit with a yellow tint from the street lamps along the path.

"Remember the days when everything was so simple? The hardest decision was the slide or the swings."

He bypasses the swings for the slide.

"I was a monkey bars girl."

"Probably because you're determined. I bet you worked forever to master those things." He lifts his eyebrows.

For being drunk, he's intuitive. Then again, I've never been drunk. Maybe that comes with the alcohol.

"A month. It was the first and last physical thing I ever beat Lauren at."

He turns from climbing the ladder and points to me. "That's why you look so familiar, you're friends with Lauren Hunt."

I mentally chastise myself. We already established he didn't really know me.

"We've been best friends since kindergarten."

"But you're so different."

Yeah, she's hot and I'm homely looking.

"Yeah, she's super athletic and I can't run without tripping over my own feet," I say instead.

He stops, sitting at the top of the slide, his long legs leaving him almost halfway down already. "I was going to say because Lauren is a ball buster and you're...sweet." He slides down the metal slide while my heart flips in my chest. "I was a slide guy. Anything to get me up high. I only did the swings if Cristian or Luca dared me they could jump farther."

He skips over the part where he kind of complimented me, but I know it's something I'll never forget.

Wandering some more, he heads toward the outfield of the baseball field and collapses on his back.

"Lay with me." He pats the spot next to him.

"I should really get home." I wind my dress in my fingers until I realize that's pulling my dress higher.

"Come on. We're just getting to know one another."

I sit down next to him and he grabs the back of my dress, pulling me down.

"You ever wonder the point of this is? Life. Why we're here? Like we both go to Catholic school. Don't you ever wonder about God's plan for you?"

"Yeah."

Suddenly, he leans on his side, holding his head up with his hand.

"I feel like I'm meant to do something meaningful. Not sit in an office, or worse, inventory and order sandwich meats. I want to live, knowing that tomorrow isn't guaranteed so I don't look back on my life and wonder what the hell I did with it, you know? I get how it is with my parents. They each came here for a better life and the sandwich place is their life." He laughs. "And me, Cristian, and Luca. It makes them happy."

"So you just want to be happy?" I continue to stare up at the sky, attempting to ignore the proximity of his body heat so close to me.

He's just a boy, he's just a boy.

I see him shrug from the corner of my eye. "That's where I'm fucked up. I want it all. The family, the house, the career. I don't want to settle, but no one gets the trifecta."

A pinch in my heart has me turning my head to look at him. How can this jock, who I never really thought much of except for his hot body and beautiful face now, break off a piece of my heart?

"What about you? Do you believe in love?" he asks.

I look away, gazing back up at the stars and trying to keep my breathing even. "I used to, but after my parents' divorce, I kind of agree with you. You can't have it all, so I'd rather choose career and screw the family."

"You don't want to get hurt?" Mauro is much more intuitive than I would have thought.

"I suppose. Both my parents hurt after the divorce." I press my lips together, remembering that time in my life.

"My parents fight like crazy, but usually their bedroom door is shut hours later. My brothers and I flee the house while they're making up."

He slides his hand down between us, running his fingers up and down my arm.

"Will you look at me?" he asks in a gentle voice.

I turn my head and lock gazes with him. His hand is suddenly on my cheek, and he's leaning over.

I squeal inside when his eyes fixate on my lips.

"Can I kiss you?"

"Okay," I practically whisper.

Lame, Maddie. Lame.

"Relax and close your eyes."

Does he know this is my first time being kissed? Is that why he asked permission and is directing my body how to respond?

As my mind is swimming with a million simultaneous thoughts, he presses his lips to mine and all those worries vanish as his tongue slowly slides into my mouth.

I've long imagined what it would feel like to be kissed at all, but the fact that my first kiss is from Mauro Bianco feels like I'm in a movie or something.

Every nerve in my body fires and he moans softly, his body weight starting to press into me as he deepens the kiss. My breasts press against his chest now and though the sensation is new and unfamiliar, I understand now why girls want to do this. I open my mouth some more, loving the sensation of our tongues brushing together.

"Shit." He pulls back, sitting up and pressing his hand to his lips. "Your braces."

Blood leaks from his lip.

"I'm sorry." My eyes are wide and my heart races as my cheeks heat.

He picks up his t-shirt, blotting his lip. "It's okay." He stands up, working to find his balance for a second. "Want to ride the slide?"

Just like that, the kiss is forgotten and he's wandering away.

"Mauro, what the fuck are you doing?" someone yells as they cross the street. "Fuck. Ma's going to kill you."

"Cris, I might have had too many, but I got a ride. Do you know....?" He glances back to where I'm unceremoniously getting myself up off the grass, his arm stretched out toward me.

I step out of the darkness and Cristian's eyes widen for a second.

"Hey, Maddie." He disregards his brother beelining it over to me. "Everything okay?"

"Um...yeah. I just gave your brother a ride."

The blood on Mauro's lip is pooling now but isn't streaming down.

"Nothing else?" Cristian dips down to see my eyes. I can barely form a coherent sentence, let alone assure him I'm good.

I just had my first kiss with the boy of my dreams and my braces cut his lip. I do live in a movie, but not a romance, rather a horror film.

"Yeah, everything's good. You can make sure he gets inside?"

"Yeah." Cristian heads over to his brother, hooking his arm over his shoulder. "Thanks a lot, Maddie."

"MADDIE!" Mauro starts singing the Barry Manilow song using my name.

"The song says Mandy, fucktard," Cristian says.

Mauro laughs for a second before dead silence fills the air. "I'm gonna puke."

I hop in my Wrangler and glance over to the park where I see Mauro's head in the trashcan and Cristian waving goodbye to me.

My phone rings in the center console and I pick it up.

"Where the hell are you?" Lauren screams when I answer.

"Sorry, I got lost," I lie and start my truck, getting the hell away from the Bianco house.

The rest of the weekend felt like it crawled by. I played our kiss over and over again in my head—both the amazing part and the embarrassment of his bleeding lip.

Even still by the time Monday rolled around I can't help that hope that blooms inside me like a fragile flower. It's right before homeroom that I first spot him walking down the hallway.

I feel half nauseous, half excited and more than anything anxious to get speaking to each other at school over with.

I pause as he approaches and smile wide at him so he'll know that it's okay to say hello. Instead, he walks right by me with nothing but a polite smile.

Mortification is swift and complete, even if no one else is the wiser.

I run to the girl's bathroom, passing Lauren on the way and hearing her call my name, but I ignore her. I don't want to be near anyone right now.

When I reach the bathroom, I race into the stall and let the waterworks loose.

I can't believe that I actually believed, even for a second, that he could have feelings for me. What a joke.

I should have known I was the only one who felt something that night.

CHAPTER ONE

Present Day

Madison

"One thousand!" Lauren stands, her paddle high in the air like she's the damn Statue of Liberty. Actually, strike that, the paddle in her hand isn't *hers*, it's mine.

"Lauren!" I scold, rising from my chair.

Whose idea was it to switch our paddles and bid on a hot bachelor for the other? Not mine, that's for sure. More importantly, why did I go along with the idea that Lauren could pick a guy for me to date at this First Responders Fallen Hero Bachelor Auction? I was out of my mind to think she'd make the right pick for me.

That's how she snuck the first couple of bids by me because when Mauro Bianco stepped foot on that stage, the multi-tasking function in my brain turned off.

He still looks like a real life model. The spotlight glows over his head, giving the appearance that his dark hair holds streaks of natural highlights. His chiseled jaw is more defined than his boyish one at eighteen.

My entire body heats with flames only he can extinguish.

It's not his broad shoulders and tight waist, the dimples in his cheeks or his luscious pink lips that undo me. It's his eyes. The way they transform from aqua to the deepest blue of the ocean depending on what feeling is spiraling around inside him. Mix those with the bronzed skin of his Italian heritage and I'm done for.

The MC goes back and forth between Lauren and another woman who wants a piece of Mauro. I'm not sure whether I want her or Lauren to win.

The gavel lands on the podium and my muscles tense as he points to Lauren and yells, "Sold!"

She drops the paddle in the middle of the table as though it's a generous bundle of hundred dollar bills.

"You can thank me at your wedding." She smirks.

Lauren saw me through my Mauro Bianco fangirl phase. I never told her what happened that fateful night I drove my drunk crush home—I was too embarrassed to tell even her.

"I don't want Mauro," I protest even though my body is literally giddy to think about another night alone with him. One where I'm not in braces and glasses. We may not be on equal footing now, but the gap is shortening.

Don't get too cocky, my inner voice warns.

"I need to be filled in." Vanessa's blonde hair swings side to side as her head swivels between Lauren and myself.

Vanessa didn't make us a trio until college after we got thrown into a quad without a fourth. She never met the Maddie who turns into a babbling mess when Mauro's within a twenty-foot perimeter. And she won't know her now. I refuse to morph back into the insecure girl who propped him up on a pedestal.

"Later," I whisper, not wanting to rehash history in this moment.

"If this is the way we're going to play it." She turns to face the MC who is now introducing Mauro's little brother, Luca. "Then game on."

At the end of the auction, once we've all pissed each other off by selecting one another's dates, somehow, we each ended up with a Bianco brother. Lauren practically tackled Vanessa to prevent her from bidding on Luca for her and Vanessa has told me that she will not be going out with Cristian, who's a police officer.

Good times all around.

After we pay for our dates, I feel a little better about things since the money is going to help such a wonderful charity. Then I spot Mauro across the room and decide I'd feel a helluva lot better if my date wasn't flirting with some blonde who won't stop touching his bicep. The two are entranced in a moment. Is she the other woman who was bidding? I narrow my eyes, but I can't be sure.

I might as well see what the action is about in the banquet room since there are more hot firefighter, police officers, and EMTs around. I leave my two roommates to fight it out with their designated dates.

Hell, maybe Mauro will have some insanely busy schedule and be unable to go on the date. Ever.

You don't really wish that.

Or maybe he'll shuck the responsibility. It's not like in high school he was one to follow the rules. Rules never seemed to apply to the prom king and quarterback. When others were being stopped for sneaking off school property for lunch, Mauro was waving his goodbye and peeling off around the corner. Everyone else had to carry around passes to be in the hallways during class time, but Mauro acted as though the hallways were his kingdom. We didn't have any classes together, but word was he was usually asleep in the back row.

A callused hand lands softly on my forearm. "Excuse me," a deep voice says.

I stop and circle around. My entire body shuts down for a second as Mauro Bianco stands front and center only a couple of feet away from me, his eyes just as transfixing as years before.

"I heard you were my winning bidder. Well, not for me, but a date. Which I guess is technically still me." He shakes his head, chuckling to himself.

I giggle.

Like I'm still sixteen. Ugh.

He holds his hand out. "Let's start over." His smile is infectious, his eyes—alluring. His muscles, worth salivating over. I'm back to being a sophomore again. "I'm Mauro Bianco. Thanks for coming out to support such a good cause."

"Hi. I'm... Ma...Ma...Mad...ison Kelly."

His smile grows and my gut twists. My palms sweat while my heart pounds against my chest like a bass drum in a rock band as I wait with baited breath.

"Nice to meet you," he says, ignoring my stutter.

My insides deflate like a balloon with a slow leak, hope streaming out with a slow hiss.

Of course, he doesn't remember me.

I was always invisible to him.

CHAPTER TWO

Mauro

Great, I get the drunk girl. I'll be calling Luca later to give her mouth-to-mouth. She's a little unstable like she can't decide if she wants to pass out or throw up.

Add on the fact she's staring at me like I approached her at a bar while she was partying with her friends, and I'm thinking either she's not the girl who bid on me or she's regretting it now.

"You know we don't have to go out. I mean if you think it was a mistake," I say, offering her an easy out.

Her eyes scrunch and her lips dip. She's cute. More than cute. The girl next door type, but there's a sexiness under her forties garb that hides her curves.

"Do you not want to go out with me?" she asks.

The weakness in her voice pulls my eyes away from her heart-shaped lips to her eyes. Gray with small specks of blue. Like a cloudy day right before a storm.

I shrug my jacket on, glancing at my watch. "Sorry, I'm due on shift in an hour."

"Oh."

"Are you free tomorrow? Maybe lunch?" I offer since she didn't take the out.

Again, her lips dip but she quickly sips from her straw. "Sunday?"

It's then I realize my days are all fucked up.

"Shit." My fingers thread through my hair. "I covered for a guy last night and we had five calls from two to four. I'm lagging. Monday then?"

"I work."

"Of course you do."

Could I be blowing this anymore? She's nice enough to bid good money on me, the least I can do is a weekend night. Let's see...I work tonight, and then Wednesday.

"I can do Friday night."

She continues to sip her drink, the liquid slowly lowering in her glass.

"So, is Friday okay?" I draw out my sentence to make sure she's understanding me. I'm starting to wonder if she'll remember this tomorrow.

She nods and her eyes pop open again. "Yes. Friday's good."

I pull out my phone. "Can I have your number? That way we can text later in the week. I can pick you up or we can meet. Whatever you're comfortable with."

Her lips stay on the straw, her eyes glued to my chest. I want to wave my hand and say 'eyes up here.'

Girls becoming tongue-tied and googly-eyed used to make me feel like king of the fucking world. Now it's a major turn off.

She swallows and places her drink on the nearby table.

"Oh." She pulls out her phone from her purse. Except

with her phone comes the entire contents of her purse. We both watch as everything falls to the floor.

Instead of bending down, her eyes fix to mine and her cheeks flush. Something oddly familiar tugs in my gut but I can't place it.

I bend down and she quickly follows suit. I scoop up the lipstick, her wallet, a pill case. Holding her checkbook up in the air, I decide to lighten this meeting up. "Plan on winning tonight no matter the cost?"

I smile.

She doesn't.

I hand it over to her and mumble, "I'm kidding."

She tucks it back into her purse along with the tampons which I ignored. "Thanks," she murmurs.

Once we're standing again, she slides her purse under her arm. Her dress reveals nothing. Not her tits or her waist or her ass. The thing hides all the goods.

She holds her phone in her hands for a moment, not asking for my number to text me hers. Instead, I pluck it from her grasp.

"Do you mind?" I ask.

Her face pales. "No."

I text myself and my phone goes off, the sound of a girl moaning and a slapping sound coming from my pocket.

"Fuck!" I hand over her phone and dig for my own. Grabbing it after all the heads in a twenty-foot perimeter turn in my direction, I press to view it before it does it again.

She giggles across from me, her eyes casting down to her phone.

"My brothers think this shit is funny."

Looking up at me through her long eyelashes, there's a brightness that wasn't there moments ago. "It kind of is."

"So, you're cool if I keep that as your text notification

ring?" I raise my eyebrows and the flush deepens to a coral across her cheeks.

"I didn't say that."

I quickly change the ringtone before I forget and she texts me when my mom's around. No need to deepen the permanent bruise from where she slaps me on the back of the head already.

Tucking the phone back into my pocket, I rock back on my heels. "I'll call you midweek and we'll set something up then."

"Sure." She's a little more alive now and I feel a small amount of hope at the prospect of our upcoming date.

I nod, the awkwardness wrapping around us like a roll of cellophane.

"Okay, talk to you then," I say and smile.

"Okay."

Finally, I walk out of the banquet center, not even bothering to say goodbye to my brothers. They can go blow themselves after putting that notification tone on my phone.

Heading to the firehouse to work my shift, I can't help but feel like that girl seemed familiar in some way, but I don't know a Madison Kelly. I really hope I didn't pull her from a burning building at some point and she's got some hero complex because I am not a hero by anyone's standards.

Walking into the fire station, the aroma of curry masks the scent of testosterone.

"Fuck Patel, that shit messed up my stomach last week." Donovan breezes through the kitchen area to the weight room.

"Then make your own dinner," Patel spits back and glances over at me as I sit down at the big table. "So, how did it go? I didn't hear SWAT being called to the Hilton on the scanner, so the ladies weren't fighting over you?"

I chuckle. "Nope. Just two bidders and the one gave up quick."

"You disappointed?" he asks before he turns his back to me to return something to the fridge.

"Please. Standing on stage being bid on based on how attractive the audience finds you? It's for a good cause though and one date isn't going to kill me." I play with the napkins in the center of the giant table.

"You expect me to feel sorry for you? You posed in the Chicago Firefighters Calendar three years in a row. I don't remember anyone knocking on my door." He moves around the kitchen like he's a professional chef. I guess in some ways he is since he's the only one willing to cook for us during our rotation.

"I'm not asking for pity." I stand to help him out as much as I can although my culinary skills are not existent. I was raised by a traditional Italian mama—you get the idea. It might be a little sexist, but it doesn't make it untrue.

"What's going on with you?" Patel asks.

"What do you mean?"

He glances over his shoulder at me while chopping up chicken. "You look like your mama just scolded you."

"First off, I'm twenty-nine, my mom doesn't scold me. Second, I'm fine, just tired of the same old routine."

Patel stops what he's doing, washing his hands and then drying them on a dishtowel before throwing it over his shoulder. "Maybe you need to speak to the shrink."

I shake my head. "This isn't about Hunter. This is just me approaching thirty and being stuck in the same damn routine."

Patel is about ten years older than me. Married, three kids, a happy life. I think he's had his shit together since he was eighteen. Whereas I still feel like I'm trying to get my shit together as I approach thirty. Ever since we lost Hunter at a fire, my life has felt less appealing, less meaningful.

Leaning against the counter, his gaze digs into mine.

"Shouldn't you be finishing the dinner?" I eye the uncooked chicken.

"They eat when they eat. What's the routine?"

I'm embarrassed to admit I brought this conversation on myself. I could've easily headed to the weight room with Donovan or sat and watched whatever the other guys are in the television room. It's like a silent plea for help when you go to Patel with a problem. Everyone knows that.

"All the shift work and then doing jack all with the other forty-eight hours. I fill it up, but something is missing. I'll spend some time with Cailin and Devin, but the labor jobs have been few and far between since I took some time after Hunter died."

Cailin is Hunter's widow. He was my best buddy in the firehouse and we ran a contracting business on the side together. After Hunter died six months ago, I've been trying to make an effort to go around her place and see if she or her son need anything. It has to be a hard adjustment for them and I want to help however I can.

Patel quirks an eyebrow at me.

"It's not like that." I know there's more bite to my tone than he deserves, but I want to make it perfectly clear so that there's no uncertainty.

"I think you don't want it to be like that, but she's sad and the baby needs a father and—"

"And nothing is going on. I'm just helping her out."

He tips his head back, letting the subject go even if it looks like I didn't convince him that I would never go there.

"Hunter and I were just getting our business off the ground. We'd planned to flip houses and now..."

I put the chicken in the frying pan, but Patel snatches the spoon away from me.

"You'll burn it."

"I was trying to help you." I wash my hands at the sink.

He laughs because we both know he doesn't want anyone's help. "If your mind is on other things it won't work out."

I lean on the counter next to him because the firehouse can be like a sorority house at times, there are ears everywhere.

"Start it yourself." He shrugs.

"What?"

"Start the flipping houses thing yourself. I've seen your work. What you did at my place was top notch. We get compliments all the time."

I shrug and he knocks me in the shoulder.

"It was just flooring."

"Yeah, and if I would've done it, it'd already be busting up at the seams." He pours the curry in with the chicken, adding a few more spices to the mix while taking the lid off the pot of rice. "I'm serious though. You don't give yourself enough credit. I get that Hunter was your partner, but you can do it by yourself, or find another partner if you have to."

The flickers of late night talks Hunter and I had in this very kitchen during a shift come to mind. The business that was going to put money in our pockets so we could live well and keep on being firefighters. God knows the pay is crap, but we loved it. We're both adrenaline junkies who never wanted to sacrifice our flexible schedule for some nine to five office job. He worried with Cailin and Devin that his salary wasn't going to be enough and he'd ultimately have no choice.

"He was the numbers guy. The guy who was going to find and make the deals, keep us on budget. I was the hands."

Patel eyes me again and shakes his head. "I never pegged you for a weakling."

"Do I have to remind you of the beating your team took last week on the court even with home team advantage?" I smirk and he chuckles to himself.

"You underestimate yourself. Start small. Find a cheap house and go at your own pace." Patel puts the rice in a huge bowl to feed anyone who's sticking around. "You need my help to invest?"

"Nah. I'm good." I wave him off.

"Are you sure because..."

I step away from the counter, digging in my pocket for my phone as it vibrates with a call. "I'm sure. Thanks, Patel."

"Think about the shrink thing." He uses his dad voice on me, but I look away, pulling my phone out as a distraction.

Cailin.

"Hey, Cailin," I answer, purposely upping the happiness vibe in my voice.

"Devin and I were wondering if you'd like to come by Friday for dinner and a movie?"

I head up the stairs into the sleeping quarters of our house with my bag over my shoulder. Every time she calls me here, it topples on another layer of guilt and grief. Probably because this is where Hunter's and my friendship was born. This is where he told me he met Cailin and that there was something different about her to him. Where we planned the flash mob for his proposal. Where I saw his eyes fill with water when he announced that he was going to be a dad.

"Sorry, that's the night I'm going out with the lucky woman who won me tonight."

There's silence on the other end and I hate the fact that she's upset.

"Maybe I can stop by after," I offer.

"Nah. If all goes well, you'll be lucky, too." I can tell she doesn't mean what she's saying, but I'm not calling bullshit on it. Patel's warning is ringing through my head and I can't say I haven't worried myself that she's looking for something I can't and won't offer. The loss is still fresh and she's clinging to anything and anyone she sees as security right now.

I promised Hunter that if anything ever happened to him that I'd make sure she and Devin were good, and I don't go back on promises.

The brunette from the charity event flashes through my head again. I'm not sure why. If I'm honest, her shyness and timidness annoyed me. I'm not sure what my type is, but someone who agrees with every fucking thing I do and say sure isn't the one for me. Lately, that's all I've been getting.

"I can give you a call," I say.

"Okay."

The alarms go off in the building.

"A fire?" she asks. "Be careful," she says before I answer. She knows the drill.

"I will. Talk to you soon."

"Text me after?" Her voice lowers and I know she's remembering the night Hunter was no longer able to do so.

"Will do."

I click the phone off and head down the stairs to put on my pants.

As I jump on the truck and we race out of the station, I push all my concerns to the back of my mind. Safety is number one when we're on a job and I can't afford to be distracted.

CHAPTER THREE

Madison

I sit in my car outside my childhood home. The weeds are as tall as the broken windows that are now replaced with plywood. The cement stairs are crumbling and slanted, making it a danger just to step foot in the house.

The need to make this a home others will love burns inside of me. One that a family will cherish and a neighborhood will smile upon. It wasn't my happily ever after, but it will be someone else's.

A black sedan pulls up right behind me so I turn off the ignition and step out of my car with my legal pad in hand.

"Miss Kelly, I'm thinking I deserve an extra percent on my commission for getting us in here so fast."

My Realtor, a man in his fifties with a heavy gold chain around his neck, his wrists and his pinky finger adorned with the same, is good at what he does and he's negotiated some amazing deals for me in the past. Especially when I'm going up against some of the most bullheaded developers in the area. Small fish in a little pond doesn't even cut it when it comes to describing me. They want the buck and I want to pull out the beauty.

"Hey, George and I've told you to call me, Madison."

He holds out short and stubby fingers for me to shake.

We do some quick small talk and then it's on to business as usual as he walks up the sidewalk I used to play childhood games on like Step on a Crack and Break Your Mother's Back.

"As you know, it's a three bedroom, one and a half bath. Basement, small kitchen. Yard is decent. It's up for auction next Tuesday."

"The last thing I need is a bidding war."

George opens the door and the foulest smell has us using the collars of our shirts to cover our noses. Staring down at the junk filled floor has me thankful I wore my boots.

"I have to say the commission checks are nice but looking at houses with you always makes me want to shower after." George stays by the front door.

He always does and it doesn't bother me. The first time he showed me a house there was a rat that had drowned in one of the toilets. It was already decomposing and explained the smell, but he was fighting his gag reflex that entire showing.

"Call the fire department if I don't come back in fifteen minutes." I put on my face mask and head through the front area to the back.

I dig through the massive amounts of newspaper and magazines on top of an old dining room table. Stepping through more floor rugs that are wet and soggy doesn't leave a lot of hope for the floorboards.

When my parents and I lived here, everything was bright and cheery. My mom would grow plants on the ledge by the front door. Herbs in small planters in the bay window of the kitchen. The smells of freshly baked cookies or pot roast were second nature while I was out playing in the yard.

Then the bad start to seep into the good. The days my mom never got out of her bed. Or the fights in the kitchen where spaghetti sauce ended up splattered all over the wall.

The bones are good in this house and has loads of potential. I refuse to let it be the ugliest house on the block.

Heading back to the front door after one quick pass through the top floor, I find George typing away on his phone, still as a statue.

"This is it," I say when he glances up at me.

"Are you sure? I think this might be the worst you've ever taken on."

He's right. I'll be digging into my savings and probably won't make nearly the profit I usually do, but I remember why I turned to flipping houses to begin with. The money at the end is nice, but it's about bringing out the best of what's already there, not building something shiny and new like a developer would.

"I'm sure. I just have to beat out Oswald. They'd cut corners and make a steal on this property."

"Yeah, I always steer my clients clear of his places."

We exit the house and I stand on the porch that I fear could cave in at any moment. I take a moment to look around my old neighborhood, staring at the houses up and down the street.

I don't understand.

"How can it be just this house in such disrepair? They have flowerbeds." I point to the house directly across from us. "They have a gate surrounding their front lawn." I point to two houses down.

George shrugs. "You know the city. There's no rhyme or reason. Sometimes someone elderly dies and they have no family to take care of their assets or their families want to hang on to it until the market goes up, but they don't maintain it." He takes the steps down and turns on the sidewalk, staring back up at the house.

"Yeah, I suppose so." We continue down the walkway and he moves to shake my hand but turns it into a fist bump instead.

"Let me know when you're ready to list."

I fist bump him, laughing out loud. "Thanks, George."

I arrive home and open the door to my house to find Lauren flying down the stairs. She puts her finger to her lips and sneaks into the hall closet.

A second later, a half-dressed Vanessa stomps down from upstairs. There's no urgency in her steps, but her eyes are bouncing all around as she descends.

"What is going on?" I ask.

"Lauren gave that Bianco guy my number." She raises a hairbrush in her hand. "Now I'm going to beat her to death."

I raise both eyebrows. The two fight like sisters and I think I'm the middle child.

"You might want to reconsider. Cristian could be the one to answer the 911 call."

She pretend swats at me with the hairbrush but I just laugh at her.

"I'm starving." I head to the kitchen, cringing at the sound of furniture sliding on the hardwood floors. "Do I need to remind you that I still need to sell this place at some point?"

"Don't worry. Those nifty felt pads you bought are doing the trick," Vanessa calls out.

I open the door and investigate what's in the fridge.

"Come out, come out wherever you are," Vanessa says in a singsong voice from the other room.

Did I say I was the middle child? I meant the mother. I'm like the damn guardian of these two women.

"Put the hairbrush down and we'll talk," Lauren says, and Vanessa must try to follow the sound of her voice because I can hear her running toward the foyer.

Lauren's small enough to hide behind the vacuum in the closet and Vanessa would miss her.

Cracking open a soda, I pour it into a glass and raise my voice so she'll hear me. "I don't get what the big deal is," I say to Vanessa. "Go on one date with the guy. I can't say enough good things about Cristian." I sit on the stool at the breakfast bar so I have a bird's eye view into the entryway and watch her continue to play this childish game of hide and seek.

"He's got two strikes against him. One, he wears a badge. Two, he honors the badge."

"Wouldn't that be the point of his job...to do it well?" I sip my drink.

Vanessa crinkles her brows. "It's admirable and I'm sure the girl he ends up with will love that about him. I'm not that girl."

"No one said anything about marriage. It's a date. For charity."

Vanessa opens up the hall closet, jumps in front of the opening and pushes back all our coats. "Hah!"

Lauren's not there, which means she's snuck off to a different hiding spot now.

"Damn you!" Vanessa hits the back of the brush on her palm.

"Back to you being upset that he has your phone number..." I say, trying to understand her issue.

"He called me today. He didn't text, he *called*."

"The nerve of the man." I sip my drink, grabbing a banana from the counter.

"Who calls anymore? It's desperate if you ask me."

"Or considerate," I offer.

She rolls her eyes, moving to the bathroom doorway now. "You date him then." She raises both eyebrows before stepping into the bathroom.

If only my heart didn't skip a beat when I look at his brother.

"Oh, that's right." She peeks her head out. "You love his brother."

"No, I don't."

She heads back into the bathroom and I can hear her opening and closing the cupboard doors. Meanwhile, a crawling Lauren still dressed in her scrubs finds refuge behind our kitchen island. Again she puts her finger to her lips like we're six and this game actually means anything.

"I saw the twinkle in your eye." Vanessa enters the kitchen, her long blonde hair half curled and half straight, and I realize she must've been in the middle of getting ready for her night. She either has a date or she's off to her mystery job. I really hope the two aren't combined together.

"There was no twinkle. Sure I had a crush on him in high school, but hello, I'm nine years older and wiser now."

"Wiser how?" Vanessa sits down at the stool next to me because this is Vanessa. She's grown bored with the game whereas Lauren would play for the rest of the night—she's *that* competitive.

"Wise to the fact that my life is not a movie where the ugly duckling turns into a swan and gets the handsome prince. This is reality and you date within your level."

"Level?" Vanessa grabs my soda and takes a sip.

"You know fives with fives, eights with eights. Sure maybe

there's a seven and six somewhere together. Tens only go with sixes when they want something from them."

Vanessa's face falls to a frown. "And what do you think you are?"

It's a test. I'm sure of it. "A six."

"A six?" Her mouth hangs open.

"Is there an echo in here?"

Vanessa slides off the stool and stands in front of me. "Stand up," she demands, using her authoritative voice she inherited from her father.

"I'm eating."

She cocks her head to the side.

I roll my eyes and stand.

"Go stand in front of the mirror." She points to the gold-framed mirror I found at a flea market and re-finished into an antique looking mirror someone would pay hundreds for at Pottery Barn.

"I'm not playing this game. Yeah, yeah, you and Lauren think I'm beautiful. I'm not saying I'm a two. A six is completely respectable."

"Just go stand in front of it." She pushes lightly on my shoulders.

I drag my feet, chomping on my banana the whole time. "Okay, what now?" I look at my reflection.

"Your eyes are stunning. Your hair is silky and smooth. Your figure is spank bank material if you'd stop hiding it. Can you honestly say you're only a six?"

I shrug. "I feel more comfortable dating in my division." Turning back around, I grab my soda and head to the couch, leaving Lauren hiding behind the island.

"Oh, Maddie, you're impossible sometimes." Vanessa follows behind me. "Ouch!"

I turn around before I can sit down to find Lauren with

the brush in her hand and Vanessa's clutching her ass with a pained look on her face. "Damn you!"

Lauren runs up the stairs laughing maniacally as though she's ready for round two, but Vanessa sits down next to me rather than follow.

"How do I blow off this guy nicely?" she asks. "I can't have him going around telling the district what a bitch the Commander's daughter is. My dad would kill me."

"Just tell him you have work. Speaking of—" I straighten my back and turn to face her, wanting to broach the subject of exactly where she's earning money since she's been so cryptic, but she stands quickly.

"Good idea. I'll just say I have no idea what my schedule is going to be like." She leans forward, kissing my cheek. "You're so smart and beautiful, you little eleven you." She winks and runs up the stairs.

A few seconds later I hear her scream, "Lauren, grow the fuck up!" A door slams.

The joys of living with my two best friends.

My phone dings next to me and when I glance at the name, my stomach flips.

Mauro: *Are we still on for Friday night?*
Me: *Yeah. I was thinking Dice and Spins. It's a cafe. Maybe around seven?*
Mauro: *Sure, I've never heard of it.*

Because you're not a dork who loves board games.

Me: *I'll text you the address.*
Mauro: *Perfect. See you then.*

My thumbs hover over the phone. Should I respond? Is he

expecting something more back from me or is that the end of our conversation?

God, I'm so terrible at this stuff.

I press the thumbs up emoji and no three dots appear. I'm ashamed to admit that I watched for them for a whole two minutes.

I have no idea how I'm going to get through our date without making a fool of myself like I did before. Maybe I should consider myself lucky that I'm the only one who remembers the first time around.

CHAPTER FOUR

Mauro

I'm leaning against my truck, waiting for my slow-ass brothers to make an appearance along with a Realtor who was nice enough to agree to show me the house.

Patel's words definitely got to me and that's why I'm outside a house Hunter and I had our eye on as it went into foreclosure. The bank owns it now and I'm hoping the fact that it's going up for auction means that not a lot of people are interested.

Cristian runs around the corner, his earbuds in, wearing his man leggings, shorts, and a skin-tight shirt. Looking about as unmanly as you can while working out.

His pace slows to a walk when he rounds the corner and he pulls his earbuds out of his ears.

"Hey," he says, leaning over with his hands on his knees, catching his breath.

"You're an embarrassment to the Bianco name." I push off my truck with my foot, open the door and grab a water, tossing it in his direction.

"An embarrassment? Hello." He pulls up his shirt to reveal his eight pack. "And I don't have the cushy twenty-four on, forty-eight off schedule. My ass sits in a patrol car for eight fucking hours straight." He gulps down half the bottle. "Thanks for this." He raises the bottle he asked me to bring him into the air.

"Whatever happened to old t-shirts and basketball shorts?"

He looks down at his attire, clearly confused over my question. "This is climate control. I sweat less and it dries fast. Hate to break it to you, brother, but no one wants sweat rings around their neck and pits that don't dry for hours anymore."

"I know what dri-fit is, I also know what size I am. Not sure you can say the same." I eye his erect nipples poking through the thin fabric.

"You're objectifying me." He covers his nipples with his hands.

I roll my eyes just as my other brother pulls his motorcycle into the four-by-four space between me and the car in front of me. Luca takes off his helmet.

"One downside to you working in the city is that you must not see many motorcycle accidents."

He puts the helmet on the bench of his bike. "I've seen plenty, but thanks, Dad."

Luca saunters up to us in his jeans and the t-shirt my mom gave him for his birthday, *I fix stupid* with a cartoon of an ambulance on it.

My youngest brother is a paramedic. He's good at his job, which is surprising once you get to know him.

"Nice shirt," I say.

He glances down. "Well, it's a hell of a lot better than *Christine* over there." He nods to Cristian.

"They're compression pants," Cristian argues.

"They're man leggings," Luca and I say in unison.

Cristian rolls his eyes and unplugs his earbuds.

"You know you're probably going to be the first of us to go down with a heart attack," Luca says. "It's always the guy with picture perfect health. 'No way Cristian had a heart attack, the man ran five miles a day, ate nothing but vegetables, he was so disciplined.'" Luca laughs.

Cristian shakes his head at him.

"This is the house." I motion toward it with my hand.

The three of us stand outside of it, just staring for a moment.

"It's a shit hole," Luca says.

"Or a treasure," I say.

I feel both their eyes on me. They think I'm delusional and they might be right. I should find a house that only needs a few upgrades, not a complete overhaul, but the return on this will be bigger if I can pull it off.

"You think you have the skill to do this?" Cristian, always the sensible one, asks the type of question I assumed he would.

"I think between me and the people we know, yes."

Luca places his hand on my shoulder. "Even I can't revive this house." He moves forward, driven by his natural curiosity toward anything that seems too big to conquer. He rarely accepts defeat.

Having brothers like Luca and Cristian is like having the angel and the devil always weighing in on a decision, which is why I invited them over.

"I hate to be the jackass here, but..." Cristian joins Luca, pretending to tiptoe up the front steps, steps that appear as if they might sink into the ground.

"Nice neighborhood though." Luca stands on the porch, tucking his sunglasses into the neckline of his t-shirt. "How much again?"

I stand there envisioning a nice fence in the front, a walkway lined with flowers and hydrangeas along the ground in front of the porch. "Twenty K to start."

"It's going to be auctioned?" Luca asks.

"Yes, it is," a female voice says behind me. "Which means you need to make sure all your finances are in order and ready by Monday. My feeling is that you won't be the only one who's looking for a steal in a nice neighborhood."

All three of us turn around and find a woman in heels and a short skirt standing on the sidewalk. Her eyes bulge out of her head and her gaze flows up and down each one of us.

"Hi, I'm Mauro, the one you talked to on the phone." I step forward and hold my hand out. She takes it while still examining Luca.

"I'm Greer and I'll be waiting outside while you guys take a look."

She wiggles between Cristian and Luca, bending over to punch the code into the lockbox for the key. One quirked eyebrow from Luca as he checks out her ass and the door opens.

Once we're inside, Cristian strips his shirt off and uses it to cover his nose and mouth. "This is horrible." His voice is muffled as he tiptoes around the room like a little girl.

"Man up." Luca kicks a rug out of the way between the dining room and kitchen. "I know I'm the optimistic one, but Mauro, this is a kick me in the nuts project." He disappears through an archway.

"This smell is almost as bad as a decomposing body." Cristian circles around, staying in the same spot.

"Afraid to get your new running shoes dirty?" I cock an eyebrow.

He ties the shirt around his face like a bandana so it's still covering his nose and mouth. "Fuck off." He heads toward the stairs, his back to the wall as he slowly moves up them like he's clearing a house. I guess none of us are ever too far removed from our day jobs.

"The backyard is killer," Luca hollers and I leave Cristian to examine the top floor and head Luca's way.

"Big? It didn't look that way from outside."

"No, I meant you're actually going to get killed. Rose bush thorns galore." He's staring out the kitchen window. "You're on your own there." He claps me on the shoulder. "Where's pretty boy?" Luca glances at the open stairway to the basement. "Let's make him be the first one to go down there."

It's dark and the stench wafting from the open door doesn't make it appealing in any way. "Please. I thought you were a man?" I slide by him.

"I'm not gonna get murdered. We all have our roles in this family. Cristian's is to beat up the perps. Mine is to save lives."

"I run into burning buildings without knowing the layout. I can handle a basement." I take one at a time, gingerly placing my foot down in case the boards won't hold and pushing cobwebs away from my face.

"Okay, but if there's some junkie down there high as a kite thinking he's Batman, remember how I told you to wait for Cristian." Luca's footsteps follow mine.

"I'm running into a building when everyone else is running out. I think I can handle a little danger. Unlike you who can't go anywhere until the scene is safe. You're hiding in your ambulance while we do the hard work."

"You chose that career," he says.

"Damn right I did."

I wouldn't change that—ever. I just need to supplement my income and since I've always been good with my hands, here I am.

"I understood that career, this one not so much." Luca stays on the bottom step glancing around the basement that looks like it's always been dirty and dingy with creepy crawlers lurking in every dark corner.

"It's a great way to make some money on my two days off between shifts."

"I have no problem filling in my off days." Luca waggles his eyebrows.

I roll my eyes. "Yeah, but you'll have a family to support one day." I direct my flashlight into the crawl space.

"Did hell freeze over?" He finally joins me, kicking a few boxes to the side with his black boots.

"No, but don't you ever think about it? I mean, I'm twenty-nine—"

"And I'm twenty-seven. You can forget about me getting married anytime soon."

"Upstairs is secure!" Cristian yells down from the top of the stairs.

"Thanks, pig!" Luca yells back.

"Real original." Cristian's footsteps barrel down the steps. "Can we get the fuck out of this nightmare now?"

I turn around, pointing the flashlight at him. "Shut the fuck up. This is gonna be someone's dream house when I'm done with it."

"If you say so." The t-shirt still tied over his nose.

"Did you know Mauro's looking for a wife?" Luca says.

I punch him in the shoulder.

"I didn't say that."

Cristian says nothing, just glancing between Luca and myself.

"Why aren't you surprised?" Luca asks. "Are you two shit-heads having meaningful conversations without me? You know if you two get sucked into the whole marriage thing, Mama's gonna double down the pressure on me."

"First of all, stop giving girls you want to blow off the number to the deli," I say. "It's getting old and it only advertises the fact to Mama that you're with a different girl every week."

"Week?" Luca asks, a smirk saying 'if you only knew' on his lips.

Cristian rolls his eyes and heads up the stairs.

"Did you hear about the girl who bought him?" Luca follows Cristian, but he's already cleared the stairs by the time we get to the first step.

Hell, he's probably out the front door.

"Can we please concentrate on the house?" I ask, exasperated.

"It's a lot of work, but I'll help you out depending on what you'll pay me." He waggles those damn eyebrows again. A move he thinks is cute, but I'm not some chick he's trying to pick up. One day he'll meet his match and I'll have a bowl of popcorn ready to watch the show.

"I have to get the house first," I say.

He picks up a dead plant on the windowsill in the kitchen and it falls to the counter in one big hunk of dried dirt.

"So, you're doing it then?" Luca asks.

"I've seen some other houses and they're not feasible. This is the only place I can afford and still make a decent return on."

He nods. "All right, I'm in. I can squeeze in a day or two."

"Don't do me any favors."

He laughs and we leave the house, the Realtor shutting and locking the door behind us.

"So the auction is next Tuesday at the courthouse," she says. "Get your funding or bring your checkbook. I doubt that many people want this house, but you never know."

She holds out her hand. "And if this is successful, maybe we can continue to do business." Her smile tips up a notch.

I shake her hand. "Thanks."

She gives one more inspection to the three of us and then heads down the stairs.

"Maybe she'll drop the commission rate if you sleep with her." Luca elbows me.

I shake my head. "Not interested right now."

"Sometimes I think I'm the mailman's kid around the two of you fucking saints." Luca jogs down the stairs heading to his bike.

Cristian and I follow. "Luca was saying something about your date from the auction?" I ask him.

His shoulders sag. "It's the fucking Commander's daughter. Out of all the luck, I get the one girl where if I don't go on the date, the Commander will be pissed and if I do go out he'll be pissed. I'm screwed either way."

"Is she good looking?" I ask.

"Does it matter?"

"Is she worth risking your job to get laid?" Luca chimes in as usual.

"She's a fucking knockout, but you guys know her," Cristian says.

Luca and I look at one another. "Who?" I ask.

"She's friends with Madison and Lauren."

"Who?" I ask again, my forehead scrunched.

"Oh that's right. They weren't cheerleaders." Cristian shakes his head and gives a wry laugh.

"What does that mean?" I ask, crossing my arms in defense.

"Lauren and Maddie went to our high school, but they weren't in *your* crowd." Luca laughs.

"Whatever. So the Commander's daughter went to St. George, too?"

"No. I don't know how she knows them, but it was Maddie who bid on me for Vanessa."

What is he talking about? Maddie, Lauren, and now Vanessa. None of the names ring a bell.

"Why would someone bid for someone else?" I ask.

"Lauren said they thought it would be fun," Luca chimes in again and I'm wondering how they're in the loop, but I'm not.

"Sucks for you two," I say with a laugh.

They both widen their stances, share a look of amusement and cock their eyebrows at me.

"Hate to break it to you, but Maddie didn't bid on you. Lauren did." Luca laughs while Cristian chuckles.

"I'm going out with a Madison and she didn't go to our high school. Which reminds me." I pull out my phone.

"Maddie is Madison, you idiot," Luca says. "Her and Lauren were my year."

"I went to high school with Madison?" I try to let her face come back to me, and though I can picture her bright blue eyes and long chestnut hair, nothing about her is familiar from high school.

"Yes, but she definitely wasn't hanging out at the bonfires and football pep rallies." Luca grabs his helmet off his bike. The only responsible thing I've seen him do in the last few years.

"Well, shit and she doesn't even want to go out with me? Her friend bid on me?"

Luca straddles his bike with a grin. I look over to Cristian, but he's putting his shirt back on and starts fiddling with his earbuds. They obviously think this conversation is over.

"Yeah, but we're all in the same boat." Cristian's thumb moves over his phone screen. "Maddie's awesome and I think you'll have a good time with her."

"She seemed pretty quiet and way too accommodating," I say.

Luca kicks his stand up, letting the bike rock a little under him.

Cristian's hands freeze on the screen of his phone. "And that's bad?" he asks.

"I want a woman who knows what she wants. Has her own damn opinions. Doesn't just agree with everything I say."

Cristian peeks over his shoulder, a look of amusement that matches Luca's. "You want a girl to come up and grab your nuts?"

"I want a girl who knows what her favorite food is, has an opinion about where she wants to go for dinner, likes whatever sports team she likes and doesn't default to my favorites." I stuff my hands into my pockets, digging out my keys for my truck.

"Well then, Maddie might not be the one. Like I said, she's nice." Cristian slaps me on the shoulder. "Treat her good though, okay?" He inserts one earbud.

"What do you think I'm going to do, leave her in Garfield Park?"

He puts his other earbud in. "That's not even funny man. I have a friend in that district and the shit that goes down there..." He shakes his head.

Cristian loses the entire point of my statement—the fact I'm not a jackass. I'm not Luca.

"It's one date," I say. "And who knows, maybe she's nice but still has a wild streak."

Christian again glances over to Luca who's smiling like he's fucking Mickey Mouse.

"Well, good luck on your date," he says.

Cristian jogs away and Luca's bike starts up.

I head to my truck.

The conversation is over, but I'm curious now.

Where's my damn yearbook?

CHAPTER FIVE

Madison

I peek through the window of Dice and Spins before deciding to wait outside. My habit of arriving ten minutes early is making me feel awkward while I wait for Mauro to show up. Maybe I should round the corner and wait to make a dramatic entrance like a woman who is fashionably late—one who struts across the pavement, her legs elegantly stepping one in front of the other as she unbuttons her coat and lets it slide down her arms behind her for the mystery man to take while she shakes out her hair. All while the man who's been waiting on pins and needles for her to show is mesmerized thinking how blessed he is to have this gorgeous woman walking toward him.

Ding.

Ding.

Ding.

"Lady!" a man yells and I look up to see a bicycle barreling right toward me. The guy seems to be about my age with a satchel over his back, a long stream of blonde hair coming out from under his helmet and a nasty 'get the fuck out of my way' look on his face.

"Sorry." I sidestep, only to run into another pedestrian on the street.

That person puts their hands on my shoulders to right me and keeps on walking without a word.

Heat scorches my cheeks and I step forward thinking I'll just wait inside and look like the girl who has no life and has been crossing days off on her calendar with big red Xs until today.

Not that I did that.

Okay, I did. But I do that every day though. It had nothing to do with Mauro.

A large hand grabs the door handle of the cafe before I can.

"Hey, Madison," Mauro says, opening the door with a polite smile.

He wore cologne. It's the first thought that comes to my head. The woodsy cedarwood scent makes the city vibe disappear behind me. That and the way his dark jeans hug his strong thighs in just the right way and the way his grey Henley shirt makes his eyes look a dusty shade of blue.

"Hi, thanks," I mumble, stepping into the cute café. One that Lauren and I have spent hours in competing with each other over Scrabble, Monopoly, or my personal favorite, Life.

The door shuts with a swoosh behind us and we stand on the welcome mat. A lot of booths are already taken with families and teenagers alike enthralled in their games, appetizers, and drinks sitting forgotten at the edge of their tables.

"I've never been here," Mauro says, extending his arm forward, allowing me to lead.

"It's fun. We pick a game, order some food and then play." I guide us to the back of the room to the ordering station.

"What game is your favorite?" he asks, his gaze roaming over the bookcases of board games to our left.

"You pick." I'm not really sure what Mauro would want to play, if anything. Maybe this was a bad idea. Maybe I should have suggested a quick tapas place. Somewhere where our date would go quickly and he wouldn't figure out what a nerd I am. He probably thinks this place is totally juvenile.

Oh, God. Sweat is starting to gather at my temples. I don't know if I can do this.

"Lady's choice," he winks and my stomach does a triple backflip worthy of an Olympic gold medal.

"How about...Boggle?"

He doesn't smile, but nods. "Sure." There's an uneasiness on his face I can't help but notice.

I should've picked something else, but Boggle doesn't take long to play. I don't think he'd enjoy being tormented with a three hour game of Monopoly.

"We can always play something else," I say.

He grabs the box from the bookcase. "No. It's your night."

The reminder that he's only here because I paid for him to be here is like a bucket of cold water on my face. He'll amuse me by playing a few games, making small talk and having a bite to eat before he disappears forever this time.

I should be happy. He's not in my sector of the dating pool. Maybe after tonight, I can finally put my childhood crush to rest.

After the mental pep talk, I order a trio of hummus with vegetables and pita bread along with a berry and pecan salad.

Mauro's still dissecting the menu as me and the girl behind the register admire him. His Adam's apple is prominent while his neck is stretched out to read the menu above us. His strong forearms that have probably axed down thousands of doors are crossed over his chest. I can't even fault the girl for staring at him like he's the latest Hollywood heartthrob because he looks exactly like that.

His head tips back down and the two of us try to act like we weren't just fantasizing about what he'd be like in bed. If he noticed or felt our stares, he ignores them.

"I'll have the combo platter with wings, moz sticks, and potato skins. And a Miller."

I guess I should order a drink. If anything, it will make me feel less intimidated by him. Liquid courage, right?

"Can you add a glass of Riesling to our order?" I ask.

The girl smiles and hands us a number.

I open my purse to grab my wallet, but Mauro hands her a card before I have a chance.

"Hey, I'm supposed to pay," I complain.

He signs his name on the electronic device. "You paid enough. My treat." He winks, but it comes across as more playful than seductive.

She hands him back his card and he puts his wallet in his back pocket.

"Thank you," I say.

He holds up the box in his hands. "Lead the way."

The girl behind the register smiles at us, though it's probably mostly to Mauro. I grab the order number which is at the top of a long metal stick and head farther back to where there are still a few empty tables.

Don't think about how he's walking right behind me.

Good thing I wore my 'bounce a quarter off my ass' jeans.

I slide into one side of the booth and his large body folds into the bench across from me.

"Would you rather a table?" I ask, wondering if this will be uncomfortable for a man his size.

"No. I'm good. But thank you."

The Boggle box sits in the middle of the table and we both stare at it for a minute.

"Would you rather eat before we play?" I ask—anything to fill the awkward silence.

He leans back in the booth. "Whatever you want."

Again a reminder that I paid for his time tonight. I could kill Lauren for this.

"You decide."

He shakes his head. "No, please."

"Well, they're usually fast with the food orders, but we can probably get one game in." I grab two notepads and two pens from the stand on the table that includes extra timers and dice in case the ones that are supposed to be in the box are missing.

"I think my brother Luca would love this place." He looks around, taking the cap off the pen.

"He is pretty competitive, right?" I ask. I can talk about Luca. I don't know a ton about him other than that he played four sports in high school and still graduated in the top five percent of our class.

"Competitive is an understatement. He's like the idiot who would challenge Hulk Hogan to an arm wrestling match and expect to win. Everything is a competition to him." Mauro's lips curl and my stomach decides it's time for some gymnastic moves again.

"I do remember him being sure of himself." *Shit. I shouldn't have said that.*

He snaps his fingers and points. That flipping in my stomach quickly stops and starts churning instead.

"Luca told me you went to St. George?" The fact he states it as a question is like a knife in my back.

Our school wasn't that big and I know he was two years older than me, and I wasn't close to his social hierarchy, but we did share that one night.

It's probably a good thing he doesn't remember me, I remind myself.

"I did."

"I don't remember you." His face doesn't hold any arrogance with his comment. It looks more like he doesn't understand how I don't ring a bell to him.

"Well, people can change a lot in nine years."

His lips tip up into a half smile. "I hope you're right. I was a little self-centered then I guess, but who isn't in high school?" He shrugs.

Me. I want to raise my hand. I wasn't.

Wanting to veer as far away from this conversation as possible, I pry the box open and shake up the pieces in the plastic container.

"Do you know how to play?" I ask.

"I think so."

"Just try to come up with as many words as you can. The letters have to touch and you can't use a letter twice in one word."

He nods and poises his pen over top of the paper.

I place the plastic container in the middle of the table, taking off the cover and flipping over the timer at the same time.

Barely able to concentrate, I come up with a few five letter words but mostly three and four ones. My eyes flicker to the timer because this whole game thing was a bad, bad idea. The silence is excruciating and the late realization that I made our date somehow educational instead of fun sets in.

"Time's up," I say.

Mauro's sheet is filled, but I can't read a lot of the words because of his bad handwriting.

He leans back, propping his paper up so I can't see his answers.

"If you want to go first." I hold my hand out and he doesn't argue.

"Okay." He rambles off his list and I pretend I don't have some of the words.

Don't ask me why. Maybe because I don't want to castrate him with the first game we play. He seems bored and losing would probably make him even less interested in being here. I feel like we're both mentally checked out from the date.

I guess it just confirms my belief that Mauro might be nice to look at and a great hero in my dreams, but in real life on a real date, we aren't compatible.

I lie, allowing him to win because I made him come on this date. I don't even bother to read off my five letter words.

Thankfully, I can tuck my notepad away and repackage the game when the waitress comes over with our food. The bartender is there as soon as she's done, placing our drinks down on the table.

Mauro eyes my food and seems to grimace. I ignore the look and spread my hummus over my pita bread while my mouth really waters for the potato skins he's piling sour cream on.

We eat mostly in silence and though I haven't been on a ton of dates, this is by far the worst.

"How is it being a firefighter?" I ask, wiping my mouth with my napkin.

He chews faster, taking a sip of his beer to wash the food down his throat.

Way to go, Maddie, you're really hitting this one out of the park.

"It's great. I love it."

"That's good. I'm glad you found something you enjoy."

He examines me for a second and then dips a mozzarella stick into the marinara sauce.

"What about you? What do you do?" he asks before taking another bite and after I've sipped my wine.

"I own my own company."

His eyes widen and a soft, genuine smile appears. "That's awesome."

He doesn't ask what exactly I do and I don't volunteer any information.

"You have a good schedule, right?" I ask, attempting another round of conversation.

"Yeah, but if we're out all day and night, it's like the first day off is recovery time. I can't complain though." He drinks from his beer. "What do you want to play after this?"

"Whatever you want," I answer.

I swear I catch a sour expression cross his face, but it disappears quickly.

His phone rings.

Here we go. The "friend" who needs him.

He presses the ignore button and places the phone face down on the table. "Sorry."

"No problem." I'm a little shocked he didn't take the out when he could.

"What brought you out to the bachelor auction?" he asks.

"My roommate's dad is a widow and she was hoping that if he gets involved with someone, he'd spend less time up in her business."

He chuckles softly.

"I understand, having a mom who doesn't understand privacy. That's how you ended up on a date with me, right? Your other friends are going out with my brothers?"

Is it possible that guys gossip just like girls?

"Um...yeah. Lauren Hunt?" I leave it open because maybe he remembers her from high school.

His lips purse, but he shakes his head. I'm about to continue, but the recollection of her crosses his face. "Soccer team?"

"Yeah." My tone might hold a tad of bitterness now that he remembers her and not me.

"She bid on you for me. I bid on Cristian for Vanessa and Vanessa bid on Luca for Lauren. It was really stupid. I have no idea why we agreed to it." I push my plate away, uncomfortable eating in front of him.

"So you didn't want to go on a date with me?"

"NO!" A few people at the tables around us glance our way so I lower my voice. "I wasn't against it."

He shakes his head. "Don't try to sweet talk me." The smile that consumes his face suggests he's just joking. "So you knew who I was when we met that night?"

The flush heats my face. "I did." I take a large sip of my wine.

"Why didn't you say anything?" He seems genuinely perplexed.

His plate is clear except for the green lettuce and ramekins with half used sauce. He picks up his beer, holding the glass to his lips.

"I don't know." I shrug.

"Do I scare you?"

"What?" His question throws me for a loop. "Why would you say that?"

"That's the loudest I've heard you speak since we met. Figure it has to be something." He leans back in the booth, a pleased smile on his face.

"And?"

"And nothing. You're a people pleaser." He finishes his beer.

"A people pleaser?" My forehead creases.

"Yah. A people pleaser. You haven't once picked anything you wanted to do this entire date."

"We're here because I chose this place. I chose Boggle."

"Where you let me win." He raises an eyebrow.

My eyes glance down at the paper. "No, I didn't."

He eyes the paper. My hands move, but he's faster,

swiping it up before I can grab it. His eyes scan the paper, his smile growing wider.

"You beat me."

I tear the sheet from his hands. "I was being polite."

"You were being accommodating. Did you think I'd get pissed off if you won? Or that it would wound my self-esteem?"

Okay, seems we've moved past the awkwardness now.

"I was just being nice."

He nods like I just confirmed something he already believes.

"I'm sick of nice." He says the word nice like it's bad.

My back straightens. "Well I'm sorry, I'm a *nice* person."

"I think you're confusing nice with a people pleaser. You didn't have to lie and pretend that you lost. You could've thrown the piece of paper in my face and told me to suck it."

At this point, I think that my jaw is hanging open. Is that the kind of girl he wants?

"That's not me."

"You sure about that?" The grin on his face makes me want to smack it off him or kiss it off him—I'm not entirely sure which.

I narrow my eyes and cross my arms over my chest. "Yes, I'm certain."

"It's too bad because you're gorgeous. I had high hopes coming into this date that I pegged you wrong." The cocky smirk on his lips might look delectable, but I'm ignoring the tug at my lady bits especially over the fact that he called me gorgeous.

"Sorry to disappoint you. I think suffice it to say this date is over."

"We could do another round of Boggle. You could just pretend that you don't spot the words again."

I throw my napkin on my plate, down the rest of my wine and slide out of the booth. "I'm done."

He catches my wrist before I can step away.

I wrench it back. "What?"

"Now this, I like." His gaze flows up and down over me.

A million swear words go off in my head, but I keep them to myself.

"Have a nice life."

I stomp away, ignoring the blatant stares from onlookers questioning why a girl would dare leave a man like Mauro Bianco in such a fashion.

Needless to say, I think I'm over my persistent high school crush.

CHAPTER SIX

Mauro

Her strawberry scent lingers after she flees from my unwarranted wrath, the crumpled up Boggle sheet still lay on top of her barely touched salad and hummus.

I tried to ignore the signs.

I let it go when she sheepishly looked at me when I opened the door for her.

Like I didn't hear her mumbled thank you.

I kept throwing the decisions her way when we had to pick a game.

The food she ordered was bird scraps at best.

And then when she wouldn't eat in front of me.

But when she let me win, I couldn't help but call her out on acting like she didn't find the word *ate*. She's way smarter than me. I realized that the minute I found her in my old yearbook.

She was the president of the Honor Society her sophomore year. I saw her picture with the glasses and braces, more meat on her bones. I'm fairly sure that's why she chose to keep her identity a secret from me. And if we were in high school again, I wouldn't have blamed her, but we're adults now. And when I called her out on it, I had high hopes she'd own who she was. Say 'yeah, I was a nerd back then but so what?' I'm still amazing and look at me now.

Hell, I'd respected her if she shot out some cocky comment that I could've had her in high school but I was too shallow so I'm not getting a piece of her now. I would've made sure to prove her wrong.

But she sat there all timid, eyes cast down and shy body language. After years of dating the same kind of woman and the fact that my ex-girlfriend Jenna screwed me over, the dam broke.

Sliding from the bench, I pocket her Boggle sheet and grab the game to place it back on the shelf on my way out. Some other poor sap can get schooled by his date.

Once I'm back outside, I walk close to the storefront windows, trying to find shelter from the light mist falling out of the dark sky.

Glancing at my phone, I see it was Luca calling me earlier. I dial him back.

"Where are you? We're heading to Rush Street tonight, want to join?" he asks.

Another night at a club? No thank you.

"Nah. Thanks though."

"When did both my brothers go pussy on me?" He doesn't bother to hide the displeasure in his tone.

Luca parties every night he isn't on shift. Never did I think two years difference would feel more like six.

"I just finished with a date." I stop at the light, waiting to cross.

"Didn't go well, huh?"

"How'd you know?"

A bachelorette party files out of a limo parked by the

curb. The poor bride who has dicks glued on every inch of her clothing stumbles into the pizza place. Yeah, she's not making it to the bar.

"Because you're talking to me. You should be on your way to your apartment, or better yet have her pressed against a brick wall in the alley. The last place you should be is on the phone with me."

I can't argue with him, he's right. The date was a bust especially when I morphed into an asshole at the end.

"I'm heading home."

"Perfect. That's where I am."

My mood sours further. Luca tends to travel in packs. Him and his freeloader pack of wolves probably drank the last of my beer.

"Why?"

"Oh, sweet brother. You gave me a key, remember?"

I step onto the red line train. The doors shut behind me. "That was for emergencies."

"I was out of beer. That *is* an emergency." One of his jackass friends laughs in the background.

"Leave my apartment and don't take the key with you," I warn, tapping end call.

I slink down into an available seat. It's too early for the train to be filled with young nightlife people like Luca but too late for commuters. Two couples sit on opposites sides of the train—one with limbs entwined and faces close. The other with backs straight and faces forward. The woman with her head in her phone and the man staring out the window. It's like seeing the before and after effects of the infatuation phase of a relationship.

Either the beer or exhaustion sets in and my eyes close as I rest my head against the glass of the window. Madison's temper those last few seconds together overtake my thoughts. The way her cheeks flushed with anger and not arousal. How her sulking shoulders straightened and her jaw jutted out. The fire that glinted in her eye of all the things I could tell she wanted to say to me.

All of it made me so rock hard, I almost pulled her into my lap and kissed her. Luckily, I refrained because I'm pretty sure she would've smacked me across the face. No matter how hot her fight got me, I realize now that it was wrong of me to take out my own frustrations on her.

I exit the train at my stop and by the time I'm walking up the steps to my apartment I can hear the music inside blaring. Of course since my day has been a suckfest, Mrs. Peterman opens up her door just as I hit the landing, her wig half-cocked on her head, Mr. Wiggles in her arms as she stares at me with a pointed glare.

"I can't hear Survivor," she tells me.

"Sorry, Mrs. Peterman. It's my brother."

"I saw him leave two hours ago." She sucks her false teeth back into place.

"Yeah, my other brother. The paramedic. Luca?"

She looks at me like I'm speaking a language she doesn't understand.

"I can't miss anything on the show. I'm trying to be nice here since you boys do so much for the city, but my show is important."

I put up my hand in apology. The last thing I need is her calling the landlord. "I know, I know. I'm sorry, Mrs. Peterman."

She nods and steps back into her apartment, shutting the door behind her. The echo of five different locks following her departure. You'd think a woman so scared wouldn't mind a little music when it meant that a cop and firefighter lived across the hall.

I open my door because unlike Mrs. Peterman's door, my

brother believes he's invincible. Or that he can take any burglar who wants to rob us.

"Turn down the music." I don't wait for him to oblige because Luca and his buddies are all out on our small porch that overlooks...nothing spectacular.

I press off on the stereo and Luca whips his head around, his attention inside the apartment immediately.

"Mrs. Peterman complained." I raise my hand before he can make some remark about what a pussy I am.

"You'd think after that time I carried her down two flights of stairs and got her to the emergency room she'd stop giving us shit," Luca says, coming in from the patio.

I open the fridge, grabbing a beer and twisting it open.

"First of all, you don't live here." I point at him with the neck of the beer.

He shrugs, propping himself up on the kitchen counter, grabbing a tortilla chip from a bag he opened from our pantry. Forever the little brother.

"We're family." He holds his arms out, inviting me into a hug I want no part of.

"There's a reason we don't live together." I inspect the kitchen, the empty beer bottles all over the table and chips and salsa strewn about the counter. "Cris is going to freak. Thanks for leaving me a Friday night of clean up."

I leave my beer on the counter and organize the beer bottles so after Luca and his dimwit friends leave, I can at least chill out and watch television.

"Cris needs to lighten up. So tell me about your date?" He hops down and tosses his empty into the recycle bin before lining up a row of four shot glasses.

"I'm not taking a shot," I say.

"Then I'll take two." He pours Jim Beam into the glasses but doesn't call his friends in. "Come on, I'm your brother and panty melter extraordinaire."

I toss the paper towel in the trash. "I was an asshole and now I have to apologize."

"You were an asshole to Maddie?" His jaw hangs open. "She was always the sweetest girl."

"Not so sweet when you piss her off." I snag my beer and tip it back. The shot is looking more appealing now when I think of how I have to make it right with her.

"How'd you piss her off? I mean after high school, jeez, you really are an asshole."

I pause with my beer halfway lifted to my lips. "Excuse me?"

"Come on. You aren't that dense, are you?" Luca's friends come in, all saying their hellos and fist bumping me. Half of them I've known just as long as my own friends. I figure this is good. Luca will leave and I don't have to hear him tell me off for how I treated her. Instead he says, "Hey guys, I'll meet you down at the club."

They all look at one another like their leader gave them a confusing order.

"Luca, go. I'm gonna clean up so I don't have to hear Cristian's bitching when he gets home. After that, I'm hitting the sheets."

Luca shakes his head and nods toward the door so his friends leave.

After the door shuts, Luca grabs a shot and hands it to me. I down it without argument and he downs another one.

"You looked her up in the yearbook, right?" Luca's eyes narrow to slits, curious to what the fuck I did. I'm not sure why he cares. It's not like he's friends with her. He's never mentioned her or her friend until the auction.

"Yeah, I looked her up."

"And?"

"And what? She looks different, I noticed that. I get what you guys were saying...that we didn't travel in the same circles and that I was a dick in high school, but none of that has anything to do with her."

He blows out a breath and lets out a cocky chuckle, suggesting I truly am the stupidest person he's ever met.

"Madison Kelly loved you, man. I mean head over heels for you. Hunt probably bid on you because she wanted to give her best friend the date she's been waiting a decade for."

"Hunt?" I have no idea who he's talking about.

"Her friend, Lauren Hunt."

"You refer to her by her last name?"

Luca shakes his head. "I don't want to talk about her. You really don't remember Maddie?"

I swig down a few more mouthfuls of beer. "She looked kind of familiar in the pictures. But I was a senior and she was a sophomore. I didn't know a ton of sophomores." I shrug and then throw my empty beer bottle into the recycling.

"You didn't know a lot of nerds." Luca tilts his head and gives me a challenging stare.

"High school was eleven years ago. I wasn't an asshole to her tonight because she wore glasses and had braces. I was an asshole because she was all shy and timid." I throw my hands in the air. "I have no fucking clue why I'm still talking to you about this."

Going out to my balcony, I pick up after Luca and his destruction crew.

His footsteps follow behind me like I assumed they would. "You're talking to me because it bothers you that you hurt that poor girl's feelings." He frowns and sticks out his bottom lip. "You came to your more knowledgeable brother for advice." He extends his arms and uses his hands to motion me in for a hug. "Come, Luca will make it all better."

I throw a cheeseball at him and it pings off his forehead. "You should probably get going to meet your friends."

He chuckles. "Tell me what's wrong with shy and timid? They're usually the kinky ones in bed."

I stop to stare at him, unamused.

"What?" He raises his hands up in a placating fashion. "It's not stereotyping if it's fact."

I plop down on one of the two chairs we have on the small outdoor space. Propping my feet up on the metal railing, I stare out at the sliver of skyline view we have before the next building blocks it. I notice a party full of girls in the condo building across the street, and it's clear what Luca and his friends were doing out here.

"Nice." I shift my eyes from Luca to the girls.

He sits down in the empty chair. "You can't blame us, they were having a sex toy party." He pushes his own long legs against the metal railing.

"I don't know why I did it, okay?" I don't turn to him, but I feel his eyes on me. "I just... I'm done with girls who try to mold themselves into a version of a woman they think I'll like. I knew she was different from the moment I met her at the auction. I mean it's nice she doesn't flaunt her amazing body. Truth is, before I approached her at the auction, I was excited that she bid on me. I can't even describe my first impression of her other than that she was out of my league. Then I approach her and she can barely say a word or keep eye contact."

"Hard life when you turn women into babbling messes."

Luca doesn't understand my dilemma or why I acted the way I did to Madison. He's still in the 'you're hot, come home with me' stage. The only thing he needs to know about her is that she's of age and that one of them has a condom. It doesn't matter if he knows whether she has siblings or not. He doesn't care what her favorite travel destination is, or if she's an early riser. Actually, he usually hopes she is an early riser so she wakes up and gets the hell out of his bed without expecting breakfast.

"Stop judging me." He points at me, like he could actually telepathically listen to my thoughts.

"Just go find your Friday night girl."

He sits up, resting his elbows on his knees and stares over at me. "I get what you're saying. You're getting older and looking for a wife."

"I'm not looking for a wife, just a girl who will be herself and has a backbone and isn't afraid to show it."

Luca just stares at me, confusion laced in his features. "Then I'd say the girl who used to write your name in her binder in high school probably isn't your girl. But you still need to apologize for no other reason than the fact that I have to go on a date with her best friend and I don't want your fuck up ruining what is already going to be a horrible night for me." With that cryptic comment, he rises out of the chair and puts his hand on my shoulder. "Your fighting girl is out there somewhere."

I let him leave and enjoy his night as my mind stays in flux. Like usual, I disagree with my brother. Madison Kelly might just be my fighting girl.

CHAPTER SEVEN

Madison

The anxiety of coming home early after my date crashed and burned like an Indy 500 car that hit the wall straight-on sets in when the dark windows of my place greet me. Vanessa must be at her mystery job and Lauren is either on a date herself or just out. Of course, I wouldn't put it past her to be doing PI work on Vanessa. She's way too worked up about Vanessa's comings and goings.

After I've driven up the alleyway and parked in the garage, I make my way through the backyard toward the house. The back door opens before I reach it and Lauren softly closes it shut behind her.

"Lauren," I say in a calm voice.

Her hand covers my mouth, and my back ends up hitting the banister of our porch. That's going to leave a bruise. Sometimes her quick reflexes make me think she was an assassin in her prior life.

Without any explanation, and with her hand still covering

my mouth, she turns me around and pushes me forward to lead me to where I just came from—our detached garage.

She doesn't remove her hand from my mouth until she callously shoves me into the backseat of her yellow Fiat which is parked in the garage.

"What the hell?"

She ignores me, throwing a blanket over us so we're concealed while peering out the back window.

We watch as Vanessa steps through the outside entrance of the garage, her heels clicking on the new cement I poured a month ago in preparation of selling this property. She doesn't give a glance to the Fiat when she presses the garage button and the large door rises.

A black town car waits idle for her in front of us and she presses the code on our keypad, making the garage door lower, leaving us with a view of her climbing into the backseat, unable to tell if there's anyone already in there.

Lauren, the little acrobat, jumps into the front seat and thrusts the keys into the ignition and hits the button on the remote for the garage door opener. The tires squeal and she peels out of the garage.

"Hello! What the hell are we doing?" I climb awkwardly into the front seat, the seatbelt my first priority.

"We're going to follow her." Her small foot presses on the gas pedal and we round the corner of the alley into the street.

"I'd like to not die tonight." I grasp for the door handle, anything to hold on to.

"Please. I know Chicago roads like a cardiologist knows the heart."

I don't even try to argue with the deranged line of thinking. Instead, I close my eyes. After a minute, I peek out of one eye because it's good to test your heart under stressful situations, right?

"Tell me about your date." Lauren tries to spur a conversation as she speeds past a biker on the right.

"Later."

"What?" She brakes hard, almost rear-ending the car between us and the town car. Her eyes stay focused on me as the red light illuminates her face through the windshield. "Maddie?"

"Nothing. We'll talk about it after this little PI move you've kidnapped me for."

She doesn't press the gas and I notice she's still in her scrubs from the physical therapist's office. "Did he treat you bad? Because I'll find him and nut check him." The pissed off expression on her face says she's serious.

"No. I mean...well...I took him to Dice and Spins."

A green light replaces the red one streaming into the car and I slam into the back of the seat when she guns it.

"Why would you take him there?" she asks.

"Because I thought it would be fun."

The town car stops at a light to turn left forcing Lauren to piss off the person beside us as she presses on the gas, squeezes in and slams on her brakes. Horns honk and I sink down in the seat.

"Seriously, you'd never be able to be a real PI person. The driver is probably on to you."

"Don't change the conversation. How did Mauro enjoy playing Life?" Her condescending tone confirms what I figured out mid-date—that it was the worst date idea ever.

"He didn't seem to care until I...lost."

"You didn't?"

The town car is moving and Lauren follows the car toward the lakefront.

"What? Women do it all the time," I insist, but even I can hear the lack of confidence in my voice.

"Not you, Maddie." She shakes her head. "I have to say

though, I'm surprised he noticed. He always seemed so self-centered."

I stare ahead as the car slows down due to the traffic around Lakeview and the masses of young people heading out for the night.

I'm not sure I want to stick up for Mauro, but if we hadn't had that small fight at the end, I never would have realized that he noticed everything about me. In truth, that might be what scared me the most. Like he could see inside me...how messed up I was from high school...how my beliefs about myself didn't catch up with my outward appearance. Lauren may believe that Mauro is all about himself, but he nailed me in one night. I can be a people pleaser and whether that had anything to do with having a mom who fell to pieces when my dad divorced her or a dad who moved miles away after the divorce so that I only saw him for a few days in the summer and maybe on holidays, I don't know. Or maybe it came from trying to make up for my lack of beauty at a time in my life when everyone is judged on how attractive they are. Regardless, his words sunk into me like tattoo ink on bare skin.

I might be a confident woman in my job, but when it comes to social situations, I am and probably always will be a people pleaser at heart.

"Duck!" Lauren says as the car comes to an abrupt stop.

She sinks down low in the car and I mimic her incognito behavior.

"I think this is a little extreme. Vanessa will tell us when she's ready," I say.

Lauren pays no attention to me, her eyes trained on the town car pulling around the front entrance to a condo building none of us would be able to afford a simple studio apartment in.

The town car driver exits the car, rounding the front until he opens up the back passenger one. A doorman heads out at the same time, holding the front door open of the condo building.

Vanessa steps out first, a raincoat I never knew she owned cinched tight around her waist, leaving only fishnet stockings and stiletto heels visible.

"It's so cliché I'm nauseous," Lauren says.

I jab her in the shoulder. "This proves nothing."

I'm fully in defense mode until a man emerges out of the town car. No suit, no tie, no clean-cut hairstyle that would suggest that he's a successful businessman. Instead, he's sporting a scruffy unkept beard and shaggy haircut with a plaid shirt untucked over a pair of jeans.

"It's so much worse than I thought," Lauren says.

"We don't know anything for sure."

Lauren's judgmental gaze flickers to mine. She's cast her verdict already.

I'm not so sure. Maybe it was my night with Mauro, that he wasn't who I pegged him for, but I'm not convinced that Vanessa is an escort.

The doorman tips his head toward Vanessa in a familiar way to suggest that this isn't her first time here. They disappear through the doors a second later, leaving the silence in the car thick like the fog on an early spring morning.

"It's worse than I thought. She's not even like Julia Roberts. There's no Edward...what was his last name?" She doesn't wait for me to answer. "I mean did you see that guy? She's going to sleep with *him* for money? Why wouldn't she just come to us? God knows I don't have a ton of extra cash because of my student loans, but I'd give her every extra penny I could."

Lauren's hand goes to the door handle.

"No!" I yell, reaching forward to stop her.

"We have to save her. If we catch her red-handed, she'll

confess. The three us can figure this out. Surely you'll give her a pass on rent."

I love Lauren, but she's wrong. "If we go in there guns blazing, Vanessa will flee. She'll move out of the house. She'll refuse to have anything to do with us."

"No, she'd never."

"Vanessa is hard-headed and after having a father who dictated her every move her entire life, she's not about to swap him out for two best friends who are going to treat her the same way. She has to come to us for help."

I don't inform Lauren that I've already told Vanessa not to pay me, but on the first of every month, there's always an envelope under my pillow stacked with small bills. It pains me each time, but Vanessa would never let either one of us flip a bill for her. She's too proud, a trait she inherited from her father, although she'd deny the accusation.

"She can't sell her body." Her tone has turned defeated.

"We don't know for sure that she is."

Lauren's fingers weave around the steering wheel, her fingernails digging into the indentations. "She's in a town car with fishnets and heels."

"Maybe it's her date. He's older. She could be embarrassed to tell us."

I'm not sure I believe the words coming out of my mouth. Vanessa has a type and the man that followed her into that condo building isn't him. She might have daddy issues, but she's not looking for another one.

"Come on. I'll buy you ice cream." My hand lands on Lauren's arm. "She's a smart girl. If she was into something bad, she'd tell us."

Lauren glances at the building again, the town car now gone, the doors closed.

"Okay," she agrees reluctantly.

Ten minutes later Lauren has processed my words about

Vanessa and although she'll never tell me I'm right, we both know that I probably am.

"If you're buying, we're going to George's."

"Then you better hit the gas if you want to make it before they close," I say.

Lauren listens to me and although she's back to her sane self, no longer weaving in and out of traffic and almost hitting parked cars, there were a few close calls with pedestrians. Lauren's justifies her near misses with the theory that it's Friday night and people shouldn't come down to the city if they don't know how to follow the traffic signals.

Twenty minutes later, the glass doors of George's are shut and locked behind us. I have my typical cookie dough ice cream bowl in hand, while Lauren opted for cookies 'n cream. Instead of hopping back in the car, we walk down the street. We pass a few couples strolling along after dinner and I'd be lying if I didn't yearn for what they have.

"Tell me what happened on your date," Lauren says, finding a park bench and sitting down.

"I made a fool of myself, but what's new about that?" I take a seat beside her.

Her shoulder knocks mine and I sway before righting myself. "I'm sure you didn't."

"I thought I was over the high school crush, you know. That I could go in there and be all 'look at me now.' But the minute he was inches away, my voice locked up and I was that girl again. The one who thought he'd never go for a girl like me."

"Is that what you were looking for? For him to want to date you?"

I shrug. "I don't know. Maybe. Probably. I at least wanted to be asked." I bury my head in my ice cream. "I know it's stupid."

"Why is that stupid? He's the one for you. Why do you think I bid on him?"

I glare at her from the corner of my eye. "Thanks for that by the way."

She giggles, spooning a big heap of the cookie into her mouth. "So you let him win and then what happened?" she mumbles over the giant cookie lodged in her mouth.

"He was angry. Called me out. Said I was a people pleaser."

"You're nice," she counters, sounding as affronted as I was at the time.

"See!" I point my spoon at her. "That's what I said, but he said I was confusing the two."

"You're not a people pleaser when it comes to me. If that was the case, Vanessa would be sitting on this bench with us."

Point proven.

"But when it comes to people you don't know, you do tend to give in too easily." Her eyes cast down and I think she's afraid of how I'll take her criticism.

"No, I'm not."

"You are," she insists.

"Sometimes I really just don't care when presented with two options." I shove a spoonful of ice cream into my mouth.

"I get that, Maddie. I probably care too much about getting my way which is why we've been best friends forever. I can take advantage of you by always getting my way."

"Hey."

She leans into me, placing her head on my shoulder. "I'm kidding. I throw you a bone every now and then." Her eyes flutter in a 'forgive me I'm beautiful' motion.

"We were only together for like two hours. I can't be that transparent to a guy who didn't even remember I existed until his brothers told him we went to high school together."

The ache from that jab returns like scar tissue under the surface of my skin.

"Maybe Mauro has changed."

"Well, I'll never find out because I told him to—"

A smirk crosses Lauren's face. "Told him to what?"

"I told him to have a nice life." Mimicking the conviction in my tone I had with Mauro hours earlier.

"Oh Mad, you are too nice. I'm not exactly shaking in my boots over here." She laughs and I join her.

"What should I have said?"

"You should have said even if I see you in my next life it's too soon."

"That's mean." I toss my empty cup of ice cream in the trashcan beside the bench then stand up.

"Yes, Maddie. Mean is the exact opposite of nice," she says with a smile on her face. "See where we're going here?" She throws away her cup and swings her arm around my shoulders. "I'll have an effect on you yet." Her hip hits mine. "It's okay to be nice, I wouldn't want you any other way. Hopefully Mauro will be in your rearview mirror now."

"Not when you marry his brother." I don't even bother to look at her because she's probably planning my death based on the glare I feel on the side of my face.

"Never."

"Stranger things have happened." I steal a glance and her eyes are narrowed to slits.

"Pigs would be flying, a snowball would not melt in hell, you'd be holding your breath and the Cubs would win the World Series and still I would never walk down the aisle with Luca Bianco."

"I hate to remind you, but the Cubs did win the World Series."

"Again!" she yells. "They'd have to win it again. Damn it."

We're laughing as we climb back into her yellow Fiat to go

home and I realize this was just what I needed after my disastrous date. But one day we won't live together anymore and no one will be around to help pick up the pieces. An ache starts up in my chest. I'm not in any rush for that day to come.

CHAPTER EIGHT

Madison

The room in the courthouse is pretty packed when I arrive, which never ends up in my favor. I'm definitely not the only one bidding on Property 1731. I go over the figures in my head again while more people file in, mentally calculating how high I can bid for my old house. I rationalize the lower than normal return I'm willing to take, telling myself that the emotional aspect of this project outweighs the profit.

To know that a family lives there whose love will saturate into the grain of the wood support beams will give me immeasurable pleasure. Yes, I know. Cheesy as hell, but my family crumbled under that roof and I'm determined to smack a new roof on that baby to bring a shelter of happiness to a new family.

Lucky for me, no one seems to want to sit in the front row. The room is filled other than a sprinkle of empty seats in the rows behind me, my row is vacant except for a man at the end who took the second seat in. Weird, why he would take the second? Maybe he's waiting for someone.

A minute later the auctioneer approaches the podium.

I straighten my back, thankful that the Oswald's have yet to make an appearance. They'd be my biggest competition for this property. Already giddiness starts to flutter my insides, thinking that maybe I'll get away with a low bid.

"Good morning, ladies and gentlemen. Are we all ready to get this auction started? I'll go over the rules for you newbies." Rachel smiles down at me. "For you regulars, be patient with the new people in town."

I smile back, my eyes on her until the door opens at the back of the room.

Tardiness is unacceptable and if it's Oscar Oswald, I hope Rachel tells him he's two minutes late so he can fly a kite. All the eyes shift in the direction of the door, but as Mauro Bianco strolls across the room, it's only my breath that's lodged in my throat. This cannot be happening to me. I close my eyes and peek out of one like he could be a figment of my imagination.

"Sir, the auction starts at ten on the dot."

Throw him out, Rachel.

Please.

"I do apologize, ma'am, but I just got off shift. We had a late call and I got here as soon as I could."

"You're a firefighter?" she asks.

I roll my eyes over the fact that he'd wear his fatigues like a fanatic fan of a sports team just to get an advantage at the auction.

"Yes, ma'am. Engine Fifty-Five."

Rachel smiles and holds out her hand for him to enter the room. "Next time try to be on time."

Try? I want to scream. Anyone else who didn't have that sexy panty-melting smile would be out on their ass.

It's bad enough that I have to share oxygen with the man, but his enticing scent hits me full force as his weight lands in the seat next to me.

"Hey," he whispers.

"Hi." I keep my eyes poised on Rachel who seems more enthralled in watching our interaction than performing her job.

"What are you doing here?" he asks, continuing the conversation even after I didn't make eye contact.

"Same as you I suppose."

"You're bidding on a property?"

"No. I thought this was people pleasers anonymous," I deadpan.

A huge boisterous laugh erupts out of him, echoing through the silent room. Rachel glances up from the papers her assistant is explaining to her.

Kick him out, Rachel.

She smiles instead because his laugh is like an aphrodisiac.

"You're funny." He leans back in the chair, his shoulder touching mine, his thigh brushing my thigh before I swing my leg over and cross them, effectively relieving some of the awareness of how close he was.

"Thanks. I'll add that to my credentials. Can be funny when I'm not busy putting other's needs before my own."

My eyes zone in on Rachel who is taking her sweet time with the paperwork, her and her assistant in the deep throes of conversation, papers shuffling. Something is going on up there.

"I meant to message you, but my schedule..."

I wonder how many times he uses his schedule or the fact he's a firefighter to gain an as an excuse or to gain an advantage.

"Will you look at me?" He asks the one thing I cannot imagine doing in this moment.

"Yes." I look over his shoulder instead of meeting his eyes. He won't be able to tell the difference.

His forefinger lands under my chin and he urges my face forward.

And there they are. Those gorgeous blue eyes staring right back at me.

His hand drops to his lap.

"I wanted to apologize. I never should've acted like that to you."

"It's fine."

"Don't do that." The kind voice he was using a moment ago now holds a tinge of irritation.

"Stop telling me what to do." I look away from him to Rachel once again.

Come on. Is this property really worth this?

"I'm sorry it's just—"

"What Mauro? I'm sorry if I'm not the girl you want me to be. If I'm not perfect enough for you. Well, guess what? I don't care."

The man at the end of our row looks beyond Mauro's squared shoulders in my direction. If I was Lauren, I'd flip him off. Say some crude comment about minding his own business in her Laurenesque way. But I'm not her. I'm Madison Kelly, the one who smiles like nothing is going on between me and the firefighter.

"Perfect? Enough for me?" He sounds more as though he's not asking me, but himself.

Whatever.

"Yes. Would you like it if I was telling you how to act?"

A smile tips his lips. "Please do."

I roll my eyes.

"Come on." He eggs me on.

I stand and head over to Rachel.

"Hey, Rachel, can you let me know how much longer until we start?"

Her vision shifts from her assistant to me. "Sorry, Madison. There are five properties that were taken out of auction and we're waiting on word before we start. Gives you more time with the hottie over there." She smiles conspiratorially at me.

"Thanks." I give her a tight smile.

Mauro's smile is wide and annoying when I sit back down in my seat. "What's the word?"

"It's going to be awhile. Some properties are coming off auction."

"What? Did she say which one?"

His easy-going casual persona morphs into an anxiety ridden one like that.

"No. She can't tell us."

"That sucks, I hope it isn't mine," he says, rubbing his hands up and down his thighs.

"Yours? You haven't won anything. What property are you here for?" I ask, knowing a newbie would never take on the house I want. He's probably here for a condo that needs a few light fixture changes.

"I'm not saying."

I chuckle. "What? You think I'm going to want it?"

"You never know." He shrugs.

"That would go against my people pleasing efforts, don't you think?"

Again with the chuckle that's an on switch for the heat between the legs.

"Shit, Maddie, I wish I would've known you better in high school. You're funny."

"Only with you, apparently."

His hand covers his heart and his head falls back. "I'm honored."

I roll my eyes for the fiftieth time since he sat down next to me.

"So, your business, is it flipping houses?" he asks.

"Yes."

"Impressive. I'm just about to start my first redo."

"Good luck. Hope you're handy."

"I'm good with my hands."

I don't miss the sexual innuendo in his tone, but I don't react.

We wait in silence for another few seconds before he stretches—his arms high above his head, his torso rising. If I dared to sneak a peek I bet his shirt is rising, too.

I wonder if he has a happy trail?

No. No, you don't.

"So you think what? That this is a way to make a quick buck by flipping a house?"

"Whoa, never saw that jab coming." He laughs again.

Why is everything so damn humorous to him?

"Everyone thinks it's so easy. Buy it on the cheap, cut a few corners and double your money. I'm going to warn you, it's hard work."

"Thanks. I'll take it into consideration."

He crosses his arms in front of him, checking his watch and yawns. "I need a bed."

Can I join you?

Bad Maddie.

Rachel approaches the microphone. "I'm sorry ladies and gentlemen. Two more minutes. We're about done."

"What are you into flipping for if not for the money?" he asks, though his eyes stay trained on the wall ahead of us.

"To take something everyone thinks is ugly and past its prime and pull the beauty out of it so that people will love it again."

He says nothing but his eyes are burning a hole in the side of my head now.

"I didn't expect that," he says.

"What?"

"An explanation so, I don't know...profound?"

"Just do me a favor and if you are going to take the time to redo a house, think outside the box. Don't just go with whatever the latest trends are. Picture a family living there and do quality renovations, imagine what their life will be like while they're enjoying each and every decision you made along the way."

"Man, you're just full of advice today."

Rachel approaches the podium again, her assistant finding her spot right next to her with a stack of papers.

"Sorry." I cringe once the word leaves my lips.

"I don't offend easily, no need for apologies."

The fact he ignored the opportunity to take another jab at my people pleaser tendencies tells me he must have meant his earlier apology.

"Property 3902 is up for auction." A picture of the house comes up on the screen. "We'll begin the bidding at fifty-six thousand dollars." Rachel is all business as usual and I sit and wait for Property 1731 to be called.

The property doesn't get called until an hour later and though a lot of people have left, Mauro is still sitting right next to me.

Rachel eyes me, knowing my go-to property type. "Property 1731."

Mauro straightens in his chair, abandoning his phone to the vacant chair next to him.

No.

He looks over at me with the same expression of disbelief that's heating the blood in my veins. Forget the Oswald brothers. Mauro Bianco is my biggest threat?

Then he raises his eyebrows as though this is a challenge for him.

"Game on," I murmur.

"Don't play nice." He waggles his eyebrows and raises his hand. "Twenty thousand."

Narrowing my eyes, I put my own hand in the air. "Twenty-two thousand."

CHAPTER NINE

Mauro

If I could turn back time, I would. I'd go back to that board game cafe and keep my mouth shut about her letting me win because she has that fire in her eyes when she makes her 'game on' comment. You can tell this is her element, which probably means she's got the advantage here.

"Twenty-four," I raise my hand.

The auctioneer smirks at her assistant and points to me. We both know I won't have the winning bid for long.

"Twenty-six." The spitfire girl next to me raises her hand like an eager teacher's pet.

Was she?

With no one else coming in to bid, I figure it must be only us.

"How high?" I whisper to her. "Twenty-eight," I say.

"What? Why? I'm not telling you." Her head is twisting between me and the auctioneer, her hand already back in the air. "Thirty."

"Because we're just raising the price up for one of us."

"That's the point," she says out of the side of her mouth.

"We have thirty. Do we have thirty-one?" The auctioneer eyes me.

"If we go too high one of us isn't going to make a dime," I say.

"Then save me the trouble and bow out."

"Thirty-one going once." The gavel is in her hand, her eyes silently asking me.

"Fine. Have it your way." I shrug. "Thirty-three."

"There's no rule about going up two k." She sneers her arm extended. "Thirty-four."

"Sorry, newbie and all." I shrug.

Her blue eyes narrow and she bites her lip. I shift in my seat from the concentrated effort it takes for me not to lean in and take that lip of hers with my own teeth.

"Thirty-five."

She huffs, her shoulders deflating in defeat for the first time since the opening bid.

We're now way over the starting bid and if one of us wouldn't have come, the other would have had it for twenty thousand.

"What are you thinking?" she whispers.

I can't stop the cocky grin from forming on my lips. Not because I knew she'd bend to my way, but because she's open to listening to my idea.

"I'm thinking we partner up."

"WHAT?"

Now, this is the type of woman I could get under.

"I'm sure you plan on hiring a contractor."

"We have thirty-five on the table. Anyone else?" The auctioneer is not leaving me much time to convince her.

"Yeah, so?"

"I can be our contractor. I know a million guys from the

firehouses who are skilled at different trades. Not to mention, I told you I have good hands." I hold them up for her to see.

"Thirty-five going twice." The auctioneer is being nice and going a lot slower than she did with previous properties. She seems to have a soft spot for Madison.

"You'll listen to me when it comes to budget and decorating decisions?" she asks, her eyes shifting from the gavel about to slam down making me the winner of the property.

I hold out my hand. "Sure thing, but you show me the ropes. We're partners. Fifty, fifty."

She stares into my eyes, for the first time not looking away. The softness of her hand slides into mine and I grip her hand. "Partners." Her tone might not hold the declaration I was hoping for, but it's a start.

She may not realize it yet, but she didn't get the bad end of this agreement. I think she'll be surprised by my skills.

"Sold." The auctioneer points to me, smiling down at our entwined hands.

Madison retracts, and the air conditioning must have blasted on because goose bumps run up my spine.

CHAPTER TEN

Madison

"Did you just pinch yourself?" Mauro asks next to me while we wait for the paperwork to be processed after we each supplied a check for half the amount of Mauro's bid on my childhood home.

I wrap my palm around the spot that I did, in fact, pinch myself at.

Wouldn't you think it was a dream if you just decided to partner up with your high school crush putting him in your proximity for months on end? My sixteen-year-old self is throwing confetti in the air and dancing the cha-cha. My current self is wary as much as she is excited.

"I had an itch," I lie.

He smirks, his signature trademark that probably has women stripping their panties off, but I need to hold him back with titanium arms because he'll railroad this project from me if I let him.

"Congratulations you two. You're proud owners of Property 1731." Rachel holds the paperwork out and I snatch it from her hands.

Mauro looks over at me incredulously.

"I'll keep everything organized."

"What makes you think I'm not organized?" he asks.

Rachel shares a look with her assistant that reads more 'aren't they cute' rather than 'this property will be up for auction again in two months.'

"I have a system."

"I'm sure you do and now I'm part of that system. Can you send me copies tonight?" His voice isn't sweet and syrupy, instead, it's almost accusatory as if I'd screw him over.

"Do you think I'm going to cheat you? Your name is on here."

"Just making sure we're in this together." A dimness dulls his eyes for a split second before they sparkle again. "No fights where you lock me out of the house or anything." The one side of his lips tip and I can't help the way my body melts under his flirtatious nature.

"No worries." I shove the papers in my purse. "Thanks, Rachel and Tracy. See you soon I'm sure."

I head out the door, hearing Mauro speak his own goodbyes and the ladies slight swoon back with we hope to see you soon, too. His footsteps loom behind me as I walk to the elevator.

"Let's go to breakfast, talk logistics."

"How about we pick up breakfast and go over to the house? The sooner we figure out our game plan, the better. I can have a dumpster there tomorrow to get all the crap out of the house."

He runs his fingers through his dark wavy hair.

Stop it, Maddie. Do not get sucked in.

"Okay. I'm off tomorrow and I can round up a crew."

"Hold up, stud. Let's go over plans before we start demolishing everything." I step into the elevator, the small box feeling even more claustrophobic with him sharing the space.

"Stud? I like it." His cocky grin appears—again.

"Don't take it as a compliment."

He steps forward, his hand landing on the silver railing at my side, his body so close to mine that my heart pounds in my chest as if it wants to reach out and touch him. "No?" he questions in a gravelly voice.

I shake my head, I haven't been this close to him since that night long ago and he still has the ability to paralyze my body.

"Stop messing around."

He chuckles and steps back out of my personal space.

Why would he even do that?

Running another hand through his hair, he stretches, bending and twisting in every direction.

"If you're tired..."

His gaze shifts to mine quickly. "No. We're in this together remember?"

"I know, but I slept eight hours last night and you... didn't."

"It's okay, I'm used to no sleep."

"If you say so." I shrug.

"Good, we should probably get some ground rules set," he says.

The elevator doors open. "Well, I'll pick up some breakfast and I'll meet you at the house. We can go over the business plan, talk about what we're going to do with improvements, so we know what walls to tear down."

"I'll grab the breakfast. What do you want?" he asks.

We exit the federal building and a man is walking toward us with a mass of media behind him. I freeze. We both shift our bodies to clear a path and it isn't until the suited man passes that I figure out who he is.

He doesn't see me, and just says "No comment" over his shoulder to the throng of reporters behind him before walking through the glass doors.

"That must be about that big fire. I know our Lieutenant said the investigation as to the cause is almost wrapped up and they're supposed to announce the findings soon," Mauro says next to me.

My gaze shifts to him because there's something about his voice...that's when I notice the flush that usually fills his cheeks is gone.

"Probably. The DA is my neighbor. That's him." I nod in the direction where Reed Warner finds solitude away from the cameras. He doesn't stop until he's through security and in the elevator.

"Good guy?" he asks, his eyes still on the media cluster that would make anyone think they're following a celebrity, not the district attorney.

"Really good guy. Did you know—"

He nods before I finish my question. "He was my buddy."

I'd read the articles six months earlier about a horrible fire where a firefighter lost his life. Even saw the funeral procession on the news with shots of a blonde woman with a son in her arms crying as they walked behind the firetruck.

My hand lands on his forearm, finding his skin cold and clammy and I don't think it has anything to do with the start of fall in Chicago. "I'm so sorry."

My touch seems to shock him back to the present and his gaze darts up to meet my own. All I want to do is hug him to my body, he looks like a newly adopted puppy shaking with anxiety.

"Hazards of the job." His hand covers mine. "Thank you though."

I slide my hand from his arm realizing that I just touched Mauro Bianco and didn't freak out.

The cameramen disperse, some going back to their vans parked along the street, others set up shots for the reporters in front of the building.

Wherever Mauro's mind ventured off to must clear. "Breakfast, right? I know just the place," he says.

His attention moves across the street and I spot the sandwich shop before he even mentions it.

"No one makes a breakfast burrito like my mama." He nods in the direction of his family's shop.

I drag my feet. "Are you sure you want to introduce me to your mom?"

He stops and smiles which is a relief after the look on his face moments ago. "She'll love you." He shrugs.

"Gee, will she approve of our shotgun wedding?" I laugh which spurs Mauro's amusement.

"You really are funny." He stares down at me while we wait for the walk symbol to appear on the streetlight.

"Thanks."

His eyes don't leave mine and my breathing picks up under his scrutiny. "I think we're going to make great partners."

I turn away first because I need to get a grip. Thankfully the pedestrian walk sign appears and I step off the corner before a hand grabs my upper arm and pulls me back as a blur of yellow streaks by me.

My back presses against his chest. Firm and strong.

"Watch it, asshole!" he yells at the cab driver.

"Thank you." I untangle from his grip as much as my body protests.

"No problem." His hand takes mine and he leads me across the street lightly jogging when the yellow hand replaces the white walking symbol.

He doesn't release my hand once we reach the other side of the street, like I assumed he would. Instead, he opens up the door for me to his parents' sandwich shop and shifts his hand to the small of my back.

He's Italian, they're touchy, I remind myself.

"Ma!" he yells into the empty restaurant.

It's a typical deli where you order and wait for your number to be called. You can have a seat at the long tables with stools along the window or in the booths that line the back wall which is painted in thirds. One with the Chicago fire department symbol, one for the police and another for paramedic. It's clear to me and their customers that their sons are their life.

"Mauro?" A woman who is shorter in stature, a little plump with dark, wavy shoulder-length hair emerges from the back, wiping her hands on her white apron that says, *My favorite hood is motherhood.*

"Hey, Mama." He smiles then hugs her and kisses her cheek. She does the same, but her gaze is fixed on where I stand behind him.

"This a friend?" she asks him in the cutest Italian accent.

Mauro steps back from his mom, holding his arm out in my direction. "Ma, this is Madison Kelly. Madison, this is my mom, Maria."

A warm smile crosses his mom's lips and her head tilts in a 'I know you' gesture. She points her finger at me. "Vale-dictorian?"

A warm flush heats my cheeks and Mauro studies me.

"Luca's class, right?" she asks.

"Yes," I answer sheepishly.

Her finger moves to Mauro and then back to me. "You two?"

"No," I quickly refute.

Her smile dims. "Oh." Her eyes shift to Mauro who shrugs like they're having a conversation between them without words.

"We're going to be business partners," he says after confusion masks her face.

"Business?" she asks, sliding behind the deli case and sifting through some paperwork.

"Remember Hunter and I were going to buy a house, fix it up and then sell it?" Mauro approaches the counter, his forearms flexing under the weight of him leaning over so his mom hears him.

"Yes." She doesn't turn around. I can't help but notice her curt demeanor after I said we weren't a couple. She rambles something in Italian and Mauro looks over his shoulder at me for a moment.

He responds back in Italian and before I realize it, she's turned back around, her voice rising, her face red again.

"Enough Mama," Mauro says, his back rod iron straight.

She tilts her head and I don't need to understand Italian because her body language says it all. It's a warning for him to watch how he talks to her.

"I'm sorry, but this isn't the time," he says, slightly chagrined.

"What is going on?" A man comes out from the back, taking plastic gloves off his hands and throwing them into a trashcan behind the counter.

"Papa," Mauro says.

The man who bears Mauro's light eyes, Cristian's nose, and Luca's mouth seeks the source of the reason for the high voices. "Hello." He rounds the deli cabinet, his hand already extended to me. "Anthony."

"Madison," I say and shake his hand.

"I was just telling Mama that Madison and I are going into business together." Mauro steps to my side, his hand finding the small of my back like he's presenting me as a gift, or a girlfriend.

I swallow past the dryness in my mouth and force on a smile that probably looks as awkward as this moment feels.

"Business?" his dad asks, a crease between his brows.

"The flipping houses thing? With Hunter...well, Madison already has her own business and we're going to work together on a house." His dad smiles down at me. I recognize it as the same smile Luca has, but his eyes are just as mesmerizing as Mauro's.

"Congratulations. That's wonderful news."

The deli phone rings. Mauro runs over and answers it before his mom can. He whispers something and hangs up. Again, he and his mom have a silent conversation, their eyes move to me and then back to each other.

"We're here for breakfast," Mauro announces. "Burritos, Mama?"

She smiles, her hand landing on his cheek as she studies his eyes. With a pat on the cheek, she smiles. "Anything for you."

"Non vedo l'ora," Mauro says.

His mom smiles and heads to the back.

"Very nice to meet you, Madison," Anthony says and follows his wife to the back of the deli.

Mauro comes over to me, sliding a chair out. "Sorry about the Italian. She's usually really good about not speaking in Italian when others are around who don't speak the language, but just hearing Hunter's name sends her in a tizzy." Mauro sits in his own chair across from me, legs sprawled out in front of him.

"That's okay."

I want to ask why that is? Was the partnership bad before he died? Is the fact that he died what angers his mom? There are a million reasons it could be, but it's none of my business. We need to keep this relationship professional.

"Your parents are nice."

A proud grin forms, revealing a mouth full of sparkling white teeth. "They're the best." He taps his fingers on the table. "What about your parents? Do they still live around here?"

My heart stumbles over a beat when I remember that he didn't know one key piece of information before we agreed on the partnership. If I were him, I would want to know. I cringe.

"There's something I have to tell you."

CHAPTER ELEVEN

Mauro

I notice the panicked look on her face and hear the anxious tone in her voice and my brows draw together.

"The house we bought is my childhood home." She presses her lips together, watching me absorb the information.

My phone vibrates in my pocket before I can ask why she bought her childhood home. Or how it ended up looking like it was previously on an episode of Hoarders. All these questions float in my head while she sheepishly stares at me with her top teeth pressed into her luscious bottom lip.

God help me, ever since the true Madison Kelly has shown her face, I've been trying to talk my dick down from the salute it wants to give her. The teeth on the lip is the last straw.

Seeing Cailin's name on the screen causes some internal conflict inside me for the first time since Hunter's death.

Usually, I'd stop whatever I'm doing to answer her call, but even I've noticed that they're becoming more frequent.

"Hold on one second." I pull the phone out of my pocket and head over to the doors. "Hey," I answer.

"Are you sleeping? I'm sorry." Cailin sounds as depressed as she usually does.

"No. I'm actually..." My eyes wander to Madison who is piling her hair up in a ponytail on top of her head. My mouth waters as the movement exposes her long neck and my lips beg for me to hang up this phone and venture over there for one taste. "I'm at The Sandwich Shop."

"Oh, tell your parents I say hello. Devin has been begging to see your mom."

"I'm sure she'd like to see him, too." The small argument we had in front of Madison surfaces in my mind. My mom and what might come out of her mouth would be too unpredictable if I let Cailin and Devin be around her right now.

"Since you're out and about anyway, how about a trip to the park with us?" Her tone is more chipper than when I first answered.

My eyes stay glued on Madison who's now pulled out a pad of paper and is scrolling through her phone. Her pen zooming along the page at warp speed like her mind is going too fast and her hand can't keep up.

"I'm sorry. I've got..." I pause because I'm not sure I want Cailin to know what I'm doing. Which is ridiculous because she wouldn't be upset. She'd probably think it was good or she'd be sad because Hunter was supposed to be a part of this venture with me. "An appointment."

Madison's pen stops and the tension in her shoulders fall.

"Oh...okay. What about dinner?" Cailin asks.

I was hoping to sleep through dinner. The only reason I'm still standing is from the pure adrenaline of starting in on this project. For the first time since Hunter's death, excitement fills my veins. I could kiss Patel for giving me the extra push I needed.

"Sure. I'll pick something up on the way over," I say.

"No. You're always spending too much money on us. I'll make dinner. How about six?"

"Sure."

"Great. Devin will be so excited."

My mom comes out from the back, her eyes taking in the situation. The fact I'm on the phone and Madison's by herself causes Ma to frown, and she shakes her head at me.

"See you then. Bye." I click the phone off.

So what if I'm still a tad scared of my mom. Italian mamas are unpredictable and scary. Don't judge unless you've been raised by one yourself.

Stuffing my phone into my pocket, I walk to the counter to pick up the burritos, but my mom turns her back on me and walks past me over to the table.

"I hope you like prosciutto?" she asks Madison. "I wrapped them in foil to stay warm." Instead of handing them to me, she hands them to Madison.

"Thank you so much." Madison drops her pen and reaches to touch my mom's shoulder in a kind gesture of appreciation.

My mom's entire face lights up. "Come back for lunch sometime. What's your favorite sandwich?"

Madison looks up to the ceiling thinking. "Honestly, I'm not much of a sandwich person." She shrugs. "If I had to give you one, I guess turkey?" The way Madison phrases it like a question brings a warm sensation to my heart. She's honest to a fault. Who knows if she'll ever see my mom again. She could have said any deli meat, but she didn't.

"Anthony will make you a sandwich lover. Come back for lunch someday." My mom pats her hand and stands.

"Thank you, Mrs. Bianco." Madison shoves all her stuff back in her bag and rises from the chair.

I grab the brown paper bag. "Bye, Mama," I say.

"Conosco I miei pollo." She touches my face again, her thumb gently rubbing my cheek the way she did when I came to her on one of the worst days of my life.

"I know, Mama." I glance to Madison who's granted us privacy and stepped closer to the door. "Business." I remind her like I did minutes ago after Luca's one-night stand from this past week called the deli. The guy can't get his shit together to save his life.

Her hand falls off my face to my heart. Her fingers drum over the organ.

Sometimes I wonder if she'd marry us off to any woman as long as it got her closer to grandkids.

My hand covers hers and I nod. Non-verbally telling her I'll think about it.

Although I have no intention to. My body might want Madison Kelly, but she agreed to a business partnership just hours ago. She'll show me the ropes and I'm not going to jeopardize my future by letting my dick get a say. So, I'll appease my mama because it will help her sleep at night, but I have no intention of ever letting Madison into my heart. Actually, I may shut that organ down until I'm six feet under at this rate.

I lean down and kiss my mom's cheek. "I'll be by Sunday."

She kisses my cheek back.

"Bye," Madison says, waving at my mom.

"Ciao," she says, the permanent smile plastered to her face.

"Where are you parked?" I ask Madison.

"On Dearborn in a parking garage."

"I'll walk you to your car and then get my truck."

"I'm fully capable of walking to my car. I've done it daily. For years now."

I laugh because she's so much more than the girl I saw on that date. I wish I wouldn't have done to her what I did at the café, but I can't help to think that if I didn't, she would've remained quiet and hidden. Whether or not it was me calling her out for letting me win or that she's just grown more comfortable with me, I can't deny that her humor and self-confidence is sexy.

"Yeah, well that's before you met me. Much to the contrary of what you witnessed on our date, I'm actually a gentleman."

She glances at me briefly and rolls her eyes. "Fine. I'll drive you to your truck after."

"Look at that, we're already compromising. What all great partners do." I smile, wrapping my arm around her shoulders.

Her neck strains as her eyes meet mine. "You have no idea how much compromising you're going to have to do to cater to my ways."

"Keep talking dirty, I like it."

She jabs me in the ribs and though I may not ever sleep with Madison, I think she'd make a killer friend.

The word friend shouldn't leave a bitter taste on my tongue though. I don't need to have been valedictorian of my class to realize that.

CHAPTER TWELVE

Madison

We arrive at my old childhood home but stay by Mauro's truck to eat our breakfast burritos since it's gross inside and I'm already fearful I'll lose the burrito minutes after walking in and dealing with the stench.

"So, you were saying...this is where you grew up?" he asks, glancing up and down the street instead of at the monstrosity in front of us.

"Yeah, when we were in high school...not that you knew me, so it's not really *we*, but you know what I mean."

"I knew you," he says probably out of obligation.

"You don't have to pretend you did. I'm fully aware of our differences."

He bites into his burrito, a low satisfactory moan leaking out of him. It makes me wish I pulled those sounds from him.

"I'm not sure I understand what you're talking about." He sips on the iced coffee he stopped to pick up on the way over.

"Mauro, you were captain of the football team and I was captain of the geek squad."

"There's a captain?" He winks.

"Hardy har har. If we're going into this, I need you to know a few things."

"You're the woman American Psycho and you're going to seek your revenge and kill me?" He devours half of his burrito when I'm only a quarter into mine.

"No. The night we saw each other at the auction, I might've been a little awestruck."

God, this is embarrassing, but I need him to know I am not some dork that he can push around.

"I thought maybe you saw me as Ogre and couldn't stand to look at my face."

He's smirking when I glance up from my burrito. If I'm going to tell him this I have to look him in the eyes, so he respects me.

"No, that's not why. A person like you is probably used to always having the advantage. Having people cower down and listen to you because...well...you're really attractive and attractive people usually get what they want fairly easily."

"You must be speaking from experience." He raises both eyebrows.

I roll my eyes at him, trying to act like we both aren't aware of where we stand.

"I just need you to know, I know what I'm doing here. This is my fifth house and I've learned from my mistakes, so I'd like it if you didn't try to intimidate me into getting your way. That you believe the decisions I suggest and make are what is best for us and come from a place of experience and knowledge."

"Did you think if I wanted a different molding stain I was going to strip off my shirt? Or if we didn't agree on what price to sell it at, I'd do a strip tease?" He hops off the back end of the truck, crumpling up his foil wrapper and tossing it in the bed. "If we're being so honest, than I'd like you to know that

I'm more than just brawn, I have some brains, too. So please respect any suggestions I make."

I've offended him.

I follow him to the passenger side of the truck. "I didn't mean—"

His head turns and his blue eyes are lit with anger. It's a side of him I've never seen before.

"You meant that you thought I'd use my looks and my charm to get my way with you. That I wouldn't respect you as an equal partner." He steps closer. I swallow down the small amount of saliva pooling in my mouth. "Let me tell you, Madison, you might think you know me, but you know nothing about the real me. I seem to remember you telling me something similar last week." His arm lands on top of the truck, effectively caging me in. "I'll tell you this, you might be hung up on what you looked like in high school, but I'm not. I'm sorry if I was an idiot and didn't notice you back then, but I could accuse you of using your looks to get what you want in our arrangement, too. "

I stare into his eyes, watching anger transform to heat.

"I would never disrespect you, Madison. We'll both get what we want out of this partnership." He winks and pushes himself off the truck, leaving me weak in the knees. "Now let's go get dirty."

God, I so want to get dirty with him right now, but not at all in the way that he means.

Two hours later, we're back to sitting on the lowered tailgate of Mauro's truck. I'm finishing up sketching what I'm imagining for the main living space after we knock down the wall between the kitchen and the dining room.

Mauro is lying next to me, his forearm over his eyes,

halfway to dreamland. Part of me wants to tell him to go home and sleep, but if we're going to start demolition tomorrow, then we have no choice but to figure this part out today.

"What do you think about the staircase?" I ask.

"It's dark and scary," he mumbles from underneath his arm.

I laugh. "When I was younger, it left a great space to eavesdrop on my parents."

A flashback of their composed conversation when they decided on a divorce overtakes the one about the Barbie dream house they put together on Christmas Eve during happier times.

"How long did you live here?" He sits up, his back slouched.

I laugh. "You can lay back down."

"Nah, I'll fall asleep on you."

"Do you want me to sketch this and send it over to you tonight?"

He slides closer to me, shifting his weight to the arm behind me. "No."

He leans in a bit more and he points to the top, where the stairway bends to go upstairs. "We could open this up. The light from the window will come through, but there's still room for a little girl to eavesdrop on her parents' conversation."

My gaze meets his and he smirks.

"I like it." I smile at him.

"You do?" The disbelief in his tone is surprising.

"I do. So..." I scribble away to show that we'll be taking out part of that wall. "That's gone."

I hop down, mostly to get away from his nearness before I drown in his scent which may only be soap and shampoo but is still intoxicating when it's on him.

"That's enough for now. It'll be a couple days of demo," I say.

He follows suit, his boots hitting the ground. "I have tomorrow off and then I'm back on shift for twenty-four hours." His fingers thread through his hair, stress lining his jaw.

"No worries. I'll hold down the fort when you're at the station. We do need to hire a crew."

"I already have guys coming tomorrow," he says, hands on his hips.

"Pretty sure you were going to get the house then?"

"Well, I didn't think there would be a lot of people vying for this much of a fixer-upper."

"Only me." I shrug.

He smiles, the one that melts my insides. "I'm glad that we're doing it together. I think it will be fun."

"Hmm...you are a newbie," I tease. "Remind me how much fun we're having in a month."

He chuckles, his hand pulling on his neck.

"Are you going to be okay to drive home?"

He nods before I finish the sentence. "I'm good. I'll probably be asleep until dinner. You've got my cell."

"Yep. We're all good. I need you rested for tomorrow. If you can tell your crew to come in at nine or so. I'll probably be here at seven, but don't feel like you have to join me. Nine is fine for you."

He quirks an eyebrow. "I'll be here at seven. Fifty-fifty, remember?"

I giggle and nod. "See you at seven."

He nods and I grab all my stuff off the bed of his truck, turning to head to my car.

"Enjoy the rest of your day, partner," he says, securing the tailgate and heading to the driver's side.

"Sweet dreams." I open my car door.

Why don't I want to leave him?

Because you're still infatuated with him.

"Probably won't even remember them if I have them. Bye, Madison."

"Bye, Mauro."

We both get into our vehicles and Mauro pulls away from the curb. Rather than follow suit, I open my purse and pull a few M&Ms from the bag I always have in there, then grab my phone and pull up Vanessa's contact. Lauren should be at work and besides, Vanessa will be more on board with the crazy decision I made to be business partners with Mauro on this project.

"What's up girlie?" Vanessa's huffing with labored breaths into the phone.

"What are you doing?" I check my blind spot and pull out onto the street.

"I'm running."

Vanessa and working out is about as common as seeing a leprechaun riding a unicorn skipping down Michigan Avenue.

"Um...why?"

"Oh, fuck it. Where are you? Can you pick me up on the way home?"

I laugh. "Where are you?"

"On the corner of Irving and Western."

"Van, that's like two blocks from home." I chuckle.

"Yeah, there's a Dunkin' Donuts, I'll be in there." There's a pause. "Large ice coffee... definitely cream and sugar."

"I'll be there in ten."

"Thanks. You're a lifesaver." Her tone sounds about as frazzled as I feel emotionally right now. "Wait, what's up? Why did you call?"

"I'll tell you when I get there." I brake at a stop light.

"No, distract me from the lack of oxygen going into my lungs."

My fingers tap the steering wheel while I wait for the light to turn green. "I got that house." I start with the really good news.

A loud screech echoes over the phone. "That's great news! I can't wait to see what you do with it."

The light changes and I accelerate through the intersection. "It is, but I decided to partner up with someone on it."

"Why? You don't need a partner. Please tell me it's not that sleazy Oswald ass you're always telling us about... Thanks." I hear her sipping through a straw so she must've just been handed her order. "Tell me it's some hot guy with a nine-inch dick."

"You do know you're in public?" I shake my head even though she can't see me and turn right at the next intersection.

"Yeah, the woman is kind of looking at me funny. I'll be waiting outside."

"You really need to be more aware, Vanessa."

She huffs. "It's not my fault if people are prudes. Like she wouldn't want a nine-inch dick. Who doesn't? Oh, crap."

"What?" I ask.

I can hear someone who's not Vanessa yelling on her end of the call.

"I'm really sorry, ma'am. I didn't see him. Yeah, I'm sorry."

"Van?"

"Hold on...I will. Promise. Yes, I will definitely try to act more like a lady. Sorry again." The phone sounds muffled for a second then she comes back on. "Okay, my lips are officially zipped."

"A mom and child?"

"Yeah." Her apologetic voice says she knows how wrong she was, but it's Vanessa and she tends to act before she thinks things completely through. "Let's get back to you. Who's the lucky partner?"

"Mauro Bianco." I bite my lip, waiting for her to either lecture me or tell me to find out if he's got a nine-inch dick.

"Really?" I get neither of those reactions. Her voice is one of concern and worry.

"Yeah. He was there and we were both bidding on the same property, increasing the cost for each other, so he proposed that we partner on it and I accepted. We're fifty-fifty."

Silence.

Deafening silence.

"And he put down half the money?"

I'm stuck behind some guy on a bike and though I know it's good for your physical health and the environment and all that, they are really annoying when you're in a car and can't get around them.

"Yeah. And he said he's good with his hands and has friends on the department who do side work."

Traffic eases in the opposite lane so I pull out and around the bike.

The lack of enthusiasm on the other end of the call is popping my balloon filled with excitement.

"Are you sure this is a good idea?" she asks after a moment.

"I am." Not entirely true, but glass half full and all that.

"But this guy is the guy you had a crush on all through high school, right?" she asks in a wary voice.

"I can handle myself, Vanessa. You would've been so proud of me. It's like after our date when he was annoyed with me, I'm not afraid to speak to him anymore."

"That's good, Mad. Has he done this before? Flipped a house?"

"No, but he wants me to show him everything there is to know."

I make a left onto the street where she's waiting.

"But don't you wonder why he wants to partner up?" she asks.

"I just told you. It just made sense for this project. I'm a big girl, Van."

"Of course you are."

"I'm excited. To have a contractor who is as invested as me can't be a bad thing. He'll want to get it flipped as quickly as I do. Time is money and since it's half his money, he won't be dragging his feet."

The more I work to convince Vanessa what a good idea this is, the more my own reservations at the back of my head ease. I could list a bunch more reasons, but I'm stopped at the light across from her. I spot her sitting on the cement block of a parking space, head in her hands.

"I just don't want you to get hurt. He could be...using you."

I don't respond right away because to be honest, I'm a little hurt that she thinks I'd let myself be manipulated like that.

"You think I'd just sit there with a smile on my face and let him fuck me over?" I ask.

"No." Her head picks up and she's shaking it. I watch her until the light turns green. "I just think this guy is your 'what if' guy and you might not even realize you're letting him take advantage of you until it's too late."

Vanessa comes from a place of caring and I have to remember that as I accelerate forward to pick her up. She doesn't think I'm weak, she just thinks my long-lasting crush on Mauro could cloud my judgment.

"I'm here," I say and she glances to her right and spots me.

Instantly, a smile overtakes her face. She slides into my car, her arms around my shoulders. "Congratulations, Maddie."

"Thanks." I pat her arms, sweaty from the two block walk. "Nice try with working out."

She falls back into my seat. "I'm done with that. It was a stupid idea."

I giggle, pushing back the deflated feeling she left me with admitting her worries with Mauro swindling me. "One day and you're calling it quits?"

She sips her pale iced coffee and shrugs.

Typical Vanessa, bored with something after two point two seconds.

CHAPTER THIRTEEN

Mauro

With two coffees in hand, praying that Madison takes her regular coffee like she does her iced coffee, I step up onto the porch, where she's already in a folding chair with her computer on her lap.

"Good morning." I hold up the coffees and danishes.

"Finally rested?" she asks, her hair in a high ponytail, exposing her neck that's like a spark to kindling.

It doesn't help that I had a dream last night about her naked wearing only a tool belt.

"Yeah. I slept, ate and then slept again."

If I wouldn't have had to go to Cailin's, I probably would've slept the entire time. Usually I function on small pockets of sleep, but I hit a wall yesterday.

"Great because you'll be using those good hands you mentioned today." She smiles. Her teeth all white and glowing. "You're going to think I'm a dork, but I drew up a list of responsibilities yesterday."

She stands up and meets me on the edge of the porch,

accepting her coffee and taking a sip before continuing. "Oh, you remembered. Thank you."

She's wearing a set of denim overalls with a white t-shirt underneath and she looks cute as hell. Not in the two-year-old sense. In the 'I wonder what she'd look like in just the overalls and no t-shirt underneath' way.

"You're welcome," I say. The stirring of happiness inside me over the fact that I got her coffee right needs to be squashed.

"I usually make my own, but of course having roommates, I came down this morning and we were out. Not a note on the chalkboard adding it to the list to buy or anything. Not that I should be surprised, I tend to be the mother hen of our trio."

"You're making me feel kind of bad for Cristian." I sip my coffee, my eyes transfixed on her dark ponytail swinging as she talks.

"You live with your brothers?"

"Just Cristian. Luca's on his own with his buddies. Partying is still everything to him so we kicked him out two years ago. Not that he doesn't use our place as his grocery store. Drives Cristian crazy, but he's still young."

"He's as old as me." She drops her pen, crossing her arms over her chest and resting her hip on the ledge.

Her eyes remain on mine. This is a nice change of pace.

"You're not in the same spectrum of maturity, I assure you."

She giggles, that curl at the end of her ponytail teasing me as it appears and disappears.

"Well, Vanessa is about the same. Can't hold a job to save her life. Scrapes by to pay the rent. Lauren is determined and has a drive like no other, but only when it comes to succeeding in her job or winning a sports game, not so much with her laundry or keeping food in the cabinet."

"I haven't even asked my brothers, have they gone on their dates yet?" I open the bag of danishes and hold them out in front of her.

"No, thank you." She might deny them, but I catch her licking her lips after seeing the cheese and strawberry pastries. "They haven't. Vanessa is delaying because her dad is the Commander of Cristian's district and Lauren is downright refusing to date Luca. What kind of brothers do you have?" She smirks, clearly joking with me.

"I wouldn't want to date them either. I'm the best of the lot in case you were wondering."

She quiets for a moment, her gaze moving down to the pad of paper.

"We really should finalize this before they get here. The dumpster should be here by ten." She turns away from me, and I take the opportunity to check her out while she isn't watching me.

Her overalls hug her ass perfectly. I just manage to move my eyes back up to her face before she spins around to say something.

"Here's the list I came up with. I'm totally flexible, but I think it gives us each multiple areas to work in. It wouldn't be fair if you did all the manual labor and I only took the decorating and redesign. I have dates down that I'd like us to go shopping for fixtures and tiles. I think I have your schedule right, but if not, we can change it up."

"I feel like I'm the slacker between us."

A frown crosses her lips before she raises the coffee to her lips and takes a sip. "I'm sure you'll be proving your worth this first week of demolition."

I wrap my hand around her bicep. "Let me feel. I bet you have biceps of steel."

Her arm lays limp.

"Come on."

Rolling her eyes but obliging, she raises her arm and flexes, showing off some serious guns for a girl her size. I press my four fingers on the top and my thumb on the bottom. More than her muscle, I notice how soft her skin is.

"I'm gonna call you Zena,"

"The warrior princess?" she asks, her eyebrow quirked so high it's near her hairline.

I laugh. "Yeah."

"I guess that's a compliment."

My hand leaves her bicep even though I don't want to pull away.

"It is."

She rolls her eyes again, but more playfully than the first time. I pick up the sheet to scan it over.

It's printed in two columns, one with my name and the other with hers, on the other side is a two month calendar of dates she'd like things to be done.

"Two months huh?"

"Well obviously there will be things out of our control, but this is the proposed schedule if everything goes smoothly. We need to talk budget. Figure out how much demolition and contracting is going to cost. If you're comfortable with it, I'm going to leave that up to you."

The piece of paper drops from my grip and floats to the ground. I scramble to pick it up.

"If you'd rather not, I can..." she rambles out quickly probably taken by my surprised response.

"No. I can do it."

She smiles and I straighten the piece of paper in my hand.

"Great. I can do the one with the new finishings once I get your figures."

Looking it over, she's right, everything is right down the middle. She didn't leave all the numbers and paperwork to her and leave me doing everything that required muscle.

"I did leave some permits for you to get because although I don't want you using that dreamy smile on me to get what you want, I figure it might work on the clerks at the city and get them pushed through faster."

I so badly want to call her out on her dreamy smile comment, but I let it slide.

"Done. If I get a male clerk, I might need your help though."

Her cheeks flush and damn it if I don't want to cage her between my arms and feel her body pressed against mine.

I fold the piece of paper and put it in my back pocket. "Oh, and you got my schedule right." I wink and the rosy blush in her cheeks deepen.

"Look at this dump you two decided to lose a shit load of money on." Cristian's voice behind me makes me curse him for always being early for everything. I would have liked a few more minutes with Madison to myself.

I turn around to see my younger brother in his damn man leggings again with earbuds hanging from his neck. "You don't look like you're ready to work."

He walks up the steps, his attention only on Madison. "I have to work in two hours. It's my weekend off, do you guys work on weekends?" He smirks in my direction and then his arms wrap around Madison, lifting her feet from the splintered wood porch. "Maddie, you look great. You really should discuss your business decisions with me first though." He chuckles into her neck, his lips in the exact place I want mine to be. "You and Mauro taking on the world together?"

Her feet fall back to the ground and she smiles up at my brother like he's a long lost friend. If they were so close, how come I never knew her? "One beat down house at a time." She laughs and he chuckles, his gaze still not leaving hers.

Finally he looks over at me. "I was on a run. Training for the marathon. Thought I'd drop by and give you guys hell."

"Thanks. You can go back to training now."

Madison playfully swats my stomach. "He's joking, Cristian. You're always welcome."

"Thanks, Maddie. You always were nice." Cristian doesn't know about the word nice and how offensive Madison finds it after the board game cafe.

"Some might say I'm a people pleaser," she says, her eyes lit with mischief glancing in my direction.

"Who? My dumbass brother?" Cristian slaps my stomach harder than I expected and I hit him right back. "Fucker."

"I carry hoses, you carry a gun."

Cristian looks up at me, shaking his head. "Let's do a quick sprint and see who's faster."

"Let's run up a flight of stairs with forty-five pounds strapped on our backs," I deadpan.

"Jump a fence holding your weight on one arm."

"Carry two hundred pounds of dead weight in your arms down a flight of stairs that's crumbling without a face mask because you gave it to the victim."

He crosses his arms. "Go into a dark building knowing some creep is there hiding, his only intent not to go back to jail and he'll do anything to make sure he achieves his goal."

"Run into a building that—"

Madison's hand covers my mouth. "I think we get the point boys. I can say that you both have extremely hard jobs."

Cristian laughs. "I like this. You're the only person I've seen able to shut him up."

I bite the inside of her palm lightly and she removes her hand, staring down at it and back to me.

"Did you just bite me?"

"Why didn't you silence him?" I nod to Cristian who I can see is enjoying whatever this is between me and Madison way too much.

"Because me and you have work to do." She opens a bag. "Do you want to come in and see the house, Cristian?"

"Cristian got sick the last time he went in." I give him a shit-eating grin. "Some tough police officer he is."

Cristian laughs, shaking his head. "You're such an ass."

Madison pulls out a hat and places it on her head, pulling her ponytail out of the back and then twisting her hair into a bun.

"Too bad you can't help, Cristian. Demolition is good for releasing aggression. You're welcome to stop by anytime, we can always use an extra set of hands." She smiles and heads to the front door. "I'll see you in there."

She disappears through the door, a groan echoing from the hinges as it opens and closes.

"What the fuck?" I whisper-yell to Cristian.

"What?" His head draws back like he has no idea what the fuck I'm talking about.

"You're flirting with her."

"No, I was saying hi to an old friend." A smirk emerges on his lips. "Oh, man." He shakes his head in disbelief.

"What?" I shift in place.

"Jealousy looks good on you."

"I'm not jealous." I peek in the door to see that she's at the back of the house in the kitchen, looking out a window. A laundry basket full of stuff sits on the dining room table.

"You are and you like her."

I look in the house again and set my narrowed gaze on Cristian. There's a good chance he'll see through my bullshit. I might have been able to pull it over on Luca, but Cristian is a tougher sell.

"I just want this to go smoothly and if you date her and fuck it up by breaking her heart, it'll screw up my chances of having something profitable outside of the department."

He crosses his arms. "Jealousy, lying, are you sure you're my brother Mauro?"

"Fine." I roll my eyes back in my sockets. "Do I want to sleep with her? Yes. Am I going to? No. We're business partners."

"Interesting." He smiles and rocks back on his new, too colorful running shoes.

"Stop it."

He holds his hands up in the air. "Stop what? I'm not doing anything."

"I can't do anything about my attraction to her and you know it."

"Yeah, I do." A small part of me thought, (hoped?) that maybe he'd tell me to go for it. "I stopped by the deli last night. Mama's already got the two of you living in this house with a kid on the way."

"Mama just wants a grandchild." I pull off my hat and run my hand through my hair.

"Keep doing that and you'll be the first bald Bianco."

I shake my head, placing my ball cap on backward. "I'm screwed."

He grips my shoulder. "Can I ask you a question? Are you into her just for her looks?"

I shouldn't be surprised by his question. Have I dated mostly tens? Sure. The fact Maddie has transformed into a ten plus is not lost on me, but it's more than that. "No. As sick as it sounds, I think it's because she sees me differently. Not at first, she didn't. But this morning she told me she'd like me to do the budget for the demolition and construction of the remodel."

My brother smiles, familiar with how people underestimated my intelligence and didn't think I was smart enough for anything other than throwing a football through high school and college. "I told you, Madison Kelly is good people."

I rock back on my own heels. "Yeah, she is." This time it isn't just my dick reacting, but my heart beats a little faster thinking about her being a permanent part of my life.

"You're right. You're screwed." He jogs down the steps. "Let me know about this weekend." Heading down the walkway, I hear the soft words of Mauro and Maddie kissing in a tree fall from his lips.

Smiling, I open the door of the house and the first thing I see is Madison's ass as she bends over to pick something up off the floor. For the first time in my life, I'm jealous of Cristian's tenacious willpower.

CHAPTER FOURTEEN

Madison

A week later, the house is bare bones. We have effectively stripped it down to the studs. This is my favorite part of the process—when I can see the inside structure of a home that's carried the weight of not only the roof and all the supporting beams, but the people's lives who lived here. It's now a clean slate, ready for a fresh start.

The stench that lingered from the refrigerator that was never cleaned out has dissipated a bit and I'm hoping that with the help of a few candles I've lit, it will disappear completely.

I'm sitting in the middle of the living room, taking in the space when the screen door opens and a big body steps in.

"Are we having a seance?" Mauro sits down across from me, placing a bag of food between us.

"Well, we *do* have to try to get the dead to move on."

He chuckles, placing all his weight on his arms as he extends them behind him, leaning back.

"My profession means that I can't help but warn you about candles and wood."

"I didn't realize you were such a rule follower," I tease.

He straightens up, opening the bag, taking out the Chinese food containers. "I'm not."

"I didn't think so."

I rise up and go to my laundry basket of essentials we might need for meals. Yeah, call me uber-organized, but this isn't my first time being so hungry I could chew my arm off in a house with no kitchen. Pulling out two plates and two plastic forks and napkins, I sit back down across from him.

In the last week, Mauro has transformed from the guy I didn't really know and yet placed on a pedestal, to a guy I'm getting to know a lot about and am really starting to like for the right reasons.

He's funny, and I like his dry sense of humor and the way he never cracks a smile when he tells a joke. He treats the workers well and somehow gets them to do a little extra work each day. Once he makes a decision, that's it. He's committed. And he always makes the best of a situation. When a wall got knocked out that wasn't supposed to, he said that it would allow more light in instead of asking me where I was when it was happening since he was at work.

"Always prepared." He chuckles to himself and opens up the containers and I'm surprised to see that it's Thai food, not Chinese.

I shrug. "It's a curse."

The curse of not having a present mother.

"You should be proud of it. I bet you've never been late on a bill." He lets me get my dish before his.

I use the fork and pull the noodles from the container.

"No."

"It's an endearing quality. Don't be ashamed of it." His words warm me. Most people would probably find it geeky.

He's fixing his plate and my gaze wanders across his body. His strong shoulders and taut waist. The way his jeans are worn just the perfect amount and hug his firm thighs. The fact that his hair is never fully done, but more styled with his fingers because no matter how neat it looks when he gets here, by day's end he's got that just-fucked hair going on. The light stubble along his cheeks and his manly jaw.

"Is there something on my face?" He sits back, wiping his face with a napkin.

Oops. My eyes cast down, heat rising up my neck. "No."

He lets it go instead of calling me out on my gawking. Just as I did earlier today when I bent over to grab something and found his eyes glued to my ass when I turned around. Let's just say, the exhilaration I felt in that moment was pretty close to when I earned Summa Cum Laude in college.

"So, tell me why you don't have a boyfriend."

My head snaps up to meet his inquisitive eyes.

He's kidding. Right?

"You tell me first," I say.

"Don't even try it. Come on."

Every fiber inside of me says this is a horrible idea, but I sit up from my plate. "I've never had a serious relationship. I've dated a few guys, but the relationships never lasted longer than a month or two."

His forehead wrinkles. "Why do you think that is?"

I tip my head back down. "I tend to date guys similar to me. Guys who want career success before a romantic relationship. We'd both understand when the other said they have to study or that they had to go to this networking event or whatever it was. The relationship was never the priority. Does that make sense?"

"Yeah, that would be a problem. What about now? You still put your career first?"

His question is innocent enough. He asks casually, but the

way he's intently waiting for me to answer has me wondering if there's more to it.

"Um...I think I use it as a crutch now. Maybe it's an excuse not to get involved with someone."

I'm not sure I've been this honest with anyone else before. There's just something about Mauro that doesn't have me wanting to give him a glazed over answer you'd give just to move on to the next topic of conversation.

"I'm with you on that one. I think I use the fact my job is dangerous as a reason sometimes not to get serious."

I look up from my plate, chewing the last of my chicken. He forks large amounts of noodles and chicken into his mouth. I'm not sure I've seen Mauro go longer than an hour without food.

"You've never had a serious relationship?" I ask.

His eyes dip back to his plate. "No, I did, sort of, I guess. We were together for a year, but I found out it was all based on lies."

"I'm sorry." I frown. "Did you love her?"

He doesn't look up from his plate as he pushes the food around.

"I think I thought I did, but I'm not so sure now. Maybe when you find out someone didn't love you, maybe that strips everything you felt for them? I don't know. Let's just say it was the ultimate betrayal."

My heart squeezes for him. Whether he loved her or not doesn't mean it didn't hurt. Whatever happened obviously affected him.

"See, so maybe I'm better off continuing to put my work first." I try to lighten the vibe, but his solemn eyes say he's having none of it.

"I learned a lot from it."

"Like?"

He stands up, heading to the cooler he brought earlier

today to make sure the crew had water. Bringing two over, he wipes the water off with his t-shirt, opens the cap, and hands it to me.

"Thank you."

He sits down, closer than he was moments ago. Not that I'm complaining.

"This is going to sound a lot like some 'I am woman hear me roar' statement, but I deserved better. She had me using my two days off as her chauffeur and errand runner. I thought I was doing it because we loved each other and I was helping her out. I realize now that she didn't care if I needed to sleep. She never even called me when I was on shift." He shakes his head. "You're going to think I'm taking estrogen tablets at this rate."

I knock my shoulder to his. "I'm going to ignore the fact that you're saying women are overly emotional."

He smirks at me. "You know that's not what I'm suggesting."

I raise my eyebrows. "Who knows if you are."

He holds up his hand with two fingers. "Scout's honor."

"You weren't a Boy Scout, were you?"

He chuckles. "For two weeks. Until all three of us got kicked out for wrestling. The leader told my mom that we'd have to be split into three different troops. That was the end of scouts for the Bianco brothers."

I lower his hand. "Then sorry, you can't use the honor salute."

"Were you a Girl Scout?" he asks, his smile already suggesting he knows the answer.

"Yes, and before you make fun of me, I did go all the way to Ambassador. It looked good on my college application."

"Ever think that's where those people pleaser skills were bred?"

"Hey." I shoot him a warning glare.

He chuckles, resting his weight on his hand. "I'm kidding. I know I've apologized, but I need to again. I should've never made fun of you because if you weren't nice, I'm pretty sure we wouldn't be sitting in this house. You wouldn't have given me this chance."

I straighten my back. "Do you think I gave you a bone? Like I agreed to be your partner as a handout?"

He straightens as well, pouring a big gulp of water down his throat while staring at me through squinted eyes. "Well, I'm the newbie and you're pretty established."

I shake my head. "Mauro, that's not true and I don't want you to think that. I agreed to this because this house means something to me and so that I'd have a partner who was just as invested as me. I'm sick of doing it alone. I thought it'd be fun, but it's been good having someone to bounce ideas off of. The fact you're good with your hands was just a bonus." I attempt to wink, but as usual, both eyes fall closed.

"Try that again?" he asks, pointing to my eyes.

"No. I can't do it." I pull my legs up and bury my head down into my knees, my long chestnut hair falling in a veil around my face.

He sweeps it back and my stomach flutters when his fingertips brush my cheek. "It's me. Come on."

"It's me? That's your explanation? That it's okay to embarrass myself. You're Mauro Bianco."

I shake my head and he tucks my hair behind my ear.

"You say that like I'm Bradley Cooper."

"To me you are," I mumble, half praying he didn't hear me, half hoping he did.

His finger lands under my chin, slowly raising my face until our eyes lock. "I'm just a firefighter from Chicago. I'm the oldest of three brothers from an immigrant father and mother who came to this country for the American dream. There's nothing special about that."

I swallow down the saliva pooling in my mouth.

Our faces inch closer.

"Don't pin me as a hero, Mad," he says in a low, gravelly voice.

My heart pitter-patters at the way he shortened my name.

"You're so much more than you realize. You're kind and sweet and generous and hardworking. The package you come in is nice eye candy, sure, and I'm ashamed to say that's all I knew about you at one time. Over the last week though, I've discovered that you're so much more."

Our faces inch closer again and I can feel his breath on my face.

"We can't do this," I murmur. "It could destroy everything we're building."

His eyes transfix on my lips. "I've been denying myself for days. Just one taste."

Another inch closer and my breathing grows shallow as my heart thumps an unsteady beat against my rib cage.

His hand molds to my cheek and I lean into his strong, callused palm.

"Mauro," I whisper. I'm not even sure if it's a plea to kiss me or to stop.

"Madison." My name rolling off his lips with so much need undoes any self-control I had left and my eyes flutter closed as I lean in.

"Mauro," a woman's voice says from outside the screen door.

We reel back from each other, my water spilling onto one of the candles. How fitting.

"Cailin?" he asks, standing to his feet.

A blonde woman walks in wearing tight skinny jeans and a top snug enough to show off some nice cleavage. She's wearing a gold necklace that draws your eyes down to her breasts just in case you didn't happen to notice them. Her hair is down—loose and curled in those waves I never seemed to master with my straight iron.

"You must be Madison." She disregards a flustered Mauro and beelines it over to me, holding her hand out. "I'm Cailin."

I wrack my brain for any recognition the name should bring me. She's definitely not the contractor we hired for the landscaping.

"Hi." I shake her dainty hand, watching her eyes wander up and down my body.

I've never been the woman other women are jealous of, so I'm not certain why she's sizing me up.

"Madison, this is Cailin Zaxby, she was the wife of my buddy, Hunter." Mauro takes up the space at our sides.

I nod hello.

"This place doesn't look very appealing." She cringes at me, a smear of lipstick on her glowing white teeth. She must be just off a whitening treatment.

"Consider this her natural look." My hand caresses a beam that separates the living room and dining room.

"Oh how cute, you refer to it like a person. Did you name her like those people who name beat up ugly cars?" I try to hide my disgust and Mauro should be thankful I'm a nice person right about now because I feel like taking her head and knocking it into a four by four.

"No, I don't." I move over to the table and pack up my computer and notebooks, shoving them in my bag. "I'll leave you two alone."

"That's not necessary." Mauro steps closer to me.

"Sorry, did I interrupt a meeting? It's just Mauro's been going on and on about this project of his and I drove by and saw his truck. Figured I'd stop in." She's lying. Not that I think she didn't just drive by and see his truck, but she's here for a reason other than to see the house.

"No worries, we were just finally taking a break after a week of demolition." I swing my bag over my shoulder.

Mauro's hands are tucked into his pockets, his eyes on the ground.

Upset that he got caught almost kissing the hermit?

"So, I know you work tomorrow, but we have that meeting the day after with the tile guy. We need to decide on stain and cabinetry so that we make sure it all flows. Just Pinterest anything you really like, okay?"

His hand touches my arm and I desperately want to lean into him. I want to finish what we started in front of Cailin and show her he's mine. But that's not me. And he's not mine. I'd do well to remember that.

"You Pinterest?" Cailin's voice bounces off the empty walls.

Mauro stares at me, his eyes conveying the apology he's yet to verbalize.

"Sounds good. Crossing fingers for a slow day tomorrow." He smiles and my belly lights up like a rocket's about to take off.

I step away from Mauro before I do something foolish like kiss him goodbye. "Very nice to meet you Cailin." I wave.

She's busy looking around like she'd rather be anywhere but here. "You too, Madison." She waves, not bothering to turn and actually look at me.

"Bye, Mad," Mauro says and I walk out the front door feeling about as empty as the house I'm leaving.

The candles. Shit.

I peek my head back in and see Cailin's hands on Mauro's shoulders giving him a massage.

Wow. They waste no time.

"I just wanted to remind you not to forget to put the candles out." I shake my head. "That seems stupid now. You're a firefighter. Of course you'll know to blow them out."

I glance at the floor to see that they're already blown out.

"I'm one step ahead of you." Mauro smiles, dislodging his shoulders from Cailin's hands.

"Have a good night." I wave and let the screen door fall closed behind me.

This time I head down the stairs to the solitude of my car.

Once I'm inside, I reach into my purse grabbing my bag of M&Ms, pour out a palm full and stuff them in my mouth.

CHAPTER FIFTEEN

Mauro

"What are you doing?" I side-step away from Cailin, still wondering why the hell she surprised me here. "Why are you acting like some jealous girlfriend?"

I keep my voice even, but anger boils inside of me. Anger I haven't seen surface since I cleaned out Hunter's locker at the firehouse.

"What are you talking about?" She plays off my question with a laugh and picks up the candles, placing them on the dining room table, familiar with fire safety.

The candles had made me uneasy, but Madison liked them, and I couldn't take my eyes off of her in the candle-light. I already installed two fire extinguishers, so I knew I'd get to it quickly should the unthinkable happen.

"Where's Devin?"

She stops and turns to me. Her lips dipping. "I was out for dinner with my girlfriends. My mom has Devin. It was my first night out."

Thank God, I was just misreading things. For a second there I thought Patel was right—that Cailin wanted to replace Hunter with me.

"I'm sorry." My hand runs along the back of my neck. "I'm just—"

"You like her?" she interrupts.

I shrug. My ability to lie is shit. Cailin wouldn't catch me like Cristian might, but she caught me about to kiss Madison so I think she knows the answer without me answering.

"We're partners. Come on, I'll show you around."

We head through the dining room to the kitchen.

"Don't lie to me, Mauro. I saw you a millisecond before you were about to kiss her."

"And yet you decided to interrupt?" I turn and cock an eyebrow at her.

Her cheeks flush. "I thought maybe she was taking advantage of you. You know you're so gorgeous women can't resist."

She pinches my bicep and I've never wanted to be away from Cailin more than right now. Even when she was knee-deep in snot and soaking my t-shirt after Hunter's death, I was good with it. She needed someone and I was willing to be that person she could lean on. Now...I don't know if that was such a good idea.

"She wasn't taking advantage of me." I stop at the stairs to the basement. It's dark and still looks haunted even with the new lighting we've put in.

"I'm not going down there. Show me the upstairs. Is there a bed?" she asks.

I squint my eyes, annoyed with her. "No."

"So you were just going to lay her down on the plywood and give her splinters in her ass? How romantic, Mauro." She laughs and the sound grates on me.

"I wasn't going to sleep with her," I bite out my words.

"Come on, you must find her attractive if you were going

to kiss her." She's smiling at me trying to play it off like she's teasing, but behind her smile there's insincerity.

"Who wouldn't?" I ask.

"Some wouldn't. I mean she has that cute, smart girl vibe, but her sense of style is a little lacking."

I've heard Cailin make fun of girl's I've gone out with. Hell, she tore Jenna apart after we broke up, but I figured she was in the grieving stage of anger at that point.

"I wasn't aware jeans and t-shirts were somehow out of style." I remind myself that she's been through hell these last few months and that I need to cut her some slack, so I walk up the stairs first, Cailin's heeled boots sounding on the stairs behind me.

"I think it was a guy's shirt."

My patience snaps. "Enough Cailin. She's my partner and yes, I find her attractive. Yes, I want to kiss her. Yes, I want to screw her. Am I screwing her? No. So put the claws away."

She draws back at the top of the stairs. "I was only suggesting..."

I raise my hand. "No. You were judging. She's a great person. Enough of the prom queen judging."

Her eyes fall to the floorboard. "I just want to protect you. After Jenna..."

"I can protect myself but thank you." I place my hand on her upper arm and squeeze. "I'm sorry, it's just..." I shake my head not wanting Cailin to know more than Madison because that's not fair. My conflicted feelings about Madison shouldn't be discussed with anyone but her. "Anyway, there are three bedrooms up here."

I flick the flashlight on since the sun has started to descend already with autumn upon us. "This will be one bedroom that shares a bathroom with this one." We head to the next bedroom before turning down a small hallway. "This is the master."

She steps into the space, eyeing the skylight. You can see right through the structure to what will be the bathroom.

"It's a nice space." She twirls around. "Hunter would have loved this." A tear slips down her cheek.

"Cailin." I sigh. "Don't."

It's the whole reason I was never really up on her coming here. This was my dream with Hunter and now I'm living it out with Madison. That has to be tough for her.

"He always told me that he'd give me the modern luxuries we'd see on the DIY channels. A house we'd be proud to host cookouts and parties at. A pool for Devin and his younger brother or sister."

Another tear spills down her cheek and I do what I've done the other hundred times I've been in this position with her. I wrap her in my arms, her head falling to my shirt, her arms tight around my middle.

"It's okay. I know it hurts, but eventually the pain will fade a bit and you'll find someone else to share your life with. I promise. And you'll be happy again. Hell, he might even be better than Hunter for you."

She pulls back, her eyes launching daggers into me. "How could you say that? He was your best friend."

Shit. Sometimes it's hard, knowing what I know, not to let my true feelings slip out around her.

I step back. "I'm just saying you'll find happiness again."

Shaking her head, she brushes the tears from her face. "Hunter was my everything."

She says it like I don't already know that little fact. She lived and breathed Hunter, practically suffocated him. Nothing was ever good enough for her. I was with him the nights he'd be exhausted on shift after being up the night before because they were fighting and Cailin wouldn't allow him to go to bed until it was settled.

"I know. I know," I say.

"If I'd had him for longer. Our time together was so short."

She cries into my chest again and I lightly rub her back.

"HA!" a voice yells into the room.

Cailin steps back, startled, but I have no chance to move before there's a body strapped to my back.

"You son of a bitch. I knew you were a loser like your brother." Little hands pull at the strands of my hair and the more I twist to remove whoever it is, the higher she climbs up me.

"Who the hell are you?" Cailin asks.

"His worst nightmare," she says, jabbing her knee in my armpit.

My t-shirt is choking me and though I could easily toss this girl off me I have no idea what the fuck is going on and it's not in my nature to launch a woman across the room, doing who knows how much damage to her.

Cailin backs up closer to the corner of the room, afraid.

"Jesus, Lauren, get off of him!" Madison runs into the room, unpeeling her arms from my throat.

The person on my back falls down to her feet, and I straighten my shirt, turning to look at the culprit of my attack.

"We are so sorry." Madison grabs Lauren's hand and tries to drag her out of the room.

"I can't stand to look at you. If you want to have some fling with some tart then go to your own apartment, don't do it here!"

Madison's cheeks flush the deepest red I've seen yet.

"Excuse me?" Cailin steps up, towering over Lauren. Not that it seems to intimidate Lauren.

"You heard me. This is theirs." She points to Madison and me. "He should have the decency not to fuck someone in their shared space."

"This is all really unnecessary." Madison pulls at Lauren, but she yanks her arm back.

"Is that what you think is happening?" I ask Madison.

"No. I mean...I didn't think she was here to you know...it's not exactly very romantic."

I want to remind her that it was a half hour ago when the two of us were surrounded with candles and Thai food declaring how much we've come to enjoy each other's company in the past week.

"Lauren drove by and decided to stop in. She saw what was going on and called me. I sped back over here as quick as I could so this wouldn't happen."

Lauren jabs me in the chest. "Do you know how great she is?"

My gaze flickers to Madison. "I'm well aware, yes."

"Well let me tell you...wait, what?" She stops talking, her eyes searching for Madison.

"Cailin isn't some girl I brought here to show off this place to. Not that it's really any of your business." I take a step in her direction, squaring off with her.

The sheepish look I expected doesn't appear on Lauren's face. Instead, she crosses her arms waiting for a better explanation.

"She's the wife of a fellow firefighter who died."

Lauren's arms fall. "Oh." She bites the inside of her cheek. "But you were pretty cozy in here." Lauren juts out her chin.

If Luca ever does go on his date with her, he's going to have his hands full. I can't fucking wait.

"Are you going to apologize now?" Cailin snarls.

"Lauren," Madison pushes and Lauren rolls her eyes.

"I'm sorry okay, but you know she's my girl and..."

"So she likes Mauro?" Cailin interjects.

"NO!" Madison screeches. "Lauren's just protective."

My eyes lock with Madison's.

"Yeah, I'm just protective of her. You know she's a hard worker and I don't want some guy taking advantage of her. This has nothing to do with personal feelings." Lauren walks backward toward the door. "Please carry on." She steps out of the room.

"I'm really super sorry for the misunderstanding." Madison follows and the sound of their footsteps trampling down the stairs echoes throughout the house.

I want to go after Madison, but I know mixing business and pleasure is a bad idea. The war inside of me rages on and I'm not sure which side will end up the victor.

"What a head case." Cailin slides her arm through mine. "I mean sending her friend here to attack you? Make sure she doesn't go all Fatal Attraction on you."

I blow out a breath and step away, letting Cailin's arm fall. "I have to go. I have work in the morning."

"Oh, okay. I should get back to Devin anyway."

We walk down the steps and I lock up, noticing that Madison's car is gone from the curb. I say goodbye to Cailin, see her drive off and climb into my truck.

My life was much simpler a week ago.

CHAPTER SIXTEEN

Madison

"Lauren, what the fuck?" I ask as we step out of each of our cars in the garage.

"What? I thought he was disrespecting you."

"I told you already, I don't look at him like that anymore."

We head into the house, void of Vanessa because it's after seven o'clock. Whatever job she's working, she's always gone by seven.

"That's bullshit, Maddie. At least be straight with *me*." Lauren sheds the shirt of her scrubs, kicks off her shoes, and heads up the stairs.

I follow her because I need to shower, too, to get a day of being at a work site off me.

"I'd be lying if I said he's not hot as hell, but I have to respect that we're partners. I'm not going to ruin that."

She strips off her pants and heads into her bathroom.

"Just be careful. I saw the way he was looking at you and I don't care what he says about that Cailin, she wants him."

Lauren shuts the door to the bathroom and I head into my bedroom to take a shower as well.

As much as Lauren can be on the impulsive side, I agree with her. Cailin's intentions don't seem pure. I'm surprised Mauro doesn't see the signs that his friend's widow is falling for him.

The water cascades over my skin, the warmth soothing muscles that have been working hard this week. I soap up my body, my mind wandering to our almost kiss.

The almost kiss I'll remember for the rest of my life. The heat between us was searing. The way his gaze dipped to my lips and then met my eyes. How his tongue slid out to lick his lips in expectation of them being on mine.

Damn that Cailin.

When he said, 'one taste' like he was begging for one drop of water in the Sierra Desert.

I drop my loofa on the floor of the marble shower and my hand slips below my belly button imagining the weight of Mauro's body over mine. His lips, his hands in exploration of every inch of my skin.

Five minutes later, my body shudders and the glass door rattles under the pressure of my other hand. An emptiness sets in, knowing my imagination and my hand are not going to ever be enough to quench my thirst for Mauro.

I liked it better when I thought he was an ass.

I step out of the shower and begin to dry off when my phone chirps from its position on the counter.

Mauro: *I want to apologize for tonight.*

I wrap myself in a towel and take my phone over to my bed, sitting down and leaning back against the headboard.

Me: *No need. It's really none of my business.*

The three dots appear immediately.

Mauro: *Should we talk about the kiss?*
Me: *There was no kiss.*
Mauro: *I wanted there to be. That's what we need to discuss.*

God, I wanted there to be, too, and if he only knew what my mind took the liberty of exploring moments ago in the shower, he'd probably be surprised at how dirty my mind could be.

Me: *It was a moment of weakness. Just forget it.*
Mauro: *I don't think it will be our last.*
Me: *We need to make sure it is.*
Mauro: *Madison, I want you.*

My nerves tingle and an unbelievable feeling of euphoria fills every cell in my body.

Me: *Mauro...*
Mauro: *Tell me you don't feel the same?*
Me: *We should talk face-to-face.*
Mauro: *If we were face-to-face right now there'd be no talking.*

I smile like a goon.

Me: *We just need to keep a firm line drawn.*
Mauro: *So that's a no?*
Me: *No to what?*
Mauro: *No to you wanting me. You don't want to jump me?*
Me: *Maybe like Lauren jumped you a few times.*
Mauro: *LOL... I'm serious. I gotta know if I'm in this alone.*
Me: *Why do you have to know?*

"Who's that?" Lauren walks by in her pajama shorts and cami, her hair still tucked into a towel.

"No one."

"Tell Mauro I can still kick his ass," she says and heads down the stairs.

Mauro: *I need to know that if I kiss you, you won't pull away.*
Me: *You can't kiss me.*
Mauro: *That wasn't part of the buying agreement.*
Me: *I added the stipulation.*
Mauro: *We're both adults here. We can handle it.*
Me: *Time to think with your other head, Mauro.*

Mauro texts a laughing gif.

Mauro: *Don't be funny, that only makes me think with the wrong head.*
Me: *I think it suffices to say this conversation is going in a circle and will never end.*
Mauro: *It will when you agree to let me kiss you.*
Me: *I have to go get some sleep. And I believe you have to get up early for a shift.*
Mauro: *You're gonna leave me hanging like that? I can describe in great detail what it will be like if you want.*

The blush encompasses my entire body.

Me: *Gotta go now. See you in a couple of days.*
Mauro: *I'll be counting the minutes.*

I shake my head and don't respond because who knows what will spill out of his mouth next.

When we began this partnership, I figured my biggest

challenge would be keeping my own attraction to him in check. I didn't consider the fact that he might like me, too.

The next night, I'm vegging on the couch after a long day of grabbing samples from textile and paint companies. And when I say vegging I mean carrots, cucumbers, and celery with ranch dip.

I'm flipping through the channels by myself—Vanessa is gone again—and Lauren is out on a date—not with Luca. I breeze by Chicago Fire since that would only remind me of Mauro, but the ticker on the bottom of the screen grabs my attention. It's a breaking news alert and with everything going on in the world today I figure I better read it in case I need to head for cover.

I sit up, squinting to see the small print when the words fire, high-rise, and danger catch my eye. It goes on to say that all available engines have been called because it's out of control and there's a chance the blaze will spread to the high-rise beside it.

All too quickly Chicago Fire disappears from the screen and a news anchor appears, the scene behind her reminds me of a war zone—emergency vehicles everywhere and a fire blazing out of control in the building behind her.

I swear my heart stills inside of my chest and I sit on the edge of my couch, my phone in hand.

One fire truck after another pulls in behind the woman, each raising their ladders up in the air. Some firefighters climb them, others run inside with hoses and masks on. Angry red and yellow flames pour out windows on the one side of the high-rise condo building.

I pick up my cell phone knowing I won't get an answer.

Me: *Mauro, please let me know when you get back to the station so I know you're okay. I saw the fire on tv.*

Is this what it's like to care about someone who works in emergency services? I have more compassion for Cailin now and what she must have gone through every night her husband was on shift and then when she eventually lost him.

I lean back on the couch, trying not to let my worst fears invade my mind.

Hours go by and the news is no longer covering the fire, they've gone back to their regular programming while I pace back and forth. This feeling of helplessness is horrible. The waiting even more so.

I pull out my phone and look up where Engine Fifty-Five is located.

I shouldn't go.

I'll look like a loon.

I don't even have to talk to him. I just need a glimpse of him when the truck pulls in.

I won't sleep until I know.

I grab the keys off the table and race out to my car.

The street the fire station is on is lined with cars. There are some reporters hovering around the red doors, but they're all shut, meaning the firetruck hasn't returned yet. I drive around the block, circling back to see the same scene as before.

I decide to park on a side street. I don't want to chance looking like a stalker around the firehouse, so I sit tight and decide that every ten minutes I'll drive around the block.

And yes, in case you're wondering, I'm fully aware that I am out of my mind.

The thought of something really bad happening to Mauro has me acting like a crazy woman. His friend Hunter died not that long ago in a fire at a commercial building that they didn't know had explosives in it because it had been abandoned. It goes to show that anything can happen.

The sixth time driving around the block the bay doors are open with two firetrucks and an ambulance inside each one. The guys are taking their gear off and cleaning up the trucks.

Double parking for a second, I catch a glimpse of Mauro stepping out of his bunker pants. His face has soot on it and there's a trace of blood from his eyebrow down to his lip, his hair a sweaty mess. But he's alive and to me, he's never looked better.

The tension dissipates from my body and I pull away before he notices my car.

On the ride home, I realize how much trouble I'm in. I've done the one thing I shouldn't have. I've fallen for him, truly fallen for him as a person, and his text messages suggest he has for me as well.

But does he want me for more than one night?

Even if he did, would the novelty wear off after he had me for a while and he figures out I'm still the nerdy girl I was in high school at heart?

Once I'm inside the house, I head to bed, falling into the softness of my mattress. My phone dings an hour later, stirring me from sleep.

Mauro: *I like you checking up on me. Tough one, but I'm okay. Maybe you can show your civil serviceman some gratitude tomorrow with a kiss.*

My girly parts go into a full five-alarm fire and I don't respond because right now the only thing I'd be texting him back would be to come straight over when he finishes his shift in the morning.

CHAPTER SEVENTEEN

Mauro

I'm not sure what I expected when I walked into the tile store. Okay, that's bullshit. I expected Madison to run into my arms, clinging to me like a damn Koala bear, thankful I was alive and standing in front of her in one piece. I didn't expect her just to tell me that she picked me up a coffee and ask if we should go with either blue or gray.

"I figure dark stained floors and cream colored cabinets in the kitchen. Since we broke down the wall between the kitchen and dining room, how about we install an island with seating for kids to eat breakfast." She taps her pen to her mouth, contemplating the idea.

"Sounds good."

She glances to the side at me. "I was thinking soapstone for the countertops?"

"Cool." I sip my coffee not looking at the textiles laid in front of me.

"Can you excuse us for a moment, Meadow?" Madison

asks the young woman who's been helping us and sneaking glances my way. She has long blonde hair that matches her long legs. She's attractive and maybe before Madison, I would've liked the looks she's been giving me. But there's only one woman who's been filling my mind this morning and that's the one whose eyes are locked on me right now.

"Certainly. Just holler when you're ready." Her heels click as she walks away.

Madison places her pen down on her pad of paper next to her coffee.

"You know I want your opinion, right? Don't just go along with whatever I suggest. Feel free to challenge me."

Her voice and her eyes are soft and sincere. Just like they always are. Maybe that's why the ache in my chest won't disappear. After her text last night, I thought she'd be more enthusiastic about seeing me this morning and would lower the wall she'd put up between us. Obviously, I was wrong.

"I know, but I'm not really good at this design stuff. Maybe I should go back to the house and get started on the drywall."

"No!" Her hand presses on my arm. "I want us to do this together."

"Okay." I shrug and stuff my hands into the pockets of my jeans, not sure what advice I can really offer.

"According to the budget you gave me, we have..."

She rattles on about square feet and inches, but I really don't care because my mind is still focused on why I give a shit if she cares.

What the fuck am I doing? Sitting here in this textile place not worried about the house anymore but why Madison Kelly who I never knew existed until a month ago doesn't seem to care that I could have lost my life last night. The flames were hot, the fire unpredictable. High-rise fires are always the riskiest when you go up through a stairway. Maybe it was the relief I felt when we were safe back at the station or the grateful look on my crews' faces when the truck pulled into the station. Everyone found their phones to contact their loved ones.

I knew I'd find a text from Ma, but Madison's message surprised me. The elation inside me grew and that's when the light bulb popped on, I want more than a kiss from this woman.

Now to arrive this morning to an all business Madison wounded me when it shouldn't. I told her not to see me as a hero and if she'd have jumped in my arms when I walked in the shop this morning, I'd know she hadn't listened to me. Having her see me as a hero only raises the expectation level and sets us up for failure.

"Honestly, I'm cool with whatever, Madison. I just want clean and streamlined and it seems like you have it handled here."

Meadow returns with more samples of stained wood, holding it up to the backsplash.

"I don't want the bathrooms to look the same as the kitchen, can we do a painted wood on the cabinetry with an epoxy that resembles marble?"

Madison doesn't bother acknowledging my comment, making me sit there through the entire ordeal, shooting me a pissed off look whenever I say cool or okay instead of giving an opinion.

By the time we're readying to leave Meadow slips me her number when Madison goes to the bathroom complaining about too much coffee. A sour feeling takes over my stomach over the fact that I accepted it. Not that I'm going to use it, but I never want to make anyone feel bad by refusing. Still, somehow the piece of paper in my pocket makes me feel dishonest.

"Do you like Meadow?" Madison asks as we stop on the

sidewalk next to our cars. "She worked with me on my last house and manages to get some really great deals. Plus, she really has an eye for modern, trendy and sleek."

"She's okay." I shrug.

Madison rolls her eyes before her fist nails me in the shoulder.

I wrap my hand around the area she hit. "Ooouucchh," I deadpan, confusion laced in my tone.

"What's with you?" She juts her hip out, her papers high in her arms.

"Nothing. Tired I guess."

I use my usual excuse of tiredness to cover up my emotions. The only woman to figure out my M.O. so far is my mom.

"You seemed chipper when you came in."

"Chipper?"

"Yes, like happy," she says.

My muscles tense in annoyance. "I know what chipper means," I bite out.

She throws her hand out. "Whatever. Why don't you go sleep it off for the rest of the day. I'll handle the house." She heads to her car, opening up the passenger side door and tossing her papers in.

"You'd like that, so you can say that I'm not carrying my weight."

I have no idea where this anger is coming from, but the words leave my lips anyway.

She glances over her shoulder, her forehead scrunching up, not understanding. "No, I wouldn't. I know how hard you work at the station. I'm sure last night shook you up a little."

So, she's finally going to acknowledge last night.

"I'm used to it. It's my job."

"I know but still..."

"Don't baby me, Madison. We signed up for this together."

She stares at me, her eyes alit with questions. "I'm not. If you want to go to the house, then go to the damn house." Her voice is raised, causing a man in a business suit to pause briefly behind us on the sidewalk.

"Do you want me to go to the house?" I ask, stepping closer.

She lightly shakes her head, her back falling to the passenger side of her car. "Truth?"

"Always."

"Not if you're going to be the jerk you're being right now." She crosses her arms and the button on her blouse slides, giving me a glimpse of her green lace bra. My mouth waters and my hands tighten into fists.

"Fine."

"Fine? What the hell do you want from me?" she asks. Her voice is low and I can tell she doesn't want to cause a scene by the way she's glancing around us.

What I want is my lips and my body pressed against hers.

"Nothing." I step back, closing my eyes to regain any amount of composure I can muster right now. "I'll see you at the house." I turn around to head to my truck.

"Mauro?" she calls out.

I circle back around, not stopping my feet, walking backward now. "I'm sorry, Madison. I think it's just the stress getting to me."

That's not even a lie. She'll think it's the job and the house, but in truth it's her.

Back in the serenity of my truck, I watch Madison slide into her car and sit for a moment.

I'm such a fucking asshole. Why would I expect her to act like a girlfriend would after last night? She's not my girlfriend and I need to keep reminding myself of that.

There are two people I can call right now and only one will give me solid, serious advice, so I dial Cristian.

"What's up?" he answers.

"You have a minute?"

"I just left the gym. You want to grab something to eat?" I hear him tell someone else it's his brother and he'll see them tomorrow.

"No. I have to be at the house."

"I can pick up some food and head over there. I'm sure you and Maddie need to take a break." My brother's always thinking of others.

I blow out a breath and run my hand through my hair. "Definitely can't talk at the house."

Silence is the only response.

"Cris?"

"You didn't?"

"Didn't what?"

"Have sex with her. Please tell me you didn't give in to the temptation and now you have a house half-finished and you guys can't stand to be in the same room with each other."

Irritation raises its head again.

"What are you, her keeper?"

"You did. Jesus, Mauro, what are you thinking? She's not like your usual girls." His disappointment is clear from his tone.

"I didn't sleep with her," I grind out.

Silence.

"But I want to."

"Do yourself a favor and go out tonight, find one of your other admirers and screw them. Leave Maddie alone."

My hands tighten on the steering wheel, wishing he was in front of me and that we were ten again when I could justify wrestling him to the ground and pounding my fist into his face.

"I don't want to screw anyone else. Hell, I just got a girl's number five minutes ago."

An exasperated breath flows over the line. "Good to know."

"What am I missing here, Cris? Why are you so protective of her and why do you always think the worst of me with her? It's not like you're talking to fucking Luca."

He's quiet for a long time, but I can hear the sounds of the city through the line—horns honking, bells ringing, and muffled conversations coming and going as he walks.

"Let me ask you something...do you really want something with her? Like something more than one night?"

Two days ago I might've said I don't know, but after last night's message and my reaction to it I can't lie to myself any longer.

"I think I do. She's different, you know?"

"I do know and that's why I'm asking because if you cross the line, Mauro, there's no going back. You're business partners and I have a feeling that if you hurt her, she'll be gone forever."

I swear Cristian is talking in code.

"So, you *don't* think us is a horrible idea then?" I look over my shoulder and pull out into traffic.

He chuckles. "No, I think you just need to make sure you'll give this an honest shot otherwise leave her alone."

I drive for a minute not responding and Cristian stays on the line, knowing me well enough to know I'm deep in thought.

"Am I missing something?" I finally ask.

I follow Madison down the street the house is on. Construction crews for the new roof are already hard at work. With the dark clouds looming I'm not sure how long their workday will be.

"What do you mean?" he asks.

"I mean, do you like her or something?"

Even if he did, I'm not sure I could hold back and do the right thing. I never thought a girl could come between my brothers and me, but a possessiveness runs through my veins whenever he and I speak about Madison.

He laughs like I'm a stand-up comedian. "No. I just don't want to see her hurt. I saw... look, just be one hundred percent sure, that's all I'm saying."

"I will, now stop lecturing me." I park a few cars down from Madison. "See you later."

I hang up the phone, hearing Cristian's sarcastic mumble of 'you're welcome asshole' before the line disconnects.

I still can't help but think I'm missing something that makes Cristian put on a big brother persona when it comes to Madison. She wasn't even in his grade. What kind of connection could they have?

Grabbing my tools I head over to Madison where she stands beside her car putting on her ball cap. She turns to me. "I think we need to talk."

My feet come to a sudden stop. There's no smile on her face, no reassuring tone, nothing in her body language that implies that everything will be fine.

Fuck, now I've done it.

CHAPTER EIGHTEEN

Madison

On the way to the house, I tried to figure out why Mauro was so angry. What had set him off? The last contact we had was a flirtatious text and I let it go because I just don't know if we should cross that line.

But one thing is for sure, we can't let any unresolved issues remain between us or it'll ruin this project. When I saw his truck parked a few cars behind me, and I made the decision to stop him before we went into the house so we could talk and leave all our toxic issues outside.

"I think we need to talk." I tuck my hair into my ball cap, flipping my ponytail out.

He drops his tool bag, the stress lined in the creases around his eyes. "I'm sorry, I can't even explain why I acted like that..."

I hold my hand for him to stop. "You know what I think?"

A smile tugs on the corner of his lips and the tension plaguing his face loosens. "What?"

"That I've done something to upset you and you didn't

think I wanted your opinion on textiles. I tried to go back through everything since this morning, but I can't figure out where I might've not treated you as an equal. It's important that we keep an open line of communication between us, so just tell me. I promise I'm a big girl and can handle it." I stand up straighter like I'm proving how tough I am.

He stands there, his head tilted like I'm a mathematical equation he's having trouble trying to figure out.

"It's okay, give it to me." I close my eyes tight waiting for him to rip the Band-Aid off.

"Give it to you?" he asks and it's true that you can hear a smile in someone's voice. "Open your eyes," he almost whispers.

I do and his blue eyes are right in front of me, a smirk on his face.

"Did you think I was going to sucker punch you?" He steps back and I miss his nearness immediately.

"No. It's stupid. Something Lauren and I do when we have to tell the other person something bad. Like if you don't see how pained their face is for having to tell you it helps you cope better."

He looks as confused as I am as to why I'm telling him this. Embarrassment heats my face.

The roofers are pounding nails into place and we're standing outside the car making spectacles of ourselves. At least I am.

"I'm not upset with anything to do with the house," he says.

Oh phew. That's a load off. I'd thought I was being fair, but of course the person writing the lists always thinks everything's split down the middle.

"You're working too hard. You're exhausted. I get it and really, I don't mind being here longer hours. I don't think..."

He laughs, shaking his head.

Now this is the us I love. Not that version back at the tile place. My sixteen-year-old self is impressed by the way I've been able to develop this growing friendship with Mauro.

"No?" I ask, taking the hint that my statement isn't correct.

"No." He shakes his head.

"What could it be then? Last night? Did the fire bring up bad memories of Hunter? Do you want to talk about it? I know we've never really talked about anything too deep, but I'm a good listener. Just ask Lauren and Van." He places his fingers over my lips, stepping forward and caging me against the car. He really likes this domineering role of having his body hovering over mine. Let's face it, I kinda like it, too.

"Close your eyes, Madison," he whispers.

One hand lands on the roof of my car and then the other one next to my head.

When my eyes are still open a few seconds later, he repeats his earlier statement. "Close your eyes." His voice is soft and sultry and could probably make me strip down for him right now if we weren't in public.

My eyelids flutter shut but pop back open. "You're not going to kiss me, are you?"

His head falls forward in defeat, his body language saying I ruined the moment.

"Well?" I prod.

His hands fall back to his sides leaving me free to escape. "Yes, Madison, I was going to kiss you."

I'm not stupid but what I just did was stupid. I effectively took the damn hose and doused the fire between us. Maybe that's a good thing. I don't even know anymore.

"I'm sorry."

He shakes his head. "Of course you are." Picking up his tool bag, he waits for me to walk up the sidewalk first.

"Wait," I say. He turns in my direction. "You still haven't explained what made you so angry earlier."

He looks up to the sky as though the answers are up there somewhere. "I think this is a longer conversation than we can have right now."

Just as I'm about to suggest we head inside to talk, Emmanuel, the contractor doing our roof, calls out to Mauro from the ladder.

"Saved by the contractor." Mauro winks and heads up the walkway.

They talk while I bundle the samples in my arms that Meadow gave us. I've almost reached them when Emmanuel climbs back up the ladder with some tarps in his hand.

Mauro approaches me before I reach him. "Bad news. Rain is coming so they're covering up and heading out for the day."

I look up at the sky, the dark clouds fast approaching. "This is what those spare days I put into the schedule are for. No worries." I slide by him to go into the house.

His tools jiggle in the box so I know he's two steps behind me.

"Just me and you today," he says once we're both in the house.

"I'm going to tackle the basement."

"I was going to start the drywall, but maybe I should go down there with you."

I laugh. "I can handle it myself."

I head through the large living room to the dining room and kitchen. We'll need to pick our paint colors soon. There is supposed to be a crew in here over the next few days to lay whatever drywall Mauro doesn't get done. He's been amazing at arranging the help. His men work all day with the strongest work ethic I've ever seen, never cutting a corner.

Compared to my other projects, this one is going a thousand times smoother.

The wooden steps creak on my way down to the basement and I remind myself for not the first time that old houses make strange noises. Nothing to freak out about.

Grabbing my sketchpad to figure out how we'll configure the basement, the fact that Mauro said he was going to kiss me outside lingers in the forefront of my mind.

I still don't understand why he was so angry earlier, but maybe it's better to just let it go unexplained.

An hour later, I've got my plans to go over with Mauro. When I step onto the top of the landing of the staircase I see that the sky appears even darker and angrier than earlier.

"A storm is definitely on its way." I shut the back door, the cool rush of air igniting a cascade of goose bumps along my skin.

I turn to find Mauro there, his shirt stripped off, long forgotten on his toolbox. Sweat glistens off the curves and crevices of his muscular body.

Did I say I was cold? It's suddenly like an oven in here. His hat is on backward which I've realized he only seems to wear when he's working. It reminds me of the high school version of himself.

It takes me a second, but I realize that Snow Patrol is playing through a small Bluetooth speaker to his right.

The night from forever ago rushes back to me. This was the song playing on the radio when I drove him home.

I sit down on the dining room table we didn't have the heart to remove and watch his corded forearms strain as he lifts a sheet of drywall. He really is a man's man. So different than any other man I've dated. They were all good with their heads. Engineers, professors, accountants. Mauro holds more sex appeal than all of them put together.

His looks are what drew me in all those years ago. The cocky quarterback every girl wanted. An Adonis of a guy that all the girls dreamed of taming. Now years later, after getting to know him better, it's clear that I never really knew him back then.

That night under the stars on that baseball field that I saw as a moment of bonding and trust on his part wasn't. The man that's standing in front of me now isn't an unsure boy taking an opportunity when it presented itself. He's so much more than a handsome face. He's smart, considerate, and hard-working. I need to get my expectations back in check.

"The storm is going to be here any minute." Mauro talks directly to the wall. "I'm trying to just finish this wall then we can head out."

I pull my legs up to my chest and let a contented sigh out. This view coupled with the promise of being unable to do anything but lay in bed listening to the rain. Or reading a book. I love these lazy days.

"Do you like thunderstorms?" I ask, never letting an opportunity pass where I can get to know him.

He shrugs. "Yeah, I guess. More just the steady rain than the thunder and lightning." His answer is nonchalant so I don't offer my own opinion and he doesn't ask.

Finishing up the wall, he drops the X-acto knife in the bin and studies his work. "The crew I hired should be able to finish over the next few days. We're really making progress."

Whereas I've always done days of framing, followed by days of drywalling, followed by days of mudding and taping, Mauro decided on a different plan of attack. One where one group immediately follows the first and so on. I think it's going to work well and it'll definitely reduce our turnaround time on the house.

"You do good work, Bianco." I nod at the wall.

He grabs his t-shirt drying the sweat from his face and tucking it into the waistband of his jeans. God, he's gorgeous. Not a stray hair anywhere on his chest and I can't help but want to run my tongue over the planes of his rippled abdomen.

"Can I ask you a question?" He takes a sip of his water.

"Sure."

"Have you hooked up with my brother before?"

"Luca?" My mouth hangs open for a second before I begin laughing. "Absolutely not, no."

Mauro doesn't laugh nor does he smile. "Cristian?"

My mood sobers a bit with the realization that he's serious. "No. Why would you ask me that?"

He tries to shrug it off, but I'm not letting this go. Is this the reason for his earlier anger?

"Mauro?"

"It's stupid, but he seems almost protective of you when I talk about you to him." He lifts the hat off his head with one hand and the fingers on his other, thread through his hair. "He's really worried about me hurting you. When I asked him if I was stepping on his toes, he said no, but I know my brother well enough to know I'm missing something."

His eyes bore into mine, asking me to clarify his brother's reaction. My initial reaction is an inward celebration that he's been talking to his brother about me. It's all clapping and jumping around and happy times inside. But my head makes its way into the conversation and I know that now is the time. I need to fill in some of the blanks for him.

I pat the table next to me. "It's time we had that talk."

He slides up beside me on the table. As embarrassing as this is going to be, he has to know the truth before anything happens between us. His reaction will solidify whether I risk taking a chance on him or not.

CHAPTER NINETEEN

Mauro

I slide up on the oak table I plan on redoing as a gift to whoever buys the house. The table deserves to have its beauty revealed. I think it's Amish made which explains how it was able to stay in decent shape since its owners beat the shit out of their house.

Madison's fidgeting scares me and I'm crossing my fingers that she didn't have a one-night stand with my brother. Or some secret crush on him. Not that I think she did, but the two of them are definitely keeping something from me.

"So, you know how you've been hinting at us kissing?" she starts.

Her tone is back to heavy and somber. I hate it. Loathe it is more like it. I can easily figure out that whatever she has to tell me, she's unsure how I'll receive the news.

"Our first kiss would have been over and done with had you let me kiss you at the car." I smile down at her, teasing, trying to purge the tension from the room.

She shoots me a soft smile and her cheeks color pink. I

love pulling that reaction out of her and I can't wait to have the opportunity to see her entire body flush in that same shade.

"That's the thing," she continues.

Her eyes focus in on her entwined hands. Just as I can't stand the wait any longer, she swivels her body to face me. Her gaze shifts from her hands to my face. Gorgeous blue eyes filled with adoration pierce mine.

"We already had our first kiss."

"What?" I scrunch my forehead in confusion.

"Back in high school."

I wave my hand in the air to stop her before she continues. "Is this some joke you're helping my brothers pull off?" It would be just like them to talk Madison into messing with my head just for a laugh.

She shakes her head, her teeth biting down on her lower lip like she does when she's nervous.

"No?" I ask, stunned.

"No."

"How could I not remember kissing you?" I slide forward, taking her hands in mine.

Rain starts beating down on the house, and light inside is dim now from the dark and stormy skies. I can't help but relate the storm to whatever story I'm about to hear because seconds ago I would've said I had a better chance of being struck by lightning than not remembering that I'd already kissed Madison at some point in my life.

"You were drunk," she says.

"Were you?"

Please tell me she was and that maybe, just maybe she was able to remember it a little but not fully because if I kissed her when I was drunk, it probably means I did a piss poor job of it.

She shakes her head.

My eyes roll into the back of my head and I look anywhere but at her. Here I've been flirting with her based on the idea that we'd never been together in any way and now I find out that we've already kissed.

"Okay, give it to me. How much of an ass did I make of myself?" I squeeze her hands and her eyes find mine once more.

"You were a senior. I was a sophomore. It was at a bonfire party." She pauses for a second and I think she's testing me to see if I remember anything at all, but my memory is still a black hole.

With my silence, she continues.

She tells me about the party, finding me in the woods, driving me home, "Chasing Cars" by Snow Patrol playing on the radio, the slide in the park across the street from my parents' house. Lastly, the outfield of the park I played Little League in.

"You were asking about God's plan. Talking about how you wanted the trifecta. The career, the family, and the house. It was sweet. Then you asked if you could kiss me."

A wistfulness fills her eyes as she recollects how she expected to see a shooting star. I wonder how many times her mind has drifted back to this memory of us? The same memory that was erased from mine because of alcohol. I feel an aching loss inside because of that that I can't comprehend.

Her soft smile leaves her face and her shoulders tense. "My braces cut you." She cringes, and for the first time her gaze shifts away from mine. "You were bleeding."

Oh Jesus, what I could have said? It was high school, so I probably reacted like a rude asshole. Did I yell at her for cutting my lip? For all that is holy, please tell me no.

"You didn't seem to care. You just touched your lip and told me like it was a fact."

Thank God I wasn't a complete jerk off. I'd better get to church on Sunday and ask for forgiveness.

"Then we stood up and you asked me if I wanted to swing." She shrugs, but her eyes are welling with tears.

"Madison." I sigh, my hand sliding up her arm, past her elbow, bypassing her shoulder, molding to her cheek. "I'm sorry I don't remember."

My heart squeezes over the fact that a moment that clearly meant so much to her wasn't even a blip on my screen.

"Cristian showed up right after, you threw up in the trash-can, and he took you home." A tear slips down her cheek. "As embarrassing as retelling this story is, you had to know before we move forward because we already had our first kiss, but I was the only one who remembered."

"And Cristian, he knows?"

She shrugs. "I think he suspected. I actually think he thought we had sex at first."

I hate that I have to ask her this question, but I need to know. "We didn't though, right?"

Her face is beet red and she slides out from my hold, her feet hitting the floor. "No. I wasn't that pathetic." She begins throwing stuff into her bag. "Telling you was a really bad idea. I need to go. We should've kept this platonic. It's not too late though. We just need to shift gears and forget all of this emotional stuff. Keep things uncomplicated."

I hop off the table. Coming up behind her, I still her hand with mine and she pauses. "I didn't mean the question as a bad thing. I hate the fact I don't remember and I had to know what I'm up against." I dip my head down into the crook of her neck, the strawberry scent of her shampoo intoxicating and arousing. "So I know what I need to do to make this right. Madison, I don't want to go back to being just business partners. Not by a long shot."

Her body loses the tension of a stretched rubber band.

"It's mortifying that I admired you from afar and you had no idea who I was."

I ease her around to face me, but her eyes focus in on my chest. Placing my finger under her chin, I nudge her to look up into my eyes. The second our gazes lock, her shoulders relax and I swear she sinks into my body. "I'm sorry that I didn't notice you in high school. All I can say is that I was a self-centered jerk, but I see you now Madison Kelly. In fact, you're all I see."

Both my hands cup her face and as badly as I want to lean in and kiss her right now, our second kiss needs to be special.

"Kiss me," she asks, her chest heaving with breath, the hard points of her nipples pressing into my chest.

My head fights my heart as I wonder if there's ever going to be a perfect time for us. She's just put her heart out there for me. Trusting me for a second time and I don't want to take advantage. I want her to know I'm in this.

My cock strains in my pants as our eyes swim together in a mix of hazy lust and need. I lick my lip in anticipation and when I can't stand the building tension between us anymore, I lose all control of my body and my head dips, my heart winning the war.

She licks her lips, her fingers wrapping around my shoulders, rising on her tiptoes. Our eyes fall closed, our lips nearing one another and I can feel her breath on my face.

The tornado sirens blare outside and like a snap of the fingers, our moment is over.

Her eyes widen in fear. "Mauro," she says my name with a soft plea.

"Basement." I grab her hand and lead her through the kitchen, down the stairs.

Large hail pounds atop the half-completed roof.

We race downstairs, turning on the lights, but I know

with the way the power lines in Chicago are, electricity will be the first thing to go.

"I'll be right back." I run back up the stairs.

"Hurry, Mauro."

Grabbing the candles she had lit before, I find the one flashlight I have in my toolbox. Shutting the front door, I run back into the basement where Madison's arms are crossed as her teeth nibble on her bottom lip.

"It's okay. We'll be fine." I wrap her in my arms.

"I just hate storms like this."

The sirens are still blaring. I don't even remember the last time I heard them sound here. I was probably a young boy.

"It will pass. Tornados don't hit Chicago." I rub my hands over her chilled arms.

As we stand in the middle of the basement, her in my arms, her story from a decade ago runs through my mind while I try to gain a flicker of recollection, but nothing surfaces.

"I'm so sorry, Madison," I whisper and she turns her head to peer up at me with those sweet blue eyes that could make me do just about anything for her.

Her hand caresses my cheek. "I made peace with it a long time ago."

"Still. I just...I had you ten years ago and let you go."

A smile plays on her lips. "Who said you had me?" Turning in my arms, she winds her arms around my neck. "Maybe I let you go."

"You're way too nice. You should be kicking me in the nuts right now."

She laughs and her forehead falls to my chest. "Then I guess you're lucky that I'm a people pleaser."

The lights flicker once, twice before blackness surrounds us. "Hold on." I turn on the flashlight and hand it to Madison.

Lighting the candles, I place them around the space and we sit down on a tarp that Madison had down here when she was working.

"Tell me about your parents." I try to do anything to get her mind off of the storm looming overhead.

She looks off over my shoulder. "They're divorced. My dad lives in Florida. My mom's in Oregon. This is where everything fell apart." She glances up at the ceiling. "My dad left and my mom lost herself for a year or so."

I reach out for her knee, my thumb rubbing back and forth. I've never experienced the repercussion of divorce, but I've heard enough stories from friends to know how bad it can mess up someone's belief in love after seeing their parents' happily ever after fall apart.

"It was so many years ago and if you didn't think I was a loser before, wait until you hear why I bought this house." She lets a self-deprecating chuckle escape her lips.

"Hey, let's get one thing clear, I never thought you were a loser."

She smiles like she doesn't really believe me. I mentally mark that down to prove her wrong.

"Reserve your judgment for a moment."

She reaches out and rubs my shoulder. It's a casual move, but one she's never done before. And I enjoyed it way too much.

"I bought the house so that someone could build a happy life here. I wanted a family to love one another and for some other little girl to get the dream I didn't."

Nothing could've blown me away more than the words that just left her mouth. I'd actually been thinking she wanted revenge of some kind on the place, but it's the opposite of that. And her reason speaks way too much for who she is. How thoughtful and kind she is right down to why she rehabs houses.

"What about the other houses?" I lean in and my arm rests behind her back. I want that kiss more than anything right now.

She locks eyes with me. "Same." Her unsure voice continues. "I just want to build a place for families to love each other in, one that reflects on the outside, the love you can find inside. A home is so much more than wood and glass, carpet and stairs. It shelters and protects the people you love most in this world."

"Madison?" I raise my hand to her cheek.

"Yeah?"

"I'm going to kiss you now."

CHAPTER TWENTY

Madison

He's slow to start, deliberate in his actions, wanting to make this a kiss to remember. Just like that night ten years ago, my body hums and heats under his soft lips. But it's different this time. It's not Mauro kissing me, it's us kissing each other. Another small piece of my heart floats out of my chest and nestles into his.

His tongue sweeps across my lips, asking without words if it's okay. Opening my mouth, my skin ignites in a wave of goose bumps when his tongue slides across mine. We entwine ourselves in one another slowly until I don't know where I stop and he begins.

I give Mauro credit, he's as patient as the saint his mama probably prays to every night. Pressing my body to his, I'm the one who deepens the kiss. His arms tighten around my back and the feel of his powerful chest against my own makes my nipples taut.

Somewhere between the butterflies roaring into an uncontrollable flutter in my stomach and all my sensory alarms flashing overload, we sink into one another. Our mouths colliding one second, gentle the next. One of his hands runs up the length of my spine until his fingers reach my hair and he manipulates my ponytail holder, my hair spilling down across my shoulders.

His dark hair is smooth as my hands run up the back of his head, trying desperately to cling to anything. My legs beg to wind around his waist, but I force myself to stay grounded. Never have I ever felt so much from one kiss.

I'm not even sure which of us slows down, but long after our lips have stopped moving, our bodies are still entangled like wild vines.

"Let's pretend that was our first kiss." He smiles down at me.

"Not a chance."

"That was a pretty spectacular kiss." He presses his lips to mine one more time. "Definitely top ten." His smirk says he's joking. I lightly punch him in the stomach. "You sure you don't want to forget that first one?"

"I'm positive, but I'll take another kiss like this one anytime."

"If you're not going to pretend that was our first kiss then I have no choice but to try to erase it from your memory." His head descends and again, the feel of his lips on mine catapult me back to euphoria.

We come up for air minutes later and I'm surprised and if I'm honest maybe a little disappointed. Mauro didn't even try to cop a feel. His hands ventured down to my ass, but he stopped short. The only part of the kiss that was NC17 was his erection pressed into my stomach.

The lights flicker back on, the soft glow of the candles disappearing.

"If this place wasn't so disgusting, I'd never want to leave,"

Mauro murmurs, his lips pressed to my temple. "I'll go check on the storm."

It's only now that I realize the sirens have stopped wailing outside.

He releases me and I miss being in his arms immediately. His footsteps pound up the stairs and I hear the back door opening.

"We're good," he calls out before he comes back down the stairs.

The first thing he does is extinguish the candles with a lick of his fingers and a press to the wick. I can't help but smile at that.

"I'm starved. You want to go somewhere for dinner?" he asks.

"Sure."

We each have an armful of candles as we head upstairs.

After walking around the house to make sure none of the windows are broken, Mauro suggests we drop off my car so he can drive us to dinner.

Right before I pull away from the curb, I let the image of the house sink into my memory. I'd never want to take back our first kiss, but this one was so much better.

I turn down the alley while Mauro parks on the street in front of the house. Lauren's yellow Fiat is in the garage and my stomach drops, wondering what she'll say if she answers the door when Mauro reaches it.

So, I do what any normal girl would do to protect the guy she's falling for from her friend's wrath—I race inside through the back door, sprinting to the front door and swinging it open.

Mauro draws back, but I press on his shoulders to turn him back down the stairs he just climbed. "What's going on?"

"Nothing, just my stomach was rumbling the entire way over here. I need food."

Mauro smiles over his shoulder.

"Whoa, whoa, whoa!" Lauren's voice at my back is like the squealing of tires locking up on dry pavement.

You know when you hear that noise followed by the sound of piercing metal crashing two seconds later?

"Taking our girl out without talking to the friends? I would have thought your mama taught you better than that, Mauro Bianco."

We both turn to find her standing on the porch, hands on her hips. She's wearing a pair of yoga pants and a baggy sweatshirt that's printed with the words *Physical Therapist - I'm here to fix your ass not kiss it*.

Mauro chuckles to himself. "Lauren Hunt, hello. I guess I should be grateful that you didn't jump on my back this time." He jogs up the steps and puts his hand out. "I heard you're going on a date with Luca. Good luck with that."

Lauren shakes his hand and rolls her eyes at the same time. "That's never going to happen."

"I'm kidding. He's a good guy. Deep down."

Lauren leans back and yells into the house. "Van! We've got company." She steps back and opens the door wider. "Come on in, Mauro."

"We were just leaving," I say from the bottom of the stairs.

Lauren peers around Mauro as he's circling around, clearly confused as to why I'm still standing at the bottom of the stairs.

"You can wait five minutes. Vanessa's never met Mauro." Lauren smiles. The one that's conniving and means she's up to trouble. "We can order pizza."

"Five minutes, Lauren." I run up the stairs, grabbing Mauro's hand and pulling him in behind me.

His eyes scour the inside of the house.

"Nice, right? Maddie redid this place." Lauren leads us to the family room and sits down on the couch, patting the cushion next to her. "Come, sit, Mauro."

His eyes veer to mine, but he sits, albeit hesitantly. "What've you been up to, Lauren?" He falls back onto the sofa, resting his ankle on his knee.

"I'm a physical therapist." She points to her sweatshirt. "But I'm much more interested in knowing how this whole partnership thing is going from your perspective?" She waggles her finger between Mauro on the couch and where I stand.

"It's going great, right Madison?" Mauro's eyes find mine, a smirk on his lips.

"Yep."

Lauren narrows her eyes, trying to dissect my inner thoughts.

"What's going on? I'm about to head out." The echo of Vanessa's heels sound down the stairs before she appears in the room wearing a skin-tight dress that ends right below her ass.

Suddenly, I feel frumpy and boring.

Mauro stands up from the couch, crossing the room, his hand already out before Vanessa has even looked up from her phone.

"If this is about your vibrator, I'm going to say it again, Lauren, I didn't take it. That's not something you borrow from someone."

"Van," I say and knock her elbow. She glances up at me, smiles. "Hey, did you get caught in that storm?"

I shift my eyes and she follows the direction of my gaze.

"Oh, shit, have you been standing there for longer than one second?"

"Well, I don't think Maddie twitched her nose and he appeared." Lauren laughs. "I didn't say you borrowed my vibrator, I was simply asking if you saw it when it was delivered. Do you ever even listen to us anymore?" Lauren blows at a hair that's fallen down onto her forehead.

Ignoring Lauren, I introduce Vanessa and Mauro. "Vanessa this is Mauro, Mauro this is Vanessa, our third roommate."

Mauro shakes her hand. "Nice to meet you. Your dad is the commander of the eighteenth district?"

Vanessa's smile falters. "He is."

"My brother Cristian says he's a good man."

Vanessa drops his hand, her focus back on her phone. "He can be."

Vanessa's a master at hiding her true feelings, but I've known her long enough to know that she's giving Mauro the answer he expects.

Mauro's eyes find mine, a smile on his lips. I hate that for a second I feared that Mauro would be attracted to Vanessa. She was definitely his type in high school. I loathe the part of me that refuses to let go of all my baggage from that time in my life.

"Have a seat, Vanessa, we're going to put Mauro through the wringer about his intentions with our girl."

"No, you're not. Mauro and I are going to get something to eat," I say.

Lauren tilts her head. "Surely, he doesn't care. You don't have anything to hide, do you?"

This is getting annoying. Does she think if he's using me he's going to divulge that to her right here and now? She acts like she's some ace detective on *Law & Order* who can squeeze a confession out of a person of interest with just a few pointed questions.

"Enough with the protective dad act," I say.

Vanessa is still buried in her phone, her fingers going a mile a minute. "One question from me and then I'm out." She surprises all of us by joining the conversation.

"No girls, we aren't going to do this." I shake my head.

Mauro puts his arm around my shoulder. "No, Mad, it's fine." He shifts his attention to Vanessa.

"Do you like our girl?" she asks.

"Yes."

"Then I'm good. I think it goes without saying that if you hurt her, you can expect a visit on your doorstep from me. And Lauren." She nods to where Lauren still sits on the couch. "Oh, and do me a favor and tell your brother to stop fucking calling me. I'm not going to go out with him." She turns and walks toward the back of the house, probably to catch another ride in a black town car.

"Are you dating someone? Is that why you won't date him?" Mauro calls out and Vanessa stops walking, slowly turning around.

Lauren and I are silent, waiting for her to answer.

"No, but I don't date people who work under my dad. That's a bad situation for all involved."

Then she's gone through the back door.

One down, one to go. Unfortunately, it's the piranha that's still circling.

"You get one question, Lauren." I turn to face her, but Mauro sits down in the chair across from her.

"Three is more than fair," she says.

"Two," I negotiate and she wiggles in her seat and rubs her hands together.

"First question. Was it a coincidence that you showed up to bid on the same property as Madison?"

Seems like a waste of a question to me. Obviously, it was a coincidence. But I'm happy that's what she asked because it could have been so much worse.

"Yes." He gives a sharp nod of his head.

"Question two. You're not using her to screw her over in the future, are you?"

"No."

"Question three—"

"No, Lauren that's it." I hold my hand out for Mauro to take. He doesn't accept it.

"It's fine. I'll answer as many questions as you want." He sits up, resting his forearms on his thighs. "But before you ask, I'll just save us each a bit of time."

Lauren sits back, crossing her arms over her chest in a way that suggests he'll never win her over, but she'll let him try and fail.

"First off, thank you for bidding on me at the bachelor auction. Though our first date didn't go as well as I'd have hoped, it put Madison on my radar. The property thing was a complete coincidence, but I'd like to think it was fate stepping in. Now, she told me what an asshole I was in high school. Don't worry, I'm still trying to figure out how I could have possibly forgotten the first time I kissed her."

Lauren's eyebrows scrunch and she glances my way.

Shut up, Mauro.

"But I plan on making that up to her. I like Madison. A helluva lot more than a friend. This is new to both of us and we have to tread carefully with the business partnership and all, but I guarantee you, my intentions are pure." He leans back into the chair, his hand out for me to take it. "Any more questions?"

"Just one." She holds up her finger. "What the hell is he talking about a kiss in high school?" She glares my way.

"Nothing."

Now both of them are looking at me. I throw my hands up in the air.

"That night of the bonfire when I drove him home..."

Please don't make me retell this story.

Her eyes narrow. I silently slice my finger across my throat. She takes my hint and gives me a quick nod.

"Oh, that time when Mauro was drunk and all over you because he wanted you so bad? I completely forgot about that time," she says.

Be jealous girls, she's all mine.

The light in Mauro's eyes dims again with that pitiful puppy look, staring up at me.

"She's kidding, Mauro." I place my hand on his arm.

Jeez does he do push-ups every night?

Lauren shakes her head and Mauro shifts his attention to her. The two share a look of 'she's way too nice.'

"What? You love me just the way I am." I stand, looking at Lauren, whose eyes move to Mauro.

My cheeks flush because now Mauro took that as I think he loves me.

Lauren busts out laughing.

"Go you two. Try to screw the niceness out of her will you, Mauro?" She grabs the remote and the television lights up.

Even Mauro's red now. Lauren has that effect on people.

"You'd rather sit at home and watch television than go out with my brother?" Mauro asks, grabbing my hand in his to lead us out of the room.

"Yes." She points to Mauro. "And what does that say about your brother?"

Mauro chuckles. "So, I have your permission to take Madison out to dinner, Warden Hunt?" He raises our hands.

"I suppose so. But, if you screw her any other way then doggie style, missionary, or reverse cowgirl, then I suggest you walk around with a jock cup permanently in place because I'll be coming for you."

Mauro gives me a look like 'is she fucking serious?'

"You've been warned," I whisper.

"Night Lauren," he says and I give her a quick wave too which she responds with two thumbs up and a million dollar smile behind his back.

I try to ignore the warm feeling in my chest once we're back outside and he's leading me to his truck.

I'm going out with Mauro Bianco, someone pinch me.

He opens his car door and I slide in. "Tough girl. But I like it that she's around to look out for you."

The door shuts and I watch him round the front of his truck.

Okay, I'll admit, I pinched myself. I had to see if this was real or not.

CHAPTER TWENTY-ONE

Mauro

"I'm sorry about Lauren," Madison mumbles when I climb into the driver's seat.

I wait to start the truck, my hand gripping hers first. "I would've answered as many questions as she had. I understand her concern, and I meant what I said, I'm glad she's there to protect you."

When I think she's appeased, I insert the keys in the ignition and start the engine.

"Now, where do you want to eat?" I ask.

Pulling away from the curb, Madison waves to her neighbors standing on their porch watching a little girl and boy jump in puddles on the sidewalk.

"That's the ADA I was telling you about, Reed Warner," she says as the kids wave and scream Maddie's name when we drive away.

"Oh yeah, and that's his family?"

She nods. "Well, his fiancée and her daughter. The little boy is around a lot so I'm not really sure if he's just a friend or a relation. They're cute though, right?"

The look of longing on her face says she wants what they have. I'd be lying if I said I didn't either, but wanting and getting are two different things.

"Very cute."

She settles in the seat, crossing her legs. "I'm not really dressed for a nice dinner, so how about Portillos?"

"Sure." I flick on my turn signal.

Once we have a destination, silence looms in the car.

"What about you? Do you want a family? I mean, I'm not implying..."

I laugh and she stops her rambling. Reaching over, I grip her hand again, entwining our fingers like the real couple we're becoming.

"I'm Italian, I'm not really sure I have a choice if I want a family." I chuckle and give her hand a squeeze. "My ma is already down all our throats for grandchildren. The Catholic guilt might crush Cristian, but not me or Luca. We'll take that step when we're ready."

My words are the truth, but I'm failing to mention one thing. That trusting someone is hard for me and after Jenna, even harder. Since that's a key component of promising yourself to someone forever, I'm not sure when I'll be ready for that huge step.

"I'd rather have that than your parents just assuming you'll never get married or have kids. My mom thinks my independence scares off men. My dad still sees me as the ugly duckling I was in high school."

"Don't say that about yourself." I let her hand go so I can put my signal on and turn a corner.

Agitation bursts through me hot and angry. We sit in silence for a minute before we pull into the parking lot of Portillos and I slam the truck into park, turning to face her.

"Beauty isn't just something you find on the outside. Besides, you weren't that bad in high school."

She raises her eyebrows at me in challenge.

"Listen, the inside of someone can make them ugly, too. Someone can be attractive and present themselves with a perfect bow on top, but if when you get to know them, they're mean and callous with your heart, you no longer see their beauty. I understand that you have your hang-ups from high school, but I noticed you the night of the auction. I'm going to lay myself on the line here." I inhale a deep breath and squeeze the steering wheel in my hands.

"When someone pointed you out as the winner of a date with me, my breath caught in my throat. Mentally I already had us in every sexual position possible, my lips on every inch of your skin as I buried myself inside of you over and over again."

She flushes and looks away, but I use my other hand to rest under her chin, bringing her eyes back on me.

"But it's these last few weeks...the beauty inside of you that has drawn me to you even more. I know I ridiculed you for being a people pleaser, but I was wrong. You genuinely care for people and how they're feeling. The way you bring water for the crew. Tell someone to take a break when you noticed they're bagged. The fact you know more than me about the guys I've been working side by side with for years. You remember their wives and kids names and ask how their little league game went the day before. How you trust me and you see the person I am inside of me. Madison, you've come to consume my thoughts, my heart, hell my life in a matter of weeks."

She smiles, beams really, her cheek leaning into the palm of my hand, the strands of her hair tickling my forearm. I lean over the center console, pressing my lips to hers. As much as I want to deepen our kiss, her stomach growls from hunger, so I pull away with a chuckle.

"Too many interruptions." She fists my shirt and pulls me closer, our lips colliding, our tongues each trying to claim dominance.

I want to slide my seat back, pull her over onto my lap, kiss her neck and nibble on her earlobe. I'd do just about anything to feel her heart beating against my chest. Who am I kidding? I want to take her home and lock her in my room for an eternity.

Slowing our kiss, our chests both heave for a breath and I rest my forehead on hers. "I'm going to feed you and then take you to your place before we lose control."

I want nothing more than to bury myself deep inside her, but I don't want to screw this up by pushing her too fast.

She giggles. "Who said I wanted to go home?" She climbs out of the truck before I have a chance to open the door, rounding the front and waiting for me.

I hop out of the driver's side, adjust my half-erect dick and quickly grab her hand when I reach her. "You're going to have to learn to wait for me to open the door for you."

She places a hand on my bicep and leans her head on my shoulder. "Oh, Mauro, I enjoy chivalry, but I don't need help in and out of the car."

"It's not about you needing help, it's gentlemanly."

"Well, when we go on a real date, I promise to wait."

I stop us before entering the rotating door to the place. "I wanted to ask you. Will you go out with me on Thursday? Me, you, and a fancy restaurant?"

Her eyes light up and she smiles so wide it encompasses her entire face. "I'd love to."

We head inside where I buy her a hot dog and fries. We talk a bit about everything including what it was like for me to grow up in a large Italian family and how much they mean to me. She actually seems excited when I talk about our Sunday dinners.

With any luck, she'll find out soon enough that they're much more than spaghetti and meatballs.

CHAPTER TWENTY-TWO

Madison

"Wear this. No this." Vanessa's throwing clothes out of her closet. "Do you want my fake eyelashes? I have the perfect shade of nude lipstick that will pull all the shades of your coloring out."

"She doesn't need all this shit. Mauro's already smitten with her." Lauren smiles at me through the mirror of Vanessa's vanity.

"Smitten?" I ask and she shrugs.

"I have to admit, I gave him a green check mark after his speech the other night." Lauren sits on the bed, leaning against the headboard pretending to relax, but I can tell her eyes are secretly taking in Vanessa's space, looking for clues.

"What speech?" Vanessa comes back out of her closet holding a simple pink dress with a beaded belt and neckline. I like that it flares at the waist so it will hide my thighs.

I stand up and grab it.

"Well, if you didn't have to run off to a mystery location

you would've been here to hear it. He basically declared that he'd take her off our hands."

I roll my eyes.

A purse hits my head. I turn and stare back at the culprit, Lauren.

"It's true, Maddie, he likes you. So, don't go all glam for him. Just be yourself."

Lauren will forever be the 'I am who I am and if you don't like it then so be it' kinda girl. She could feel sexy in a track-suit, but I don't think there's anything wrong with putting in a little effort and I can't wait to see Mauro's eyes when he sees me out of my overalls and baseball cap.

"Thank you, but I want to dress up to feel sexy for him." I take a seat on the bed. Vanessa stands on the other side, after months of being absent, she's really here, present in this moment with us. "I'm not worried about not being good enough for him."

Lauren purses her lips and crosses her arms over her chest.

"Okay, not like I once was. But this dress and that makeup will show everyone that I belong with him."

Lauren stares at me for a moment and Vanessa's hand lands on my thigh. "You don't need other people to think you belong with him. You're more than worthy of Mauro. You know that, right Mad?"

Vanessa glances at Lauren, the two of them on the same line of thinking.

"I do."

Lauren slides up to me and wraps the three of us in a hug. "Close your eyes, Madison," she whispers.

"No. Not tonight, Lauren." I try to get out of their circle of truth, but they tighten their hold.

"Close them," Vanessa orders.

I do as they say, my heart pounding, waiting for what they're going to tell me.

"You are perfect. You have no reason to feel insecure when you're with him." Lauren speaks first.

"You're gorgeous. Though I do wish you'd wear a tighter dress and show off that ass."

The three of us laugh at Vanessa's comment.

I love these girls.

They release me from their hold and my gaze veers to the clock on Vanessa's nightstand.

Shit, it's almost time for him to pick me up.

I collapse on the mattress, my hand on my stomach. "I can't believe I'm going out with Mauro Bianco and it's not some sick joke. Pinch me, girls." I hold out my arms.

They both grab pillows and smack me on the head.

"Hey," I say, standing up.

"It's not a dream and he should be the one pinching himself." Lauren smiles and Vanessa takes the dress off the hanger.

"Come on, let's get you ready. He'll be here soon." Vanessa holds it out for me.

I take a deep breath and grab it from her hands.

Unlike when I was sixteen, or our time at the café, this date feels like it means something and I'm surprised to find that anticipation and excitement are at the forefront of my emotions, not anxiety or nerves.

That has to mean something good, right?

CHAPTER TWENTY-THREE

Mauro

"You need to leave." I grab one of Luca's friends by the shoulders and push him toward the door. "Luca, the gang needs to leave."

Cristian comes in fresh off shift, his uniform still on.

"Shit the cops are here." Luca pretends to weave like he's about to run.

Cristian tosses his keys on the side table. "Funny asshole. I'm beat."

"Great, then get changed and head to Mom's. I need the apartment tonight." I grab the empty beer bottles off the coffee table.

"Hell no. I want my bed." He walks down the hall.

"All of you." I circle my finger to the guys. "Out." I point to the door.

Luca laughs. "Are you bringing a girl home?"

I give him my fuck off expression. It's one he knows well by now.

"Go ahead, guys. We'll have to watch the fight at the bar," Luca says to his pack of followers.

His friends whine and complain in response, but I don't give one shit.

"Here's an idea, why don't all of you get your own apartments." I toss the beer bottles and put the dirty dishes in the dishwasher. Seriously, Cristian usually does all this shit. He plans the night before I'm taking Madison out to act like a slob.

One of Luca's friends flips me off and the other one makes a comment about how I used to be fun and then they shut the door behind themselves.

"I'm not joking, Luca, this has got to stop. This place is not a frat house."

"I agree." Cristian reappears in a pair of athletic pants and a t-shirt that says, *I'm no hero, but I've walked beside a few*. He buries his head in the fridge, pulling out a Vitamin water. "I'm done with this shit. You made a huge-ass mess last night."

Luca holds up his hands in the air. "What is this 'pick on Luca day?'"

Cristian blows out an exasperated breath. "This is 'stop using our damn apartment' day. We kicked you out because of your parties, why are you bringing them to us?"

"Jeez, can't a guy miss his brothers." He flops down on the couch and props his feet up on the table. "Let's talk about Mauro wanting the apartment to himself. Do I hear bells?" He inches his head toward the window like an idiot.

I smack him on the back of the head as I pass.

He holds it like I really hurt him. "Hey, that spot is exclusive for Ma." He rubs at it like the baby brother he is.

"Is all this for Maddie?" Cristian peers into the brown paper bag with a box of condoms in it that I left on the counter.

I walk over and snatch it away. "Just go so I can set up, shower and get ready for her."

"Oh, are you doing the deed tonight? Man, you move fast," Luca says, who's now relaxed with his hands behind his head and his feet on our coffee table.

"Right. Should I use your timetable? Wait two grinding songs and four shots?"

Cristian smiles over his bottle. "So, things are good if you're going to this much trouble." He checks out the apartment. It's cleaner than I've ever made it.

Luca jumps over the back of the couch. "Oh, I bet he's planning some kinky—" I run over, but Luca gets the fridge open before I can. "Someone's planning on making breakfast in the morning. Cut up fruit, eggs, bacon. I think those *are* bells I'm hearing."

I shut the fridge door. "Stop with the wedding bells shit."

He claps me on the shoulder. "It's not wedding bells, it's warning bells. They're trying to warn you this path you're headed down is the wrong way."

"Stop being such a commitment-phobe." Cristian hits Luca in the head with the top of the bottle.

"I am not. I'm a realist. One who says I'm much too young and much too attractive to settle down with one woman yet."

Cristian rolls his eyes. "Whatever. Anyway, you're really going to sleep with Madison tonight?" he asks me.

I look around and glance at my watch. "Did I just warp back to two thousand and eight where I would actually discuss my sex life with you?" I deadpan.

The two of them share a look and shrug.

A smile forms on Cristian's face. "That means he's serious about her." He gulps down the rest of his water.

"None of your fucking business. Now leave so I can set up."

"Where are you taking her for dinner?" Luca leans back, snagging a chip before I can take the bag away.

"Eddie V's."

"Pulling out the big guns." Luca chomps down on his chip. "You're willing to max out your credit card for her. Mama's going to be so proud when you pop the question." He claps me on the shoulder and steps closer to Cristian. "I'm just going to head over here because I don't want whatever you caught rubbing off on me."

"You're an asshole."

Cristian glances at Luca and then to me. "I think it's awesome. I'll go pack a bag and get out of your way."

"Seriously, you're not going to give him hell for this?" Luca calls out to Cristian's back. "You guys should thank your stars that Ma and Pa had me because otherwise your lives would be boring as hell."

"You do know you were a mistake, right?" Cristian calls down the hall.

Luca's face pales slightly, Cristian having hit his Achille's heel.

This is really a topic no one knows the answer to for sure because my parents would never admit it, but who plans to have three kids back to back? I'll let you ponder that for a minute while I razz my brother.

"I was not. If anyone was, you were." He points to Cristian's bedroom.

"Keep telling yourself that," I say.

"Either that or you were so ugly, Mom and Dad didn't want to take any more chances," Cristian says, popping his head out from his bedroom door.

Luca narrows his eyes. "Mama loves me the most anyways."

"Everyone knows I'm her favorite. Firstborn." I thumb at myself.

"I'm the baby. I'm the favorite. She hugs me tighter."

"Whatever, I'm the one who goes over there and checks on her all the time," Cristian says. "I go to the deli almost every day for lunch."

"Sorry, but I'm not sitting on my ass in a car my entire shift. I'm busy saving lives, not ruining people's days."

I purse my lips because Luca's got a point, but Cristian is doing me a solid by leaving so willingly so I don't say that out loud.

"You know who her favorite will be?" I say instead.

They both stare over at me.

"The one who gives her the first grandchild." I hold up my brown paper bag. "I'm a lot closer than either of you, so feel free to invest in a plaque with my name on it."

"Shit, you're going to make Luca take a redeye to Vegas and marry the first girl who says she's ovulating." Cristian laughs as he comes back down the hall, swinging his duffle bag over his shoulder.

"Fuck that. You can have the title then." Luca grabs his coat off the back of the couch. Standing by the door he pretends to rub his eyes. "It's just so hard, our boy is growing up." He opens the door, smiles and leaves.

"He's so competitive, I hope he doesn't take it as a challenge," I say.

We both laugh. I don't think either of us will be surprised if in nine months the first Bianco grandchild to be introduced to the world belongs to Luca.

"Let's hope it's the first time he can let a challenge go." Cristian's eyes find the bag in my hands. "I'll leave you to it. I'm on shift tomorrow so I won't be home until dinner. If for some reason you need more time, text me."

"Nah, I'm sure we'll be heading to the house in the morning. Thanks for staying with Mom and Dad for the night. I owe you one."

He heads to the front door. "Who said I'm staying at their house?" He waggles his eyebrows.

I tilt my head in confusion, I didn't think he was seeing anyone. "Then I don't owe you one."

He laughs and leaves but before the door can shut I hear him say hello to Mrs. Peterson. He just got stuck in that hallway for at least fifteen minutes.

Not wasting any time, I get everything set up for when I bring Madison back here tonight, then quickly shower and get ready.

This is the first time I've been really nervous for a date. This revelation should probably concern me, but instead it makes the smile on my face grow wider.

And just like that, I realize that I'm all in.

CHAPTER TWENTY-FOUR

Madison

The doorbell rings and the inside of my stomach feels like a bunch of monkeys climbing around a jungle gym.

Lauren and Vanessa each smile at me from where they sit on the bed.

"Do you want me to do the whole I answer and we make him wait thing?" Lauren slides off the mattress to stand.

"No, but thanks for the offer."

I leave Vanessa's room, descending the stairs while staring at the outline of Mauro in the small window next to the door.

"Stop staring you two. Go do something."

I don't turn around, but I don't have to in order to know that they don't move from their positions at the top of the stairs.

When I open the door, I almost can't believe what's waiting there for me.

Mauro's hair is gelled into a tousle of loose waves. He

wears a pair of dark jeans, a light sweater, and a jacket over top. Delectable doesn't even do him justice.

His gaze slowly roams up and down my body, his smile growing as his attention travels past the hem of my dress to my exposed legs. When he meets my eyes again, a calmness settles over me.

"You look breathtaking, Madison." He steps up, wrapping his arm around my back, pressing his lips to mine. "I want you to know that you absolutely take my breath away."

The scent of his cologne that I've only had the pleasure of smelling that one night at the game café, sends a zing of awareness to my lady parts and I clench my thighs.

"You don't look so bad yourself."

He smiles, not releasing me. "Thank you." He kisses my temple and his fingers run up and down my spine before settling on the small of my back.

We take each other's presence in for another moment until we head down my walkway to his truck. As promised, I wait for him to open up my door. When he slides in the driver's side he leans over and kisses me, teasing me with a swipe of his tongue. "I'm not sure I'm going to make it through dinner."

"We can skip dinner if you prefer." I wink, teasing him because I'm more than ready to feel him between my legs.

"Nope. I'm feeding you first. You're going to need your energy for what I have in mind."

All the papers and empty cups that usually fill Mauro's car are gone and the warm sensation in my chest reappears over the fact that he cleaned his truck for me.

"Where are we headed?" I ask once he's driving downtown.

"Eddie V's. Are you okay with seafood?"

"Definitely, but Mauro, that place is so expensive."

We're talking four dollar signs expensive. He doesn't need to spend that much money to impress me.

"It's where I *want* to take you." His fingers strum on the steering wheel as we wind through the traffic of downtown.

I watch him as he drives, casual and in control.

"Have you ever not been sure of yourself?" I ask, curious.

He glances over for a second. "You mean whether I could accomplish something?"

"Yeah, I guess. You always seem so confident in everything you do."

He shakes his head, almost to himself and stops at a red light. Turning to look right at me, I'm transfixed by him, those blue eyes are alive and bright tonight. My favorite shade.

"I wasn't confident with you. I mean I doubted myself when it came to the house at first, but I still felt comfortable that I'd finish it well. But with you...I don't know if it's because I have no control over your feelings or what, but the idea of me screwing up what's happening between us keeps me up at night."

The light turns green and without warning wetness coats my eyes.

You will not cry on your first date with him.

"Mauro," I sigh, my brain unable to process everything as my beating heart floats out of my chest and places itself in his lap, flopping around, begging to be his. I never knew a man like Mauro could be so sentimental and sweet, too.

"Jesus, I'm just full of cheesy shit lately. I could act arrogant and say how I don't care what you think, but it'd be a lie. I don't want to play games with you."

I reach over and touch his thigh, the roughness of the denim like light sandpaper on my palm. "I don't want to play games with you either."

He glances to the side at me and smiles. "I'm glad."

His hand comes down over top of mine and he webs our fingers together. We sit in the truck, letting the moment soak in. We just might be creating something worth fighting our demons for. If only those demons weren't so big and scary.

Stop it. I will not ruin this for myself.

Moments later, he pulls onto a street that's clearly marked permit parking only. Finding a spot, he puts a ballcap with CFD embroidered on the bill on the dashboard.

He eyes me for a second. "Remember the deal?"

I move my hand away from the handle of the door. "Yep." I act as though I wasn't about to push the door open and hop out.

He smirks and rounds the front of his truck until he reaches my door, opening it and offering me a hand.

As elegantly as someone can, I climb out of the large truck and he shuts the door behind me.

"So that works? The hat?" I ask.

He shrugs. "If it doesn't, Cristian will try to work his magic. One perk of being a civil serviceman." His hand finds mine again and we walk side by side on the sidewalk toward Rush street.

"I need one of those."

He chuckles. "You get a parking ticket and I'll handle it." His tone is all macho and I only find it utterly charming.

We arrive at the restaurant and are seated along the windows. After he orders steak and scallops, and I order tilapia, we laugh and enjoy each other's company as our legs brush along one another's and heated glances are exchanged over the rims of our wine glasses by candlelight. Mauro's ability to carry a conversation and also be a great listener shines through the entire meal. We opt to take a slice of cheesecake to go, both of us anxious to leave.

Once we're outside his apartment door, he pauses before inserting his key.

"I'm not being too presumptuous, am I?" he asks.

Who is he kidding? We've been working our way up to this all night and we both know it.

I slide my arm through his, snuggling into the warmth of his big body. "Not at all."

He smiles and inserts his key, pushing the door open for me.

"Is Cris..." The name dies on my lips when the line of small tea light candles that lead to his bathroom come into view.

The door shuts and his hands land on my arms, his lips coming down to my shoulder. "He's gone for the night."

My hand covers his and I fall back into his chest, taking in the scene of what I thought at first glance were real candles but I now see are actually those battery operated ones. Bending down I pick one up and laugh.

"I'm a firefighter." He shrugs and a flush of embarrassment washes over his face.

I place the faux candle back down and stand on my tiptoes, reaching up to rest my hand behind his neck. "I love it. Thank you so much." Pressing my lips to his, I let my body follow suit, needing the feel of him more than my next breath.

"You're worth it." He circles me around. "Follow the path."

I kick off my shoes leaving them at the door and follow the lighted path he made for me, past a bedroom and a bathroom to the end of the hall. The flickering of faux candlelight dies and I'm overcome by the vision of a million stars glowing all over his bedroom from a tiny projector he's set up in the corner.

"This is virgin worthy," I say in awe.

My heart beats a mile a minute as I take in his queen size bed in the middle of the room with a dark comforter slung over. A dresser and television are placed along the wall. The space is very minimalistic, but it suits him.

I circle around and he's staring at me, waiting for my reaction. "I absolutely love it, Mauro. You didn't have to do this all for me."

"Don't you see? I want you to know how much you mean to me. I don't want to just sleep with you, I want to make love to you."

I close my eyes, wondering if I'll ever not feel like this is all a dream. My hand runs along his cheek, and I meet his gaze, letting myself get lost in him. My other hand slides around my back, finding the zipper of my dress and pulling it down. The dress falls off my shoulders and cascades to the floor. I step out of it, leaving me in my black bra and panty set.

"What are you waiting for?" I ask in a soft voice.

His gaze dips and a low growl escapes his throat. "Damn, Madison. You are so fucking hot."

I smile at the compliment knowing he probably didn't want it to come out that way. Gorgeous and beautiful are amazing words, but the fact he couldn't control himself is so much better.

He pushes the hair off my neck, his eyes still taking me in. "I think you need to pinch me." He chuckles, bringing his lips to my neck as his hands slide up and down my back before resting on my hips.

I pinch him and he chuckles into my skin.

"You're still here," he murmurs, his teeth scraping along my collarbone.

"I am." Tightening my arms around him, I close my eyes at the feeling of his hands and mouth worshiping me.

He steps us back until the back of my legs hit the mattress and he stops, shrugging out of his jacket and tossing it into the corner of the room. Kicking off his shoes, he pulls his sweater off, revealing abs I'd like to explore for days before coming up for air. Mesmerized by the indentations, it's not until his jeans fall to the ground that I realize he's now in front of me in only his boxer briefs.

No one would blame me if I passed out right now because he really is the perfect specimen of a man, right down to his heart of gold.

His eyes land on mine, keeping contact as he inches toward me, his hands taking my face in them, making sure I'm where he wants me once his lips reach mine. Our tongues tangle and he nudges my body to move onto the mattress.

I lower myself to the bed and he follows. We climb up until my head hits the pillow. The space between my thighs throbs when the weight of his body finally rests on top of mine. Our legs tangle and our hands explore, both of us surrendering to the desire ebbing and flowing between us.

His mouth is hot and sinful, and a moan escapes my throat when his steel length grinds into my core. My pelvis rises, desperate to feel the result of his desire for me again. His fingers thread into my hair, our mouths now frantic. Never in my life have I lost myself in a man so quickly.

A thrill shoots through my body when his fingers pull down the straps of my bra, his lips following the path of his hands so they don't miss an inch of my bare flesh. My fingers scrape at his back and my hips continue to rise and fall.

At this rate, I won't make it to the finish line. This man, the boy I dreamed of when I was a teen, is worshiping my body like I'm his favorite dessert—tasting and savoring until he's licking the bowl for one last morsel.

"I'm never going to get enough of you, Madison." His voice is a throaty whisper and I dig my fingernails into his back.

My other bra strap falls off my shoulder and his hands reach around my back to undo the clasp. Picking up the fabric, he tosses it aside and his hands cup my breasts, his thumbs running over my nipples while he licks his lips.

"Mauro." My fingers tighten on his strong shoulders as they flex with his movements.

His mouth covers my nipple and he sucks and twirls his tongue around the hard bud. Need consumes me. Wrapping my legs around his torso, he looks up at me, a smile teasing his lips as he moves to my other nipple.

Just when I think I'm going to lose all control, he flips over on his back, rolling me over on top of him. His hands burrow under my panties and grab at the delicate flesh of my ass.

I grind against his thick cock, my just-out-of-reach orgasm pulsating between my legs, begging for more.

"I want you over and over again tonight." My lips crash against his and his hands squeeze my ass cheeks, pushing me down harder into him.

"Not a problem." He stops the kiss for a moment, his eyes finding mine. "Tonight is ours."

I can have him over and over again.

The realization coils the need inside of me like a tight elastic band on the verge of breaking.

"Take me now, Mauro," I beg, our lips devouring one another again.

His fingers slide my panties down my legs and I help by kicking them off. He reaches over to the side, taking a condom from the nightstand.

Flipping me back over, his palms slide over my legs, forcing them wide and his face nestles between my legs.

"Mauro," I plead.

"There's no way I'm not tasting you first." That cocky smirk that once drew my attention to him spreads across his face.

Dipping down, his tongue slides along my slit, teasing my

clit and then sucking the greedy flesh into his mouth. His hands slide up my bare stomach, each palm taking control of a breast, tweaking my nipple while his mouth works me into sheer bliss.

Pushing all thoughts away, my hands burrow into his hair, gripping tight as my orgasm crests then spirals out of control.

I scream out, all the tension in my body falling away as I melt into the bed, melt into him. I open my eyes to the sound of foil ripping. Mauro's removed his boxer briefs and has positioned himself between my legs.

I don't want to stare or anything, but this is the first chance I've had to look at his cock. I have to say—no complaints.

Tentatively, his body lowers to mine, inching his way into my depths as he kisses me senseless until he's fully inside me, filling me completely.

"Mad, you feel so fucking good." He rocks a little and I pull my knees up, my toes curling from the euphoria of his hard length rocking into me.

"So do you."

Our bodies move as one as the pressure of our release threads through our veins, tugging at our nerve endings in a desperate attempt to erupt. His heated body on top of me, the light stubble on his face running along my jaw, the sinful moans falling from his lips the deeper and harder he claims me—all of it makes my head spin as I lose myself in pleasure with him once again.

"Ohhhh, Mauro!" The thread that Mauro wound so tight inside of me snaps and my toes curl on top of his comforter.

He stares down, watching while I lose myself. His breathing labors for a second and he props himself up on his elbows, his gaze locking with mine.

"Trust me, Mad. I know we can make it. Just stick with me."

I reach up and grab his face between my hands, smashing our mouths together until he thrusts and then stills inside of me on a groan I catch with my lips.

Both of us spent, Mauro falls on top of me and slides off, his fingers grazing down my glistening skin, kissing me slowly and sweetly.

There's no chance I haven't already fallen hopelessly for this man. Not when the reality is even better than what I'd conjured up in my imagination all those years ago.

CHAPTER TWENTY-FIVE

Mauro

I'm still wrapping my brain around our first time together. Never have I felt that close to someone during the act. Like I wanted to crawl inside of her and make myself a home so I could stay there forever.

My hands wouldn't move fast enough, my mouth unable to get enough of exploring every inch of her skin. There's so much more that I want to discover about what makes her cry out, what makes her whimper, even better, what makes her beg.

"Cheesecake?" I ask, throwing on a pair of sweats as I return from the bathroom.

"Perfect." She moves to get up, holding the sheet tight against her body.

Modest now, huh? An hour ago she was the one who stripped her dress off.

"Here." I grab a t-shirt out of my drawer and place it over her head.

She looks down at it and smiles. "Where do you guys get

these?" She holds the cotton away from her chest and reads it out loud. "Firemen do it with a big hose?" She quirks an eyebrow at me.

"My mom bought it. I don't think she understood what hose was referring to."

She laughs. "She doesn't seem like the kind of woman who would let you walk around like that."

I put my hand out in front of me and help her up from the bed.

Damn. I like how she looks in my shirt way too much.

Cute as hell with the neck draping over and almost exposing her shoulder while the length of it reaches down to her knees.

I could get used to this.

I usher her forward down the hall, letting the faux candles stay lit because I'm way too lazy at the moment to turn off one hundred tea lights.

"She gets them for us every Christmas. My brothers and I each get one for our career. Half the time we're cracking up and she has no idea why we think they're so funny." I grab the cheesecake I left abandoned in the takeout bag on the end table before following her down the hallway.

With two forks, I meet her at the counter. Forking off a bite, I place it in front of her lips.

She opens her mouth and allows me to feed her. I didn't realize this would be so damn hot that I'd have a chub again after only five minutes.

"You know what this needs, right?" she asks after swallowing down her bite.

"Tastes pretty good as it is. Not as good as you though." I wink at her and like I knew she would, she blushes.

She walks toward her purse. "Chocolate. Always chocolate." Opening a smaller purse than I usually see her carrying around, she pulls out a bag of half eaten M&Ms.

With dedication and precision, she presses them into the top of the cheesecake, pops one in her mouth and then opens her mouth for me to give her another bite.

I do as requested because I'd be an idiot if I didn't. A moan that would put me at full salute escapes her and her eyes close.

Fuck me right now.

"So good." She grabs an M&M and holds it up in front of my mouth.

I open and she places it gently on my tongue. Without any hesitation, she takes the fork from my hands and this time she feeds me. She's right, it needed the chocolate.

I've been eating cheesecake my entire life plain without knowing what I was missing.

Reminds me of my life pre-Madison.

"Should I ask why you carry around a half-eaten bag of M&Ms in your purse?" I pick her up by her hips and prop her up on the kitchen counter and then find my spot right between her legs, picking up the fork to continue feeding her.

If this was my life, I'd die a happy man.

"Well, I have a bit of a chocolate addiction so when I have a hankering for something sweet or I'm stressed out, I grab a handful."

"Why not eat the entire bag at one time?"

She tilts her head and for the first time ever she looks at me like I'm stupid. Except this is Madison, so it somehow looks like a polite gesture coming from her. "Did you see my high school yearbook picture?"

I set the cheesecake down on the counter, reaching my hands behind her, pulling her center toward my stomach. My fingers delve under my t-shirt to cup her ass.

"What's your point?"

Again with the head tilt. I'm a smart enough man not to

fight this issue with her, so I'll let it go, but I'll make it my mission to let her know I'll take her however she comes.

"How perfect that we have a candy made after us." I nod at the package. "M&Ms. Mauro and Madison."

She giggles. "I think it would be Madison and Mauro."

"You do, do you?" My fingers skim up the t-shirt to tickle her ribs.

She squirms and her arms are rigid at her sides, trying to free herself from my torturous hands, all the while her sweet and melodic laugh echoes through my apartment.

Unable to stop myself, I allow my hands to run up the length of her torso, forgetting the tickling and cupping her breasts.

"You play dirty," she says in a breathy voice as she stops fighting me.

"You complaining?" My mouth salivates I want to taste her again so bad.

"Never." Her arms loop around my shoulders and her thighs tighten around my stomach. "You can tease me whenever you like, as long as you finish what you start."

"Hmm...I like the sound of that." I dip my mouth to her neck, licking up her jaw to her earlobe. "I'm going to run to my room, wait here until I get back."

"Why?" she asks when I dislodge from her hold.

"Condom. We're doing it right where you are."

A soft smile crosses her lips. "But there's some right there." She points to a box of condoms with a bow on them at the edge of the kitchen counter.

How did I miss those?

I pick up the box and sure enough, there's a sticky note attached that says, 'Be safe, Love Ma's favorite.'

I rip the box open and take out one of the foil wrappers. "Luca," I sigh as I eliminate the distance between us.

"They're Luca's?" she asks, stopping me from opening the foil packet.

"No, he bought them for us."

A horrified look crosses her face. "Maybe you guys are too close."

"No, no. It's not like that. We were talking about who was my mom's favorite and a comment was made about grandchildren." The hell if I'm going to tell her that comment was made by me. "This is his way of trying to secure his spot as number one son."

"Oh." She still looks surprised and a little worried that I'm going to rate her performance with my brother's tomorrow.

Ten plus if you're wondering.

"Hey." I place my hand on her cheek. "We don't talk about women like conquests or judging our partners or anything like that. It's literally his joke."

She smiles and I lean forward biting lightly on her bottom lip with my teeth. Once I'm there I figure I need to seduce her all over again, so I keep the kiss going until the worrying that's occupying her retreats and I'm all she's thinking about.

Her arms wind around my shoulders again and I slide her forward more, needing her as close to me as I can have her. Our tongues tangle and slide as one, eliciting moans from each of us.

I grab the hem of the t-shirt pulling it off her. A shiver runs through her body, but her feet press on the waistband of my sweats and I take my hands off her ass for a moment to help. I slide the condom down my length and wrap my arms around her again.

"Jesus, Mad, you're everything and more. So much more than I dreamed of." Holding her up, I swing us around so her back is pressed against the wall. Keeping her in place with my thigh, I position myself at her entrance and sink into her again with a groan.

Her fingers dig into my shoulder blades and her teeth tug on my ear as I fill her up. Never will I get enough of her. Making love to her in my bed was something, but under the kitchen lights when I can watch myself moving in and out of her is making me lose control. Her tits bounce in my face and shatter my small reserve of self-control.

Her blue eyes are laced with arousal and need for me and it's my undoing. I slam into her over and over again, claiming her as mine.

"Mauro." My name slips from her lips like a plea to never stop and as much as I'd love that, I'm close to blowing my load right now.

Rotating my hips, sweat trickles down my face dripping between our bodies and I thrust into her again and again, switching between watching her expressions and where we're joined.

"Mauro!" she screams, her fingernails digging into my flesh, her slick heat convulsing around my shaft.

Her sweet cries and the sound of me sliding in and out of her body throws me over the edge I was teetering on. Inaudible words ring out between the two of us as I spill into the condom and she crashes in my arms, spent and exhausted.

"You want to go to bed?" I ask after I've regained my ability to form a complete thought.

She nods, holding on to me.

Carrying her to my bedroom along the lit path, her breathing slow and steady against me, might be the highlight of my night. I lay her down on my bed, slide the covers out and tuck her in.

"I'll be right back." I kiss her forehead and disappear into my bathroom to dispose of the condom.

When I return to the room, she's wide-eyed and watching me. Joining her under the covers, I waste no time in pulling her into my arms.

After what we just shared, I know it's time for me to explain to her my hesitation to get close to anyone. Even though I've let her in, and I'll hurt no matter what happens to us, I need her to know. I just pray she doesn't judge me for the decisions I've made.

"You tire me out." She kisses my chest, placing her hand over where she kissed like she's sealing her affection into my skin. Little does she know, but she's already branded me. Not in a way that anyone else can see, but in a way that only I can feel.

I brush my knuckles down her arm. "Do you ever wonder why I'm scared of love?"

She rests her chin on my chest, staring up at me. "I knew you had reservations, but I didn't think you were scared."

I tuck a strand of her long hair behind her ear, memorizing the different shades of blue in her eyes. "I need you to know something about me before we move forward and I'm hoping that it doesn't change anything."

She bolts up, pulling the sheet with her, effectively leaving me exposed and naked.

"Calm down." I loosen the grip of her hands on the sheets and they fall back in place, as does she. "It's not like I murdered someone."

"Do you have a kid?" she asks.

"Remember the whole conversation before I took you up against the wall?" I raise an eyebrow.

She laughs. "Oh yeah. Okay just tell me. Is this something I should close my eyes for?"

"No, baby, no."

The affectionate pet name falls from my lips unexpectedly and I'm as surprised as she looks. She doesn't say anything, just smiles, and I take that to mean that it's okay to use it from this point forward.

Inhaling a deep breath, I decide to let it all out. Tell her the truth and wait for her judgment. "My buddy Hunter, the one who died in the fire...the one I was going to partner up with?"

She nods.

"After he passed, I was tasked with cleaning out his locker so that Cailin wouldn't have to do it. She was already falling deeper and deeper into a depression as each day passed. The surprise of his death was too much for her to take. I mean there's always the worry in the back of your mind, but you don't let that fear stop you from living your life. Anyway..."

She's silent in my arms, her hands running up the side of my stomach. Back and forth like she's assuring me that she's here.

"He had a cell phone in there. One I'd never seen him use before. I didn't think much of it because it didn't turn on right away, so I figured maybe it was an old one and he was going to trade it in or donate it to the battered women's shelter. I took it home and charged it up to make sure it worked. Other than the phone there was just his personal stuff, some notes from Cailin, the card we put on his locker after Devin was born. I packed it all in a box and took it over to their house."

"So, I'm guessing the cell phone wasn't what you thought, but I'm unsure what this has to do with you." She slides up closer to look me in the eye.

"Remember I mentioned that I had an ex-girlfriend named Jenna?"

She nods.

"We broke up six months ago."

She nods.

"Hunter died six months ago."

"I know." Her sweet, innocent eyes look on at me, not getting where I'm going with this.

"Put those two things together and add the cell phone."

"You're making me solve a case to figure out the answer. Wouldn't that be Cris—" She abruptly stops talking. "Oh my God, Mauro." She covers her mouth. "No way!"

This time it's me nodding. "Yeah. They'd been having an affair for months before he died. The text messages were excruciating to read. I'm thinking he'd gotten the phone well after their first night had started, but there were sexts and shit talking about me and Cailin on there."

She rests her body on top me, squeezing me in her arms. "I'm so sorry, that's like the ultimate betrayal."

I love the fact she's trying to make me feel better. "I'm good now, Mad, thanks though."

She falls back to her side. "I see why you'd have trouble trusting people."

"You've helped me get over that. There's something about you...I know you'd never purposely hurt me. But that's not why I told you all this." Again, I tuck a strand of hair behind her ear, delaying the inevitable. "Cailin doesn't know."

"What?" Her head rears back, judgment clear in her tone.

"I couldn't hurt her and Devin that way. Destroy the man he was to them for what? It wouldn't change anything—he was dead. There were no text messages about him wanting to desert his family for Jenna. He's gone and Cailin doesn't need that baggage to deal with on top of everything else it will take for her to move on with her life."

"But..."

"I'm not changing my mind. All I need to know is if that changes the way you see me."

She sits up, straddling me, her hands on my cheeks. "I understand. I do. Did you think I wouldn't?"

"The only person who knows besides you is my mom. When we were at the deli, that's what we were arguing about. She thinks Cailin needs to know because she believes all women know when their husbands stray and it would confirm what she believes Cailin already knows deep down. But Cailin's never mentioned any suspicions to me so I'm not going there. Other than you and my mom, I've told no one and I want to keep it that way."

She nods. "Okay."

"You're really not going to argue with me?"

She shakes her head. "No. It's your decision, but what *I* need to know, is whether that experience makes you distrust not only the women you date but your other co-workers? I need to know that you're safe on the job." She runs a hand through my hair as she waits for me to answer.

"I can't say it doesn't fuck with my head a little, but you'll never do that to me, right?"

She collapses on top of me, her hair a veil on either side of my head. "Never," she says with conviction.

I roll us over and spread her legs, ready for round three before we find sleep. She happily obliges and after tonight, I know I'll never be prepared to give her up.

CHAPTER TWENTY-SIX

Madison

With a few weeks of bliss between me and Mauro, fall has rolled into Chicago, bringing the changing colors of the leaves, cooler weather, and stores full of items in preparation for Halloween and Thanksgiving.

The house is ready for the interiors to be installed and I'm practically giddy. This is my favorite part of any flip—when things start to look pretty.

"This house needs some color," Mauro comments, grabbing my ass on his way to the kitchen.

I pull the paint roller away from the wall. "It's neutral. Neutral sells."

"How about red? Red hot just like you babe."

"Spare us, please," Luca groans walking into the house with a sub in his hand.

"You don't see enough heart attacks that you decide to witness your own after eating all that processed meat?" I bring the roller back to the wall, running the cool gray color on the surface.

"Yeah, Ma's not gonna like you. This is the Italian." He holds up his sub. "You keep lecturing people about deli meat and you'll drive them out of business. Then Mauro will be on the black list. Actually." He pauses to think. "Go ahead and put up a sign in the front window saying how bad deli meat is for your health."

Mauro comes back into the room, pushing him with his shoulder and then wrapping his arms around my waist, lifting my feet from the ground. I let the roller drop in the paint tray and his lips find mine as they often do these days.

"Get a room." Luca disappears and Mauro quickly carries me to the half of bath that's yet to be finished.

He cradles me in the corner where the sink and cabinet will go, his hands making quick work of my overalls, letting them fall to my waist.

"Hold up cowboy, we've got a house full of people," I say with a smile.

This isn't to say we haven't already made quick work of most of the rooms in this house. The dining room table has been our favorite spot this week.

"So what? Like none of them have sex." His lips are exploring my neck, his hands halfway up my chest, prepped and ready to cup me.

"Ew! Come on guys," Cristian says as he walks in the room with his uniform on.

If Mauro had closed the door, there's a good chance he would have had this way with me. You snooze, you lose.

Mauro glances behind him quickly and his hands might fall to my hips, but his lips are still traveling over my neck. "Aren't you out of district?"

"I just got off, but if this is why you need my help tonight, then I'm out. If you'd keep your hands off each other, the house would probably be done by now."

Mauro stops and puts me all back together, fastening my

overalls back in place and kissing me on the forehead. "We'll continue this later."

Leading me out first, I go back to painting the wall. "Hi, Cristian. Thanks for helping."

"Yeah, yeah. You owe me. Your friend is still giving me the cold shoulder and her dad keeps asking when I'm going to make good on our date. I'd lie, but I think he's having me tailed." Cristian sits on the dining room table.

Mauro and I share a look that has me biting my lip remembering how he took me from behind last night right where Cristian is sitting.

"Jesus." Cristian hops off the table. "Is there anywhere I can sit in here?"

Mauro and I laugh uncontrollably. "Not really." Mauro shrugs like it's no big deal, while my face heats with embarrassment.

"I have to hear you screaming my brother's name like he's God all fucking night and now you drag me to a place where I have to imagine the two of you fucking in every corner?"

"Tell me about it. He grabs her ass every time he passes her." Luca joins the party, crumpling up the sub wrapper in his hands. "It's disgusting. These innocent eyes cannot unsee what these two do."

We all laugh because Luca's eyes have probably seen more than all of us combined.

"Come to the backyard. I need your help with this fountain." Mauro winks at me. "Be right back."

I place the roller down in the tray, not willing to let them handle this huge-ass fountain alone. It could very well land on all three of them. I linger by the window looking from afar to make it seem like I think they're macho, but I'm ready to lend a hand at any second.

They each evaluate the situation and offer their take on how to move it. Cristian even looks like he's doing a little diagram with his hands, directing the other two. Luca and Mauro squint their eyes and lift the edge, quickly putting it down. I told Mauro we should hire a service but he swears him and his brothers can handle this.

The statue isn't even lifted off the base yet and they're arguing.

"You bringing Maddie to dinner on Sunday?" Cristian asks, pretending to see what's under the fountain.

They're all delaying the inevitable.

"Yeah."

"Big step." Luca chimes in.

He's right, it is. And though I'm looking forward to it, I am a bit nervous still.

"Ma's already met her. I had her at the sandwich shop, she loved her, told me she saw our future together. I'm not shaking in my boots." Mauro's confidence shines through and I can only hope he's right.

"What about the firehouse? You take her there yet?" Luca asks.

Mauro's already shaking his head. "Not yet." The sureness of his tone evaporates like sun beating down on a puddle.

"She knows you're a firefighter, what could you possibly be afraid of?" Cristian asks.

I hate that I'm eavesdropping. Especially since I've shifted so that I'm not right in front of the window anymore, proving how badly I still feel like I need reassurance that he likes me.

"Let's just move this fucking monstrosity, okay? You're always jabbering on like a bunch of chicks." If I wasn't supposed to hear their conversation, I'd scold him for his depiction of women. Besides, I know what he's afraid of and they don't.

I give it to the three of them, they somehow get the fountain moved to the outside of the yard where the service is supposed to pick it up tomorrow.

The three of them walk toward the house and I run back to my roller, trying to lather on some layers.

"Let's order pizza," Luca says, finding his spot on the table, watching me paint.

The rest of the crew is packing up for the day and we all wave and say goodbye.

"You just ate," I say, not turning around.

"I'm a growing boy, Maddie."

"I can't eat all that cheese, it'll upset my stomach. I'll get a salad," Cristian says.

"Pussy," Mauro coughs out.

Cristian comes up to my side and grabs the edger, stepping up on the ladder and helping out. He's changed out of his uniform now and is in a tapered pair of athletic pants and a t-shirt that says *Cop-A-Feel* and an arrow pointing down. For some reason, he's still wearing his belt with his gun on it.

"There's something about a police officer out of uniform with his gun still on his belt painting a wall. Where's a camera when you need it?" Luca pretends to snap a picture.

"I'm not going to lay this thing down just anywhere. Besides, it's better than the two of you idiots watching her work."

Mauro comes up behind me, his hand covering mine on the roller handle, moving it up and down the wall as he grinds against me. "Here, I'll help."

I slide my ass out, effectively moving him away. "That's not helping."

He laughs, pulling his phone out. "Gino's or Lou's?"

"Gino's," we all agree.

"Damn, we're all Gino's?" Luca asks, disbelief in his tone.

"I told you, she's already like a Bianco," Mauro says and I

try not to let my heart leap out my chest, purposely ignoring his comment.

Madison Bianco.

I already knew when I was sixteen years old writing it on my binders that it had a nice ring to it.

CHAPTER TWENTY-SEVEN

Mauro

This is a first for me. I've never brought a girl to my parents' for Sunday dinner. Not even Jenna. Ma never really cared for Jenna. Women's intuition I think.

Opening the door to my parents' place, the aromas that still make my mouth water hit me full force. I still feel the anticipation of sitting down for a meal that will stuff me full for days. Okay, I'll eat the leftovers she sends us home with later tonight.

Madison's hand is clammy in my own. I squeeze it to tell her not to worry, but her teeth are still nibbling at her bottom lip like they did most of the drive over here.

I purposely got here before Luca and Cristian. It's a rarity that we'll all be present for the dinner—usually one or two of us are on shift.

My dad comes out of the kitchen, his apron already stained red but sadly not enough to cover up the writing on it.

Madison giggles but tries to hide her response when she

sees the words, *If you like my meatballs you should taste my sausage*. I'm not sure my mom understands the humor in the English language sometimes.

"Madison, the smarty pants. Welcome." He extends his arms, gripping her by the shoulders and pressing a kiss on each cheek. "Mauro." He ruffles my hair and kisses me on each cheek as well. "Come. Come." He disappears through the archway of the kitchen, where I know Mama will be found.

Our house is small, a typical Chicago bungalow with three bedrooms. Each room smaller than the next. My bedroom moved to the basement as soon as I could escape Cristian at fourteen.

I'm eager to give her the tour, wanting more alone time with her even though we just got here.

In the kitchen, my mom is breading and frying chicken breasts while gravy simmers on the stove. She has all the salad preparations for Cristian on the small butcher block.

"Ma," I say, coming up behind her and pressing my lips to her cheek. She pats my hand on her shoulder. The one she's not currently using to hold the chicken.

"Mauro," she says my name like she usually does, with love pouring out of every syllable, like I've done something to make her proud just by saying hello.

"Madison is here," I whisper and she must've momentarily forgotten because she seems a little alarmed.

"Oh." She whips around, chicken dripping down to the floor. "Hi. Hold on." She hems and haws on what to do so I take the chicken from her hands and place it on the plate.

Rushing to the sink, she thoroughly washes her hands for thirty-seconds—as always—singing the happy birthday song in Italian. Madison probably already thinks we're a bunch of nut cases.

"Hi Madison, right?" she asks before greeting her much

the way my father did except she pulls her into her arms catching Madison by surprise.

"Maddie is fine. Thank you for having me."

"I'm so happy you came. You're welcome anytime." Her eyes find mine across the room and she smiles her proudest grin, the one that says I did good, like when I joined the Chicago Fire Department.

I wash my hands at the sink, drying them on a towel.

"Can I help?" Madison asks like the good guest I knew she'd be.

"No. You go sit and enjoy yourself with Mauro." She shoos us out of the kitchen as usual. It's her domain.

We leave my parents much to Maddie's argument about helping and earning her meal.

"Come on, I'll show you where I slept in high school. Your fantasy come to life."

She swats me in the stomach and I corner her before the basement stairs, caging her into the wall like I love to do. "Tell me no part of you wants to know where I slept in high school. Did you ever imagine it for yourself?"

Her cheeks redden. "Keep it up and you'll be using your hand like you did in high school instead of my mouth," she whispers in my ear.

My head falls back in laughter. "This is me backing off." I hold up my hands in the air and nod to the basement stairs.

She follows behind me down to the wood-paneled basement. The smell down here is the same as I remember it and it makes me a little nostalgic for a time when this house was crawling with so much testosterone I thought it'd bust the walls down.

My parents haven't changed the space at all. My bed still sits in the corner, a small table next to it with an alarm clock. The guitar I pretended to play to impress girls in the corner.

The chair I played my video games in sitting front and center of the television.

I drop down to the bed. "This is where it all went down. Lube, my hand and a lot of dirty magazines lost their lives here."

She sits down in the chair, watching me like I'm a different person than the one she walked in with.

"Come." I pat the spot next to me. "I promise I don't bite."

She laughs, standing and coming over to my side. "I kind of like it when you do."

Rolling her over, I kiss her lips, nibbling at her bottom lip. "You know I aim to please." I gently bite all over her neck and jaw.

She swats me away. "We are not doing this in your parents' house."

I slide my hands up her sweater, finding a camisole that's fitted to her body. "Double wrapped? Not cool. I'm supposed to have easy access all the time." I let my thumbs trace over her breasts, finding two peaked nipples hungrily looking for attention. "Maybe I'm wrong."

"Maybe you should reserve judgment until you've investigated the situation." She eyes me, smiling over the fact she's not wearing a bra under her camisole.

Great. Now I'm hard.

"You going commando on me, too?" I fiddle with the button and zipper of her jeans.

"You'll have to wait to find that out." Her hand lands on mine, stopping me.

"You expect me to go all day without knowing?"

She slides out from under me. "This is my first time in your parents' house. I'm not about to let you get to third base." As she stands at the side of my bed, footsteps start to sound from overhead. Seconds later they're joined by loud Italians talking.

Madison winks and unbuttons her jeans and pries the edges open. A simple pair of red panties greet me that say, *Hose Connection Here* with an arrow pointing down.

"Come." I wave her over, sitting on the edge of my bed now, adjusting my hard-on.

Surprisingly she obliges and stands in front of me as I pull down her jeans a little bit.

"I love them." I press my lips right below her belly button.

She doesn't fight me, so I take the opportunity to slide my finger under the crotch of her panties, feeling how wet she already is.

"Hey." She backs up, zipping up her jeans, my obsession quickly covered up.

"What did I do to you that you're punishing me so?" I haul her onto my lap and she winds her arms around my neck.

"Gotta keep you on your toes." She kisses my cheek and the scent of her perfume overwhelms me in the best way possible.

I will never get enough of this, of us.

Small feet scurry down the stairs and she bolts up off my lap.

"Uncle Mauro! Uncle Mauro!" Devin runs across the room right into my arms.

I'm surprised to see him, but I hug him back. "What's up Little Man? I didn't know you were coming today." I ruffle his blonde locks and hold my hand up for a high five. "This is Madison, my girlfriend."

He stares her down and turns back to me without saying hello.

Another set of footsteps come down the stairs, a voice calling for Devin and my entire body tenses.

Cailin turns the corner and her head rears back in shock for a second.

I know things are about to get complicated when I hear Madison's sigh.

CHAPTER TWENTY-EIGHT

Madison

"Hey, Cailin." Mauro stands, holding her son, Devin, in his arms.

"Hi. We were at the sandwich shop and your mom invited me to dinner. I hope it's okay that we came."

Mauro glances at me, letting Devin slide down to the floor. He runs to his mother as Mauro settles at my side. "You remember Madison?"

Cailin's eyes set on Mauro's hand on my hip and then raises to meet my eyes. "I do. Nice to see you."

"You as well." I slide an inch closer to Mauro.

Jealousy? Maybe.

As if the uncomfortable static suffocating the room wasn't enough, two more footsteps sound on the stairs and Luca stops at the bottom, a piece of bread in his hand.

His gaze investigates the scene, his eyes shifting in each of our directions.

"What's up guys?" He steps farther into the room, leaning

toward Cailin and placing a kiss on her cheek. "Ma said you were coming today. How are you doing?"

Cailin kisses his cheek back and the sad expression that crosses her face has me feeling bad for feeling possessive over Mauro. She's grieving and here I am thinking she wants to steal my boyfriend. She just needs support from someone who understands what she's going through.

"What's up, Maddie?" Luca greets me with the same kiss on the cheek. "Mauro." He nods.

"Hey." Devin tugs on Luca's Bears jersey.

Luca pretends to circle around completely missing Devin. Cailin smiles watching the scene unfold as Devin runs to the other side of Luca, but he turns around the other direction.

"Here!" Devin yells, his hands reaching up in the air.

Luca finally glances down with a surprised look on his face. "Oh. I didn't see you down there." He picks him up and flies him around the room like he's an airplane, complete with zooming noises.

Devin laughs uncontrollably, drool falling from his mouth. "Let's go steal a meatball," Luca whispers and the two fly upstairs.

Leaving the tension to suffocate us again.

"I'm going to go insist that your mom let me help in the kitchen." I kiss Mauro on the cheek, his hand firm on my hip in a gesture that tells me he doesn't want me to leave. But I can't handle this tension and if Mauro can trust me after what Jenna did to him, I can surely trust him.

"She never lets anyone help her," Cailin comments as I pass her by to reach the stairs. "I've tried and she always pushes me out of the kitchen."

I didn't really need her opinion. I mean, I'm doing this to be nice so she can have some alone time with Mauro. I'd much rather be here in the basement making out with my boyfriend than cutting up lettuce.

"I'll give it a shot. I think she's just used to having boys around. Maybe with a woman coming around now, she'll appreciate the help."

"And that woman is you?" A hollow laugh leaks out of her. "Slow down there, *Madison*, you two aren't married."

"Cailin," Mauro warns, his eyes shooting me a look of apology.

"What? I was just saying you guys have been dating for like two days..."

Mauro removes his attention from her causing her gaze to fall at her feet.

"Madison, I'm sure my mom would love the help. I'll be right up to join you."

I walk up the steps wondering what their conversation will consist of now.

"I thought we were clear about this," Mauro says to Cailin before I'm out of earshot.

"I know you said you like her, but come on, Mauro, you just broke up with Jenna. She's a rebound and she's acting like—"

"Enough, Cailin. I'm not sure where you think you get any say in the person I decide to spend time with."

Not really interested in hearing any more from Cailin's mouth, I wind my way back to the kitchen. I will busy myself with whatever task Mrs. Bianco deems me worthy of.

I wasn't expecting the small space to be packed full of people, all speaking Italian with their hands moving around like rapid fire. There are mostly women, but a few men are sprinkled around the table, eating the samples the woman are shoving in their faces.

"Welcome to Italian life." Cristian's voice from behind surprises me and I jump. He grins. "Where's Mauro?"

"He's downstairs with Cailin," I say.

His lips draw straight, but he smiles to try and cover it up.

Yeah, I feel the same.

For the next three minutes, Cristian introduces me to his aunts and uncles, cousins and family friends who don't have family nearby. Everyone seems confused as to why if I belong to Mauro, Cristian is the one introducing me. I ignore the ache in the pit of my stomach as I wonder whether Cailin might always be a problem for us.

Quickly, I refute my assumptions. She lost her husband, I can't be that heartless to not have empathy for what she's going through. Finding comfort with the man closest to her husband doesn't seem that strange. Even if her husband was a piece of shit, but she doesn't know that.

Mrs. Bianco sits me at the table, placing lettuce on a cutting board. "Salad?" she asks like this is the only thing I could really help her with.

"Got it."

She smiles, her palm rubbing on my shoulders before she walks away.

I'm busy cutting the lettuce and the tomatoes up while running through the possibilities of what could be going on downstairs. Eventually Mauro appears in the doorway.

At this point I've worked myself up so much I'm not sure I can even look at him. All those doubts from ten years ago have resurfaced. Cailin is the tall, curvy blonde that someone like him belongs with.

"Mauro!" an uncle hollers and pulls him into his arms. He smacks his cheek, says something in Italian and both their eyes wander to me.

Mauro's lips tip down and he nods to his uncle, responding in Italian. An aunt smacks him on the back of the head on his way over to me, but then grabs his head and kisses him on the cheek. The entire way, Mauro ignores the pats, hugs, and kisses from his family as his gaze stays glued on me.

Once he reaches me, I'm a ball of nerves, trying to cut up a cucumber nonchalantly. I don't even know how that's supposed to look, but I don't want him to know all the messed up things that have been going through my head.

Bending down, he kisses my cheek. "Sorry about that," he whispers and sits down next to me. The air between us crackles with electricity like it usually does when we're less than six feet apart.

I shrug, continuing my job of making the salad.

"So Ma gave you a job?" He smiles, watching me.

"I think this might be the only thing she trusted me with, but it's something."

His arm stretches across the back of my chair, his lips landing right below my ear. "I want you so bad right now," he says softly.

The heat he stirs in my body rises up to my cheeks. "Sure, elbow deep in lettuce? That's your turn on?" I whisper.

He slides his chair closer to me, his knee pressing against mine, his hand finding my thigh. Way too high on my thigh I may add.

"I want you every second of every day, but the fact that my mom trusted you to make anything says how much you already fit in here. My uncles scorned me for leaving you alone. Said I'm lucky my uncle Mikey isn't here. He'd kick my ass. Or hit on you." He winks and I can't help but smile. "They're right. I shouldn't have left you alone." His teeth snatch my earlobe and when he pulls, shudders travel all the way down to my clit.

I hope this phase of never getting enough of one another never dies. Though I know in the back of my head that I'm bound to lose my shine as far as Mauro is concerned at some point.

"Mama!" Cristian yells and Mauro bolts up out of his chair.

I turn to find Mrs. Bianco's hand on the counter as though she's holding herself up. Cristian grabs her by the waist and she lets him hold her until Mr. Bianco comes over and takes the place of his son.

"Maria. Maria," he says her name like it's a prayer.

"LUCA!" Mauro yells. Everyone else is looking around for the paramedic in the family.

"A fire again? That's Mauro's department..." His voice dips seeing his mom in the arms of his dad, pale and tired. "What's going on?" He rushes to her side, his fingers already on her neck. "Ma?"

She shakes her head, speaking in Italian and shooing all of them away from her.

"No. Let me grab my bag."

"I'll get it." Mauro claps him on the shoulder and then weaves through the throes of people.

"It's too hot, that's all," his mom says. "Everyone give me some space."

The aunts and uncles yell at one another or what sounds like they are since it's all in Italian and I'm quickly figuring out that if I want to come to more of these dinners, I really need to learn the language.

I join the family in the dining room right as Mauro comes back in with his brother's backpack. He shoots me a look of worry, but I try to reassure him with my eyes that she'll be fine.

"I'm sorry, Madison," Cailin says, coming to stand next to me as I wait along the wall.

I give her a small smile. She seems sincere and I have no choice but to give her the benefit of the doubt.

"It's just his last girlfriend treated him so poorly. Always making him do everything, making him take her to the latest restaurants and shows. He spent so much money on her it was ridiculous. I mean firemen don't make a ton of money, I'm sure you know that."

"It seems unfair since the job they do puts their lives at risk."

She nods, looking behind her to find Devin playing with Legos with one of the aunts.

"Exactly. She liked him for the title he had, not that man he is."

I desperately want to ask who she thinks that man is, but that would be wrong. If I want Mauro to be part of my life, Cailin and Devin come with him, so I need to learn to play nice.

"Well, I assure you that's not me. If anything, his profession scares the crap out of me."

Her lips dip to a frown.

"I'm so sorry, Cailin. I'm an idiot. I shouldn't have..."

"No, you're right. The danger is there every time they leave the house. I think I took the years of safe returns for granted. It becomes a part of your life. I wish I would've hugged him hard every day he came home. Instead, I usually handed him Devin and said he's yours for twenty-four hours now."

My hand finds her shoulder and I let her vent as long as she needs to.

"I'm sorry."

It's now that I understand Mauro's decision to not tell her about Jenna and Hunter. She already holds enough guilt, and although she shouldn't hold any guilt that he cheated on her, let's be real, she would dissect their relationship from beginning to its end.

Mauro comes out of the kitchen and the two of us approach him at the same time. I'm not sure I'll ever get used to that.

"She said she just felt faint and that her heart was racing, but Luca said she seems good right now. He'll make a doctor's appointment for her. I guess it could have just been the heat in the kitchen." Mauro doesn't seem completely convinced and if I had to guess, he's realizing that his parents are growing older.

I hug him. "I'm sure she's fine. I was sweating in there. It is really hot."

Mauro glances down at me a small smile in place. "I like you sweaty," he says.

"And that's my cue to leave." Cailin turns around as Mauro's lips descend down on mine.

For the entire meal, everyone's eyes stay on Mrs. Bianco instead of their overfilled plates. The aunts don't let her clean up one dish even though she seems okay by that point.

Thankfully, Cailin and Devin leave right after dinner which gives me some time with his family without the awkwardness of feeling like she's watching my every move.

When we leave his parents' house, I'm so exhausted I fall asleep in his truck, content and happy.

CHAPTER TWENTY-NINE

Mauro

"Lunch delivery?" I ask Madison as she hands me a bag of food.

"Well, I want to see where you work." She steps into the garage. "You do eat lunch, right?"

"I do." I smile down at her.

"So, are you going to show me all your cool tools?"

She's covered up today, thank God. Jeans, ankle boots, and a jacket. Perfect to keep what's mine from being seen around here.

I wrap my arms around her waist. "I think you've become well acquainted with my biggest and best tool."

She giggles, her forehead falling to my chest. "True." I love the blush my comments pull out of her.

"Do you want me to put on the sirens?" I ask, holding my arm out for her to enter the truck.

She takes no time at all to hoist herself up and pretend she's driving the truck.

"Press the button right there." She follows the direction

my finger is pointing and the sirens blare. She quickly retracts her finger and covers her mouth with her hand, eyes wide.

A few guys head into the garage, seeing her in the truck.

"Bianco, you hiding gorgeous women from us today?" Lloyd calls out.

I roll my eyes. "I'm hiding my girlfriend."

Madison climbs out and I catch her in my arms as she slides down my body before her feet land on the cement floor.

"You make it impossible not to hold onto my hero complex. Just an FYI." She kisses me briefly and then walks over to my buddies. "Hi, I'm Madison."

The guys each shake her hand in turn.

"Jack."

"Lloyd."

"Trevor."

The three youngest members of our squad blatantly appraise her and I'd like to gouge their eyes out of their sockets.

"You dating this guy?" Lloyd asks, running his hand through his short blonde hair.

Madison looks at me, smiling widely. "I am."

"How did he manage to get you?" Jack asks.

Madison scrunches her eyebrows. "I think you mean, how did I get him?"

Trevor bends over laughing. "You're a ten and he's like a six."

I wrap my arms around her, my hands resting on her stomach. "Even so, she's mine and don't you forget it. We're going to eat. The three of you, make sure everything's ready to go in case we get a call."

The three probies walk past us and I grab my girl's hand, leading her into the firehouse.

"I agree with their line of thinking but..."

I cage her against the wall, swallowing her doubt with a kiss. Her hands never miss a chance to thread into my hair and she does just that as she grinds against me, lifting one leg to wrap around my thigh.

"Every night away from you is excruciating," I mumble along her lips, closing our kiss.

"I know, but the good news is that the countertops are coming in today."

I draw back. "Here I am laying my feelings out there and you're thinking countertops?"

We walk up the stairs and I drop the bag of Portillo's on the table and take a seat. Patel isn't on shift tonight so I expect dinner will be nothing special.

"Well, you or the countertops." She pretends to weigh the options with her hands teetering up and down like a scale.

"I don't think countertops can make you scream like I do." I wink at her.

She pretends to look at the ceiling, nibbling on her lip. The one move that drives me batshit crazy. "I might scream when they get installed. I'm really excited about them."

Standing from my chair, it falls down to the linoleum floor and I take her head in my hands, kissing her feverishly until her head spins. By the time I release her, her eyes are dilated and dark with arousal. Exactly what I was going for.

"Okay, one point for Bianco." She swipes an imaginary line in the air.

I pick up my chair and unwrap the food she brought me.

"Why is there nothing in here for you?" I ask, taking a second glance in the now empty bag.

"I already ate." She sits down and crosses her legs, placing her phone on the table.

"What? A granola bar?"

She cocks her head to the side. "I'm sorry, are you judging me?"

I unwrap my beef sandwich. "I'm just saying you need to eat more. I hate that you watch everything that goes into your mouth."

She digs into her purse and wiggles the bag of M&Ms in her hand until some fall out, like that's proving a fact.

"Case in point. You don't even eat the entire bag. You eat five in a sitting."

"Hey now, don't ruin my M&Ms for me," she warns.

The conversation is turning to where it might not go the way I want it to.

"One bite of my beef and I'll leave you alone." I smile at her.

"You act like I have an eating disorder. I don't."

I blow out a breath. There's no turning back from this conversation.

"I don't think you do. I just hate that you worry so much about it. I'll like you no matter what."

"You didn't even notice me when I was 'Fatty Maddy' with braces and glasses, Mauro, let's be realistic."

Anger boils inside of me. She just doesn't get that I might not have noticed her back then, but that doesn't mean it was right. That right now, in this moment, it's not her beauty that has me, it's her heart, her mind, her personality. I could list twenty things about her that I've fallen for but it feels like she'll always see the most important of them as her beauty.

"That's so unfair." I slide out my chair, patting my leg, needing to feel her body because I do not want us to spend a night apart in a fucking fight over how much she eats.

"No." She crosses her arms over her chest.

"Come here, you know you want to." I hold out my arms, inviting her.

"No."

Stubborn, one quality that I haven't fallen for. Yet.

"I'm sorry, I just want you to see why I'm with you and how it has nothing to do with your perky tits and great ass."

A slight smile forms at the corner of her lips.

"I need to feel you."

She looks around, stands and then sits on my lap.

Moving her hair off her shoulder, my lips find the spot right under her earlobe that gives her goose bumps. She wiggles in my lap, stirring my dick in my pants.

"I'm sorry, baby, but I need you to know that I don't care about your body. You're so much more than just a beautiful woman and I want you to see that when you look in the mirror."

She nods, but I know she doesn't believe me.

I turn her face toward me and capture her lips with my own.

My tongue slides through the part of her lips and the anxiety in my chest brought on by our fight diminishes. I know it won't always be this easy to end our fights, but I'll take what I can get tonight.

My fingers push through her hair, the silky strands wrapping around my hand. I swallow her moan and my hand slides up the side of her ribcage.

The bell goes off and I blink my eyes open to see Madison's eyes shifting in every direction as men from all different areas in the house head in one general direction.

She jumps up from my lap.

"I gotta go, babe. Grab your things."

She frantically gets her cell phone, puts it in her purse and positions it crossways over her body.

Some guys are heading down the pole and others the stairs. Madison runs down the stairs trying to stay out of everyone's way before I even see that she's left. I slide down the pole, then get my gear on. All the guys pile into the truck.

I spot her off to the side so I race over to her.

"Like I said...hero complex." She smiles as I kiss her one last time.

"This is just my job."

The horn honks on the truck, the sirens blaring.

"Go." She shoves me but I slide my tongue into her mouth one last time, my body not wanting to leave her.

"BIANCO!" someone shouts.

"Gotta go. Remember, no hero." I shake my head.

"Call me after?" she hollers out as the truck starts to leave and I grab on to the handle and climb into my seat.

"I will." I wink and she watches the truck race out of the station.

I'm always concerned about returning whenever we leave on a call. But watching the look on her face as I race toward danger makes coming back feel that much more important.

CHAPTER THIRTY

Madison

I was torn whether to be worried or horny watching Mauro hop on that truck as it was pulling out of the station. It was like a scene from a movie and he was the heartthrob hero.

Pulling into my own garage, I climb out of my car and for the first time in a long time, I'm home at a decent hour. Walking the path from the detached garage to the back door I see my neighbors out in their yard.

"Maddie," the little girl says, jumping up and heading to the fence line.

"Hey, Jade." I see she's holding a cute white puppy in her arms. "You got a puppy?"

Her eyes light up, a smile so big I can see why Reed finally caved. Jade's been begging for a dog for months.

I pet the dog's head, and it leans in already too used to getting a lot of attention.

"I named him Snowball." Jade holds him up in her arms.

"He's adorable." I continue petting him thinking maybe a

dog would be a good idea if I stayed in a house for any length of time.

"I know. I can't believe my mom and Reed agreed. My daddy brought him as a good luck in school gift this past weekend."

I cringe inwardly, wondering how pissed off Reed must have been.

Speaking of the man, he walks out of their house and over to us in jeans and long sleeve t-shirt. He's definitely an attractive man and talk about a potentially dangerous job. Assistant DA isn't exactly a cakewalk either.

"Hey Maddie, I see you met our new addition." He drinks from his cup, staring down at the furball in Jade's arms.

"I did. Snowball is a cutie."

"Not so cute when he can't figure out that he needs to pee and poop outside," he says.

"Not much of a dog person, huh?"

"Reed says Snowball is going to ruin our house so he's stopped all renovations until he's potty trained," Jade says.

Reed shakes his head with a smile.

"It's a nice gift," I offer.

"From a person who doesn't have to deal with it, of course." He raises an eyebrow.

Jade drops Snowball to the ground, following the puppy as it wanders around their small yard.

"Sorry, ex-husbands, huh?"

He shrugs. "Did you see her smile though? How can I argue with that?"

"And Victoria?"

"She's the same as me. Jade's got us wrapped around her finger. She's wanted it and we'd thought about it. Pete just beat us to it."

Pete must be Jade's father and if memory serves he lives in California. From what I can tell, they all get along pretty well.

"I'm glad I ran into you, I've been meaning to talk to you about something." Reed glances behind him to make sure Jade isn't within earshot. Which is hard in our small yards but she's so consumed with Snowball, I don't think we have to worry.

"What's going on? If it's about the sale, I'm waiting for another project to be finished and then I'll be putting this house on the market. I'll let you know what I list it at."

He waves off my concern. Usually I don't know the neighbors of the houses I rehab, but Reed, Victoria, and Jade are outgoing and it's summer so we've had more interaction than I normally would.

"No, I saw a black truck picking you up and dropping you off a few times. Is that a new boyfriend?" I can tell he's uncomfortable asking me.

"He is."

"A firefighter? I saw the sticker in the back window." He sips from his cup again, his eyes looking over his shoulder one more time.

"Yes. Engine Fifty-Five."

"The one with Hunter Zaxby?"

"Cut to the chase, Reed. I feel like you're about to ruin my day."

He chuckles. "I'm not. The case is pretty clear-cut—it was arson that killed Hunter. I'm not sure if your boyfriend knows that yet. The case is finalized tomorrow, but I have some concerns, off the record."

He takes a deep breath. "I don't think this was the owner of an abandoned building wanting his problems to burn up. Just tell your boyfriend and his buddies to be careful. We're having another look at some other fires that were originally ruled as accidents, but his job might be a lot more dangerous than usual if an arsonist is using ingredients to make fires uncontrollable and unpredictable."

"Why would anyone purposely go after the fire department?" My stomach churns and my chest is tight thinking about someone trying to harm innocent workers who lay their lives on the line.

"I don't know, but I intend to find out. It could be anything from a disgruntled former employee to a psychopath. There's just too much coincidence in what I'm seeing. I wondered if he'd be willing to sit down and talk at some point."

My hands grip the fence. Mauro's in even more danger than he normally is?

"I'll ask him. Hunter was a good friend of his so I'm sure he'd do anything to help you figure this out."

"Reed, Snowball just threw up," Jade calls out.

Reed rolls his eyes. "Remind me to thank Pete again."

I laugh.

"You can give him my number or if he'd rather you're there, the two of you are welcome over anytime. I just really want to pick his brain." He walks away from the fence line, placing his cup down and unwinding the hose.

"I'll ask him tonight and get back to you."

"Thanks, Maddie."

"Anytime."

The house is empty, which I already suspected since Lauren's Fiat isn't in the garage. I dig through my purse for my M&Ms and flip on the television to see if there's any news about the fire Mauro had to run off to. Reed's fears become my own that he'll have the same fate as Hunter if there's some crazy person out there setting fires to harm firefighter.

There's nothing on the news about it except what Reed already said about the announcement tomorrow morning on the fire that took the life of a firefighter. No mention of arson yet. Once that's decided they'll start the investigation.

I can't help but worry about how this will all affect Mauro.

Will it churn up feelings of anger toward someone he considered a best friend and betrayed him? One thing is for sure, our easy road of lovemaking and small disagreements is about to be turned on its head.

I hope we're strong enough to get through it.

CHAPTER THIRTY-ONE

Mauro

"Your girlfriend seems nice," Trevor says on our way back to the firehouse.

The small kitchen fire wasn't anything much, and it sucks that what one person could have easily taken care of stole me away from my lunch date with Madison.

"She is and you can stop thinking about her right now."

He rumbles with laughter. The kid is overzealous to say the least. Always at a ten.

"You worried I'm going to steal her away?" He moves his eyebrows up and down.

"No. Because you wouldn't stand a chance with her."

"I never said I wanted her. All I said was she was nice." He holds up his left hand with a ring attached.

Well, I've been fooled before. That piece of metal means nothing.

"And I'm just confirming that she's mine."

"Jeez, lay off the testosterone."

We sit in silence for the rest of the ride. I know I'm being a jealous prick. I've seen Trevor and his wife, Ariel. They're much like me and Madison where they can't keep their hands off each other. She's all bright eyes and huge smiles, bouncing around next to Trevor when she comes in. That's one thing Cailin and Hunter never had. They never did seem that happy, but they were married and in my opinion that held more weight than the affection they shared.

The truck is about to turn into the station, a few passersby watching us as always. A little boy waves and Big Gus honks the horn. The kid's face lights up.

I'll be thankful to get back to the station, call Madison and if I'm lucky, get each other off with some dirty talk.

"Engine Fifty-Five," a dispatcher comes in over the radio.

Big Gus pulls the radio down to his mouth, pressing the button.

"Another call. A warehouse on..." My mind drifts with the word warehouse.

Trevor pales across from me, his eyes finding no serenity at the kid jumping up and down on the sidewalk. He was there that night. Being a newbie, he was only able to assist in hose preparation. Tonight, he'll be in on the action.

My LT turns to us from the front, his eyes finding mine.

"They're calling in other engines for back up. It's a big one boys."

As we back up onto the streets of Chicago, another set of guys head to the ladder truck, climbing in. The ladder truck hasn't been used since that night and all of us in the cab of this truck know it.

Fuck, uneasiness unsettles my stomach as the truck sirens blare down the street. It's a bad omen when you have to go into a call with a monkey on your back like this. I try to shake it off as we whip through traffic, but it's impossible.

Ten minutes later, the thick, dark smoke billows out into the blue sky and we've arrived at our destination. The ladder truck goes first, positioning itself to spray down into the structure.

At three stories, this one is bigger than the one six months ago.

My lieutenant jumps out, as we all do, the physical aspects of the job second nature by now. It's putting the mental mind fuck aside to function as the team we're trained to, that's the challenge.

A car is parked in front of the fire hydrant, so Trevor breaks one window and I the other as I pass him the hose to hook up. The car alarm joins the chorus of fire trucks approaching the scene.

"Bianco!" Lieutenant waves me over. "You and Conley handle hose."

I nod to Trevor Conley who looks like he's about to puke in the middle of the street.

I grab the hose, put on my helmet and button my jacket up.

We head up the sidewalk, following the other fighters with axes to break down anything that blocks our way.

All that's on my mind is Madison. The way her eyelashes flutter when I kiss her good morning. How her body seeks mine, her arms and legs anchoring my body down in bed like she's afraid I'll disappear.

The heat of the flames hits my face, and I switch the hose on, cementing my legs to keep control of the water, spraying down the uncontrollable rager in front of me. I'm fighting the fire physically but my mind wanders to her.

I remember two mornings ago when I woke up to her hands sliding down the waistband of my boxer briefs.

How her heated gaze stayed on me while her tongue licked up my length and she settled between my legs.

Her soft hair wrapped around my fingers as I rocked into

her mouth. The tension that stiffened my legs as my balls drew up while her soft hands massaged them.

The name Madison falling from my lips while the morning light flowed into my bedroom.

The warmth of her body as she slides up to meet me.

The way I tasted on her tongue.

Her giggle as I flipped her over and returned her good morning wake-up call.

I never wanted to leave that room.

"BIANCO!" Trevor yells and I wake up from my daydream to hit the flames about to melt our boots on the floor. "It's everywhere, man!" Fear laces every word.

It takes us a while but when the front room is clear, we head upstairs while another team covers the first floor.

"Just keep the hose firm in your grip. It will be over before you know it." I say to him.

"Second floor is practically nonexistent," another firefighter says over our line. "Need another hose ASAP."

"Coming," I say, increasing my speed.

Trevor keeps up and we find two guys outside a door, one with an axe in his hand.

"One, two, three." The guy beats it down and we all stay on the side to see what kind of flames will emerge.

When it's clear, me and Trevor head in, spraying down the rapid rupture of flames climbing the walls. Again, as I extinguish the hungry beast, Madison enters my mind once again.

Last week when she went over to my mom's and they discussed options to expand their kitchen. A ventilation system that would ensure it did not get so hot. She even suggested a double oven. The call from my mom after her visit, proud that I found such a keeper.

That's exactly what she is, a keeper and I have to make sure she doesn't slip away.

From room to room, we combat the fire, making ground

and all I want is for this to be over so I can see Madison. I'll call her as soon as I get back and ask her to come to the station just so I can hold her in my arms.

We break down another door, waiting for the flames to emerge before we spray it down and enter. We've already done this more times than I can count but based on the other rooms I wasn't prepared for the flames to cover every surface like an out of control vein on steroids. Within seconds, every surface around us was covered.

"What do we do?" Trevor asks as I try to spray each corner, only to have it covered by fire again immediately. The flames aren't going out and panic starts to bubble in my throat. "It's closing in on us, Mauro. What do we do?" Trevor is in a full panic.

"Conley! Bianco! You need to get out. It's way too dangerous. We're going to have to fight it from the outside only!" the lieutenant shouts in my ear.

I turn around for a second to signal to Conley for us to find some way out of this, but he's as baffled as me. "We've got nowhere to go. We're caged."

"Find a way, goddamn it. Find a fucking way, Bianco!"

My eyes search, spraying the hose in all different directions trying to get enough control of the fire to allow us a moment to escape. It feels hopeless as I watch the water-sprayed wood feed the fire down the path we came.

"We have no choice. We have to go forward to get out."

"We'll never survive," Trevor says behind me.

"Look behind you, Conley, we'll never survive that way. We have no choice." Moving forward, the heat becomes almost unbearable.

"If you live and I die, tell Ariel I love her. Tell her I'm there with her when the baby is born. There's a letter in my locker, in case anything like this happens. Give it to her."

I don't want to hear this shit because I've never told the

woman I love that I love her. I've been too chicken shit in case she doesn't feel the same way about me yet.

"I will, but we're getting out of here, you hear me?"

"Watch out!" Conley yells and a wall falls down to the right of us, sending embers in all directions.

I have to get it together, but visions of Madison at my funeral plague me as we search for escape. Visions of the flag draped over my coffin and her walking behind the truck assault my mind as each room brightens with more intense flames.

She'd never know how much I love her. If I get out this, I'm telling her, to hell with the consequences.

"BIANCO!" Conley bellows and this time I have no time to react.

CHAPTER THIRTY-TWO

Madison

"A firefighter from Engine Fifty-Five has been taken to hospital," the anchor on the news channel says.

I stare at my phone, wishing, pleading, praying that it will ring.

"The fire is finally out, but it took a lot of resources and crews to accomplish. Many in charge are comparing it to the fire six months ago that took the life of Firefighter Hunter Zaxby."

Nope. I'm not waiting.

I grab my purse and my keys, not caring that I'm in my pajamas.

Racing over to the fire station is scarier than when I checked up on Mauro the first time. I'm so much more invested in our future now. Which I'm not sure I realized until this moment. It always takes something big like this, right? How fucking stupid.

Pulling up, I park on a side street and head up the sidewalk, with each footstep unsure of my decision, but he's my boyfriend, and I need to know he's okay.

I round the corner and the truck pulls in, some of the guys hopping out, hugging the women waiting for them. Mumblings of I love you and I was so worried can be heard coming from the women while the men give them assurances of how they were safe and had the fire beat the entire time.

I smile at the man with soot all over his face, cradling his wife's stomach, relief etched in his face.

"They were trapped and couldn't get out," one man says to his wife. "The ambulance took him before I saw anything. They called his brother."

My heart stops beating and blood rushes in my ears.

Oh my God, it was Mauro. They called Cristian or Luca, I know it.

Why would they not call me?

Because they don't have my number.

"Excuse me?" I approach the man, needing to know. "The injured firefighter?"

The big man raises his eyebrows and purses his lips like he's not going to tell me shit.

"Do you know if Mauro Bianco is back yet?" I ask.

"MAURO!" a woman's voice screeches from behind me.

I turn to see Cailin running across two lanes of traffic, not stopping, heading right to the other side of the truck.

"He's right there, ma'am," the guy says to my back and then continues his conversation about whoever the injured firefighter is.

My eyes are glued to the end of the truck, watching Mauro emerge and drop his gear, opening his arms to Cailin. Burrowing his head into her neck, he picks her up like a man coming home from war.

My mouth hangs open and tears prick my eyes.

Mauro places her back on her feet and she looks into his

eyes, her hands on his face, his shoulders, like she's trying to make sure he's real. It's like I'm having an out of body experience or peering into an intimate moment between lovers.

Nausea rumbles in my stomach.

She raises on her tiptoes, keeping his head firmly between her hands.

I watch the scene unfold and I can't look away even though it's torture and I know I'll never be able to clear the visual out of my head.

Their lips meet and I close my eyes, tears spilling down my cheeks. The roller coaster of emotions my body went through in the last five minutes too much to deal with.

Turning around, I walk away.

"Hey, Madison, right?" One of the guys from earlier today reaches out to me. "Your guy was quite the hero today. He saved my ass."

I nod. His pregnant wife looks at me with sympathy, probably because I'm crying and walking away from the scene. She obviously sees something her husband doesn't.

"I'm glad you're safe," I say and step away.

"Wait. I'm sure he'll want to see you." His hand lands on my forearm, but his wife hits his arm and he turns to see what she's talking about. "Oh."

Sympathy that matches his wife's tells me I don't need a second look.

Instead, I round the corner of the street and when I get into the safety of my car, I down the entire bag of M&Ms in my purse, before ripping the wrapper into small pieces. I never want to see those initials again.

CHAPTER THIRTY-THREE

Mauro

"Cailin!" I push her shoulders and remove her hands from my cheeks. "What are you doing?"

She falls back to her heels, her cheeks red with embarrassment.

"I'm just so happy you're okay and in one piece. They kept comparing it to the fire, and Hunter's name and picture were all over the news again. I had to make sure you were okay."

I blow out a breath.

"We need to talk." I shake my head, staring down at the ground.

"Maybe I got too carried away, but I'm just so relieved." She heaves for breath and her mascara is trailing in waves down her cheeks.

"I get that, but you know I'm with Madison."

The other guys with their significant others are lingering around and my eyes do a quick scan of the area. No sign of Madison. I'd hoped she'd see the news and come.

"I know," Cailin says in a small voice.

"Do you?" I take her by the hand, pulling her to the side of the building away from prying eyes.

"I do," she says with her back against the wall.

"I think you're transferring your feelings for Hunter on to me or something."

She shakes her head and rubs her face with her hands. "I just don't want to be alone. It's so hard, Mauro. Raising Devin, going to bed alone every night."

I hug her. "I know. But I'm not going to take his place. My heart isn't up for grabs."

She nods into the crook of my neck, sobs wracking her body.

As I'm consoling her, I look off onto the road and spot Madison's car parked down the street. It can't be her, can it?

"Hold on. I'll be right back."

Cailin keeps her head down, tears continuing down her face as I jog down the street.

Approaching the small SUV, I figure it's a car similar to, but not hers, because if she's here, why isn't she in my arms?

When I bend over and look through the window, her head is on the steering wheel, the keys in her hands, resting in her lap.

"Fuck," I murmur, looking back at Cailin and then at my girl.

She came. I smile at the fact that she came to make sure I was okay.

My knock on her window startles her and she straightens her back.

"Madison, what's wrong?" I ask.

She doesn't take time to wipe her own tears but puts the keys in the ignition.

My hand tries to open up the passenger door, but it's

locked. She quickly puts the car in reverse to get out of the parallel parking spot. I bang on the window. "Madison!"

She ignores me, her eyes set on her task of getting the fuck away from me.

Realization makes my gut clench and panic tightens my throat.

"It's not what it looks like. Let me explain. Don't leave!" I bang on the window again.

She reverses again, the asshole in front of her way too close to give her any room. Of course, I'm thanking that asshole as I round the hood of her car and plead through the window.

"Come on Madison. I promise you it isn't what you're assuming. Hear me out." Our eyes meet and she stills.

"What are you doing, Mauro?" Cailin approaches the car.

I place my hand up in the air. "Stop."

"Is that Maddie?" she asks, continuing to walk toward us.

Hasn't she caused enough trouble tonight?

Madison catches me looking away and turns her head, looking out her side mirror.

A fresh set of tears fall and she moves not caring if she hits me or not.

"FUCK!" I yell as she pulls out of the spot and her tail-lights round the corner.

"Did she see us?" Cailin asks.

"No, she always drives away from me like that. What do you think?"

From the tone of my voice anyone else would know to leave me the fuck alone, but Cailin follows me as I jog back to the firehouse.

"I'm sick and going home," I say to my lieutenant passing him by.

"No, you're not. We have to unpack the truck, get it ready

in case we're going back out. You're on shift until the morning." He follows me. "Oh, hello, Cailin."

She stops him long enough for me to strip out of my gear and head upstairs to grab my keys and phone.

"Bianco, you can't leave," the lieutenant says.

"Then fire me."

I run out of the fire station down the street with Cailin yelling my name behind me.

I don't give a shit about any of it. I just need Madison to understand.

I call her, not surprised when it goes to voicemail over and over again. I leave pleading messages for her to listen to me and explain that it was a one-way kiss.

What seems like a lifetime later, my tires squeal to a stop outside her house and I jog up the steps, ringing the doorbell over and over again until it finally swings open.

I instinctively cover my nuts.

"Lauren."

No smile this time around which means Madison is home.

"You are such an asshole. I trusted you and here you're having an affair with your partner's widow? You sick motherfucker. Do you enjoy torturing Madison?" She steps out onto the porch and my gaze flickers past her, wondering how I can get around her.

"It's all a misunderstanding."

"Were your lips on hers?" she asks, her hands on her hips, eyebrows raised in question.

"For a millisecond until I threw her off me. Where is she? I need to speak with her." I look into the house again and still see no sign of Madison.

"Nope. You're not going near her again. I gave you the benefit of the doubt, Bianco and you fucked it up." She turns her back to me, but I slide by her, shutting and locking the door behind me.

She is going to have my nuts, I know that as I hear her banging and yelling my name, but I'll deal with that later.

Madison isn't in the family room, or the kitchen, so I run upstairs, finding her bedroom door shut. I knock.

"Just give me tonight, Lauren, okay? We can talk in the morning."

I try the knob and it's locked. Fuck.

"I'm serious, I just can't tonight. Please understand."

No fucking way I'm letting her go a whole night thinking I'd hurt her like that.

I reach up on top of the door and retrieve the key she was adamant about us keeping on the ledges of all the doorframes at our flip house.

Trying to be quiet so she can't put a dresser in front of the door, I insert the key into the lock and turn until the click sounds.

The pounding on the outside door and ringing doorbell sounds below, Lauren voicing all the ways she's going to torture me when she gets her hands on me.

When I open the door, Madison is on her bed, a pillow tucked in her lap.

"Madison?" I ask, walking in and shutting and locking the door just in case Lauren gets into the house.

"If you're here, who's knocking?" she asks, startled to see me.

"I might have outplayed Lauren at a game of chicken."

She doesn't find it as funny as I do and this isn't the moment for me to be raising my fist in victory. We'll laugh tomorrow morning when all this behind us.

"Cailin kissed me and I pushed her away immediately. I told her I'm with you." I sit on the edge of the bed, wanting this fight to be over so we can go back to being us.

"I believe you. It took me a minute to process, but I knew

you wouldn't do that to me because it was done to you." She wipes at the tears on her cheeks.

Relief fills my insides.

"Never. I'd never do that to you." I reach for her, needing to feel her, but she leans away from me.

"But it made me realize something, Mauro." She leans over and grabs a Kleenex from her nightstand and blows her nose while all the relief I was feeling a moment ago flees.

"For a moment I felt like that girl again...the nerd in high school and she was like the cheerleader. I think I'm always going to be screwed up like this. It's not fair to you. You shouldn't have to reassure me all the time and feel like you have to prove that it's me you want." A tear trickles down her cheek, but she swipes it away.

"I don't feel like that and I'm happy to tell you every morning we wake up together and every night before we go to bed. As long as I have you, I don't care about any of that." I slide closer, but she moves back, keeping the same distance between us.

"This is never going to work. I'll forever be that girl at the bonfire staring at you while you're thinking of someone else. At least in my own head. We tried and I thought maybe it could work, but I see now that girl will always live on inside of me. She's not going anywhere."

"This is ridiculous. As I was fighting that fire tonight, do you know what I was thinking about?"

I want her to know that I love her, but at the same time I can't tell her right now. I'm afraid I'll scare her away and she'll think I'm just saying it to make her feel better.

"What?"

"How much I wanted to be with you. I wanted you wrapped in my arms. It was scary there for a second and I fought to get out of that building just to hold you. That's what got me through. Madison, don't do this. It's all high school bullshit that doesn't matter. Who cares if I was the jock and you were the nerd, we're here now. And what we have, few people get."

"Ha! You asshole, get the fuck out." Lauren storms into the room, a key in hand.

"I'm not going anywhere without her." I look between the two of them, determined to make this right.

"First of all, you're stinking up our entire house with the smell of smoke. Second, she doesn't want you here."

Madison's gaze shifts to her friend and then back down to her lap.

Maybe it's good that her friend is here.

"Tell her, Lauren," I beg. "Tell her how good we are together. I'm with her because of the person she is inside. That I was a blind bastard ten years ago and I'll spend the rest of my life making it up to her."

Lauren's rigid stance falters and her gaze lands on Madison who is busy sniffling and wiping away tears again.

"I thought he cheated on you?" Lauren asks.

Madison says nothing.

"She caught my buddy's widow kissing me. I pushed her away, told her I didn't want her and I was with Madison. But now she's saying we'll never work because we're too different."

Lauren's head falls back in what appears to be exasperation, like this isn't the first time she's dealt with this issue when it comes to Madison.

"Maddie." She makes her way across the room and when she reaches her friend, she wraps her arm around her shoulders. They sit there in silence for a minute, Lauren must see something I don't because she moves off the bed and nods for me to meet her in the hall.

Is she crazy? I'm not leaving without making this right.

Lauren grabs my shirt and pulls me out into the hall, shutting the door behind her.

"Just give her tonight to be by herself and process her thoughts. I'm sure she'll come to her senses tomorrow," Lauren says.

"You're kidding me, right?" I take one step toward the door and Lauren's hand presses into my chest. "I'm not leaving. She needs to know I'm not going anywhere when things get tough."

"I understand, but you won't get through to her tonight. Trust me, I've known her my whole life. Her wounds are deep, Mauro, and I wish she didn't see herself as that girl in high school, but the rejection she felt during those years still lingers. She never even told me about whatever happened between the two of you at the bonfire party. I'm her best friend, and she didn't think she could tell me which means it hurt bad. So bad she chose to pretend it never happened. Now here you are, telling her you want her. It's hard for her to believe that deep down. That the one thing she wished for every night for years before bed is coming true. When it comes to you, she feels second best."

Lauren's words make me realize how deeply I hurt her and how far I'll have to go to make it up to her.

I push my hands through my hair. "I still don't want to leave."

Lauren gives me a small smile. "Listen, Maddie is a thinker. Always has been. Let her sort this out a bit in her head and you can try to talk some sense into her again."

"I need to come up with a plan to make her realize."

"Good luck with that." Lauren pats my back like she pities me because whatever I come up with will never work.

She obviously doesn't understand my competitive drive. Madison Kelly is mine and I intend to keep it that way.

CHAPTER THIRTY-FOUR

Madison

Lucky for me, Mauro is stuck in an interview today about last night's fire, so I don't have to worry about him coming to the house. The only reason I know this is because he texted me since I'm still not answering the phone.

He's upset and doesn't understand why I'm pushing him away. I'm not sure why he doesn't see how this will never work out between us. We're nothing alike and sooner or later he's going to realize I'm not worthy of him.

Tonight killed me when he showed up at my house smelling of smoke, the soot still lining his jaw and forehead. The urge to wrap my arms around him because he was okay nearly catapulted me off that bed, but what good would that do? Just delay the inevitable.

As I'm walking around the house, writing out a list of everything that needs to be finished before we can put the place on the market, I hear a car pull up outside. I sigh, worried that he got out of the interview early and has decided to plead his case again.

It's not even just him. Somehow, he's won Lauren over because she left me a note on my dresser about not wasting true love. Who knew she was such a romantic?

Even Vanessa sat me down earlier today telling me that I had to put the past behind me and live for the present. That I was giving up something special not many people share. Easy for the beauty queen to say.

"Hello?" a feminine voice calls out into the house.

"Yes?" I walk down the stairs, stopping mid-flight when I see Cailin.

The vision of her lips on Mauro's is still vivid in my mind.

"He's not here," I say, walking down the rest of the way, rounding the bottom stairway and heading to the kitchen.

She holds up a thermos and two cups. "I'm here to see you."

Her blonde hair is pulled back into a high ponytail, no makeup on her face.

"I'm not sure why? I'm out of your way now. He's all yours." I cock my hip and stare her down.

"Even if you broke up with him, we both know he's not mine. He's still yours." She sets the thermos on the dining room table that has somehow become a staple of this home.

"Sometimes things just don't work out. He'll find someone else. Someone more suitable."

She places the two cups she brought and fills them up with tea from the thermos. I take a few tentative steps over toward the table.

"I need to apologize, I was an evil witch and I deserve it if you want me to have no contact with Mauro, but don't take what I did out on him. He didn't want that kiss. I convinced myself he did, hell that I did, for that matter, but I was just trying to replace what I'd lost."

She slides the cup my way.

Dropping the pad of paper on the table, I sip the tea, crossing my fingers it's not poisoned.

"When Hunter died, we weren't the happiest of couples. We fought a lot. About money and his schedule and the new business venture he was going into with Mauro. We argued about parenting, sleeping times, me not wanting sex enough. In my head, I thought that was just marriage....we had a young child and this is what happens with couples at that stage of life. There were times it felt like we were headed for divorce, but he'd always come home with a bouquet of flowers, telling me how much he loved me. We'd make love and we'd be back in our happy place until the next fight."

If she only knew what he was doing behind her back.

"After he died, I propped him up on this pedestal as a man who could do no wrong. A man who fought fires and saved lives. A man who gave up his own life helping others."

A tear slips down her cheek and I can't help the compassion I feel for her, much as I'd prefer it weren't there.

"I morphed him into the perfect father, the perfect husband in my head. And I believed it for a minute there because I hated that I ever thought ill of him now that he was gone. But you know what? Everyone has their flaws. Look what I did...treated you terribly. Kissed your boyfriend. Tried to steal him away from you. I know you don't know me, but that's not me. I never would have done that six months ago."

I swallow down the revelation I want to give her about Hunter.

"I don't know why you and Mauro broke up but if it's because of the kiss, don't. He didn't even reciprocate. He told me you held his heart, Madison. I'm sorry that I was so lonely and wounded that I tried to ruin what you two have."

The pained look on her face has me telling her that I

accept her apology. And I do. She seems sincere and I do feel awful for what she's going through. But it doesn't change the fact that at some point Mauro is going to come to his senses.

"You're the one for him, Madison. Mauro told me that you went to high school together, but he didn't know you at the time. He was over one evening to fix my garbage disposal and he stayed for a drink after Devin went to bed."

I really don't want to hear this.

"He went on and on about you. How he wished he did know you. That it felt like he'd wasted these past ten years because the woman he's meant to be with, he'd already met years prior."

She smiles like that should appease me in some way.

It kind of does.

I clear my throat. "Nice of him to say."

She laughs in an exasperated way that asks 'how much more convincing do I need to give you?' "I don't know who brought Hunter into my life, but he was there for a purpose. He gave me Devin and for that I'm grateful. People come in and out of our lives, some return, some you never see again. I like to think there's a reason that this is your time with Mauro. Maybe back then it wasn't the right timing. Do you really want to take the chance that the paths you're on don't meet again?"

I sip the tea and allow her words to soak in.

"We don't know each other well, but I *do* know Mauro. He and Hunter were close since the academy. I've seen women come and go in and out of his life and none of them have had anything like what you two do." Her hand covers mine and I see she still wears her wedding band. "I promise you, his feelings are genuine and true."

With a squeeze on my hand, she turns around and leaves as I lower myself to the wood floor wondering what the hell I'm doing. My eyes shift around the room, taking in what we built together. This house was a bid away from being bulldozed and now it's a bright and happy home, ready for a family to build memories, a life in.

Cailin's right. Something brought Mauro into my life. We could've had that date and then never saw each other again, but he showed up at that auction.

Regret and determination fill me and I stand up, finding my phone and calling his number.

No answer.

I hammer out a text message for him to call me as soon as he's out of the interview.

Locking all the doors and shutting all the windows, I run out to my car, peeling away from the curb to wait for him outside his apartment.

I have to make this right. I just hope it's not too late and my issues haven't scared him away.

CHAPTER THIRTY-FIVE

Mauro

"Just get as many people there as possible. I don't care who they are. Did you leave the outfit on her bed?" I ask Lauren, who thankfully has moved over to Team Mauro.

Our agendas match—make Madison see she's deserving of love. I have no doubt that if I pull this off, she'll be back to giving me hell tomorrow.

"It's all set, but she hasn't returned home yet," she says.

"I drove by after my interview and her car wasn't there."

I pace around the grass, wondering where the hell she could be.

"What's up, man?" One of my buddies arrives to help me set this entire thing up.

"Hey." I nod toward the area where the other guys are lingering.

"Did you call her?" she asks.

"I texted her. I'll call her now." Lauren hangs up and I see that there's a text message from Cristian waiting for me.

Cris: *She's outside the apartment waiting for you. I just woke up from my double shift.*

Fuck. She's come to talk to me and I can't even make it to her.

Me: *Tell her to go home. That I'm not there.*
Cris: *Pretty sure she's going to stick around and wait.*
Me: *Do whatever you have to do, just get her home so Lauren can do what she needs to do.*
Cris: *I'll try.*

I pull up Lauren's contact and send her a message so she'll know what's going on.

Me: *She's at my apartment. Cristian is going to try to get her to go home. Did you get a hold of her?*

I pace a path from one side to the other. I need to pull this off.

Lauren: *She said she's an idiot and she's going to wait for you until you come home. I don't think she's budging on this.*

Damn it. I thread my fingers through my hair.

Me: *Okay. She had texted me so I'm going to tell her to meet me at your house.*
Lauren: *Then I'll kidnap her. Perfect.*

Starting a new thread, I pull up her earlier text that I was going to ignore until she got here.

Me: *I can't talk right now but let's meet at your house in a half hour?*

The three dots appear immediately.

Madison: *I'm at your apartment. Just come here. Your brother just left. I don't want to talk in front of Vanessa or Lauren.*

I stare up at the sky silently asking why this woman is determined to be so stubborn.

Me: *I'll get to your place quicker. We can go somewhere and talk.*

That's the best I have before begging her to go home.

Madison: *Okay, I'll head over there now.*

Finally. I pull my thread with Lauren back up on my phone.

Me: *She's heading home now. Make sure you get her in that dress before you bring her.*
Lauren: *On it.*

I spend the next hour preparing a scene going off someone else's memory. It's time to redo history.

CHAPTER THIRTY-SIX

Madison

I walk into my bedroom, Lauren on my heels from the moment I opened the front door.

"I know I've been stupid so you can stop your lectures. I'm apologizing and I'm going to try and put all the past behind us..." I trail off as I spot a dress I've never seen before laid out on my bed with a small note placed on it.

I glance back to Lauren, who's smiling.

Come back to two thousand and eight and let's start fresh. Put on the dress and have Lauren drive you to me.

Love,

Mauro

"I'll let you change." She shuts the door behind her and I have the passing thought that I now realize she's wearing a pair of baggy pants and a tight t-shirt that shows a sliver of her stomach.

Puzzled but hopeful, I strip out of my jeans and sweatshirt, putting on a dress very similar to the one I wore ten years ago. The one that ended up drenched in beer. I'm tying my shoes when my bedroom door opens and there stands Vanessa and Lauren.

Vanessa's decked out in a gold headband and a babydoll top.

"Are you ready, Maddie?" she asks. "I heard there's a bonfire going down tonight and Mauro Bianco is going to be there." She flutters her eyes. "He's so dreamy."

Lauren knocks her shoulder. "Two thousand and eight, not nineteen sixty-eight."

Vanessa laughs.

"I'm ready."

Hope feels like it's filling my chest from the inside out, expanding my chest with every breath. I stare in the mirror for a moment reflecting on the differences between the person I was a decade ago and the one that stands here now, not just in appearance, but personality, too.

A decade ago I never would have been able to hold a conversation with Mauro. Kissing him just about made me mute, never mind sleeping with him. I would have agreed with everything he said because that's what I thought you were supposed to do with boys. Now I fight for what I believe in. I didn't know what I wanted out of life back then, but I do now.

And I can't let my fears and insecurities stop me from having them. Mauro is a good man and if he says that he cares for me, I have to trust in that. The same way he was trusting me not to hurt him.

I realize now that there are no guarantees in life. The best any of us can do is try. And if we fail, well...at least we had our moment in the sun. It's better than withering away to nothing in the shadows.

The three of us head out of the house to the garage where Lauren's Fiat awaits.

"Your parents are so great to buy you this car, Lauren." Apparently, Vanessa is still pretending we're in high school. "My dad told me no car until I'm eighteen. I'll get him to cave though."

The three of us continue to make jokes like we really are sixteen again and living with our parents.

"Did you know that all the Bianco brothers are going to be there tonight?" I ask because now that I've figured out what's going on, the outfit I saw Cristian in earlier at his apartment makes more sense. He was wearing his jeans halfway down his ass with a brown belt and plaid shirt. Totally ten years ago.

"Whatever. The only one worth anyone's time is Mauro. You should totally talk to him tonight, Mad." Vanessa nudges my shoulder.

"I don't know, I think they all have their own redeeming qualities," I say.

"Luca can suck my tit. He'll never have a chance with me. He's so cocky and thinks he's great at everything he does," Lauren says.

I raise my eyebrows at her.

Finally, we arrive at the same place high school bonfires were held ten years prior and Lauren parks on the grass.

There's a bonfire roaring in the middle of the field between two sets of trees. People are scattered over the grass, Solo cups in hand, laughing and having a good time.

"Party time!" Vanessa hollers. She wasn't there originally when I begged Lauren to go home, but I wish now that she were.

We all file out and I'm not sure how he managed it, but

everyone acts like they don't know why we're there, barely giving us a glance. Searching the area, I spot Mauro talking to a group of guys.

A smile crosses his lips, his eyes flowing over my body like it's the first time he's seen me.

I blush, of course I do, and shake my head at the absurdity of this entire situation.

He's wearing what he wore that night minus the backward hat which I'm kind of happy about because I love his hair so much. Oh and he's added his letterman jacket, though it's a little snug now with all his muscles.

"Come on, let's get a drink." Lauren tugs me the other way.

We head into the woods where the conversations we pass consist of topics like kids, date nights, and save the dates rather than SATs, parents, and midterms.

Lauren fills her cup but makes me leave mine empty. I'm surprised Lauren remembers or maybe she's going off of what I told Mauro about that night.

Regardless, I end up on a log in front of the fire. As I watch the flames, I assume he'll appear across from me and our eyes will meet.

"Do you mind?" his voice says from next to me and my body hums with the awareness of him.

I look up and his smile is so wide I'm ready to throw myself into his arms, begging him to forgive me for my stupidity and take me back to his apartment. I just want to go back to where we were.

"No," I say, playing my part although he's changed the script.

He sits down and sips his beer. "I'm Mauro." He holds out his hand.

"Madison."

"Nice to meet you." He stares ahead. "I saw you earlier

with your friends."

"Yeah, we're sophomores. You're a senior right?" I can't help but smirk at him.

He nods. "I am. You want some M&Ms?" He pulls a bag out of his letterman jacket.

I smile wide. "My favorite, how did you know?"

He pours some in my hand. "I didn't. They're my favorite, too. Kind of cool the way they're our initials huh?" He pops a few into his mouth. "I heard they're great with cheesecake." He winks at me.

"Really? I'll have to try that sometime." I bump his shoulder with my own.

"Maybe we can try it together?" His thigh presses to mine and the cage to the butterflies in my stomach is opened. How can he still have this effect on me?

"Are you not drinking?" he asks, noticing me flipping my Solo cup around.

"No, I'm the driver."

"Great, I've had a few, not too many but I shouldn't drive. Do you mind giving me a ride? You can drive my truck." He pulls his keys out of his jacket.

"Sure, let me find my friends to let them know."

"Cool. I'll wait by the truck. It's over there." He points off into the distance.

We both stand and he steps closer to me, tucking a strand of hair behind my ear. "Thanks for this."

"You're welcome," I croak out because I'm torn on wanting to finish this scene to see what else he has planned and jumping him right now.

"Hurry, okay?"

I nod and he steps back until he disappears into the darkness.

God, I miss him already.

Turning around, I survey the crowd to find Vanessa and

Lauren. At first, I spot no one and I'm about to tell Luca who's pretending to arm wrestle someone to fill Lauren in for me. Then I see she's the one standing behind Luca's competitor screaming at him to kick Bianco's ass.

I head over to her and tap her on the shoulder. "Hey, can you get a ride home? Mauro just asked me if I could drive him home."

"Um, no you agreed to be my DD. The hell if you're going off with that shithead."

Luca stands up. "That *shithead* would be my brother."

"Okay, funny guys. This didn't actually happen so I'm driving Mauro home. Lauren you have your car and I played the game, so...thanks."

They both smile at me but quickly narrow their eyes at each other again.

"I was kidding." She hugs me. "Go get him, Mad," she whispers in my ear before releasing me.

Luca places his hand on my shoulder. "Give him hell and I mean it. Don't make it easy on him."

I smack his hand and walk away from them, looking around for Vanessa, but when I don't see her, I figure Lauren will tell her and so I head toward the truck, walking faster the closer I get.

Just like that night ten years ago, he's leaning on the passenger side waiting for me. This time he isn't swaying or looking like he might throw up.

"Thanks for this, Madison." He hands me the keys.

"Mauro," I say being done with the game, but he places his fingers on my lips.

"We need to play the song." He leans forward, his hands on either side of my face and he closes his eyes. "Just listen to the lyrics of the song, okay? It says everything I want to on this night." He kisses my forehead and then releases me.

I climb into the driver's seat, a little intimidated by the

size of his truck. Once we're on the road the song, "Chasing Cars" by Snow Patrol starts to play. The lyrics speak so much to my heart and the two of us. The irony that it played ten years ago when we were strangers to one another isn't lost on me.

By the time I'm pulling up to his parents' house, tears are falling down my face.

"I'm so sorry, Mauro," I choke out.

He takes the keys out of the ignition, gets out of his car and then opens my door.

"Come on. Let's go to the park."

He entwines our hands, his callused palms giving me comfort and letting me know that he's already accepted my apology.

We walk across the street. The park equipment is newer now and a locked fence surrounds the outfield.

"Well, we'll have to do this a little differently this time around." Mauro releases my hand and climbs the fence. "Come on." He waits for me as I do my best to get over the fence without flashing him. Not that he hasn't already seen all of me.

"We'll pretend the fence wasn't there." He laughs, taking my hand again and guiding me to centerfield.

He sits down first and pats the grass next to him. I silently oblige and we both lay back in the grass.

"Do you know what you want to be?" he asks, staring at a sky that's littered with stars to wish on tonight.

"I'm not sure. What about you?"

He rolls on his side. "I want the trifecta—the house, the family, and the career. Hopefully one day I get it."

"I'm sure you will. You're a pretty great guy."

He slides closer, his hand touching my cheek. "I have a vision that in ten years I'm going to meet a woman who will change my life forever."

"Really? A vision?"

He chuckles. "Yeah, I think she'll look a lot like you."

"Weird, I had the same vision of you."

Our eyes lock, blue on blue, and the feelings that pass between us without words feel more powerful in this moment than anything the world can throw at us.

"Can I kiss you?" he whispers.

I nod, swallowing down my excitement, my joy of finally being able to kiss him.

He's hesitant at first like he was the first time our lips met, but the fire, the time apart quickly consume us and he rolls me onto my back. His thigh separates my legs as our mouths claim one another.

Finally, I'm back to where I feel like I fit—with Mauro.

Peace travels through my body even as my arousal pulsates out of control.

"Man, that's some kiss. Will you come to my bedroom?"

I smack his shoulder. "A little forward don't you think?"

He nibbles at my neck. "What I want to do to you can't be done in public."

I place my hands on either side of his face and pull him away from my neck so that he's looking at me. "Take me home, Mauro."

"I love those four words," he says, springing to his feet and hauling me up with him.

We rush to get back to the truck, him driving this time instead of me. I'm so busy staring at him the entire ride I don't even pay attention to the time it's taking to get to his apartment.

"You didn't have to do all that," I say, my hand in his as the song plays on repeat.

"I did. It's how that night should have gone." He stops at a light and he bends over to kiss me. "I'll forever regret those ten years I missed out on with you, but I'm not going to dwell on that if I'm lucky enough to have an entire future with you."

The light turns green and he accelerates and I'm still unable to take my eyes off of him.

"We're home," he says, parking by the curb.

I move to open my door.

"Hey, that's my job." He quickly takes the keys out of the ignition and exits his truck, and I look out the window.

We're not at my house and we're not at his apartment, we're at the flip house.

He opens my door, asking for my hand then leading halfway up the walkway and taking both my hands in his.

"Why are we here?" I ask.

"Because this is where I want to start our life together. We gutted this place and pieced it place back together at the same time as our love for one another grew. I only want to stay here and build a life with you until this house is overflowing with kids, pets, and grandkids."

"You want to move in together?" I can barely push the words past the growing lump in my throat.

"This is *our* home. It's not just a house, it's what brought us together, Madison, and I want to finally give you the happily ever after you deserve here. What do you say?"

I stare up at the house that reminds me a lot of myself—good bones, a little disastrous at first, but now with some love and attention, the best parts of it are clear to see—inside and out.

"I say...yes!" I jump up in his arms and he catches me, circling me around.

"I love you, Madison."

"I love you."

"M and M forever," he says and leans in to kiss me like a seal to all my wishes coming true.

EPILOGUE

Mauro

It's been three weeks since we moved into our home. I love the sound of that—*our* home.

Next week is Thanksgiving and we thought about hosting—strike that—Madison wanted to host, but that isn't going to happen. My ma likes to cook and I'm not having my family, aka Luca, mess up our new home.

We've been looking for another property to rehab together, one that will hopefully be on the cheap since we didn't end up pulling our money out of this one, but in the end, it was worth it. We built this home together.

Madison's car pulls up along the curb since we've yet to get the detached garage we weren't thinking about adding when it was a flip property. Lucky for us the parking isn't terrible on this street.

I hide behind the doorway of the bathroom and hear her turn the key in the lock. She enters and flips the light switch that doesn't work.

"Damn it, we couldn't have blown a fuse. Where is he when I'm stuck in the dark?"

I flip on the switch of twinkle lights, the same ones I used the first time we made love. I'm hoping she'll see the rose petals lining a pathway for her follow and take the hint. I peek around the corner.

"Mauro," she sighs, her hand covering her mouth.

I'll never grow tired of my name falling from her lips.

She walks down the pink rose petal path, dropping her purse, jacket, and bag of groceries on a chair as she goes.

Stopping at the dining room table, I see tears prick her eyes from the glow of the real candles I've set along the table, illuminating the words I've spelled out with custom-made M&Ms.

The message is short. Two simple words that hold the key to my happiness.

Marry me?

I emerge from the bathroom and she looks at me, her eyes pouring with love. I already know what she's going to say.

"It's so quick..."

"No, it's not." I round the dining room table I ended up refinishing for us. "I don't want to waste any more time. I want us to be married. I want you to have my name. I want to see your belly swell and watch our kids grow alongside you. I want the bath time, the goodnight stories, the scraped knees. The learning to ride a bike, building a snowman."

"I'd love to be Mrs. Mauro Bianco." She smiles and I grab her, swinging her around, my lips finding hers.

"You've made me so happy."

Her feet fall to the floor as I lower her.

"How did you do this in M&Ms?" she asks, placing one on her tongue.

"Hey, you can't eat the ones I used to ask you to marry

me." She laughs into my chest. "I had to use M&Ms, they're our candy."

I pick up one from the bowl I set beside my question, holding it up for her.

"Maddie and Mauro." She sighs again and I put it in my mouth. She steps closer and wraps her arms around my neck. "You're too romantic, you know that, right? How will you ever top this one?"

I kiss her, and unlock her hands from around my waist, falling down onto my knees and grabbing the ring box from the chair on the table. Taking out the one-carat diamond with white gold band, I present it to her, sliding it on her left hand.

"It's perfect," she says, gazing down at her hand.

"It was a hard decision, but I thought simple and classic like my girl, worked best."

She presses her lips together and I think she's trying not to cry.

"The best part is that now everyone knows you're mine."

She falls to her knees, her hands cradling my cheeks. "I've always been yours."

"And I'll always be yours," I promise.

I brush my lips along hers.

"Pinch me, Mauro?" she asks once I have her laying down on our hardwood floors.

"I'll do more than pinch you, baby."

"I mean it. Tell me this is real?" Her fingers massage the back of my head.

"It's real. We're in love and we're going to live happily ever after."

"I couldn't love you more," she whispers like it's a secret between the two of us.

I lay on top of her, kissing her neck. "Words I'll never grow tired of hearing. But just so you know, I love you more."

Then before she can object, I crash my lips down on hers, swallowing down her moans.

What fun is marriage without a couple fights over who loves who more?

Later that night, I'm eating a row of M&Ms off my fiancée's stomach, when my phone rings.

I'm not on call so I won't be answering it. Whoever it is, has lousy timing.

The ringing stops and starts right back up.

"It must be important," Madison says, sitting up and ruining what I had planned once I passed her belly button.

"Stay there." I point to her and she giggles, falling back down to the mattress, three lonely M&Ms right above her small patch of hair.

I reach for my phone, seeing Cristian's name.

"This better be important because I'm..."

Madison's knee nudges my ribcage and I stop talking. She's still shy about giving my brothers any confirmation that we're sleeping together. Pretty sure they've figured it out.

"A call came through," he says.

"Another warehouse fire?" I ask and Madison sits up, the M&Ms falling off her body.

There are still no leads on who is setting the fires, but the one that almost took my life was found to be arson as well.

"No."

"Okay, Cris, stop fucking around so I can go back to eating M&Ms off my fiancée."

"First off, way too much information. Second, congratulations. She decided to ruin her life and accept your proposal?"

"Did you call me to piss me off?"

"No, like I said, a call came in tonight. It was Mom and

Pop's house." I jump up from the bed, throwing Madison's clothes at her as I try to locate my own from the pile on the floor.

"Ma?" I ask.

"She passed out and she's on her way to the hospital. I'm on my way over from the station, said I had to leave for a family emergency. Luca's doing the same. I'm sorry to ruin your night with Maddie. We tried to wait and see, but when the paramedics decided she needed to be checked out at the hospital, we had to call you."

"Cris, you call me ASAP always. Madison will understand."

"She's heading to Mercy," he says.

I click the phone off without saying goodbye and Madison is already pulling up her pants.

"What happened?"

"Ma's being transported to Mercy. She passed out." I finally find my boxers and pull them on.

Madison comes over, pulling me into a hug, calming my nerves a bit. "It's going to be okay, Mauro. They'll figure it out."

I hold her a little tighter, hoping and praying she's right.

Whatever happens, at least I'll have her by my side.

The End

ABOUT PIPER & RAYNE

Piper Rayne, or Piper and Rayne, whichever you prefer because we're not one author, we're two. Yep, you get two USA Today Bestselling authors for the price of one. Our goal is to bring you romance stories that have "Heartwarming Humor With a Side of Sizzle" (okay...you caught us, that's our tagline). A little about us... We both have kindle's full of one-clickable books. We're both married to husbands who drive us to drink. We're both chauffeurs to our kids. Most of all, we love hot heroes and quirky heroines that make us laugh, and we hope you do, too.

www.piperrayne.com
Amazon
Goodreads
Facebook
Instagram
Pinterest
Bookbub

ALSO BY PIPER RAYNE

The Modern Love World

Charmed by the Bartender

Hooked by the Boxer

Mad about the Banker

The Single Dad's Club

Real Deal

Dirty Talker

Sexy Beast

Dirty Truth

The Manny

Doggie Style

Chore Play

Bedroom Games

Cold as Ice

On Thin Ice

Break the Ice

Charity Case

Manic Monday

Afternoon Delight

Happy Hour

Blue Collar Brothers

Flirting with Fire

Crushing on the Cop

Engaged to the EMT